AFTER APPOMATTOX

AFTER APPOMATTOX

Military Occupation and the Ends of War

GREGORY P. DOWNS

HARVARD UNIVERSITY PRESS
Cambridge, Massachusetts, and London, England

First Harvard University Press paperback edition, 2019

Second printing

Publication of this book has been supported through the generous provisions of the
Maurice and Lula Bradley Smith Memorial Fund.

Library of Congress Cataloging-in-Publication Data

Downs, Gregory P.

After Appomattox : military occupation and the ends of war / Gregory P. Downs.

pages cm

Includes bibliographical references and index.

ISBN 978-0-674-74398-4 (cloth : alk. paper) | ISBN 9780674241626 (pbk.)

1. Reconstruction (U.S. history, 1865–1877)   2. Southern States—Politics and government—
1865–1950.   3. United States—Politics and government—1865–1877.   4. United States—History—
Civil War, 1861–1865—Occupied territories.   5. United States—History—Civil War, 1861–1865—
Peace.   6. Military occupation—Social aspects—Southern States—History—19th century.
7. Civil-military relations—Southern States—History—19th century.   8. Freedmen—Southern
States—History—19th century.   9. Southern States—Race relations—History—1865–1950.
10. Social conflict—Southern States—History—19th century.   I. Title.

E668.D74 2015

973.7'14—dc23

2014038048

To my father, William Montague (Monty) Downs,
who always believed

CONTENTS

NOTE ON SOURCES

Statistics regarding U.S. Army deployments from 1865 to 1870, cited in the text and presented in the maps and appendixes, are drawn from a database the author personally compiled from tens of thousands of departmental and divisional returns in RG 94, Entry 62, and RG 94, Entry 65, as well as from returns scattered through the individual department entries in RG 393, Part 1, all at National Archives I, Washington, D.C. Because numerical data on the hundreds of outposts are culled from thousands of monthly and biweekly reports, the information in those charts and maps will not all be cited individually, although full citations will be provided for any descriptive text utilized from any reports. The author has developed a website with digital maps, datasets, and full citations for the numerical data that is available at http://mappingoccupation.org.

THE WAR THAT COULD NOT END

O N APRIL 8, 1865, after almost four years of fighting and nearly three-quarters of a million deaths, Robert E. Lee wrote to Ulysses S. Grant to ask for "peace." As the U.S. Army closed in on Confederate forces near Appomattox Court House, Virginia, Lee sought a way to end not just the fighting but the entire conflict. With this letter from the Confederate general to the U.S. commander, the Civil War at last seemed near its close. If Grant had accepted Lee's proposal, the two generals might have negotiated not just an army's surrender but a nation's peace, not just an end to fighting but an end to war. But Grant's aides dismissed Lee's offer out of hand. The rebel general "wants to entrap us into making a treaty of peace," one of Grant's aides said, but "that is the prerogative of the President, or the Senate." A month earlier, President Abraham Lincoln had reminded Grant that politicians, not generals, would set the terms of peace. Even though Grant had referred to his own "great desire" for peace in a previous letter to Lee, he knew he did not have the power to make that decision. Taking Lee's reference to peace as a sign that the rebel would not actually surrender and "still means to fight," Grant went to sleep without sending a response. Upon waking, Grant decided to send a reply to Lee, writing that "I have no authority to treat on the subject of peace." They could, however, discuss surrender. Even as he dismissed peace, Grant acknowledged that he was "equally anxious for peace." Trying to appeal to Lee without making any promises, Grant stated that surrender would hasten but not bring peace.[1]

The distinction between Lee's "peace" and Grant's "surrender" would make a great deal of difference over the next five years. Denying peace was among the most important decisions made during the Civil War. It confirmed that the war was fundamentally a political, not just a military, conflict, and its terms would be set by politicians. By allowing the United States to utilize war powers years after battlefield fighting stopped, the continuation of wartime gave the national government the necessary authority to suppress the rebellion, consolidate its forces, and fashion effective civil rights. The United States would not declare peace because it could not be certain of the national government's own safety. Beyond that, with nearly 3 million people still enslaved, with the Thirteenth Amendment not yet part of the Constitution, and with state laws on the books defending slavery, the U.S. government would not end the war because slavery had not died. Destroying slavery and constructing freedom depended upon the military's authority to override state laws, displace judges and sheriffs, arrest outlaws, proclaim emancipation, oblige planters to provide contracts, transfer freedpeople's legal cases to military-backed courts, and try violent white Southerners in front of military commissions—in short, to run an occupation of the South that would have been illegal in peacetime. From that occupation would emerge new rights, new governments, and a newly expanded democracy. Constitutional protections that we still take for granted—due process, equal protection, birthright citizenship, the vote—were by-products of martial law. All of this was on the line as Grant and Lee met in April 1865, yet no one could have predicted how long it would actually take to end the war.[2]

Looking at Appomattox in this way forces us to rethink the commonsense view that wars are defined by soldiers meeting in battle. Even though wars are primarily narrated around campaigns and clashes, they are also moments when countries step away from normal legal restraints and grant the military extraordinary power over daily life. To describe a period that is neither peacetime nor active battlefield conflict, lawyers and politicians sometimes constructed names for the time after fighting but before peace. One influential Republican congressman called the period war *cessante;* another termed it a time of constructive war. To explain Reconstruction, a leading early twentieth-century historian quoted British Prime Minister William Ewart Gladstone on the difference between "war and a state of war." For the purposes of this book, I distinguish among battle time, postsurrender wartime, and peacetime. For four years, between 1861 and 1865, the United States waged an open, flagrant war against the Confederate rebellion. But the United States remained in a state of wartime for three years after surrender in some rebel states and for more than five years in others before finally returning to peacetime in 1871.[3]

Defining the years after Appomattox as a continuation of wartime allows us to understand war powers as the participants did, using the definitions they advanced. Although it seems commonsensical now to define wartime as battles, and Democrats and white Southerners frequently defined it that way then, in some ways this assumption—like much of what passes for common sense—is a product of World War II and other twentieth-century wars. In 1865, congressmen, generals, and lawyers utilized the word wartime more broadly because they understood the usefulness, even necessity, of war powers. In the summer of 1865, a general dismissed soldiers' claims that the war was over by reminding them that the war would not be "brought to a close" until civil authority was fully restored, and the states had returned to Congress. Republican congressmen frequently defended the Reconstruction of the rebel states on the grounds that "peace has not yet come," the people of the South "are yet subject to military control," and the "war powers" should be "continued and exercised" until civil authority was reestablished. As late as 1869, the attorney general flatly affirmed that the war continued since it was up to Congress "to determine when the war has . . . ended." In 1870 one of the most careful lawyers in the U.S. Senate argued that wartime endured until Congress seated the final representatives from the rebel states. They followed eminent philosophers of war from Cicero to Hugo Grotius, who defined war as "a state of affairs" which "may exist even while its operations are not continued." Thomas Hobbes likewise wrote that "the nature of war consisteth not in actual fighting but in the known disposition thereto." Weeks after Appomattox, the architect of the United States' code of war, Francis Lieber, drew upon this well-established tradition as he dismissed the "erroneous fallacy" that surrender could "take the place of treaties of peace." This was a mistake so "profound" that he found it barely worth mentioning. To lawyers and policy makers, wartime did not necessarily mean battles, nor did it mean their expansive cultural consequences; it meant a legal state that shaped government power and ended at a precise moment with the dawn of peace.[4]

To understand why the terminology of wartime was so weighty and why war powers mattered so much, we have to ask what, precisely, wartime and peacetime are. War had to be legally defined because it opened up useful but dangerous powers for government. Under U.S. law, peacetime generally means that courts, elected officials, and laws are supreme; the military serves rather than supplants local government. In the Constitution, Americans defended their republican experiment from centralized military tyranny by protecting trial by jury and the privilege of habeas corpus, the centuries-old English right to petition a court to either be charged with a crime or released from custody. Although Congress gave the president the power to call out the militia and (after 1807) the army, it placed the armed forces at the service of local government by generally making the president's intervention dependent upon a request from a legislature, governor, or federal judge. Even before the Civil War, however, some of these restrictions were loosening. Southern congressmen had implicitly expanded the military's power in the 1850 Fugitive Slave Law. Still, the military remained a tool of civil officials. It generally could respond to requests but not act on its own.[5]

But the Civil War was not fought under peacetime limits. Wartime gave President Abraham Lincoln authority that he believed he needed to defeat the rebellion. Soon after proclaiming that "combinations too powerful to be suppressed" had obstructed the execution of the law in the rebel states, Lincoln turned to the "extraordinary powers which the Constitution confides to him in cases of insurrection." Under these war powers, Lincoln suspended the privilege of the writ of habeas corpus, closed newspapers, and created army-regulated military commissions to bypass juries and try Northern and Southern civilians for undermining the war effort. Defending his actions in a widely distributed 1863 letter, Lincoln argued that "certain proceedings are constitutional when, in cases of rebellion or Invasion, the public Safety requires them, which would not be constitutional" otherwise. "I can no more be persuaded that the Government can constitutionally take no strong measures in time of rebellion, because it can be shown that the same could not be lawfully taken in time of peace, than I can be persuaded that a particular drug is not good medicine for a sick man, because it can be shown to not be good food for a well one."[6]

As the U.S. Army moved south during the conflict, these war powers helped it reestablish governments and end slavery. Drawing upon and quickly going beyond its experiences in the Mexican-American War, the army took control of towns and cities, either dismissing officials or placing them under its control. As the United States turned toward broad emancipation of slaves, the military had to go farther; ending slavery required disregarding state laws and local officials. For this reason some scholars have called Lincoln or the military tyrannical, but this is a vast overstatement. War powers did not mean unlimited powers; commanders ordered officers to behave honorably and to follow the Constitution whenever possible. Politicians did not believe that war powers allowed them to do whatever they wanted; their actions had to be plausibly tied to military necessity. The United States avoided large-scale executions or displacement or property seizures. In defending Lincoln and the army from charges of tyranny, however, we sometimes lose sight of the fact that war powers were substantial, as was the threat they posed to the country's system of government. The ultimate protection against that threat would be the dawn of peacetime. Because the state of war was temporary, military interventions during wartime did not set a precedent or topple the foundations of government. Peacetime would mean the restoration of normal legal restraints.[7]

But that was precisely the dilemma. Returning to peacetime meant giving up powers that still seemed necessary as battlefield fighting closed. In April 1865, basic order, human freedom, and civil rights depended upon not reestablishing courts' peacetime authority. While everyone knows that Reconstruction was crucial for the expansion of rights, the story is often domesticated into a tale of courtrooms and congressional debates, of laws, amendments, conventions, petitions, and voting booths. These new rights, however, had other origin stories. They were fashioned in the armed struggle among freedpeople, soldiers, and rebel insurgents. They were created in legal rhetoric and also in blood, sometimes at gunpoint and frequently through martial law. As long as the national government retained its war powers, it could save rights from becoming what James Madison had presciently described as mere "parchment barriers." Through the war powers, the government exercised the crucial, if sometimes dismaying, attribute of force, in keeping with Madison's definition of government as "an institution to make people do their duty." The government needed this force after Appomattox if it meant to defend itself or to construct a reliable freedom. From places like Alexandria, Virginia, freedpeople in the weeks after surrender asked the president to sustain military authority over local governments that still recognized slavery and discriminated against black people. These letters posed a conundrum. In 1865, the government could protect freedpeople or it could return to peacetime, but it could not do both.[8]

As the national government continued its war powers over places like Alexandria, it launched a bold and sometimes revolutionary experiment. Approaching Reconstruction through the extension of war powers instead of searching for explanations for its ultimate disappointments, we see rights born in the face of bayonets, and a Constitution remade through the subservience of civil law. We also see the power of the violent insurgency that arose in the South to displace the military's authority. The occupation of the South, despite its limitations, created narrow but precious space for freedpeople to organize economically, socially, and politically. The fruits of the occupation were new constitutional amendments passed with the aid of military rule that fundamentally altered American law and created new categories of rights. For a brief but still meaningful time, the fruits of occupation also included new governments on the ground that began to remake Southern politics and the South's political economy.[9]

 Calling the post-Appomattox period an occupation goes against some venerable ways of thinking about occupations in general and Reconstruction in particular. Operating under a narrow definition of occupation, some scholars of occupation now—and some politicians then—argue that a country cannot occupy its own territory. While logical, this distinction was highly contested during the Civil War era. Drawing from French theories of a state of siege and from British notions of martial law, many Republicans claimed that rebellious territories could be occupied almost as if they were foreign as long as the victorious nation maintained the state of war. While residents retained their citizenship, they in other ways could be treated essentially as an occupied people.[10] Other analysts are skeptical of treating Reconstruction as an occupation because of the relatively small numbers of troops used. Now, scholars believe effective occupations require one soldier for every twenty residents, but this contemporary measure confuses our ability to understand the nineteenth century. Reconstruction had similar staffing levels as contemporaneous military actions in India or Ireland or postrebellion Hungary.[11] Finally, historians have underplayed the occupation during Reconstruction because it often worked through civilian officials. In the wake of the large, successful, and thoroughly disruptive U.S.- and Soviet Union–led occupations of the 1940s and 1950s, historians downplayed the size and effectiveness of the understaffed and restrained post-Appomattox effort. Instead of a tyrannical occupation, as white Southerners had claimed, scholars wondered whether there had been an occupation at all. But in fact most occupations work through elite collaborators, and we must guard against judging the nineteenth century by twentieth-century standards. In general the skepticism about Reconstruction's occupation is due to an absence of information. Without good data on where soldiers were, it has been hard to know how the occupation worked or what it looked like. Through extensive work in National Archives records and many other sources, and with an eye on the burgeoning literature on contemporary occupations, this book portrays an occupation that was stymied but still in many ways successful.[12]

The boldness of the occupation of the South, however, raises other, disturbing questions about the contemporary use of war powers. In light of the apparent overextension of war powers over the past decade, it is almost irresistible to draw bright lines between civilian law and military rule and to see war powers as illegitimate and unnecessary. But looking at the story after Appomattox forces us to confront the dismaying, necessary fact that our own contemporary freedom and civil rights are in some ways the products of war powers. Even the rights we cherish are often fashioned by coercion.

After Appomattox, that coercion made rights meaningful, but it also threatened the republican system of government. As the Civil War opened the possibility for the realization of freedpeople's and Republicans' fondest dreams, it also raised understandable fears—often among the same people— that the republican experiment could collapse under the strain. Fearful of the vulnerable state of the national government and the contingent nature of the American experiment, Republicans tried to go beyond the law and yet not risk destroying the law. They wished to create a bounded, exceptional time when they could go to extremes but remain secure in the knowledge that they would return to peacetime normalcy. But this shared goal masked deep divisions over the precise terms and timing of the return of peace.

Beyond congressional Republicans, there was no consensus at all. The extension of wartime sparked an extraordinarily bitter political fight over who had the power to end a war, the president or Congress. They fought over a silence in the Constitution. Although Congress declares wars and then the Senate ends them by ratifying treaties, civil wars and rebellions present peculiar problems, since they do not conclude with treaties. Lincoln and President Andrew Johnson both claimed a now-familiar executive branch authority over questions of war and peace as commanders in chief. But Congress did not accede to those claims. Congressional Republicans insisted, and the army acknowledged, that Congress controlled the end of the war. Peace returned when representatives from the Confederate states were seated in the House of Representatives and the Senate. Until that day, a post-surrender wartime endured. In the struggle between Congress and the president, Johnson vetoed key bills, removed generals and cabinet officers, declared Congress illegitimate, and proclaimed peacetime. In response, congressional Republicans extended wartime for more than three years, stripped away presidential power over the army, impeached Johnson, and came within a single vote of conviction and removal in one of the gravest constitutional crises of the country's history. Even after that, the fight to define wartime and the powers of war dragged on for another two years.

If measured by wartime legal authority and by the absence of representatives from rebel states, the Civil War ended with the seating of a senator from Georgia on February 1, 1871, almost ten years after the attack on Fort Sumter. On that day, a Democratic senator called out, "Let us have peace."[13] What followed the legal end of war powers was not quiet but a battle to shape the peacetime that resulted. As the Supreme Court, voters, and white Southern insurgents hemmed in federal power, Republicans and freedpeople learned that they could construct a new peace, but they could not hold it.

When Grant and Lee did meet on April 9, Palm Sunday, in Wilmer McLean's parlor, the two negotiated the terms not of peace but of surrender. Still, it was hard not to read the scene as a sign of something larger. There are good reasons why we have treated the moment as a return of peace; many people at the time did. That day, U.S. officers waved Confederate money, "shouted, screamed, yelled, threw up their hats and hopped madly up and down." Perhaps carried away by events, Grant said: "The war is over. The Rebels are our countrymen again." By legend, although perhaps not in reality, at the famous surrender ceremony three days later, U.S. and Confederate troops signaled their mutual respect when they each sounded the marching salute, "honor answering honor." "Reluctantly, with agony of expression," the Confederates stacked arms, lay down their "battle-worn and torn" flags, and turned toward home. Behind them would trail myths and misunderstandings that confound our sense of the Civil War and Reconstruction to this day. Stories circulated of gestures of reconciliation and peace. Some said that Lee surrendered his fine sword to Grant, and then Grant handed it back. "It is the purest romance," Grant later wrote. "Wars produce many stories of fiction, some of which are told until they are believed to be true."[14]

So, too, and still, from Appomattox a great many more significant and troubling stories bloom that would be very good if only they were true. The most important is the notion that the war ended at Appomattox, an idea so powerful that it seeps into the words of historians, documentarians, and even the National Park Service. The Appomattox myth is a mighty one that draws people to a message of mercy and reconciliation in the encounter between the two generals. In American history, the Appomattox myth carries the weight of the birth of the new nation, forged in sacrifice and respect and forgiveness, the family returned home under one roof.

But that story of a quick peace misleads us about key developments of the post-Appomattox era. It is easy, but inaccurate, to see rebels stacking their arms as proof that they had surrendered their cause. In fact, they returned home from fighting still fighting. There was no time when most rebels were willing to concede to whatever terms the federal government suggested, no moment when the problems of a postsurrender Reconstruction might have been easily solved. Although many ex-Confederates were careful to avoid trouble after surrender, they were biding their time. Soon they would launch a powerful insurgency to undermine the army's rule and then topple the military-backed freedpeople's governments in the South.[15]

Likewise, it is tempting to misread the U.S. soldiers' alleged salute to the rebels as proof that the U.S. military disappeared from the story and retreated into peace, or even felt a sense of brotherhood with their Confederate enemies. The famous parade of 200,000 soldiers through Washington, D.C., in the Grand Review in May 1865, when Herman Melville compared the soldiers' alleged disappearance to the natural force of daylight dispersing the stars "at their steely play," seems to confirm this. Although many soldiers did return home, the army did not actually disappear. It launched a widespread and intermittently effective occupation of the U.S. South. The army maintained more than a hundred thousand soldiers in the rebel states for the remainder of the year, and more than twenty thousand for the next four to five years. There, the occupying army used its legal powers over civil governments and its geographic reach into the Southern countryside to try to set the terms for the end of slavery and the meaning of freedom.[16]

The conventional image of the surrender at Appomattox Court House also erases the 4 million African Americans whose freedom had become crucial to the war effort. Grant may well have encountered some of these fleeing ex-slaves as he rode to meet Lee along roads so choked with people that he could barely make headway and had to cut across fields and Confederate lines. Freedpeople on the move had launched strikes that crippled the Confederate economy, delivered information to U.S. forces, enlisted by the hundreds of thousands in the U.S. Army, pressed for an expansive vision of their freedom, lobbied for land, and begun to reconstitute societies in the coastal belt where planters had fled. Before we too quickly transform all of the men and women and wagons on the road in April 1865 into warriors or strikers, however, we might also ask where freedpeople were going. Throughout the South, before and after surrender, freedpeople moved in the direction of the U.S. Army. The army, despite its many limitations, was their most proximate, powerful ally in the battle to assert the rights of freedom. Ex-slaves did not move to the blank space of freedom but to the government that seemed to have the power to defend their rights.

At Appomattox, and then afterward, the war seemed almost over, and yet the war could not end. The day after Lee surrendered, as Grant prepared to rush to Washington to "begin the reduction of the military establishment, and the enormous expense attending it," he asked to meet with Lee one more time. The two men talked on horseback atop a knoll that overlooked the lines. There, Lee reminded Grant that the South "was a big country and that we might have to march over it three or four times before the war entirely ended." To this Grant suggested that Lee might calm the "whole people" by urging them to surrender. But Lee would not and could not do it. Like Grant, Lee now recognized that civilians, not soldiers, would have to determine the timing of peace. Parting, Lee returned to his lines, Grant to Wilmer McLean's house, where Confederate and U.S. officers—many of whom had been classmates before the war—reunited. After an hour or so of listening to their conversations, Grant headed toward Burkesville Junction, the nearest working railroad depot. The men in Appomattox had a surrender ceremony to prepare, but Grant had more important work. At Burkesville, he caught a train toward Washington for a cabinet meeting about the conquered states, planning what would come next.[17]

– 1 –

AFTER SURRENDER

BEFORE GRANT REACHED Washington, D.C., the question of what followed surrender surfaced 170 miles north of Appomattox in the town of Winchester, Virginia. Occupied numerous times by both U.S. and Confederate forces, the people of Winchester knew what wartime meant: soldiers walking the streets, military officers overruling courts, civilians sitting in jails under army orders. What they did not know was whether wartime conditions continued now that the battles in Virginia were over. On April 11, two days after the surrender agreement at Appomattox, U.S. Major General Winfield Scott Hancock decided that peace had now arrived in Winchester. A conservative who consistently fought against postsurrender occupations, Hancock asked permission to withdraw his men from the town limits to avoid clashes with paroled Confederate soldiers and to give the white people "every freedom consistent with the situation." If surrender marked the break in time between war and peace, Hancock's suggestion made sense. In peacetime, the United States must restore civil rule and normal social life. But surrender did not end the war, army chief of staff Major General Henry W. Halleck responded. An architect of the military justice system, Halleck peremptorily denied Hancock's request without even bothering "to trouble" Grant with the question. In exasperation, Hancock argued that it was best to "occupy as little ground as possible," but Halleck remained unmoved.[1]

The end of battles did not end the occupation of the rebel states. Surrender marked a turning point, not an end point, for the state of war. While battlefield fighting would close over April and May 1865, wartime did not. The questions that surfaced first in Winchester materialized within weeks in small towns and rural districts across the former Confederacy. As other armies surrendered in the Carolinas and then in the Southwest, commanders faced the same issue that Hancock confronted: Did the conclusion of combat conclude the war? The answer remained the same: the army did not intend to give up its war powers simply because the fighting had stopped. Rather than breaking sharply at the end of surrender, military policy toward the conquered states in many ways stayed intact. Although the national policy would not be clear until the end of April, when President Johnson and the cabinet firmly rejected the opportunity for an armistice with Confederate forces, its roots were laid in the orders, like Halleck's, that immediately followed Appomattox.

The crucial question that the U.S. government faced was who controlled those defeated rebel states. In time, the issue of civil rights—and the way to make them meaningful—would take center stage in the postsurrender era. That would be the crucible for war powers, the brake against a return to peace, and the prelude to a deep constitutional crisis. But in the first days after Lee's surrender, the problem was even simpler and more concrete. Did the local officials in the rebel states have normal, peacetime power over their regions? If the United States answered yes, if it retained local officials in office and acknowledged their ultimate power, then the army would be hamstrung. It could not constitutionally use its force against governments in peacetime and would be powerless to put down outlaws, squelch trials of U.S. soldiers, and provide basic protection to freedpeople unless it received a request from a local or federal official. Absent another declaration of insurrection that established a new state of war, the national government would be simply a bystander. Freedpeople's civil rights may not have shaped the initial decision to continue the state of war, but they depended upon it. It was the necessary prelude for everything that would follow.

What first shaped the decision to extend wartime was the military's wariness about the quiescence of rebel soldiers and the possibility of ongoing fighting in the rebel states. As the Confederate armies surrendered, the U.S. government grappled with an enormous set of challenges in the rebel states. It was reacquiring control over a vast, largely unconquered territory filled with newly freed slaves and newly returning soldiers. While some regions— especially the eastern coast, the Mississippi valley, and western and central Tennessee—had been ruled by a mixture of military and loyal civilian governments for years, large sections of the ex-Confederate states had been nearly untouched by the armies. They were, essentially, terra incognita, regions where the army knew very little about the quiescence of the white people or the actions of the ex-slaves.

In that context the army had reason to fear additional uprisings or ongoing guerrilla wars. Confederate president Jefferson Davis remained at large; by rumor, he was heading to Mexico or as-yet-unconquered Texas to rebuild the Confederate nation. Into the vast, unknown space of the South would soon march hundreds of thousands of rebel soldiers heading home. Young, isolated, unpaid, angry, and well armed, these white men could easily join uprisings or launch guerrilla wars. Northern generals and politicians well knew that civil wars often sparked spiraling conflicts, echo wars that sounded for years or for generations as ex-soldiers continued to strike back against the victors.

Beyond the problems that confront every society at the end of a civil war, the United States faced the particular challenge of managing a quick transition from a society shaped by slavery to one structured around freedom. For the more than 3.5 million slaves in the Confederate states, the war's end meant a revolution in their status, an opening to a new form of freedom they claimed whenever and however they could. For white planters, the war's end meant the recognition that slavery—the basis of their economy, political system, theological beliefs, and self-image—seemed to be on the verge of disappearing. Although Northern planners hoped for a smooth transition from slave to free labor, they had every reason to fear violence from one side or from both. Finally, there was the crucial issue of the political world that would follow peace. Unless the U.S. government planned to overhaul the constitutional system, the end of wartime meant the return of law and civil governments that would regulate their localities and, when Congress returned in December, send representatives to vote on national policy. On the ground, this would mean magistrates charging soldiers with kidnapping their slaves by setting them free, judges ruling on contracts, and sheriffs delivering public whippings of freedpeople. In Washington, this might mean the end of the advances of the war; peacetime even threatened the passage of the Thirteenth Amendment, which had not received the approval of a sufficient number of states.

Fearful that rebel soldiers would launch a guerrilla campaign, that planters would reestablish slavery, and that Southern courts would indict soldiers, the War Department continued to operate on a war footing. U.S. officers generally claimed the common political and police authority of mid-nineteenth-century militaries over the places they occupied during a period of wartime, though, in keeping with military practices, fairly little control over property titles. The army could replace, vacate, or overrule existing civil officials; it could retain, dismiss, or topple local courts; it could arrest civilians, interpret contracts, temporarily seize property, close newspapers, restrict commerce, overturn laws, regulate movement, levy fines, and in many other ways either directly assume the powers of local government or supervise civilians in those positions. Most controversially, it could try civilians in front of military commissions. The army could be police, judge, jury, council, and mayor, or it could permit locals to fill those offices while retaining the power to oversee them. Although the army tried to avoid direct violence, its forceful claims of authority and its recourse to military justice raised the specter of what one contemporary scholar of occupation calls "latent violence," a threat meant to quiet the subject population. Even at the beginning, the United States never punished many people, but it relied upon its ultimate power to frighten people into acquiescence.[2]

As the military's focus shifted from winning battles to governing territory, it began reassigning its soldiers to reach into the expansive Southern territory and assert the nation's power. When the U.S. Army extended its lines across the entire Confederacy, it found itself responsible for more than 800 county governments spread over 750,000 square miles, containing about 9 million people. Slowly but surely, the military spread out toward regions far from the war's front lines. From about 120 towns in March 1865, the army extended to 218 reported posts by the end of May and 334 by the end of August.[3] From a narrow range of posts along coasts and rivers, and a series of posts in southern Louisiana, middle Tennessee, central Arkansas, northern Alabama, and northern Virginia, the army moved deep into the Confederate countryside over the spring and summer. There they tried to create a new social order on the ground. Peace would follow, not create, the birth of the new world.

The Civil War endured because everyone from the president down to the army staff dismissed efforts to declare it finished. There was no proclamation that the war continued; there did not need to be one. The old proclamations were still in effect. The army's code of war stated that martial law did not end with a surrender or armistice but continued until the commander in chief proclaimed it over. Therefore, the decision not to announce a policy was a decision to continue the powers of occupation.[4]

At Appomattox, there were simple, practical reasons to understand that the war continued. In the field, the Confederacy's other large army still held North Carolina, having fled northward through Georgia and South Carolina as U.S. Major General William T. Sherman's men pursued it. Other scattered armies of Confederate regulars and irregulars operated throughout the South, and General Edmund Kirby Smith commanded the forces west of the Mississippi in Texas. Confederate president Jefferson Davis fled southward, driven by the hope of sustaining the rebellion. Still, it seemed possible that surrender in Texas or the capture of Jefferson Davis would signal the end of wartime.

Instead, the war powers endured, in large part because of the government's response to the second major surrender in the field. In North Carolina, the famously tough-minded Sherman pursued the last large rebel army under Confederate general Joseph Johnston into central North Carolina. As word of Lee's surrender reached the outnumbered Johnston, Sherman moved boldly—and it turned out foolishly—toward peace by offering not surrender but an armistice and political restoration to the Confederacy. Sherman's terms raised fundamental questions about the endurance of the government's war powers over the rebel states. This proposed armistice tested the new government of President Andrew Johnson and forced him to declare unambiguously that the state of war continued and that the South would be ruled by the army.[5]

Sherman's offer of peace unfolded from the clear, commonsensical way he distinguished wartime from peace. "I will fight as long as the enemy shows fight, but when he gives up and asks quarter I cannot go further," he wrote in late April 1865. When Lee surrendered, Sherman's men rejoiced at what seemed like the dawn of peace. Sherman regarded "the war as over, for I well knew that General Johnston had no army with which to oppose mine." Turning from war to peace, Sherman pondered "the only questions that remained." Would Johnston surrender, or "would he allow his army to disperse into guerrilla-bands, to 'die in the last ditch,' and entail on his country an indefinite and prolonged military occupation?"[6]

To hasten peace and prevent a guerrilla uprising, Sherman began to overstep his authority and act on political matters. Even before he met with General

Johnston, Sherman urged North Carolina governor Zebulon Vance to remain in his office, since "the war was substantially over." Vance wisely disregarded Sherman's advice and fled. On the Confederate side, Johnston convinced President Jefferson Davis to seek peace terms rather than continuing the fight. When Sherman and Johnston finally met, an additional factor complicated the situation. As he left for the meeting, Sherman learned that President Abraham Lincoln had been assassinated; the news was not yet known in most of the South. Recognizing the danger of a Northern reaction, Sherman passed Johnston a confidential note with the news. Alarmed, Johnston asked if they "might arrange terms that would embrace *all* the Confederate armies." The terms Johnston sought were political. Would the rebels be "denied representation to Congress" and made "slaves to the people of the North?" Sherman replied, "No."[7]

With that settled, the two generals resolved to end the war. Grandiosely, Sherman proclaimed that their agreement would lead to peace from "the Potomac to the Rio Grande." Their agreement ordered Confederate soldiers to return to their state capitals to deposit weapons in the state arsenals. In exchange the federal government would recognize the existing state governments as legitimate once the officers took an oath of allegiance. The white men of the states, including soldiers, would be guaranteed the right to vote, and new president Andrew Johnson would pledge "not to disturb any of the people by reason of the late war." Although General Johnston admitted that slavery was dead, Sherman did not include any promises of abolition in the agreement. Summing up, Sherman wrote, "In general terms—the war to cease; a general amnesty" and the "resumption of peaceful pursuits." This agreement would sustain rebels in control of county courts and state capitals. Within months, returning Confederate soldiers would cast votes for new officers. State adjutants would manage large stores of arms to be used against guerrillas or rebellious freedpeople. Even if the Thirteenth Amendment successfully ended slavery, the rebel states would be free to regulate black people through explicitly unequal legal systems and to deny them the right to testify in court. The U.S. Army would presumably retreat to a few state capitals, port cities, and major depots as a guard against any future uprising. Against ex-Confederates, the federal government would have no more power than it did anywhere else. That was the fruit of peacetime. Sherman began to ponder which corps he could muster out first.[8]

More than perhaps any document of the war, Sherman's agreement suggested how clearly an immediate end to war would maintain the power of white Southerners over their governments, their lands, and their slaves and ex-slaves. While evaluations of Reconstruction contrast its disappointments to better potential outcomes, Sherman's offer illustrates an alternative in 1865 that would have eliminated Reconstruction and constrained emancipation in ways that far exceeded the effects of Jim Crow. If Sherman's offer had stood, if the United States had only pursued peace and reunion, then there would be no Civil Rights Act, no Fourteenth Amendment, no black enfranchisement, and no constitutional and legal legacy of civil rights to draw upon in the twentieth century. There might not even be a Thirteenth Amendment. Sherman's agreement therefore revealed the dilemmas of peace. A premature peace would not mean harmony; it would mean acquiescence.

Sherman understood the hard hand of war, but he did not think it applied any longer. During battlefield conflict, he had hanged guerrillas, obliterated an entire town in Tennessee for harboring outlaws, led the notorious March to the Sea to demoralize white Georgians, and distributed South Carolina planters' lands to ex-slaves. Eight months earlier, he had ordered all civilians to evacuate Atlanta and warned the mayor that "war is cruelty, and you cannot refine it." But Sherman sharply distinguished between war and peace. "*During* War the Conqueror of a Country may use the local government & authorities already in existence, or create new ones subordinate to his Use," he wrote to Chief Justice Salmon P. Chase. "That is not the question now, for War has Ceased."[9]

The U.S. general sought a quick restoration of peace because he did not believe the United States could govern the rebel states by military force. He was not sure that any country could. To understand what was possible, Sherman and other Americans looked to what they believed was a Roman imperial model of very light occupation, holding provincial capitals and strategic sites along waterways and roads, and extracting nothing more than loyalty, taxes, trade, and men for warfare. Beyond those cities and trade routes, local elites remained in control because it was impossible to displace them. If the government declared peace, the rebels would "pay taxes, live in Peace," and defend the country, he believed. In that case all the army needed to do was hold "forts, arms, and strategic points" and leave the rest of the region to local sheriffs and judges. But if Washington vacated state and local offices, it would leave people "without any government at all." There would be "pure anarchy." Unable to rely upon these local elites to stabilize society and enforce law, the government would depend solely upon a "military occupation" which could not possibly reach 9 million people in "all the recesses of their unhappy country."[10]

While Sherman understood the difficulty of occupation, he had misread the political moment. When Sherman's armistice offer reached Washington on April 21, it created a sensation. A crestfallen Grant sensed at once that his friend had misjudged the national mood. Even before Lincoln's assassination, the tide had turned against easy peace terms. At first, Lincoln had encouraged Virginia's rebel legislature to meet and revoke secession, but after intense pushback from his cabinet, he had changed his mind, suggesting that he did not intend to recognize local governments. The terms Lincoln might have accepted with formidable armies arrayed against him were no longer enough now that those forces had disappeared. In his final speech, Lincoln publicly suggested, for the first time, voting rights for some black men. Lincoln's assassination hardened this national turn against peace. Blaming the rebels, and especially Jefferson Davis, for the killing, Northern politicians and editors called for punishment and revenge.

Lincoln's assassination had also concretely changed the political situation. Most obviously, new president Andrew Johnson was now the final voice. Although Johnson would later disappoint Northern Republicans and Southern freedpeople, in these early days he seemed guided by his wartime experiences as a lonely white Southern loyalist. In the war's early days, Johnson led the fight against secession in Tennessee and then returned to the state as military governor. There he gained fame for his harsh attacks on Southern rebels. In ways often submerged in public memory of Reconstruction, Johnson defended military power in 1865. But the assassination had changed more than just the man in the White House. Another would-be assassin seriously injured the influential and increasingly conservative secretary of state, William Seward. During Johnson's first weeks in office, the new president therefore leaned heavily upon the brilliant and dour secretary of war, Edwin Stanton, a champion of war powers. Stanton "was a man who never questioned his own authority, and who always did in war time what he wanted to do," Grant later wrote. "He was an able constitutional lawyer and jurist; but the Constitution was not an impediment to him while the war lasted." In the cabinet, Stanton led an assault on Sherman's agreement. If Stanton's tone was particularly fierce, his positions were commonplace; every cabinet member and President Johnson supported him. Stanton instructed Grant to take charge of the surrender negotiations personally, and ordered generals in the field to ignore directives from Sherman. Outraged but obedient, Sherman offered Johnston the Appomattox terms: unconditional surrender with no promises of peace. At first, Jefferson

Davis urged Johnston to refuse surrender and let the soldiers flee to Texas or Mexico. But Johnston had had enough of fighting for a cause that could no longer be won.[11]

Unlike Sherman, many politicians and the Northern public did not believe that the work of the Civil War was complete. Reconstruction illuminated tensions between two powerful goals: to find peace and to maintain the victories of the recent past. If peace and reunion were the nation's only goals, the ending of war powers would have come much sooner. But there was more work to be done. The rebel army had dissolved, but the rebel people had not been subdued. Beyond that, slavery had not come to an end, and the terms of freedom had not been defined. While these challenges remained, abandoning the powers of war seemed suicidal.[12]

One of the clearest voices for this position came from the *Army & Navy Journal*, a New York–based weekly newspaper that was the forerunner to the current *Armed Forces Journal.* Founded by former brevet lieutenant colonel William C. Church and his brother Francis (who would later write the famous "Yes, Virginia, there is a Santa Claus" editorial for the *New York Sun*), the *Army & Navy Journal* served its audience of active-duty officers and soldiers by collecting official reports and serving as a sounding board for their opinions. Typically moderate and supportive of the administration, the paper had just urged the government not to "be hasty" in making terms. Better to let soldiers "thoroughly finish their work" through "military rule" before "the civil power is brought in to interfere with them in any form." When Sherman reached his ill-fated agreement with Johnston, the paper mourned that the general "still stands, politically, where he did four years ago, untaught by events," while the nation "has drifted forward, and he is left hopelessly in the rear." After the *New York Times* published a version of Sherman's armistice terms, the furor overshadowed even the coverage of Lincoln's funeral train. Politicians who had recently created a special rank in the army for Sherman now called for his dismissal or termed him a traitor.[13]

By laying out what he thought the government should not do, Sherman inadvertently captured the boldness of the postsurrender extension of the war. Had the United States sought conciliation, it could have obtained taxes and professions of loyalty with very little cost. There would have been no reason to sustain posts in towns like Winchester, much less to expand to hundreds of other towns like it.

But the fear of more rebel uprisings led the United States' leaders to act in ways that astounded Sherman. As they surveyed the rebel states, military and civilian officials had reason to worry that combat would not end with surrenders. From their history books and their newspapers, they knew that quiescence did not always follow defeat. In the French counterrevolutionary War of the Vendée, regionally based conservatives had resisted the republican army for years. In Ireland, Poland, Hungary, and other parts of the world, they saw proof that partisans did not always lay down their arms. In parts of the South, including in sections of the loyal states of Kentucky, West Virginia, and Missouri, bands of outlaws attacked U.S. soldiers and loyalists. Guerrillas operated in regions where neither the Confederacy nor the United States had been able to establish control, especially in the North and South Carolina Piedmont, in western Louisiana, in eastern Tennessee, and in Arkansas. As the rebel soldiers returned home, the U.S. government had good reason to hold its power and watch carefully to see what would follow surrender.

Therefore, in April 1865, the United States launched a little-understood, intermittently effective, and spatially ambitious postsurrender occupation of the American South. It began by doing what Sherman had thought unthinkable: vacating governments. Within a few days after the failed armistice at Durham, Chief Justice Chase wrote to Sherman that Andrew Johnson had not decided whether to enfranchise black people but was "clear and settled in the opinion that no civil authority should be recognized which has its source in rebel election or appointment." As rebel state governors tried to call legislators back into session and rescind secession, Secretary of War Stanton ordered his generals to block them. No one yet knew the federal government's plans, but it was apparent that the Confederates would not at first be part of the discussion. When Georgia governor Joseph Brown ordered the state government into session, Stanton had him arrested. Although Sherman had assured North Carolina governor Vance that he would remain in office, Vance was arrested next, followed by a slew of other governors and Confederate cabinet members. In Texas, the army displaced state authorities in mid-June after the rebel governor fled to Mexico. "Notify the people of Texas that all acts of the Governor and Legislature of Texas since the ordinance of secession are illegitimate," Major General Philip Sheridan ordered his commander there. The Confederate state governments were disappearing.[14]

In four states, the issue was complicated by the presence of loyal, but tenuous, governments. Backed by Lincoln's direct encouragement, Unionists in Virginia, Louisiana, Arkansas, and Tennessee had created shadow states that were powerful in Louisiana and Tennessee, and weak in Virginia and Arkansas. In Louisiana and Tennessee, Johnson ordered the military to aid but not interfere with the loyal governments. Despite his rhetoric, Johnson did not lift martial law there. To aid the weaker apparatuses in Virginia and Arkansas, the United States displaced competing Confederate governments, offering a reward for the arrest of Virginia's rebel governor and vacating county officeholders. In Arkansas, Confederate governor Harris Flanagin— whom the U.S. Army had driven into the southern section of the state in 1863—offered to call the legislature into session, repeal secession, and recognize the loyal government's appointees; in exchange he wanted the loyal government to accept his county officers in the southern portion of the state. Instead, U.S. Major General Joseph J. Reynolds ordered the army to arrest any Confederate legislators who tried to meet.[15]

For the first six to twelve weeks, the contours of the occupation were unclear. President Andrew Johnson reopened trade with the rebel states, but did not further spell out his plans. The army's policy could be read best in what it did not permit. No one could claim office based upon a Confederate appointment. Beyond that, officers had only the vaguest guidelines to treat rebels as friends but also to enforce laws and protect the peace. Without clear orders, generals often just acknowledged that the old order was gone. In eastern Virginia, the commander put it simply: "For a time there was no method in the work. It was a jumble of collisions." On the whole, "each commander used his own discretion." In Richmond, this meant chaos, as Major General Marsena Patrick spent the first four weeks after Lee's surrender "mixed and muddy." "I know not what we are to do, inasmuch as there are so many contradictory orders" and no clear policy, he wrote. In North Carolina, Major General John Schofield tried to set a plan for regulating the state through established local officials, but Grant rejected it. "Until a uniform policy is adopted for reestablishing civil government in the rebellious States, the military authorities can do nothing but keep the peace," Grant wrote. In some regions, as around Natchez, Mississippi, officers would neither hear cases nor recognize local judges and magistrates. Law simply lapsed. When one Southerner complained about this absence of law, Attorney General James Speed instructed his clerk to tell him that he would simply have to wait; for now, he was "without remedy."[16]

In the silence from Washington, many commanders acted as they had in occupations before the surrenders. Although some officers looked back to the occupation of Mexico and the military government over the annexed lands of the Southwest for precedents, the United States' occupation policy had primarily developed in the war's second year, especially after disappointments in the Peninsula campaign dashed hopes for a quick victory. As the United States captured New Orleans, Memphis, and Nashville in 1862, generals like Benjamin Butler and William T. Sherman and civilian military governors like Andrew Johnson experimented with broad, multifaceted plans of occupation. At times different commanders followed each of what an occupation scholar calls the three strategies for occupation: accommodation to existing elites, inducement to encourage people to stop fighting, and latent coercion to inspire fear. As inducement, officers tried to restore municipal services, including public health, social welfare, and daily governance. Coercion arose as a strategy where opposition was the sharpest. Major General John Pope carried western antiguerrilla warfare eastward in 1862 to Virginia, where he imposed harsh martial law on places like Augusta County. Rather than exerting military power over disloyal individuals, the government regulated geographic areas in rebellion, treating inhabitants—whether soldiers or not—as "enemies, though not foreigners," in Supreme Court Justice Robert C. Grier's phrase. Over 1862, officers tied occupation policies to emancipation, and occupied towns became havens for escaping slaves.[17]

Against complaints that martial law, foraging, and emancipation went beyond the laws of war, the United States developed the Lieber Code. The code paradoxically both restrained and unleashed occupations. On the one hand, it declared that the army should be governed by "justice, honor, and humanity" and avoid enslaving or murdering innocent civilians. At the same time it also justified displacing law for "force," starving or exiling recalcitrant populations, and killing guerrillas as "highway robbers or pirates." While armies should behave honorably, nothing could restrain "military necessity."[18]

As they judged necessity, commanders tried forms of both direct and indirect rule. At times U.S. officers worked through local officials they supervised. At other times, especially after 1863, they directly emancipated slaves, seized food, exiled traitors, shuttered newspapers, hanged outlaws, starved regions, and developed a policy of hard war meant to sap Confederates' will or capacity to fight. In Savannah, Sherman laid out the common framework for military and civil control. "During the war the military is superior to civil authority, and where interests clash the civil must give way." But "where there is no conflict, every encouragement should be given to well-disposed and peaceful inhabitants." As Sherman cut across Georgia and turned to the hotbed of rebellion in South Carolina, he expanded his powers, eventually distributing roughly 400,000 acres of land along the South Carolina coast for the use of 40,000 freedpeople. In Missouri, Sherman's foster brother, Colonel Thomas Ewing, exiled traitors and resettled loyalists in several counties, while a colonel in Arkansas moved loyalists onto fortified plantations.[19]

With the surrenders, generals acknowledged the new moment but did not change many of their policies. There were a few crucial exceptions: Washington ordered the troops to permit most commerce, cease foraging on local supplies, and stop requiring passes for civilian travel, an early effort at accommodation to the local whites. In the aftermath of the surrenders, U.S. soldiers could still take white Southerners' liberty but could not take their corn without compensation. Halleck hoped this policy would lead to a new, cooperative interaction between the army and white Southerners. The expectation of peace was genuine, yet it was also ephemeral. Something had changed with the passing of battles, but the military's power had not evaporated.[20]

On the ground, in fact, the army's power expanded dramatically. As politicians and officers celebrated markers of the war's end, the army launched an intrusive, expansive occupation of the Southern countryside. Prior to surrender, the U.S. Army held strategically important towns; now it aimed to regulate the entire Confederacy. The continuation of wartime drew the U.S. Army deep into the recesses and crossroads of the South, into the regions now left without clear or functional civil government. Surrender scattered not just Confederate but U.S. armies. As paroled Confederates returned to their farms and villages, U.S. soldiers spun into the same countryside as if they were still pursuing the very men they had just defeated. Through May and June, the military tried to extend its authority over a rural, inaccessible region the size of the United Kingdom, France, Spain, Germany, and Italy combined. "Station troops in all important towns," Major General Quincy Adams Gillmore ordered officers along the coast, to "keep the whole country under military surveillance." Using cavalry, Gillmore hoped to "at any time reach any remote point where disorder may occur" to "effectually punish all crime, and

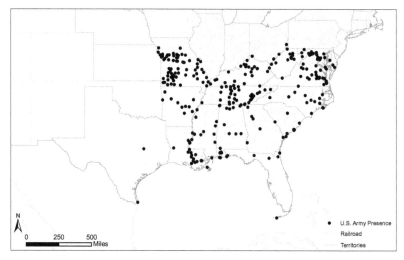

U.S. Army presence, March–April 1865. University of Richmond Digital Scholarship Laboratory.

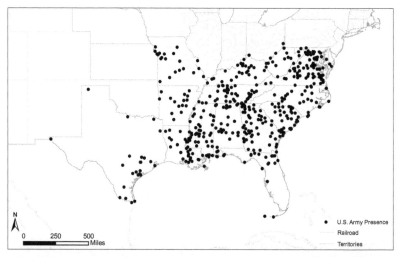

U.S. Army presence, June–August 1865. University of Richmond Digital Scholarship Laboratory.

to do justice." In parts of Virginia, commanders sent cavalry to every county seat, where they could conduct military courts and "shoot guerillas, horse-thieves, or marauders."[21]

The very expansion of the military into the countryside that Sherman feared had become the United States' policy. By the summer of 1865, army companies quickly came to resemble spokes on a wheel, attached by highway or rail line or river to powerful regiments in cities or central places. The largest groups were typically stationed in capital cities and the larger towns. Others were often dispatched to key rail lines, like the troops who held the L&N line at Pulaski, Tennessee, or railroad lines at Stevenson's Depot, Alabama. Others covered river transportation, like the troops at Ship Island, Mississippi, or at De Valls Bluff in Arkansas. From central cities and rivers and railroad lines, the units moved outward in more ambitious and unpredictable ways. From 120 outposts at the end of March, they eventually reached more than 630 posts in the former Confederacy. Across the South, the army occupied seven different Lexingtons and six Franklins, as well as three Fayettevilles, two Fayettes, and two LaFayettes. In South Carolina, companies quickly occupied not only large towns but also smaller places like Gillisonville, Grahamville, and McPherson-ville. In Georgia, Gillmore's orders dispatched men up the Altamaha, Ocmulgee, and Savannah rivers and along the Atlantic and Gulf Railroad from Doctortown to Thomasville. In eastern and southern Florida, soldiers quickly spread beyond Tallahassee to places like Palatka and Mellonville. The total number of outposts swelled over the summer in South Carolina from ten to forty-two, in Georgia from seven to sixty-nine, and in Florida from seven to twenty-one. In places where the army was already present, the growth was slower: from about a dozen to twenty-six in North Carolina, from thirty to sixty in Virginia, and from thirty-five to forty in Tennessee. These reported outposts almost certainly understated the geographic spread of power. One Mississippi commander confessed that he listed only officers' headquarters, not permanent stations in surrounding counties, to save paperwork.[22]

These intrusions into the countryside created a new, uneven, temporary, but meaningful national sovereignty on the ground. If we think of sovereignty as defined by statute books, by the aspirational power of judges or congressmen, then it does not make sense to think of occupation as a new type of sover-eignty. The clean lines of a ladder of sovereignty rising from the local through the district to the state and the nation, mirroring the limits of court jurisdic-tion, do not capture the way people experienced legal power in the United

U.S. Army encampment, Baton Rouge, Louisiana, during the Civil War. Andrew D. Lytle Album Photograph Collection, MS 3708, Louisiana and Lower Mississippi Valley Collections, Louisiana State University Library, Baton Rouge, Louisiana.

States or other nineteenth-century countries. Instead, the question of who had the authority to make decisions that would stick—whether a magistrate, a local layman, a state official, or a federal judge—was fraught and open ended. Before the Civil War, national power existed primarily in anomalous enclaves around federal courts and customs houses. Sending soldiers made natural rivers and the steel rivers of railroad tracks into corridors of sovereignty and created hundreds of enclaves where the federal government's power had concrete meaning. The nation's capacity to exert authority over river towns, upcountry regions, coastal plantation belts, and high mountains varied dramatically, creating an uneven occupation and a patchwork sovereignty over the South.[23]

In the Southwest, the occupation expanded along similar lines but at a slower pace because of the confusing situation in Texas. When Confederate general Edmund Kirby Smith refused to surrender Texas, U.S. generals in the southwestern states did not scatter troops like their eastern peers. Instead, they consolidated their forces to prepare an invasion. Only after Kirby Smith finally admitted defeat on May 26 did the army direct an occupation of the Gulf that mirrored that of the eastern coast. With the threat from Texas diminished, Major General Philip Sheridan ordered the occupation of those sections of Louisiana not already under federal control, sending garrisons to Shreveport and Alexandria to "maintain peace and order." In a series of orders on May 29, soldiers headed toward Washington, New Iberia, Thibodeaux, Donaldsonville, Plaquemine, Shreveport, Alexandria, and Natchitoches, Louisiana. Troops at New Orleans and Carrollton branched out to Bayou Saint John and Ponchatoula and Pass Manchac. In a slippage of language that often surfaced in the months after Appomattox, the army order forbidding foraging stated that "the war"—not just battlefield conflict or the insurgency—"is over." Therefore the military should "teach" Southerners "we are their friends." Nevertheless, a great many wartime powers remained. The same order urged the soldiers to prove that "wherever the authority of the United States exists there is ample security for persons and property." Farther north in Arkansas, the commanding general dispatched companies in late May to each county around Pine Bluff, and other troops occupied Jacksonport, Augusta, Batesville, and Searcy. Another commander wrote, "The peace and quietude, as well as the police, of the stations will for the present be entirely in the hands of the military."[24]

In Mississippi, bureaucratic confusion delayed the spread of troops into the interior counties until the middle of June. Then soldiers moved out into the state along the railroad lines. The army expanded from twelve mostly riverine towns in April to at least fifty by the end of the summer. There, the army's occupation clearly reflected its ambitious goals; one officer wrote that he needed only 3,000 soldiers if the military shifted to a peacetime footing and restored local law. But if the government intended something more ambitious, "it will take a considerable force of cavalry to suppress out-laws, and of infantry to hold certain interior posts or depots."[25] Rather than withdrawing to 3,000 troops, it kept more than 16,000 in Mississippi in July 1865 and maintained levels over 3,000 for a full year.

Once finally occupied, Texas presented many challenges as the site of multiple threats: Confederate, international, and Indian. The rebels there had never been conquered, and slavery still thrived in the eastern plantation belts. Slavery had actually expanded in Texas during the Civil War as planters moved refugee slaves away from the fighting to the safety of the Lone Star State. Across the Rio Grande in Mexico, the French-backed forces of Emperor Maximilian fought to displace the Liberal government of Benito Juárez. In the western part of the state, Comanche raiders took advantage of the war to seize horses, drive off white settlers, and claim control. The end of fighting in the Southwest was not a transition from war to peace but from one war to multiple wars, from a unifying narrative of struggle against the Confederacy to a pluralism of problems that beset the nation. From the time France and other European powers attacked Mexico in the winter of 1861–1862, some Americans and Mexican Liberals had vocally tied the two wars together. The French-backed Mexican Empire was "part and parcel of the late rebellion in the United States, and a necessary part of it to suppress before entire peace can be assured," Grant wrote.[26]

To defend itself against both the Mexican Empire and the unconquered status of Texas, the U.S. Army moved nearly 50,000 troops in June and July 1865, 25,000 by ship from Virginia alone. At first the largest concentrations were in the border regions of Galveston, Brownsville, and Brazos Island as well as the important town of San Antonio. "The great army of observation is step by step moving towards the Mexican frontier, seizing the strategic positions, and deploying along the hither bank of the Rio Grande," the *Army & Navy Journal* wrote. These troops all but erased the border between Texas and Mexico, patrolling the Rio Grande to frighten fleeing Confederates, crossing into Mexican territory to claim material that Confederates had carried away after surrender, and dumping tens of thousands of muskets for Mexican Liberal forces to use. In the Texas interior, troops aimed to restrain guerrilla warfare and arrest "desperadoes" and insurgent Indians. Tellingly, the *Army & Navy Journal* thought the military ought to teach Texans the "lesson of the Shenandoah Valley," where commanders had forcefully occupied Virginia towns from 1862 onward. What Texas lacked, in this formulation, was the true experience of occupation. To deliver on that promise, the army swelled to forty-two posts by the spring of 1866. Although many Americans expected open war against the Mexican Empire, and perhaps France, Secretary of State William Seward played for time while he tried to negotiate France's withdrawal from the country.[27]

As soldiers arrived in places that had not hitherto been occupied, they transformed the nature of everyday life in these regions simply by their presence. Even if they behaved generously, their arrival marked a new moment, a breakage in time. The army called an end to anarchy, the state of not being governed, and proclaimed a new order, recognizing "for the present no authority but its own." Whites who lived within rebel lines had "lost their rights as citizens," commanders warned people in Pocotaligo and Grahamville, South Carolina. "The country is under martial law and the civil authority is dormant." In the first days, army outposts enforced emancipation, prevented Confederate uprisings, provided rations, policed the countryside, and helped oversee railroad construction. Army officers directly intervened in the Southern economy by remaking labor contracts, providing an outlet for complaints, and forcing freedmen to work on farms rather than flee to cities. In South Carolina and Georgia, Major General Quincy Adams Gillmore directed his subordinates to exercise wide powers. "Lawlessness must be suppressed, industry encouraged, and confidence in the beneficence of the Government established." In some states, lawyers, physicians, ministers, and merchants could not practice until they took an oath of allegiance. In others, commanders banned the use of the word "Confederate" or arrested people for insulting the nation or the flag. In Raleigh, Sherman suspended the newspaper *Progress* for publishing critical pieces. "There is one thing I want your newspapermen to understand," he wrote the editor. "And that is you are not conducting a newspaper in Massachusetts or New York, but in a conquered territory."[28]

At first, the army's power was murky. In these early months, some commanders did not convene military courts or permit civil courts to meet. Law fell into abeyance. There, the army simply kept the peace by serving as a police force to arrest and hold criminals. In some places, the army swept aside local officers and named new ones whom it empowered to act. Under the newly passed bill creating the Bureau of Refugees, Freedmen, and Abandoned Lands (the Freedmen's Bureau) to oversee the transition of ex-slaves to freedom, the army also had the authority to take control of any cases involving freedpeople, but the bureau did not yet have a staff or orders. In other places, the army relied upon indirect rule and allowed local authorities to continue to hear both criminal and civil cases in the first months, as they awaited instructions. Even where it worked through local magistrates, the army exercised ultimate authority over their decisions. Unlike in peacetime, magistrates and clerks were "directly responsible to the military power." When the officer commanding Farmville, Virginia, asked in April 1865 whether the mayor could exercise "civil authority," his superiors told him the mayor could act as long as he "does not conflict with the military" but that the commander had the final authority. Military oversight of the law changed the dynamics of Southern life; magistrates who once held vast powers to regulate their neighborhoods (and whose decisions were rarely tested by appeal to higher courts) suddenly could be called to answer to nearby military authorities who could overrule and even depose them. This was an extraordinary intervention into forms of local law that even states had barely regulated. It undermined the broad power that local white elites had often exercised over their neighborhoods.[29]

From these posts, the army kept an eye on paroled rebel soldiers, looking for signs of additional uprisings. To tamp down any expressions of public disloyalty, the military banned Confederate emblems and uniforms. By his perhaps exaggerated account, it arrested rebel officer Henry Kyd Douglas for having a photograph taken in his Confederate uniform. In Norfolk, Brigadier General George H. Gordon ordered his provost marshals to remove every vestige of rebel attire they encountered on the streets and to give every returning soldier forty-eight hours to obtain a citizen's dress. Writing after the war, Gordon reflected upon the peculiar importance of clothing. Seeing free men in Confederate garb on the streets of Norfolk "was so offensive to the eyes of Union men, that I felt constrained to suppress it upon its first appearance."[30] Banning rebel attire was in part a simple effort to make disloyalty disrespectable. What the army aimed to control was not private opinion but public expression in the form of speeches, newspaper columns, and uniforms. By wearing uniforms after the end of battle, rebels not only celebrated the Confederacy but also blurred the meaning of surrender in ways that outraged U.S. soldiers.

Although romances of reunion emphasize close collaboration between Northern soldiers and white Southern civilians, the early weeks were defined by mistrust, fear, and apprehension. "Not a drop of sympathy do they have from me," one soldier in Louisiana wrote in April. "May not one single person who voluntarily took up arms against our Flag ever return to his home, but may their bones be left to bleach upon the earth forgotten and alone." A soldier on occupation duty in Alabama and Mississippi threatened to bayonet a white woman in the abdomen to prevent her from conceiving any more "traitors." When soldiers forced women to dance in front of a U.S. flag at a town ball, one soldier bitterly commented that "Bayonets taught them a lesson." Many Northerners blamed all rebels for Lincoln's assassination or the deaths of their fellow U.S. soldiers.[31]

Because the army's policies were still unfolding during the weeks after surrender, it can be hard to grasp the concrete implications of the continuation of wartime. In the late spring of 1865, the machinery of postsurrender occupation was not yet in place in most regions; few parallel court systems were functioning. But one could see the impact of wartime in what did not happen. One place where the endurance of wartime mattered was St. Catherines Island, Georgia, where the remarkable Tunis Campbell, a New Jersey–born African American lecturer and organizer, had become the leader of an extraordinary experiment in black self-rule. When Major General William T. Sherman issued Field Order 15 setting aside the coastal region of South Carolina and Georgia for freedpeople to set up farms during the duration of the war, Campbell became superintendent of several Georgia islands. He established a black-run government, founded schools, and organized a black militia. While the bold and brilliant Campbell worked from his own understanding of freedom, his experiment still depended on the space wartime created. The right to occupy the land was based on Sherman's field order giving the freedpeople a possessory title that depended either upon wartime or a determination in court that the land had been abandoned. Had Sherman's armistice prevailed, judges in Georgia and South Carolina would undoubtedly have ruled that the land still belonged to the planters, and, at minimum, hampered the federal government's authority. The rebel governors of Georgia and South Carolina, who also still would have been in office by virtue of Sherman's armistice, would have likely dispatched former rebel soldiers as a militia to reclaim the land. Facing Campbell's well-drilled militia, there would have been pitched battles; had Confederates prevailed, it would likely have ended in a massacre. But judges could not make those rulings, sheriffs could not enforce them, and the rebel governor of Georgia could not call out the militia since he was under arrest. While President Johnson eventually betrayed the residents of the Sea Islands, Johnson's decision to extend wartime created time and space that was crucial for Campbell's experimentation and prevented a gloomy story from turning out even worse. In Wilmington, North Carolina, the radical ex-slave Abraham Galloway established Equal Rights League chapters within weeks after Lee's surrender. They, too, did not look to white soldiers for advice as they acted upon their own vision of freedom to petition the president for the right to vote. But they, too, depended upon the continuation of legal wartime. If peace had been restored, sheriffs and magistrates would have assuredly broken up the meetings and arrested Galloway under state law. More narrowly, the force of wartime was obvious to Reuben E. Wilson, a rebel captain who in March 1865 had ordered his men to execute two deserters, two white Unionists, and a black man in the North Carolina Piedmont for disloyalty to the Confederacy. When federal soldiers arrived in

Forsyth County at the end of April, they arrested Wilson. For the time being, no civilian court in North Carolina had jurisdiction, no judge could release him, and he remained in military prison in Richmond. In the spring of 1865, Campbell, Galloway, Wilson, and millions of other Southerners did not know the ultimate consequences of extending wartime, but they knew that there had been a change in who ruled the places where they lived.[32]

The army's presence and its power transformed the way that white Southerners understood their condition. "To say that Shreveport was upside down hardly expresses the situation," a Confederate there wrote. "Negro guards were placed at nearly every street corner." White Southerners understood that the presence of troops signaled that they were on soil occupied "by the enemy."[33] People who had never seen a federal officer other than a postmaster suddenly found companies of troops in crossroads villages and county seats. Company commanders represented the first effective face of federal power. Their ubiquity was not a prelude to their power; it was itself their power. In the South, many people lived their lives within relatively narrow confines even though the goods they bought and sold embedded them within global commerce. Placing these posts within walking distance made the army suddenly, shockingly present. As white and black Southerners struggled to define their rights and powers in the period after surrender, the army figured in these conversations, and in some areas powerfully reshaped them, not just because it had guns but because it was there. Practically, sovereignty was not just a legal but a geographical term.

But if proximity was at the heart of the army's power, the military was nearly powerless in places it did not reach. In regions far from military stations, guerrilla warfare raged. In coastal South Carolina, regular and irregular bands swept in after Sherman's men marched northward, attacking slaves with ruthless abandon. In Saint Paul's Parish, South Carolina, a band of guerrillas under Dick Sims slaughtered at least four freedpeople and planned to kill any white Southerner who took an oath of allegiance. There, defeat erased the line between maintaining slavery and murdering slaves. Most explicitly, this was true in Missouri and Arkansas, where the war lifted ongoing regional and personal tensions to new planes. Bands of outlaws like Quantrill's raiders practiced what at times looked like indiscriminate bloodshed and thievery. Although few portions of the Confederacy resembled Missouri or Arkansas, outlaws flourished in upcountry North and South Carolina, northern Alabama, and the Appalachian regions of West Virginia, Virginia, Kentucky, and Tennessee.[34]

In parts of the South, it was legally and practically anarchy. If Confederate officials had no standing, and if the United States had not replaced them, then there was no law at all. Surrender had stripped away the foundations of law that propertied people relied upon to naturalize their privilege. Absent law, they quickly recognized, they lacked the hegemonic ability to regulate daily life to protect their property and status. Southern society "resolved to its original elements," one Virginian wrote. "Every social bond had been ruptured. . . . All laws had become inoperative for want of officers to enforce them. All the safeguards of life, liberty and property had been uprooted." It seemed a return to the state of nature, thousands of years of civilization erased in a flash. A white Georgia woman wrote in her diary: "We have no currency, no law, save the primitive code that might makes right. The props that hold society are broken." Parts of Georgia were literally "without civil government," a public meeting in Savannah proclaimed, "exposed to repeated depredations and violence" and subjected to "the peril of famine and anarchy." Josiah Gorgas, who had overseen armaments for the Confederacy, described this transformation vividly. "I am as one walking in a dream," he wrote. "It is marvelous that a people that a month ago had money, armies, and the attributes of a nation should today be no more, and that we live[,] breathe, move, talk as before— will it be so when the soul leaves the body behind it?"[35]

In the face of this anarchy, many ex-rebels, no matter how much they disliked the Yankees, tried to claim military power for their own benefit. Even as some ex-rebels attacked soldiers, many others tried to ally with the U.S. government to create peace on their own terms. In Staunton, Virginia, townspeople "quietly took the reins of government" from fleeing officeholders, reached out to U.S. officials for recognition, and refused help from the fleeing rebel governor. In other regions, where guerrillas and outlaws held sway, white Southerners depended entirely on the U.S. Army to create order. For six weeks after surrender, one Arkansas judge waited for the resumption of law, which would come, he believed, only when troops proclaimed the new regime. In Jackson, Mississippi, in May 1865, the leading citizens desperately wanted U.S. soldiers to arrive from Vicksburg because they could not feel secure until the troops shot "the devils down where they can be found."[36]

Because rebels sometimes asked for military assistance and generally stopped shooting, some contemporaries and later historians have confused their tactical silence with acquiescence. No one worked harder to prove that rebels were willing to accept any terms after surrender than Chief Justice Chase.

As he toured the coastal South and drummed up support for black suffrage, Chase wrote that white Southerners would "just as clearly, accommodate themselves to any mode of reorganization the National Government may think best—even including the restoration to the blacks of the right of suffrage." Chase's argument for black suffrage, however, should not be confused with reliable analysis. One of his fellow travelers on this tour, the reporter Whitelaw Reid, found rebels much more resistant to change. Other Northern travelers described a white South in active rebellion, "seething and boiling, as if a volcano were struggling beneath it." While many rebels pledged loyalty, white loyalists thought these sentiments were illusory. A former Texas legislator wrote in late May that not a "tittle of the spirit" of rebellion "is eradicated." Although officers generally believed that rebels were done with organized fighting, many found evidence of continued hostility toward the government. Over time, however, as conditions worsened in the South and as President Johnson fought against Republicans, a myth developed that the period after surrender had been a golden age when rebels might have accepted anything. But this myth had a thin foundation. Many people who later claimed that there was acquiescence in May or June 1865, including Whitelaw Reid, had actually written very different things at the time. For example, Alabama loyalist J. J. Giers wrote in May 1865 that "secessionists are as bitter and hostile against the Government as ever." By the next year, however, Giers retrospectively made the period after surrender a time when the Southern white people were willing to "submit to anything and to everything."[37]

From later claims that rebels would have acquiesced in the spring of 1865, some historians imagine a Reconstruction that could have been an easy remaking of Southern society. By presuming that white rebels would truly have acquiesced, they make the time a "window of enormous opportunity."[38] But in fact, many white Southerners would not accept the end of slavery, much less the birth of civil rights for freedpeople. They were already on their way to launching their insurgent campaign to dislodge federal and military power in the South. By misreading white Southern opinion, contemporaries back then found an easy scapegoat for the disappointments of Reconstruction in President Andrew Johnson; he had failed to take advantage of the golden moment. While Johnson's actions would in fact later undermine Reconstruction, his behavior in the spring of 1865 was actually quite bold. He blocked white Southerners' dreams of complete restoration. Johnson surely performed badly after 1866; had he performed better, Reconstruction still would have remained an extraordinarily difficult challenge. White Southerners only acceded to federal rule when it did not threaten what they most valued. As soon as it infringed upon their power over freedpeople, even in the narrow ways Johnson intervened, they resisted vigorously and violently. There was no easy path to peace over a white Southern population who—by and large—continued to resist changes to their legal, racial, and economic order.[39]

Rebels did demonstrate dread in the face of force. Very few were willing to launch suicidal direct assaults upon large bands of soldiers; the era of open combat had passed. But this dread was not the same thing as acquiescence; it was situational, contingent, and temporary. The army could convince them of its power, but only by continual presence and firm action. Even then the fear of the army's authority would not persuade rebels to accept a broad transformation of their society. As soon as they saw any sign of vulnerability, rebels quickly began to assert their authority. One window into these sentiments can be seen in the letters Confederate navy commander Matthew Fontaine Maury received after surrender. From Europe, where he had been purchasing ships for the rebels, Maury wrote in April and May to his scattered family and friends across Virginia. He wanted to know whether he should return home or flee to Mexico. Particularly he feared that he would be hanged as a traitor.

The answers he received reveal the importance of proximity and symbolic power in shaping white Southerners' responses to occupation. One relative who lived near federal barracks reported that the South "stands in the light of a conquered province and has no rights." Others, farther from troops, were certain that they were "not practically oppressed." This judgment turned, however, when troops suddenly marched into town and camped there. The experience of occupation was more one of psychological than physical coercion; another Virginian found himself "shocked beyond measure, beyond measure, at the ease which people because of nothing but pure fear come under the yoke."[40]

For a brief time, the federal government through the army was clothed in might and mystery because of its victory in the war. There seemed literally no limit to what it could do. "The rebels are frightened at the very sight or name of Yankee," a Northern agent wrote later. As the army marched through the South after the surrenders, it often succeeded in inspiring the first flash of fear. But sustaining that dread was a more difficult problem. Rebels were frightened, the U.S. agent wrote, "but they need to be kept in awe." The letters back to Matthew Maury revealed its evanescence. As soldiers departed from central Virginia, Maury's correspondents noted that "now it is different." With the departure of the provost marshal, the power of the army seemed slack, one cousin wrote. "Time will help me." Many ex-Confederates became confident that time was on their side; surely, the departure of the troops would allow landowners like the Maurys to once again claim their old rights. Only if we understand the thinness of rebel acquiescence can we see why it could not be the basis for an easy Reconstruction. No occupation could work through constant forceful presence everywhere, all the time. Unless the United States restored all the rebels' power, they would resist both politically and violently.[41]

If the United States' power depended on ubiquitous presence, it seemed to ebb in the last week of May 1865. Tens of thousands of soldiers marched through Washington, D.C.'s broad avenues over two long days in what would become known as the Grand Review. Standing densely on sidewalks, leaning from balconies, and sitting on tree limbs, civilians witnessed a procession that seemed to translate war into peace. Instead of haunted, ruddy men in blood-caked uniforms and mud-eaten shoes, the soldiers were newly scrubbed in their "cleaned boots, blackened equipments, polished arms," casting themselves both forward and backward in time to be once again mild, respectable men, not warriors. Calling upon a peacetime tradition that reached at least as far back as the Roman triumphal marches, spectators threw flowers into the air. As the flowers descended, they fell on the newly cleaned uniforms, the "battle-rent flags," the bayonets, and the "rumbling field-pieces, from whose black muzzles death had so often hurled," now "gaily decorated with wreaths and bouquets." The flowers that lay thickly upon the soldiers buried the past in the present, the old graves in the promise of new growth.[42] As the soldiers reached the final stand, they saluted the president, the cabinet, and a few generals, and then marched onward to camps from which many would begin to head home. The Grand Review promised to deliver upon the promise of the nation's seal, to make of many one. From a war which made two nations, two fronts, a multitude of armies, and an immensity of experiences, the review offered unity in the form of a peace that drowned rivalries and treason and bondage in a tide of progress. Marching on separate days, western and eastern armies sent the same message: the army's work was well done and nearly done.

The expectation of peace was general all over the United States. Five days later, on May 29, President Andrew Johnson proclaimed the insurrection "almost entirely overcome." Starting with North Carolina, Johnson marked a transition from anarchy to order by appointing a provisional governor whom the army would "assist." As he began to restore government, Johnson also moved to restore individuals in a second proclamation offering amnesty and pardon to many ex-Confederates who took an oath of allegiance to the United States. There were reasons to think the war was ended. U.S. troops had captured Jefferson Davis in Irwinville, Georgia, on May 10. A series of smaller surrenders swept away the remainder of the Confederate armies. Since Appomattox, the Confederacy had lost its leadership and its armed forces.[43]

Therefore, many people in late May embraced the Grand Review and the provisional governments as the end to the war. Confident that they lived now in something approaching normal time, Northerners increasingly spoke of the war in the past tense. Johnson, however, had slipped the stubborn "almost" before "overcome" as a brake against the achievement of peace. As Johnson leaned yearningly toward the war's end—as if it had all but arrived—he also unequivocally, if quietly, signaled that this moment had not yet come. In late May, one might have supposed that Johnson's "almost" was a product of geography; organized battles were still possible in Texas or Arkansas or Indian Territory. Bands of guerrillas roamed the South. As Johnson continued to issue proclamations for the remaining ungoverned states, however, he included the "almost" each time. As the spring ended and summer arrived, the insurrection remained "almost" ended. The Grand Review and presidential proclamations began, not completed, the processes of army demobilization and restoration of state governments. For the spring and summer of 1865, the word "almost" marked the hope for peace but the continuation of wartime. In ways that confounded his contemporaries, Johnson desired peace but would not relinquish the powers of war.

– 2 –

EMANCIPATION AT GUNPOINT

T HE MAURY FAMILY celebrated the withdrawal of troops too soon. Although they expressed relief in May at the retreat of federal soldiers, by the summer they learned that the government continued to intervene between planters and their former slaves. Instead of ending with the first mustering out of troops, the military occupation had only just begun. In Charlottesville, soldiers arrested a Maury family friend for slapping his former slave. "They fill our land with military government and garrisons thus evidencing still more the great breach that now yawnes between us," one of Maury's cousins complained late in the summer.[1]

Soldiers could not retreat from Maury's Virginia, nor could the war powers cease, because slavery had not died and freedom had not yet been defined. While spectators in Washington expected parades and proclamations to lessen the army's role, military commanders instead expanded their interventions in daily life in the South in the late spring and summer of 1865. They did so because they learned that slavery endured. Embedded in legal, political, and social supports, slavery had to be pried away from the body politic like a tick from the skin. On May 26, two days after the Grand Review, Alabama's commissioner for the newly created Freedmen's Bureau described problems of emancipation that could not be resolved by mere words. When he arrived in Montgomery, he found a society in chaos. Plantation owners "appeared disinclined to offer employment, except with guarantees that would practically reduce the Freedmen again to a state of bondage." Freedpeople in turn clustered in cities and towns for safety. Attempting to terrorize workers into submission, a group of newly returned Confederates "took some Freedmen and cut off their ears." As he toured the region, the bureau administrator found not peace but fresh wounds, angry words, crops left to rot in the fields. Like other army commanders and bureau officials, he realized that labor contracts and admonitions alone would neither end slavery nor restore peace. As one general wrote in June, "To announce their freedom is not to make them free."[2] The only reliable mechanism to attack slavery on the ground was the army, and the crucial tool the military could use was its wartime authority over civil government.

As freedpeople taught officers about the enduring power of slavery, soldiers and ex-slaves together developed the notion that freedom meant accessible rights. In the process, they helped to expand the meaning of both freedom and rights, keywords in American life then and now. Although freedom is not necessarily defined around rights, in the political language of the day ex-slaves found it easy to invoke rights as the measure of what it meant not to be enslaved. As slaves, they had virtually no rights they could defend in court. Looking to the experience of free people around them, they defined freedom in part as the opportunity to have those basic rights—marriage, control of children, property ownership, travel, and contract—protected by the government. This was the bare minimum. Ex-slaves pressed for broader rights, too. In the spring and summer of 1865, however, even these minimal rights were aspirational, not rights at all in a legal sense but mere claims upon military power. They recognized that their rights depended in part upon access to government. This statist understanding of freedom as attachment to government, instead of separation from government, proved crucial in sustaining support for the occupation of the rebel states and in shaping the development of civil rights over the next decade. Instead of a march to freedom, with its connotations of separation from the state, freedpeople and soldiers described a walk toward government.[3] Because the military was the only force that could render these aspirations meaningful in much of the Southern countryside, the development of these rights was inseparable from military power on the ground. The occupation therefore inaugurated a temporary but important expansion of government's intervention in daily life. Rooted in the military, rather than in the courts or bureaucracies, it provided a different, and in the end unsustainable, model of government compared to the better-studied twentieth-century development of the U.S. state.[4]

Although the United States might have extended its authority over the rebel states purely through a strategy of accommodation and inducement, its determination to strike against slavery's vestiges forced the government toward coercion. Facing a white Southern population that was determined to hold on to slavery, the United States could topple it only by disregarding white public opinion in the South. In the process, the United States attempted a laudable but risky effort to go beyond most occupiers and attempt to remake the society it had conquered. But the United States did not possess many options. Either it could disrupt slavery and risk a rebel insurgency, or it could accommodate white rebels and accept the persistence of either slavery or the vestiges of slavery. From the moment the United States committed to overturning Southern society, the die was cast for a long, violent struggle that would be decided as much by force as by law or politics.[5]

Slavery needed to be killed because it had not died. Although it is natural to think of the Emancipation Proclamation as the end of slavery, its impact was limited to slaves who could reach U.S. forces. While the Thirteenth Amendment passed Congress in early 1865, it had not yet been ratified by a sufficient number of states to join it to the Constitution. Therefore, slavery endured on the ground well after the end of fighting. Of the nearly 4 million slaves in the United States in 1860, the vast majority were still held in bondage as the Confederate armies surrendered. Historians estimate that 474,000 former slaves were federally sponsored free laborers as soldiers, camp residents, or farmworkers on government-run plantations. The Freedmen and Southern Society Project suggests that about 125,000 of these ex-slaves lived in the Mississippi valley, 98,000 in southern Louisiana, 48,000 on the Atlantic coast, 74,000 in tidewater Virginia and North Carolina, 40,000 in the Washington, D.C., area, about 37,000 in middle and eastern Tennessee and northern Alabama, and about 52,000 in the border states. In the winter of 1864–1865, the border states of Missouri, Maryland, and West Virginia eliminated slavery; this freed perhaps another 185,000 people, not counting black soldiers already enlisted from those states. Andrew Johnson's Tennessee government likewise ended slavery in early 1865, freeing perhaps 200,000 more people. While Arkansas's and Louisiana's loyal governments abolished slavery, they had at best limited control over large sections of their states, and their laws freed relatively few people. Soldiers found people held in slavery there deep into the summer. The number of slaves who reached the North or who were actually freed by Arkansas or Louisiana is unknown, but we might estimate that perhaps 1 million of the nation's 4 million slaves had been actually freed by Appomattox. Of the rest, somewhat less than 200,000 remained in unencumbered legal slavery in the loyal states of Kentucky and Delaware. The remaining 2.75 million slaves were largely scattered across the Confederacy's vast interior, in regions that the U.S. Army either had not reached or had quickly passed through. The persistence of slavery reminds us of slavery's resilience. Although scholars once presumed— like many 1850s Republicans—that slavery was weak, unprofitable, and backward, we now know what many officers discovered in 1865. Slavery was profitable, efficient, and powerful, embedded within a modernizing world, not a relic of the past. Slavery would not simply die; it would have to be killed.[6]

For weeks and months after surrender, soldiers confronted slavery in areas that had not yet been occupied by U.S. troops. When German-born Colonel Charles Bentzoni reached eastern Arkansas with his 56th U.S. Colored Infantry, he found "slavery everywhere." The planters "understand that slavery will remain in some form or other." In a series of exasperated letters, Bentzoni captured slavery's tenacious survival against both state laws and army policies. Unless "slavery is broken up by the strong arm of the Government," he wrote, "it will continue to exist in its worst forms all law and proclamations to the contrary." In isolated Eastport, Mississippi, one hundred miles from other outposts, a general believed that proclamations could not lead to "the actual immediate emancipation of a large mass of plantation slaves." The end of slavery depended on force. As late as September, Arkansas's Freedmen's Bureau commissioner reported that "there are large portions of Arkansas where the freedmen are still treated as Slaves, the former slave owners in some cases proclaiming that 'Slavery has not been abolished by any competent authority.'" Not until November did an Arkansas soldier who discovered two slave girls explain the situation as an anomaly; before that the endurance of slavery was simply a fact of life.[7]

From many other parts of the South, soldiers discovered the difference between announcing the end of slavery and actually destroying the institution. In South Carolina, Sherman's mighty army of invasion had blasted through the coastal region and Columbia, but as late as July 1865 "the authority of the United States" had "not yet permeated every part of the interior." Major General Quincy Adams Gillmore thought that "in remote sections the relation of master and slave does, in some cases, practically exist." While inspecting South Carolina, Carl Schurz found that "the people adhere not only to their former opinions, but to a certain extent also their former practices." Around Winnsboro, South Carolina, people tried to "hold the negro in a state of slavery until the arrival of our troops put an end to it." In far-off Texas, former masters worked to ensure that "slavery in some form will continue to exist" by murdering the blacks who tried to leave. As late as October, one observer noted, slave owners "still claim and control them as property, and in two or three instances have recently bought and sold them as in former years."[8]

Although slavery had collapsed in some regions of the South under the force of the war, planters worked quickly to restore it. They acted from their desire to protect their economic system but also from their broader belief that slavery was at the center of their way of life, even of their religious faith. To abandon slavery would mean something worse than losing a war; it would mean losing an entire culture. Some relied upon brute force to create the expectation that slavery endured. Describing the situation in Virginia after surrender, former slave Peter Randolph wrote that "some of the masters were very reluctant in giving up their servants, and tried to defraud and rob them out of their freedom, and many of the slaves had to run away from their masters to be free."[9] The scars on the backs of slaves, like the sliced ears of slaves attacked in Mississippi and Alabama, were meant to mark them as still enslaved.

But planters' hopes for salvaging slavery depended upon the resumption of peacetime. If the rebel states were restored to civil government, as Sherman's armistice promised, their political leaders would likely reject the Thirteenth Amendment and stop soldiers from intervening. Soon, they believed, they would be able to sue for their property in federal courts. Throughout the summer, officers and agents in Alabama complained that planters declared that the "ceasing of hostilities had made void the Emancipation proclamation." Months after Congress passed the Thirteenth Amendment, Alabama planters openly said that "they prefer gradual emancipation," as if the issue had not yet been decided. Many believed that slavery could be "restored in full sway in 18 months." From Jackson, one Mississippian wrote that "the troops should *not* be removed until the FACT, that the negro is free, is recognized and respected. For rest assured that this truth stands fast—*Slavery* is not yet broken up."[10]

Since President Johnson did not end the war, soldiers continued to use wartime powers to ensure slavery's destruction. Rather than relying solely upon law, they turned to an expansive and vaguely defined force. As Colonel Bentzoni surveyed the grim survival of slavery in Arkansas, his prescription was simple: "This evil can be suppressed at once by sending a military officer in every county with a small force." From Alabama, another wrote, "If you mean freedom, it is your power that will insure it." Surveying the vast and unoccupied region around Eastport, Mississippi, one general claimed that only "mounted soldiers" could enforce U.S. policy. They turned to force both from pessimism about law's power and optimism about the military's. Fresh from their battlefield victories, army commanders possessed an exaggerated confidence in their ability to reshape white Southerners' behavior through wartime maneuvers. As Carl Schurz recorded the persistence of slavery in his tour of the South, he noted the key difference between the unhappy but acquiescent rebels who had "come into direct contact with our forces" and those who had not. Ex-Confederates who had never encountered U.S. troops showed a "spirit of bitterness and persecution." "Everything is in a transition state. . . . Their action will be governed, not by the Spirit of the Emancipation Proclamation, but by an experience."[11]

As the military confronted the persistence of slavery, it exposed deeply laid tensions in the relationship among slavery, freedom, and the state. Wartime emancipation and the postsurrender struggle against slavery forced Northerners to examine the question of whether people could be free without the intervention of the government. Although Northerners had long understood that slavery depended upon state support, many only learned during the war that emancipation, too, would require ongoing government action. Adamantly antislavery politicians, including William Seward and Salmon Chase, had pictured a slavery whose tentacles were long but slippery; pry them loose, and freedom would emerge naturally. Even in 1865, some Republicans described the end of slavery in nearly magical terms. "The deliverer came, and at the sound of her voice every shackle fell and the slave was transformed quickly into a freeman," one Republican congressman said in 1865. In a similarly minded poem celebrating slavery's demise, poet and editor William Cullen

Bryant denounced slavery's "guilty power" but imagined that at "the appointed hour," a slave's shackles fell "and he whose limbs they galled / Stands in his native manhood, disenthralled." Emancipation would break the spell of slavery.[12]

Educated by wartime experiences and slaves' testimony, however, institutionally oriented officials learned to see emancipation not as a moment of delivery but as the beginning of a process that would require consistent government intervention. Some of these institutionalists had not been antislavery activists before the war; they included previously apathetic people like Secretary of War Edwin Stanton and Lieutenant General Ulysses S. Grant. But once ending slavery seemed both possible and necessary, people like Stanton and Grant committed to pulling it out by the roots. They recognized, as anti-institutionalists sometimes did not, that slavery would not die of natural causes. Slavery was simultaneously the product of government action and an institution that government could not easily unmake.

A crucial training ground for the development of this institutional thinking was wartime experiences in the Mississippi valley. While many owners fled from the coastal regions that the United States occupied, leaving control to the slaves and the army, the situation in the interior was different. There, the American Freedmen's Inquiry Commission reported, the army for the first time on a large scale encountered planters and ex-slaves on the same ground, "still face to face in the presence of the great revolution." The conditions there forced antislavery thinkers to see the "true nature of the mastership, and the order of slavery founded upon it." Emancipation required "not only the release of the slave population from their bonds and the degradation thereby imposed upon them; but the deliverance of the master population also, wholly and forever, from their mastership." Government would have to go beyond nullifying the laws of slavery and instead guarantee black civil and voting rights, break up large plantations, and establish "some uniform system of supervision and guardianship for the emancipated population in the interim of their transition from slavery to freedom."[13]

Over 1864 and 1865, these fights over the relationship among freedom, rights, and the role of government took center stage in Washington. As Congress attacked slavery through the Thirteenth Amendment and the Freedmen's Bureau bill in the lame-duck session of 1864–1865, politicians explored ongoing state intervention in destroying the institution. The first Freedmen's Bureau bill created a temporary government role by permitting the bureau to distribute clothes and food, regulate contracts, and set apart abandoned lands that white loyal refugees and freedpeople could rent and eventually own. Although some Republicans complained that the bills "virtually give the lie to the whole teaching of the anti-slavery men and women" and "say that the colored race are not competent to take care of themselves, that they want guardians," most Republicans increasingly reckoned with the structures necessary to support freedom. Slavery "had an infernal strength greater than any of us supposed," one said. Even "emancipation is not enough," Republican senator Charles Sumner said about the bureau. "You must see to it especially that the new-made freedmen are protected in those rights which are now assured to them. . . . The power of the Government must be to them like a shield."[14]

Democrats denounced the newly intrusive government that followed emancipation. The Thirteenth Amendment's enforcement clause would "annul the municipal control of each State over domestic matters," they complained. In a sweeping condemnation, New York Democratic congressman James Brooks called the acts a stride toward "homogeneity," a doomed effort to create—for the first time—uniformity across the nation. If the United States aimed to enforce national rights across the countryside, it would overstretch itself and provoke more rebellions, Brooks argued. Homogeneity "was not possible for Rome; it was not possible for Athens; it will not be possible for the Government at Washington, with all the telescopes which they may mount upon the highest pinnacles in this city . . . to regulate the local rights and privileges of the millions and millions of people." But Republicans mocked this assertion of government weakness. "We want 'homogeneity' as a nation," one answered.[15]

To make emancipation's new rights concrete, soldiers and agents of the newly formed Bureau of Refugees, Freedmen, and Abandoned Lands reached deep into the Southern countryside to impose the force of government. Because the Freedmen's Bureau was charged with overseeing the freedpeople, it is commonplace to emphasize the bureau's particular role in shaping emancipation. The Freedmen's Bureau did in fact have broad authority over labor contracts, rations, and the establishment of schools, hospitals, and local courts. For a time, the bureau even had jurisdiction over land that the federal government controlled during the war. On paper, it seemed as if the bureau was the crucial force for remaking the South, and bureau offices were in fact places that ex-slaves immediately sought out when they needed food, wanted a contract enforced, or feared the rulings of a local court. But the bureau was hamstrung by its size and composition. National commissioner O. O. Howard was only appointed in May 1865, and many states had no assistant commissioners until the late summer. In the crucial period of transition, the bureau simply did not exist in most places. Additionally, the bureau was housed within the War Department and was barred from employing many civilians. Therefore, it depended almost entirely upon detached soldiers. Even after the bureau was established, it had a small footprint. The Freedmen and Southern Society Project estimates that there were only 310 men in district and subdistrict bureau field offices at the end of 1865. Georgia had only thirteen, Texas merely ten. From the beginning, but especially during the winter of 1865, the bureau relied upon post commanders and provost marshals who were cross-appointed to the bureau or simply charged with responsibility for freedpeople. While some agents ran important offices, many others simply functioned within army posts, doing bureau business as they conducted military justice and other affairs.[16]

Because the army remained the crucial instrument of emancipation, the end of slavery demanded the expansion of its reach into the countryside. If occupation only meant to assert order in ungoverned counties, it might have shrunk by late June, as soldiers reached many county seats. Having established or recognized magistrates or, in some states, created police forces, they might have then departed for centralized posts. Instead, the army extended into the countryside, especially into regions with significant ex-slave populations. Over the summer, outposts continued to spread until there were up to 409 in total, and stayed roughly even at 403 in the fall. (See Appendix 1.)

To create practical rather than abstract rights, the United States depended on, in the words of the aptly named Major General Manning F. Force, a "general policy of ramifying these small posts through the country."[17] This meant ongoing occupation at outposts where the presence of soldiers changed both freedpeople's organizing strategies and their sense of the power of the national government. Freedpeople carried their complaints to soldiers, who came to define occupation as, in part, the defense of their rights. Many freedpeople, in turn, judged their freedom by proximity to someone who recognized and would defend it. Like many white Southerners, ex-slaves had learned through hard experience in the antebellum South to see power as personalized and geographically constrained. In the slave South, power often worked through

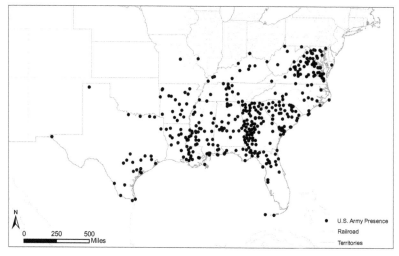

U.S. Army presence, September–November 1865. University of Richmond Digital
Scholarship Laboratory.

individual planters and magistrates who wielded both formal and informal
authority. In the complex postsurrender period, as people struggled to understand the relationship between individual officers and broader bureaucracies, the federal government could likewise seem both powerful and
personalized.[18]

To gain access to soldiers, freedpeople voted with their feet, moving toward Southern towns where occupying forces were stationed. A former slave
felt "safe, in his new-found freedom, nowhere out of the immediate presence
of the national forces," two Norfolk freedmen wrote. Freedpeople were "always fleeing to the nearest Military post and seeking protection of the law."
In Mississippi, freedpeople's actions varied with their wartime experiences.
Where the army had occupied, freedpeople stayed on their plantations; in regions the army had not reached, and where there was "no civil or military
law," they fled "to the nearest military post with all their children and effects."[19]
This raised grave fears for white Northerners who hoped to sustain a Southern
cotton economy and who believed that free labor would increase productivity.
For that to happen, the army would have to slow the movement of agricul-
tural workers into towns.

Desperate to ease the town overcrowding, relieve themselves from providing rations, and sustain the crop picking in the fall harvests, soldiers and

bureau agents took their message to the people in the countryside. Recognizing that many ex-slaves believed that "to secure perfect freedom they must get to some place occupied by U.S. troops," army chaplain Homer H. Moore and two Florida agents traveled from Jacksonville to Lake City and from there to Suwanee, Silver Springs, Madison, Tallahassee, Crawfordville, Monticello, and Quincy, stopping at plantation after plantation, speaking at times to dozens of slaves. They "taught the colored people that they were free, they and their children, and would remain so for ever: that freedom was brought to them and they need not leave their homes to find it." Similarly, when Alabama freedpeople streamed into Montgomery from one hundred miles away, a bureau agent realized the necessity of "trips into the country," talking to freedpeople where they were on large plantations and small towns. That personal presence was necessary because freedpeople were understandably skeptical of the power of proclamations to overturn power relationships around plantations. By making the government's might and its individual agents visible in the countryside, soldiers and agents hoped to convince ex-slaves that they did not need to move to find freedom; freedom could exist where they were.[20]

Hard experience taught ex-slaves that freedom depended upon the recognition of people in position to defend it. That meant freedom depended on proximity and force. Rather than either self-emancipation or a gift from above, freedom was a process in which ex-slaves asserted their new status through proximity to powerful defenders. Although slaves' actions were crucial to their freedom, especially as they fled to U.S. lines and fought for the U.S. Army, they—like all people—could not fashion their own freedom without the force of the state behind them. Although particular governments may violate a person's freedom, freedom in the contemporary sense is only possible within the state, not just for freedpeople but for all people. Ambrose Douglass, held a slave in North Carolina, captured the relationship between emancipation and soldiers' presence. In his area, "I guess we musta celebrated 'mancipation about twelve time. . . . Every time a bunch of No'thern sojers would come through they would tell us we was free and we'd begin celebratin'. Before we would get through somebody else would tell us to go back to work, and we would go."[21]

One of the most poignant efforts to balance slave agency and federal authority in shaping emancipation came from the pen of Louis Hughes, who was a slave in Mississippi and Alabama during the war. Hughes had tried to escape four times, but wrote that he still found himself enslaved a month after Johnston's surrender to Sherman. Well into June, he waited and "tried to be content" as U.S. soldiers were "still raiding all through that section. Every day some town would be taken, and the slaves would secretly rejoice." Rather than giving up after surrender, masters held their slaves "with a tighter rein than ever" and demanded passes from slaves "long after the proclamation making them free had gone into effect beyond all question!" To find freedom, Hughes had to look beyond northern Mississippi, since a postsurrender detachment did not arrive in Oxford until July. "We knew that Memphis was headquarters for the Union troops, but how to reach it was the great question." One day in late June, he and a fellow slave fled to Memphis and waited in a long line of black people to ask the officer for help emancipating their wives. The officer replied that they needed no permission, as "you are both free men to go and come as you please." But the officer's conception of freedom did not capture their reality. "Why," Hughes replied, "Colonel, if we go back to Mississippi they will shoot the gizzards out of us." As they walked back into Mississippi, Hughes and his friend met two soldiers in Senatobia who, in exchange for twenty dollars, rode with them to the master's house. To scare the master, the soldiers suggested that there were 75 cavalrymen behind them. Had their master "thought that there were but two soldiers, it is certain that they would have endeavored to prevent us getting away again, and one or more of us would undoubtedly have been killed," Hughes wrote. With this assistance, Hughes and his family then headed toward Memphis, "the city of refuge," around the Fourth of July with "thousands of others, in search of the freedom of which they had so long dreamed."[22]

Like Hughes, ex-slaves did not need the army to understand that they deserved to be free. From the beginning of American slavery, enslaved people sought their own emancipation. With the intense political fights of the 1850s, and then the start of the Civil War, slaves interpreted the conflict as a fight over their freedom and helped make it so by undercutting planters' power and serving in the U.S. Army. For Booker T. Washington, a nine-year-old boy in southwestern Virginia at war's end, "freedom was in the air, and had been for months." As slaves saw Confederate soldiers returning home, "the news and mutterings of great events were swiftly carried from one plantation to another." Slaves sang freedom songs more boldly. Around Franklinton, North Carolina, "news went from plantation to plantation," and slaves "prayed for freedom," Mary Anderson remembered in an interview seventy years later. "We all felt like heroes and nobody had made us that way but ourselves," a Texas man recalled. "We was free. Just like that, we was free."[23]

Nevertheless, soldiers' presence mattered. Actual freedom occurred at the moment when ex-slaves' hopes met external confirmation. While Booker T. Washington celebrated slaves' understanding of freedom, he emphasized the role that soldiers played in making it concrete. Even after the masters told them that they had been freed, "the most distinct thing that I now recall in connection with the scene was that some man who seemed to be a stranger (a United States soldier, I presume) made a little speech and then read a rather long paper—the Emancipation Proclamation, I think," Washington wrote. "After the reading we were told that we were all free, and could go when and where we pleased. My mother, who was standing by my side, leaned over and kissed her children, while tears of joy ran down her cheeks. She explained to us what it all meant, that this was the day for which she had been so long praying, but fearing that she would never live to see." Then "there was great rejoicing, and thanksgiving, and wild scenes of ecstasy."[24]

After Mary Anderson's master told them that they were free, she and her family waited until they saw a long line of U.S. soldiers marching from Louisburg. Then, "slaves were whooping and laughing and acting like they were crazy. Yankee soldiers were shaking hands with the Negroes and calling them Sam, Dinah, Sarah, and asking them questions." When soldiers announced emancipation on Sallie Paul's plantation near Marion, South Carolina, they captured both the importance and the limits of the ritual. "Yankees tell de colored people dey was free as dey was, but just didn't know it." The soldiers did not bring freedom; they brought affirmation of their freedom. When other ex-slaves celebrated a soldier's announcement, Sara Brown did not "see why dey want to carry on like dat for. I been free all de time."[25]

Although everyone understood that emancipation meant the end of slave sales, the constitution of legal families, and the beginning of wage labor, the full meaning of freedom was largely undetermined. Freedpeople taught soldiers over time the many other attributes of freedom. The questions spilled out during the fighting and in the months after surrender: Could free people be whipped by their employer? Was a right to testify integral to freedom? Did freedom demand a general sense of fair play? Were people subject to campaigns of violence truly free? Over and over again, freedpeople carried these issues to bureau agents and army outposts. While the question of property ownership would be settled later in the summer by the president, many other policies had to be worked out on the ground. "Neither the North nor the South have yet defined what is included in that emancipation," former Confederate treasury secretary Christopher Memminger wrote in the fall. "The boundaries are widely apart which mark on the one side, political equality with the white races, and on the other, a simple recognition of personal liberty."[26]

In their first encounters, many officers described freedom narrowly. Some said freedom simply meant the end of sales. Freedpeople might be required to stay on their plantations and work the same fields for minimal wages. Other soldiers, however, gestured more broadly. From Montgomery, Alabama, a bureau agent told 2,000 people that freedom meant "no abuse, no personal violence, no selling, no buying, no breaking up families by force." Still, there were strict limits to his version of freedom. "They were not free to be insolent, to be idle, to pilfer, to steal or do anything contrary to good order. They were free to come under the restraints of law." After the surrenders, soldiers told Thomas Ruffin that "you didn't have to stay where you was, that you didn't have no master, that you could go and come as you pleased." Other soldiers went beyond movement to bodily autonomy. Isaiah Green recalled that officers told him, "If your mistress calls you 'John,' call her 'Sally.' You are as free as she is and she can't whip you any more."[27]

Freedpeople quickly expanded the meaning of freedom. Booker T. Washington believed ex-slaves expressed their self-ownership first in concrete ways. "They must change their names" and "they must leave the old plantation for at least a few days or weeks in order that they might feel really sure that they were free." Most concretely, many wished for land. "The current view among many, directly after the war was, that they would receive so much land from the government to help them in the new life," Peter Randolph wrote. When U.S. senator Henry Wilson visited Richmond and gave them advice, Randolph responded that "they were not looking for advice, however, but land to plant corn and potatoes, for their wives and children." Beyond money, many saw in freedom a new world, what former slave and White House seamstress Elizabeth Keckley skeptically called "a land of sunshine, rest and glorious promise."[28]

Black soldiers in turn encouraged freedpeople to press more expansive definitions of freedom. Trained by their own experiences protesting discriminatory army policies, they provided both models and access to government for freedpeople. In Yazoo City, Mississippi, blacks ran to "town to make complaint" once a black unit occupied the town. In Nottoway, Virginia, freedpeople met for church and school at the black soldiers' barracks. Black soldiers taught freedpeople to expect voting rights and land redistribution. Landowners, meanwhile, complained that proximity to black soldiers demoralized black workers by giving them broad ideas of their rights and future prospects.[29]

Although some directives came down from Washington, the *Army & Navy Journal* wrote, "It is Division and Department Commanders . . . who are settling the grand question of the future of the freedmen, and burying slavery so deep that no trump will ever bring it to resurrection." This led to a wide range of outcomes as commanders pursued different definitions. From Richmond, Major General Henry Halleck and Major General Edward Ord deployed soldiers to implement a constrained version of freedom. Halleck began by cutting rations to freedpeople, barring rural blacks from moving to the city, putting the roughly 40,000 blacks in the city to work, encouraging other freedpeople to return to their homes, and ordering soldiers to keep freedpeople off the streets unless they had a pass. After a series of indignant meetings, a committee of Richmond black men traveled to Washington, D.C., on June 16 to complain about Halleck's system. Calling the soldiers and police who checked them for passes a "daily mounted patrol," they complained that "all that is needed to restore Slavery in full is the auction-block as it used to be." Likewise in Lynchburg, the commander extended to freedpeople only the narrow rights that free men of color had before the war. If freedom depended upon the government's coercive power, then it was inevitable that this coercion could turn back upon the freedpeople. Emancipation was not a moment of lifting the hands of the government but of extending the federal government into areas it had previously not regulated. The same authority that permitted some commanders to aid freedpeople would permit others to harm them.[30]

But the United States did not follow the Halleck plan. Within weeks the army sent both Halleck and Ord elsewhere, and a second model of postsurrender emancipation emerged in Virginia. The new general in charge, Major General Alfred Terry, issued sweeping orders on June 23 that used the military's authority over civil government to aid freedpeople. Interpreting wartime powers broadly, Terry overrode state law and implemented a color-blind scheme. Since the restrictive antebellum laws for free people of color were "substantially parts of the slave code," the abolition of slavery by military order vacated not just slavery but those laws too. "People of color will henceforth enjoy the same personal liberty that other citizens and inhabitants enjoy; they will be subject to the same restraints and to the same punishments for crime that are imposed on whites, and to no others." Taking control of criminal cases, Terry ordered the military courts to disregard the state law against blacks giving evidence.[31]

In Georgia, war powers provided even broader latitude for Major General Quincy Adams Gillmore. Learning that Savannah's city government established free public schools for whites only, Gillmore used his military authority to vacate the city's law. "Both soldierly honor and simple justice require that during our military occupation of this department, no unjust distinctions as to privileges and favors be made against a loyal race resident therein." Gillmore's goal was "to enforce and exact military justice and extend equal and exact military protection to all loyal persons, without regard to color or race."[32] Under Gillmore, freedom would mean the right not to be discriminated against by the government.

The crucial test of freedom was not orders but enforcement. Freedom was a set of "acquired rights" that would take shape as soldiers paid "proper attention to complaints," Florida's commander wrote. In standalone Freedmen's Bureau offices or, more frequently, in army posts where provost marshals or post commanders were detailed as bureau agents, they responded to grievances about the treatment of freedpeople by developing a newly concrete notion of freedom. As they heard complaints, bureau agents and army officers quickly began to wrestle with the persistence of "plantation discipline" through whipping or other forms of ritual punishment. Turning from actual enslavement to the feel of freedom, agents and officers warned that unchecked planter power "would render the position of the negro more grievous than before." Military officials therefore banned whipping, dispatched troops into the countryside to respond to complaints of bad treatment, overruled discriminatory laws, and arrested violent planters. The bureau's national commissioner acknowledged that blacks and loyal whites "universally desire the presence of United States troops" and "distrust their ability to maintain their rights without them."[33]

These rights, Colonel Bentzoni wrote from Arkansas, supported not just legal but "practical freedom." Practical freedom, however, was spatially constrained and only meaningful "within the line of permanent military occupation." Even Northerners who rented plantations would whip freedpeople "were it not for the military authorities constantly keeping an eye on them." This posed a problem. If practical freedom depended upon the proximity of the army, what would happen when the army went home? To this question, Bentzoni proposed a simple answer: soldiers should never leave. He suggested a plan to establish military colonies in the South by distributing land to U.S. soldiers as they left the army. "In this manner a nucleus of strength of Free Government will be formed in each county in a short time." With an army of 200,000 "colony soldiers" in a state of reserve while they farmed in the South, the government would have "all the assistance which might be required to enforce law and order, and the black people would through it become free in deed."[34] Bentzoni's proposals carried the logic of wartime emancipation to an intriguing conclusion. If freedom could be sustained only through proximate protectors, then one logical outcome was the extension of war; the other, which Bentzoni argued for, was a permanent colonization that would place armed white Northerners within reach of many freedpeople.

White Southerners responded violently to this attack on their society. In South Carolina agents and officers found "the bodies of murdered negroes" scattered through the woods. "The southern people seem to have transferred their spite at the government to the colored people," a traveling clergyman said. When a white man captured a black woman and her children running to the U.S. forces, he "drew his bowie-knife and cut her throat; also the throat of her boy, nine years old; also the throat of her girl, seven years of age; threw their bodies into the river, and the live baby after them." Another rebel nailed a black woman and her children into a chicken coop and threw them into a river for trying to escape. In parts of Alabama, Mississippi, and Texas, rebels killed an average of one black man per day during the summer of 1865. In western South Carolina, the number of attacks on freedpeople grew from two in July 1865 to nine in August, fourteen in September, and seventeen in December. In Charleston alone, there were 138 reported attacks on freedmen between May and December 1865.[35]

Believing that their society grew from and depended upon slavery, white Southerners who might accept nominal U.S. rule were moved to violence to defend as much of slavery as they could. These assaults convinced officers that in some way the war had not ended. "It is a continuation of the war, not against the armed defenders of the Government, but against its unarmed friends," Carl Schurz wrote. Hearing of attacks on freedpeople or schoolteachers, soldiers called the assailants guerrillas "waging a war against the invaders." Near

Atlanta, a mob drove away a detachment of army soldiers. A major in the 69th New York Volunteers reported that he had been attacked several times while guarding government cotton seven miles away from the post. In Jefferson County, Mississippi, outlaws broke into a lieutenant's office and destroyed his papers, and attacked a military escort and forced him to marry a black woman. Near Summit, Mississippi, two white men with guns demonstrated their own control over territory when they stopped a black soldier and asked "by what authority he was there." When the soldier showed his military pass, they cut off the buttons on his coat and ordered him to leave. These attacks were intended to make the U.S. Army appear helpless, its authority illusory, its pretensions to power contemptible. Instead, the violence taught most commanders—whether moderates or radicals—to support an ongoing occupation with troops "stationed in that section of the country."[36]

Soldiers' developing alliance with African Americans was rooted less in personal sympathy than in the firm, if less inspiring, political ground of a common enemy. Occupation was not a test of personal racial beliefs, but of power. Only a scattering of soldiers were committed antiracists like Colonel Bentzoni, but large numbers of prejudiced U.S. soldiers provided crucial assistance to freedpeople because of their shared hatred of ex-Confederates. U.S. soldiers listened to black complaints because many saw white Southerners as disloyal traitors. Following the initial swell of fellow feeling upon surrender, many officers hardened their views once again as they watched white Southerners launch bloody assaults on both loyal freedpeople and U.S. soldiers. After a time in Hawkinsville, Georgia, Lieutenant Colonel Nelson Shaurman called Georgians the "most ignorant, degraded white people I have ever seen. . . . Were it not for the military power—of which they have a wholesome fear—there would be scenes of cruelty enacted that would disgrace savages." In Richmond, Major General Wesley Merritt yelled, "What is this!" when he saw a wounded girl brought into the Freedmen's Bureau. She had been "shamefully whipped and her back burned with a hot iron." The officer who was taking care of the girl replied, "It is the devil." One casually racist U.S. soldier found that his dislike for black people bred no sympathy toward rebels. "There is not 9 out of 10 of these so called 'Whiped' traitors that I would trust until I saw the rope applied to their Necks, then I would only have Faith in the quality of the rope." While people told him to love and forgive the South, "I can never do it only in the way I have been doing for the last four years."[37]

By responding to freedpeople's complaints, the army disrupted white Southerners' plans to reconstruct a system of near-slavery. Where planters hoped to restrict freedpeople's movement, impose penurious contracts that required obedience, and use the whip to inflict discipline, soldiers' presence generally restrained them. White Southerners responded with resignation but not acceptance. Many denounced what they called the army's "Eastern despotism." While ex-Confederates had "undergone no change," they tacitly acquiesced because they were "compelled to by the power of the Union Armies," a former slave owner in Arkansas argued. "He who stands between the late master and the freedmen for their protection must be backed by the power of the bayonet." In Texas, the relative quiet near army posts suggested that it was possible to familiarize ex-Confederates with "the idea of law as an irresistible power to which all must bow." They were, in one general's words, "submissive but not loyal." Ex-Confederate congressman Josiah Turner bitterly compared the military rule to the East India Company's reign over Bengal in the decade after the American Revolution. Randolph Shotwell, returning to North Carolina after his confinement as a prisoner of war, complained of "petty despotism in every Southern village." "There is no longer any Union. . . . The South is no more a real partner in the so-called Union than Poland is a part of Russia, or India of England, or Cuba of Spain." Given planters' partial reassertions of their power and President Johnson's sympathy for them, it is tempting to dismiss these hyperbolic statements altogether. If they do not give us an accurate portrayal of the precise facts on the ground, however, they do give a window into the way Southern planters experienced the breakup of slavery not as a continuation of their power but as a government-enforced assault upon their customary rights.[38]

Farther from the direct force of government, former slave owners and their allies exerted their control. Before a garrison arrived in Attala County, Mississippi, it was "the theatre of gross outrages" against black men. Although troops temporarily restored "tranquility and order," "four murders happened in quick succession" once the soldiers left. In Opelousas, Louisiana, a soldier was killed while visiting a friend a few miles away from a post. "The protection afforded to loyal men by the presence of the Federal troops does not extend to the whole country," a resident complained. In the early fall, soldiers at Tuskegee, Alabama, controlled that town but had little impact on neighboring Tallapoosa County. There, "where there are no troops and civil authority not reestablished," murder was "almost dissolving society." In South

Carolina regions where soldiers preserved order "in their precincts," planters
and freedpeople made contracts and adjusted to the new world, but around
Barnwell, "where few troops have been stationed . . . the sectional bitterness
is as extreme as ever."[39]

If the army's coercive war powers provided hope for freedpeople, they also
posed a terrible dilemma. The very authority to go beyond normal law empowered soldiers to abuse freedpeople. Some grim cases remind us that coercive
powers, once unleashed, cannot easily be restrained. From Columbus, Georgia,
a U.S. private wrote to complain that blacks were "killed daily" with the "full
knowledge of the post commandant. . . . The negros say that they were never
treated So in life as since we garrisoned the place." In Savannah, U.S. cavalry
assaulted freedpeople, and officials were "uncivil" and "cruel," while the Beaufort, South Carolina, agent was "too meen to live and . . . not meen enough to
die." Freedpeople generally responded to these cases by pleading not for withdrawal but for new officers. They needed a powerful government; they wished
it in the hands of their friends since they knew the dangers of turning that
authority over to their enemies. An official in Louisiana captured this dilemma
as he responded to complaints from free people of color in New Orleans. "Are
you willing with your knowledge of society here to have the military officers
withdraw all control?" he asked. "You well know that you are not."[40]

In the city of Charleston, one regiment of U.S. soldiers seemed to be
fighting not against rebels but against black people. In June, after some of
the 165th New York Zouaves refused to serve with black troops, the army arrested forty-three mutineers and stationed the remainder in Charleston. On
July 8, after one white soldier quarreled with a black civilian at the city market,
a squad attacked black people there and demolished their stands. When a
black man named John Bean complained, they bayoneted him to death. Soon
a detachment of the 21st U.S. Colored Troops arrived to reinforce the black
Charlestonians, and there was open fighting among soldiers and civilians. For
a time, the army hoped to quiet the incident by sending both the black and
white units from the city, but black citizens protested to local commanders and
threatened to carry their appeal to Washington, D.C. In time Major General
Quincy Adams Gillmore confined the entire 165th to Fort Sumter, arrested its
lieutenant colonel, and sent them home without arms as a sign of disgrace.[41]

A particularly observant traveler in Georgia captured the complexity of
depending upon war powers to define freedom. He had no illusions that soldiers would always use their power wisely; he knew of terrible outrages by

cavalry in Savannah. Still, he saw that freedpeople flocked to the outposts, viewing soldiers as imperfect but accessible vessels for justice. "Withdraw our troops and I question whether any man who trusted solely to the local law would not be courting death at the hands of the first knife-swinging vagabond he might chance to offend." Whatever its limitations, the army opened up a new vision of rights making that reached into many precincts and crevices. "We are establishing an American nationality; let us at the same time establish an American citizenship." To be meaningful, rights would have to be enforceable, which meant that government would have to be visibly present. He could see only one hope for the future: the extension of war powers into peacetime. "The protection we have now only under the abnormal war powers of the President . . . should become part of the fundamental law of the nation."[42]

The situation in Kentucky revealed the centrality of war powers to emancipation. It seemed strange that war powers existed in Kentucky at all by the summer of 1865, for the state had never joined the Confederacy. But the enduring presence of slavery led the army to continue to assert its authority over civil government even after battlefield fighting had stopped. The dilemma arose because Kentucky stood with Delaware as the last lone loyal states with legal slavery. From the war's beginning, Kentucky politicians argued that staying in the United States would help them preserve slavery. By 1863 the enlistment of 25,000 black troops from the state undercut white popular support and sparked conflict between soldiers and white civilians. In 1865, when Louisville's mayor began enforcing strict vagrancy laws, Major General John Palmer, a native Kentuckian raised in Illinois, struck back by ferrying 5,000 black people to freedom in Ohio. Black Louisvillians in turn traveled to Washington to ask the president to sustain military power. Otherwise, they claimed, "the People of colour Have No Rights *whatever* Either in Law or in fact." President Johnson assured them that he would not lift martial law. On July 4, black Kentuckians flocked to army outposts in hopes of hearing a proclamation of their freedom. Palmer told one group they were "substantially free," and then wrote, "My countrymen you are free." White Kentuckians complained bitterly that Palmer was changing the "Organic Law of Kentucky" at "the point of the bayonet." But even after Johnson lifted martial law, the government upheld

Palmer's power to proclaim that all people were "presumed to be free." Even in a loyal state, the end of slavery turned on the presence of war powers.[43]

When it came to regulating democracy, however, Palmer encountered more resistance. In late summer Palmer tried to limit voter participation in state elections to loyal white men. To Palmer, this action was merely an extension of his attacks on slavery. Barring Confederates would make it possible to elect a government that would end slavery. To President Johnson, however, this extended military power into areas it should not touch, at least in a loyal state. Although Palmer was sustained, he was warned to tread lightly. Here too lay a harbinger of the future. If Palmer's actions against slavery in Kentucky demonstrated President Johnson's support for aggressive intervention to ensure emancipation, so too did the response to the election suggest the president's wariness of soldiers' involvement in politics. But, as Palmer found, untangling the fight against slavery from politics would turn out to be nearly impossible. Ending slavery was inherently political and depended upon federal amendments and new state laws.

The army had played a key role in undermining slavery during the summer, when Southern governments were nonexistent or weak. Soldiers had created pockets of alternative law where ex-slaves could demand new rights to family reconstitution, movement, labor contracts, education, and bodily autonomy. The military had listened to freedpeople and exerted its war powers to strike down laws and issue orders to planters. Without that authority, the military would have been hamstrung, emancipation limited or in some places reversed.

But as summer turned to fall, and as provisional governments began to take shape and hold their first elections, maintaining that wartime authority would prove difficult. The struggle to reconcile democracy and military rule would become much more fraught. Soon the conflicts between civil authorities in Kentucky spread to all the former Confederate states. There, the military wrestled with the challenge of sustaining military oversight in the face of newly reborn civil governments that sought to retain as much of slavery as they could. The balance between military-backed emancipation and civil government was about to enter a new phase.

– 3 –

THE CHALLENGE OF CIVIL GOVERNMENT

ON OCTOBER 13, 1865, a former Confederate colonel named Drury Brown burst into the Freedmen's Bureau office in Hazlehurst, Mississippi, to complain about a tax the agent had imposed on local planters. After Brown became "boisterous and defiant," that agent—Captain Warren Peck—and three soldiers arrested him. This small act soon prompted a large-scale confrontation between civil and military authority. Five days later, a deputy sheriff tried to arrest Peck for assault. After Peck denied the deputy's authority, the sheriff and a posse of fifty armed men surrounded him on the outskirts of town. Hearing Peck's cries for help, the seven U.S. soldiers stationed in Hazlehurst raced out with their guns leveled. For a moment, it seemed possible that there would be open gunfire between the army and local law. But Peck defused the situation by agreeing to let the posse carry him to the county seat, where a judge held him in a small iron cell under a $2,000 bond. For a week, while Peck languished in jail, civil and military authorities in Mississippi argued about the powers of the army and of local law enforcement.[1]

What was at stake was not just Peck's freedom but the nature of military rule. If peacetime had returned, soldiers could not hold citizens like Brown, and sheriffs and judges indeed had the authority to arrest military men who broke the law. But if war powers continued, then Captain Peck had been within his rights to detain Brown, and the sheriff and judge had no power to charge Peck with a crime. In the end, force prevailed over form. After the elected governor refused to intervene, the state's military commander sent four companies to free Peck from jail and arrest the judge and deputy sheriff. Despite threats that they would resist the military, county officers stood down in the face of the army's power. The military's triumph was real but also limited; although leading army officers recommended trying the judge and deputy before a military tribunal, the two were released after a short time in jail.[2]

Peck's case raised the question of who was in control of the rebel states, the army or local officials. In May, the Peck incident might have ended quickly as the army asserted its authority. What had changed by October, however, was that Mississippi and many other rebel states had held elections. The new governor argued that his election restored "civil government"; therefore the army had improperly defied the rightful civil authority. Soon, Mississippi's newly elected legislature asked the federal government to withdraw all soldiers from the state. Captain Peck and his superiors, however, saw elections not as the solution but as the problem. The act of voting had convinced white Mississippians that the Freedmen's Bureau and the army had no power over them. In the face of their confidence, the army could no longer rely upon awe. "Only force" would make white Southerners comply with military orders, a bureau inspector wrote.[3]

Over the late summer and fall of 1865, the Peck case and other struggles between civil and military authorities provoked deep debates about the relationship among military power, democracy, and rights. It had been one thing in May to presume that the army could exert power over conquered lands, and another in June to argue that the military could thwart a presidentially appointed provisional governor. By the fall the nation faced the still-deeper issue of whether the army could overrule an elected official. What was at stake seemed the nature of self-rule, the legitimacy granted by elections. These elections over the late summer and fall both strengthened and diverted the white Southern effort to reclaim authority over the region's freedpeople. Politics provided a form for ex-rebels to lobby Washington, D.C.

But democracy did not end military rule in Mississippi or elsewhere in the South. In response to the Peck case, President Andrew Johnson supported his agent, not the judge. More broadly, he refused to withdraw troops from Mississippi until "in the opinion of the Government, that peace and order, and the Civil Authority has been restored and can be maintained, without them." The next month, the national Freedmen's Bureau commissioner authorized the head of the Mississippi bureau to "use all the power of the Bureau, to see that the Freedmen are protected," the "whole power of the Government being pledged to sustain the actual freedom of the negro." Whenever state officials infringed on black people's rights or "refuse[d] them equal justice," he should call upon the state's military commander and "take such measures as may seem best to guard and protect their interests."[4]

The U.S. government faced a dilemma in the rebel states in the months after surrender. The ex-Confederates could not be allowed to rule unimpeded because they would refuse to acknowledge the rights of freedpeople. Military authority had to remain in place if those basic civil rights were to be meaningful. But the army could not regulate the entire South without some government to work through. More broadly, the absence of elected governments in the rebel states in the summer seemed to violate deeply held American expectations of local self-rule. Even if access to the ballot was limited by gender, race, or wealth, the authority of locally chosen officials was the ultimate check on tyranny. Even in the Western territories, elected governments wielded a great deal of power during this era. In the fall of 1865, the U.S. government therefore faced a conflict between two basic American values: self rule and civil rights.[5]

In the 1865 fights for control between civil and military officers, President Johnson and his administration often favored the army. Although Southern officeholders claimed that they possessed the normal powers of a legitimate government, the president did not agree. Rather than ushering in civil control, democracy brought an unusual form of dual government, where armies and elected officials worked side by side, but not hand in hand, with overlapping jurisdictions. Conflicts between the army and elected officials could not be contained in the normal language of jurisdiction or states' rights but instead were open fights between competing forms of sovereignty: civil and military. Although the reviving state governments won some of the contests, the military ultimately prevailed in 1865. The so-called states had the form but not the substance of civil government.

President Andrew Johnson deserves both blame and credit for the fights between civil and military governments in the fall of 1865. It was Johnson who created the conflict by appointing provisional governments and requiring quick elections, but so too was it Johnson who ultimately—although not always—sustained the military's power in the South in 1865. Johnson's 1865 actions have often been obscured behind his increasingly bitter fights with Congress between 1866 and 1868, his public opposition to black voting rights, and his ultimate impeachment and near-removal from office. Reading backward from those conflicts, many historians have presumed that Johnson favored immediate home rule. Therefore, Southern-sympathizing scholars in the early twentieth century assumed that Johnson was a wise Unionist whom wild-eyed Northern Republicans foolishly ignored.[6] As historians came to see the virtues of Reconstruction, Johnson was reinterpreted as a virulently racist appeaser who quickly betrayed the promise of Reconstruction by favoring the rebels.[7] With his open racism, vituperative tongue, bullish stubbornness, and absurd misjudgments, Johnson seemed malevolent enough to explain almost anything that went wrong.[8] The tendency to treat racism as not merely evil but uniquely powerful in explaining American history also fed overconfident judgments about Johnson's effectiveness in restraining Reconstruction. But Johnson was neither as important nor as single-minded as those narratives suggest. To a surprising degree, Johnson regularly sustained the military throughout 1865 and even into 1866. The white Southern insurgency that would stymie Reconstruction was not the product of Johnson's actions, nor were his decisions so uniformly opposed to military power and the creation of black civil rights. There is not one but a thousand roads to grief.

We must first step back to ask whether Johnson's policies were in fact mild during 1865. The entire Confederacy remained under the nebulous but still meaningful state of martial law. Even in Kentucky, the privilege of the writ of habeas corpus remained suspended after martial law was lifted. Freedmen's Bureau agents oversaw a range of parallel court systems for freedpeople, and military commanders arrested and sometimes tried whites for assaults. State commanders continued to vacate laws, silence opposition newspapers, disregard judges' orders, and even overturn elections. Beneath the veneer of provisional governments, a great deal of authority remained in the hands of the army and the bureau. Even after states elected governments in the fall, Johnson treated them as provisional, delaying the inauguration of elected governors at his whim, all but ordering legislators to approve laws he supported, urging them to pass the Thirteenth Amendment, and supporting commanders who continued martial law. Throughout the fall of 1865, he oversaw a South where freedpeople made marked, if painfully limited, gains.

When Johnson assumed the presidency, he inherited a confused set of policies toward the occupied South. In North Carolina in 1862, President Lincoln had experimented with a civilian military governor, then turned the state back over to the army. In Tennessee, Johnson himself served three tumultuous years as military governor before holding statewide elections in early 1865 to create a democratic loyalist government. Virginia, Arkansas, and Louisiana all had governments of varying authority elected by small numbers of loyalists. After Lincoln proposed to restore Louisiana if 10 percent of the former voting population participated, congressional Republicans tried to grasp control of Reconstruction through the Wade-Davis bill, which would have slowed the rebirth of governments by requiring the participation of a majority of the former electorate, barring rebel soldiers from voting, obligating the state to eliminate slavery, forbidding rebel leaders from holding office, sweeping away discriminatory laws, and granting Congress the right to approve the appointment of provisional governors. Fearful of delaying the progress in Arkansas and Louisiana, Lincoln pocket vetoed the bill. But Congress did not recognize Louisiana's government or seat its delegates in the winter 1864–1865 session. In early 1865 the question remained unsettled. In his final days, Abraham Lincoln called Reconstruction "fraught with great difficulty" and asked Secretary of War Edwin Stanton to draft proclamations for provisional governments in Virginia and North Carolina. When Johnson was sworn in as president, he inherited an administration that had declined to engage with Confederate state governments, left some areas to military rule, appointed provisional governors over other states, and recognized elected governments in yet others.[9]

In the absence of a clear plan for restoration, war powers served as the tool for governing the rebel states. Although Republicans tied themselves in knots debating the status of defeated states within the Union, in fact the question did not generally determine the outcome of Reconstruction. The status of the states—whether they were technically inside or outside the Union during the war—had important legal consequences in maritime law and in international relations. Domestically, however, the administration largely treated the issue as a practical one. In the face of necessity, no one behaved consistently. Even as Lincoln claimed that "the States have their *status* IN the Union, and they have no other *legal status*," the administration practically treated them as conquered regions under military rule. Over the course of the war and Reconstruction, politicians created intricate ways of describing rebel states as suicidal, somnolent, territorialized, conquered, or intact, but these positions obscured the pragmatism that shaped Republican positions. Some Republicans—and even Andrew Johnson himself—supported handling the states as territories early in the war. But this was primarily a method to end slavery, a power which Congress had over territories but not states. Once the Thirteenth Amendment passed, even staunch territorialization supporter Senator Charles Sumner lost interest in the idea. He dismissed "metaphysical" arguments about state status as "only worthy of schoolmen." In particular moments, these ideas about the status of the states mattered as ways to advance programs for emancipation, land confiscation, black enfranchisement, and congressional control, but almost no one followed any theory consistently. Dismissing the question of whether the defeated states remained states in the Union, Lincoln himself called the issue "good for nothing at all—a merely pernicious abstraction." A year later, when Congress's Joint Committee on Reconstruction issued its report, Radical Republican Thaddeus Stevens and the committee's majority similarly cast aside the question of state status as a "profitless"—though not pernicious—abstraction.[10]

The crucial question was not the status of the states but control over war powers. Lincoln's actions between 1862 and 1865 established the president's broad authority, but Congress also staked its claim. And Congress held an important trump card. If peace meant normalcy, then peace would not be restored until the rebel states were once again represented in Congress. Explicitly in generals' orders and politicians' speeches, and implicitly in Johnson's early messages to Southern states, this message was clear. The president had extended wartime and would direct the war powers through the army, but in some way, Congress would have a say over its close. Keeping rebel states out of Congress did not just deny them votes; it denied them peace.

Although Johnson would have an important influence over postsurrender policy, his own views at first were mysterious. Early in the secession crisis, Johnson had actually spoken in favor of turning the rebel states into territories, but once war came he argued vociferously that states could not change their status by leaving the Union. In his bitter arguments against secessionists in Tennessee, Johnson became a renowned spokesman for the idea that the states remained in the Union and that secession was unlawful. This did not restrain his acts as military commander, as it did not restrain his behavior as president. After Lincoln's assassination, Johnson at first kept silent. In the absence of information, hopeful politicians assumed that Johnson agreed with them. Famously radical senator Charles Sumner wrote on May 1 that after a long conversation with Johnson, "there is no difference between us." Johnson "deprecates haste; is unwilling that States should be precipitated back; thinks there must be a period of probation, but that meanwhile all loyal people, without distinction of color, must be treated as citizens, and must take part in any proceedings for reorganization." Some Republicans were even glad that Johnson had replaced Abraham Lincoln, since Lincoln had restrained congressional oversight of the defeated states.[11]

Radical Republicans lobbied Johnson to solve the problems of rights and war powers in one fell swoop by enfranchising freedpeople as he recreated state governments. If Johnson called new constitutional conventions and authorized the military to help register freedpeople, the gains of the war might be sustained by votes, not by force. At a mass meeting in support of black enfranchisement at Boston's Faneuil Hall in June 1865, the eminent lawyer Richard Henry Dana Jr. offered the most elaborate defense of war powers to support enfranchisement. Dana argued that a victorious combatant "holds the conquered enemy in the grasp of war until it has secured whatever it has a right to require." To secure its victory, the nation could require the enfranchisement of freedpeople. Although intervening in state election law would be constitutionally impermissible in normal times, Dana believed that it would be justified under "war powers."[12]

With the power seemingly in Johnson's hands, Radical Republicans and freedpeople launched a mass movement to put voting on the agenda. Although many Northern states disfranchised African Americans at the war's beginning, black service in the army and a strong lobbying campaign by freedpeople had changed the minds of many Republicans. From plantation belts in South Carolina to Boston debating societies, freedpeople and some Northern Republicans made the vote both a right and a method for defending rights. From South Carolina, letters and petitions asked for the "protection of the *ballot*, as their only security against those whose hands are still red with the life blood of the Nation." Supreme Court Chief Justice Salmon Chase met with Johnson at least five times to lobby for black enfranchisement and then toured the South to relay his belief that rebels would accept black voting if the president required it. By summer, the Republican Party had coalesced around the use of war powers to enfranchise Southern freedpeople, with former moderates like William Fessenden, John Sherman, and Collis Huntington and Radical Republicans like Charles Sumner, Carl Schurz, and Salmon Chase all essentially agreeing. "If we can put negro regiments there and give them bayonets, why can't we give them votes?" Senator John Sherman asked.[13]

Against the call for enfranchisement and a quick restoration of civil government, other Republicans urged Johnson to hold the states under military rule and prevent everyone—white and black—from voting. Enfranchisement, they feared, would not be enough to remake the South. "Let the national authority be exerted and administered over the conquered districts, by the military arm so far as necessary, by temporary civil organizations as far as practicable, until a spontaneous and natural growth of social order begets a local civil government," Republican Stanley Matthews urged. The *Army & Navy Journal* likewise argued that generals would need to be the "supreme ruler" in Southern states for "many months to come." "Military occupation will be a necessity throughout nearly all the South." One captain stationed in North Carolina suggested two or three years of such rule; a leading Republican called for twenty-five. For some period of time, however, these skeptics of voting believed the military would have to remain in charge. Meanwhile, Democrats argued that the states had restored themselves by surrender and needed neither military oversight nor presidential action. All they had to do was send representatives to Congress in December.[14]

Before he made any decisions about the state governments, Johnson extended war powers past surrender. This emerged first in his decision to try Lincoln's assassins in front of a military commission, not a civilian court. In his opinion for the president, Attorney General James Speed argued that the existence of courts in Southern states did not mean that martial law was at an end. "The civil courts have no more right to prevent the military, in time of war, from trying an offender against the laws of war than they have a right to interfere with and prevent a battle," he wrote. Johnson's decision outraged strict constitutionalists in the Democratic Party. It raised the specter, as one correspondent said, that "you may keep your military courts running forever!" Although Johnson stood by his decision, the backlash bothered him. No longer did he look ahead to military commission trials for Jefferson Davis or leading Confederate officers. If they were to be tried—as Johnson hoped—they should be charged in criminal courts. But here Johnson faced a bind. According to the terms of their parole, soldiers like Lee were exempt from prosecution during wartime; Johnson could charge them only if he was willing to end the war powers. But if he ended the war, he could not keep control of the South. Lieutenant General Ulysses S. Grant threatened to resign if Johnson tried Lee and his officers. For the time being, trials waited for the return of peace.[15]

As Johnson kept quiet, the cabinet prepared plans for the South. Secretary of War Edwin Stanton in April presented two proclamations for remaking the region, one that asserted federal authority over Virginia and North Carolina, another that presented a path to restore state governments through military-regulated elections. Because Stanton grouped states together and granted the army authority to regulate elections, his nemesis, Secretary of the Navy Gideon Welles, would later see this plan as the harbinger of Radical Reconstruction. Stanton was trying to "reduce states to a condition of territorial dependence," Welles later wrote. "War had justified the exercise of extraordinary power which they would not relinquish on the return of peace." Welles argued for severing Virginia from North Carolina to recognize Virginia's nascent loyal government and to preserve the state's integrity. On May 9, Johnson accepted Welles's position by recognizing the small loyal government in Virginia as legitimate. But Johnson did not restore civil government there; he stated that the military would have a continuing presence. The key fight then turned to North Carolina, the other state covered by Stanton's initial proclamations. With no existing state government there, the United States started from scratch. Therefore, Stanton claimed that the president could extend the right to vote to black men as he called for a new constitutional convention. But at a May 9 cabinet meeting, Welles argued that the president could not alter state voting laws even in time of war. While the war might authorize temporary infringements on other laws, state voting rules were sacrosanct.[16]

After keeping his silence for twenty days, Johnson finally intervened in late May with two oddly mixed proclamations. In one, he offered clemency to some, but not all, ex-Confederates. While most could swear future loyalty to the United States and pledge support of emancipation to restore their status, leading government and military officials were exempted. To this point, Johnson followed Lincoln's precedent, but then, in a nod to his long-standing struggle against Southern planters, Johnson excluded all who owned at least $20,000 in taxable property. By doing so, he denied amnesty to many men whom Lincoln almost certainly would have extended it to. Then Johnson turned to North Carolina. Invoking both his peacetime, constitutional obligation to guarantee republican government and his wartime powers, Johnson appointed a civilian provisional governor to organize the state by calling a constitutional convention. The proclamation ordered military officials to "assist" the provisional governor but did not spell out the nature of those powers. Johnson had rejected pleas from North Carolina rebels to simply call the Confederate legislature into session and recognize the old government. But Johnson had also rejected Radical Republican petitions for enfranchising freedmen.[17]

Since he left few written records, Johnson's thinking is difficult to determine. Had Radicals like Sumner and Chase been tricked by a wily politician? Or had Johnson actually expressed openness toward enfranchisement early in May? Perhaps one piece of information helps explain a seeming change of heart. On May 19, William Seward returned to his offices at the State Department for the first time since the failed attempt to assassinate him. In his private meetings with Johnson, noted but not described by Gideon Welles, Seward presumably discussed the proclamations. Although Seward had fought vigorously against slavery, he "placed no high estimate on the question of suffrage," Welles later wrote. Scalded by years of criticism and by his bitter rivalry with Salmon Chase, Seward soon steered Johnson toward alliances with loyal Democrats, moderate white Southerners, and the most conservative Republicans, the very groups who could accept a provisional government but not black suffrage. If Seward's voice was crucial, and if Johnson truly had been open to some enfranchisement, then Seward's heroic survival of the attempt on his life may be one of the less acknowledged turning points in Reconstruction.[18]

Johnson's proclamations and orders established the framework for revitalizing states and moving toward peace. Those with existing loyal governments—Arkansas, Louisiana, Tennessee, and Virginia—extended their authority over their territories. The other Confederate states followed the North Carolina path, as additional provisional governors came online between June 13 and July 13. It would be left to the states to voluntarily remake themselves and submit their representatives to Congress in December. In the interim, all state residents would have to take the oath of allegiance to participate, and high-ranking or wealthy people would need to seek individual pardons from the president. Voting rights would be left to the states, which meant to white men. While some white Southerners wanted Johnson simply to recognize existing state governments, most celebrated his decision not to extend the vote. "The document removes the blackest cloud that hung over us," one North Carolinian exulted. Many Republicans saw the proclamations as failures, even as abdications of military rule. "You had just as well undertake to reconstruct the rattle Snakes of South America, before you pull out their fangs," one wrote in disgust.[19]

The provisional governors were an effort to find collaborators. Most were politicians, including a number of moderate and antisecession former Whigs. The most radical selection was North Carolina's William Holden, who ran on a peace platform in the state's 1863 election. Another transformative pick, Texas's Andrew Jackson Hamilton, was actually a holdover from a failed Lincoln effort to govern Texas from afar. In Alabama, Mississippi, Georgia, and South Carolina, Johnson named prominent men who had opposed secession at the war's beginning but stayed in the Confederacy, even though he could have selected from the loyal politicians concentrated in northern Alabama and Georgia. In the sparsely populated state of Florida, he picked a candidate based on the recommendation of New York businessmen. If these provisional governors were not, generally, outsiders or enemies to the white planter class, they were also, in some rebels' eyes, collaborators with the victorious nation who ruled by virtue of military power. In North Carolina, where many elite whites deeply hated provisional governor Holden, one rebel groused that Johnson gave Holden more powers "than ever were claimed for an English monarch" since the Glorious Revolution in 1688.[20]

Since then, it has been common to claim that Johnson was guided by a belief in state sovereignty. But in fact Johnson relied upon war powers, as a legal theorist named John Codman Hurd immediately grasped. Author of a well-known study of slavery, *The Law of Freedom and Bondage*, Hurd appears to have written a lengthy, learned analysis of Johnson's proclamations in the *Army & Navy Journal*. Although attributed only to "JCH," it overlaps with Hurd's later writings on the development of the American nation. Hurd immediately captured the contradiction within Johnson's stance. Although Johnson spoke about state survival, he did not acknowledge the existence of state governments or even leave it to the states' residents to remake their governments. Instead, he swept away governments and established procedures for how the residents should call for constitutional conventions, something a president could not normally do. In every aspect except the retention of state names and boundaries, "every thing in the Presidential scheme is inconsistent with State existence." Hurd therefore dismissed Johnson's invocation of state survival and the Constitution's guarantee of a republican form of government. What tied together Johnson's actions was a different assumption: "The war is not yet ended." The provisional government "depends upon a military necessity, not a political expediency; upon the President's war powers, not upon his ordinary powers. . . . Hence the President's course is something not so much constitutional or un-constitutional as extra-constitutional." While Johnson was more bellicose in his defense of state survival, Lincoln "would have taken the same course," Hurd wrote, because both men wished to use war powers to keep control in the hands of the executive, not of Congress. Watching the use of the military in the Southern states over the summer, the *Army & Navy Journal* noted that "force, in the beginning and in the end, is the constitutional means of establishing republican government. . . . State government is thus the gift of the Nation."[21]

In late June, the War Department confirmed the existence of the states but also constructed a competing power center as it reorganized the army's departments. On June 27, the army broke up the wartime commands, which did not conform to state lines. Instead, the army created a military system that paralleled the provisional one. Each state was a department with a single commander who oversaw a series of districts and subdistricts. Above the states were divisional commanders—major generals George Meade, Philip Sheridan, William Sherman, and George Thomas. The Carolinas and Virginia answered to the Division of the Atlantic; Florida, Louisiana, Mississippi, and Texas to the Division of the Gulf; Arkansas to the Division of the Mississippi; and Alabama, Georgia, and Tennessee (and after an October reorganization Mississippi) to the Division of the Tennessee. At once, the army's reorganization emphasized the endurance of the states and also established clear competitors for provisional governors. Instead of calling upon different officers to help in different regions, they negotiated with single commanders often located in the capital city.[22]

Nothing proved that Johnson in fact relied upon war powers more clearly than the continuation of martial law over the ex-Confederacy. Many white Southerners presumed that Johnson had ended martial law and placed the new states under civil authority when he appointed provisional governors, but martial law and the suspension of the privilege of habeas corpus continued over the South for all of 1865 and part of 1866. As provisional governments began to extend their reach, their conflicts with the army illustrated the "extreme indeterminateness and vagueness" of martial law. In an 1857 legal opinion, Attorney General Caleb Cushing had written that it was "not easy to find satisfactory" answers to very basic questions about it, either from U.S. statutes or English common law. From Wellington's occupation of Europe and the United States' occupation of Mexico, Cushing argued that martial law included but was not limited to the suspension of the privilege of habeas corpus. It "suspends, for the time being, all the laws of the land, and substitutes in their place no law, that is, the mere will of the military commander." But this seemed too broad to capture the way that military rule actually worked; only occasionally, and in extreme cases of government breakdown, did the army actually fulfill all the tasks of government. Instead, martial law was premised upon ultimate authority. Even under martial law, a commander should allow courts to function; he did not have to be bound by them or by the statutes in case of emergency. Although one might expect a clear break between the time of civil government and of martial law, Cushing argued that commanders need not proclaim martial law. A public notification was "the statement of an existing fact, rather than the legal creation of that fact." During the Civil War, Francis Lieber's famous code of war reenforced the idea that martial law existed "whether any proclamation declaring Martial Law, or any public warning to the inhabitants, has been issued or not." Although Lieber carefully distinguished martial law from oppression, since soldiers should behave honorably, he also emphasized the vast powers that followed from necessity. "To save the country is paramount to all other considerations," he wrote.[23]

Martial law in the postsurrender South was less a fixed status than a state of mind. What martial law meant on the ground was what commanders thought it meant, not what legal scholars wrote on a page. Many officers never figured out the basic difference between courts-martial, which covered soldiers, and military commissions, which oversaw trials of civilians in areas governed by martial law. Even officers who navigated that thicket frequently made basic errors that indicated their ignorance of procedure; most had no training in law and so made it up as they went along. Throughout the war, commanders tried dozens of civilians—illegally—in front of post courts-martial instead of military commissions, made a slew of procedural errors that the judge advocates tried to correct, and in many other ways demonstrated that they simply did not understand how military law worked. An army full of judges might not have fared better. Even Supreme Court Justice David Davis confused himself by talking about the "Law of Courts Martial" when he actually was referring to the different institution of military commissions. Lieutenant General Ulysses S. Grant confirmed the mystifying nature of martial law when he testified about the pursuit of the Lincoln assassins in Maryland in April 1865. He had used martial law's powers, he said, even though he "never saw the order" that placed the loyal region under martial law. To the amazement of his congressional interlocutor, but in keeping with Lieber's understanding of the term, Grant had "just an understanding that it does exist."[24]

After surrender, martial law assumed a new importance and a new layer of complexity as the military came up against developing governments. Two forms of sovereignty competed on the ground, one military and one civil, one based on war powers, one on courts. The struggles between these two forms tested whether provisional governments were normal governments. In a summer 1865 opinion, Attorney General James Speed denied that the provisional governments were governments at all. They were empowered to call conventions, but "there is an obvious and plain distinction betwixt the right and duty to organize a government and that of administering a government already organized." Since the president "had no right to create courts and judges," he could not bestow that power on provisional governors. If governors appointed judges, the president might accept this fiction in hopes that "good will come," but he cannot "recognize such courts as absolutely legal and authoritative, and cannot order and enforce obedience to the mandates of the judges." With no other reliable civil government, it was therefore "the duty of the army to keep the peace. The peace cannot be kept without the power to punish for offences."[25]

The path to establishing civil authority was confused and ill-defined. In about half the states under provisional rule, the governors at first assumed that the old government had simply vanished with surrender. In Georgia, James Johnson refused to do anything beyond calling the constitutional convention since, he said, President Johnson had "advised me to appoint as few officers as possible," and the attorney general "was of the opinion that I did not have the power." After local leaders complained that the state was completely ungoverned, Governor Johnson belatedly directed incumbent civil officers to resume their duties. Florida's provisional governor likewise did not recognize the old magistrates until the state constitutional convention met in October. In Texas, Governor Hamilton could not communicate with, much less govern, large sections of the state and held off making appointments until he had better knowledge of the situation.[26]

The most active provisional governor, North Carolina's William Holden, shared the disdain for the powers of the old government but had an entirely different vision of his own authority. Assuming that the proclamation voided all the Confederate officials down to magistrates, Holden sought to remake the state by appointing a completely new slate of officers. Holden alone had met with Johnson before his appointment and may have received the president's approval. Within two months, he had appointed 3,500 magistrates and sheriffs and local officials.[27] In South Carolina, Alabama, and Mississippi, governors oversaw awakened but not transformed local governments. Following neither the Georgia nor the North Carolina model, they reappointed most—or in South Carolina all—the Confederate officials who would take the oath.

President Johnson gave few indications of his goals or expectations. If Georgia appointed no officers, Johnson said very little. If Holden appointed thousands, Johnson kept quiet about that as well. If most states reinstituted the magistrates who remained and simply filled vacancies, that, too, provoked no response. If army commanders appointed magistrates to fill vacancies, that also seemed to pass muster. Johnson's acquiescence to a vast range of styles suggests that he treated the states as experiments and watched to see how they would develop. In North and South Carolina, provisional governors issued exactly contradictory proclamations about the persistence of the old local governments, and Johnson approved both courses of action.[28]

Civil governments fought most vigorously against the military in Virginia and Louisiana, where they could claim office by election. In Louisiana, after Major General Nathaniel Banks dismissed the New Orleans mayor for his ill-treatment of freedpeople, Governor J. Madison Wells complained about the "flagrant abuse of Military power" that destroyed the "substance" of "civil authority." Johnson then replaced Banks. But the governor's celebration was short-lived. By July, he complained that day-to-day power remained in the hands of officers who voided discriminatory town laws, overruled restrictions on freedpeople's travel, and seized levees. This time Johnson ignored him. In Virginia, Major General Alfred Terry exercised military authority broadly despite the existence of the loyal government. After arresting one newspaper editor and suspending another publication, Terry hoped these actions gave "warning to all of exactly what the military control of the Department requires." When white Richmond residents treated a July 25 city election as proof of their "restoration" and elected ex-Confederates, the commander voided the results and assumed control of the police, reminding white Virginians that "they are on probation."[29]

In states with provisional governments, the military not only regulated but at times displaced them. Generals took the place of civil government by managing daily life, banning the sale of liquor, and requiring all citizens in Georgia and South Carolina to apply for a sporting permit if they wanted to keep guns and ammunition. Commanders also went beyond normal civil authority when they monitored newspapers and churches. When Major General Thomas Ruger suspended the Salisbury *Banner* newspaper, he aimed to teach Southerners that they "will not be permitted to discuss and criticize the actions of the military authorities." Among the most startling impositions were suspensions of ministers, including the Episcopal bishop of Alabama, who refused to pray for the national government. White and black Southerners could still carve out large sections of time and space apart from military oversight, but actions like these reminded people that they were under occupation and still living in wartime.[30]

The power of occupation was evident in the military's shadow court system. This system largely, although not exclusively, radiated down from the military police called provosts. To resolve the problems of occupation early in the war, army officials ordered military courts called provost courts to try civilians for smaller offenses. It employed military commissions to try them for major crimes. By 1864, more than 4,000 provost judges—the vast majority of whom had no legal training—heard criminal cases. At surrender, beleaguered commanders hoped to turn cases over to courts, but they still retained ultimate power over court judgments. Supreme Court Justice Salmon P. Chase acknowledged that the military remained superior to courts "until the President should see fit to declare the insurrection at an end & the civil government fully reestablished."[31] Civilian courts in occupied lands filled the form but not the ultimate function of civil government.

Military commanders frequently overrode courts in order to release soldiers from jail and to try civilians for assaulting military men. When Sheriff Josiah Daniel of Cherokee County, Alabama, called out a posse to arrest a detachment of U.S. soldiers and then killed one in a gun battle, the army arrested the sheriff and held him for military trial. When a Dandridge, Tennessee, sheriff arrested two former soldiers in the winter of 1865 and then fought back a detachment of U.S. soldiers sent to free him, the army dispatched 200 troops to liberate the soldiers and to awe the town. Intervening to protect soldiers created a reservoir of military power that could then be turned toward freedpeople. In Georgia, soldiers tried three white men for killing three black men in McIntosh County. Although the defendants complained that "being strictly civilians" they were "not subject to be tried" by military court, they were arraigned before a military commission anyway. In North Carolina, the military refused Governor Holden's request to release three white men charged with assaulting a freedman because courts did not take "notice of unlawful violence toward freedmen."[32]

The military court system expanded over 1865 because freedpeople helped officers realize that the Southern courts dismissed their rights. Freedpeople could not testify in many court cases in many Southern states, and juries frequently imposed separate, unequal punishments on them. Officers and Freedmen's Bureau agents therefore constructed a mirror court system run by the military to handle their cases. Even as courts reopened in the South, most commanders continued to grant provost courts exclusive jurisdiction over freedpeople's trials. But taking direct control of proceedings overwhelmed the bureau and the provost officers. When bureau agents could not handle the slack, commanders in Alabama, Georgia, and Tennessee tried to create a new civil system that reported directly to the military. Sheriffs and magistrates were appointed as bureau officers so that they could accept the testimony of blacks. As freedpeople complained that the civilians were biased, all the army departments but Alabama either restored the cases to provost courts or appointed new slates of agents. In Florida, Louisiana, Virginia, and Mississippi, bureau commissioners dealt with the overwhelming number of cases by making army post commanders bureau agents; every outpost was also a bureau office capable of hearing cases or referring them to provost courts. In North Carolina, problems with the provost system led to the creation of a hybrid bureau court system. Despite the different forms, the message was generally the same. When the mayor of Portsmouth, Virginia, complained that the military overturned a verdict by a municipal court that accepted black testimony, the local commander brusquely responded that his order giving the military control over all cases involving freedpeople "means what it says," then arrested the mayor.[33]

The army and the courts fought most bitterly over the right of habeas corpus, which requires that the government bring the suspect in front of a court so that the judge can determine whether sufficient evidence exists to hold him. A treasured safeguard of individual liberty from state oppression, the writ of habeas corpus had been utilized in England since at least the fourteenth century to prevent the government from imprisoning people without evidence. Although the president continued the general suspension of habeas corpus, judges tested the policy by issuing writs anyway. In Alabama, federal judge Richard Busteed fumed after a general refused his order. But Chief Justice Chase reminded him that "laws must be silent amid arms." If the army retained control, a writ was simply a suggestion, not an order. For this reason, Chase himself declined to hold federal circuit courts in Virginia during military rule. In Mississippi, a fight over habeas corpus led to sharp conflict. Provisional governor William Sharkey ordered a judge to issue a writ of habeas corpus for a white planter charged with murder. In response Major General Henry Slocum arrested the judge. What had started as a legal question turned into a political test when Sharkey threatened to resign. Out of this conflict, Sharkey and Slocum negotiated a resolution to the tension; Sharkey would order state judges to take black testimony, and Slocum would dismantle Freedmen's Bureau courts in Mississippi.[34]

By appointing provisional governors, President Andrew Johnson had not created civilian control; he had, however, bestowed titles and stature that could be used against the military. After months of backing the military, in three important decisions in August and September 1865 Johnson seemed to tilt the balance of power toward civil governments. Johnson's most consequential judgments were on land redistribution. Over the course of the war, the U.S. government acquired at least temporary control of 850,000 acres of land, which had fallen under the Direct Tax of 1862, the Confiscation Act of 1862, and the 1864 law on abandoned lands. Almost half the land lay along the coasts of South Carolina, Georgia, and north Florida. Major General William T. Sherman had divvied up these parcels into forty-acre tracts for freedpeople in early 1865, including on the Georgia islands where Tunis Campbell directed a black government. Deeper inland, thousands of freedpeople lived on leased properties at Davis Bend, Mississippi; Norfolk, Virginia; and New Bern and Roanoke Island, North Carolina. With the battles' end, several possibilities arose. The United States could rush to court to try to take peacetime possession of the confiscated and abandoned land for the life span of the owners. It could sustain its temporary hold over the land for the legal duration of wartime, giving freedpeople two to three years to work to accumulate capital. Or it could begin to return land immediately. By excluding people with $20,000 in property from his amnesty proclamation, Johnson opened the possibility of widespread land allocation. But by the late summer of 1865, Johnson pardoned hundreds of people a day and returned their lands to them.[35]

By ending the war between the nation and individual traitors, pardons restored title to the land and thus destroyed the hopes of property redistribution. National Freedmen's Bureau commissioner major general O. O. Howard directed his state commissioners to allocate property to freedpeople as quickly as possible, but Johnson blocked these efforts. He had been swayed not just by his racism but also by lies his former neighbors in Tennessee told him about the ways lands were being used there. The impact of Johnson's orders was quick and devastating. On the Donelson plantation near Nashville, almost 450 freedpeople—including thirty-five families of killed black soldiers—had been promised they could work the land until the end of harvest; by September 1 only 23 people remained. From Tennessee, the decision spread quickly across the South. Although Howard suggested that pardoned people be required to allocate five- to ten-acre plots for their former slaves, Johnson on September 12 made it easier for ex-Confederates to regain all property that had not been sold under court decree. When Howard informed freedpeople in the South Carolina Sea Islands that they would have to turn over the land to the former owners, the heartbroken crowd chanted, "No, never," and formulated petitions to Johnson and Howard demanding title to land they believed they had earned with their blood and their sweat. But these pleas fell on deaf ears. By April 1866, the bureau had returned more than 400,000 acres. Soon the islands where Tunis Campbell directed a black-run settlement were themselves in line to be returned to the planters who held legal title. In the interim, Campbell had established himself as a self-styled governor, written a constitution, and established a government based at St. Catherines. With Johnson's orders, all that lay in jeopardy; in the next year, Campbell would be dismissed and the land returned.[36]

Johnson's next major decision was in South Carolina. There Governor Ben-jamin Perry restored all civil officers, even men not covered by the amnesty proclamation. Major General Quincy Adams Gillmore responded brusquely, asserting that martial law was still the "supreme and only law in South Carolina." When Perry complained to Johnson that the military refused "to let the civil officers act, at all," Johnson at first urged Perry to appoint loyal men but then directed the military not to interfere with Perry "without orders from me." Although this seemed a prelude to the full restoration of the state, in fact the outcome was more mixed. Major General George Meade, sent south on a fact-finding trip, brokered a truce between Gillmore and Perry; freedpeople's cases would remain in provost courts, but the army would not interfere in trials involving whites. "It will in my judgment be necessary for the Government to exercise a quasi military jurisdiction" at least until freedmen could testify, Meade wrote. The military's power had been restrained but not overturned.[37]

The third crucial decision Johnson faced was in Mississippi, where he granted the state government the fateful power to organize a militia. This tipped the scales of power from the army toward provisional governments. More even than the court system, militias promised provisional governments something akin to a defensible state sovereignty, a level of force that could make the army irrelevant. Militias were a state's line of defense; in a Southern state, an armed militia could oppress freedpeople under the name of putting down an alleged slave rebellion. It was a startling setback for the army. But the story was a mixed one. In mid-August, Mississippi governor William Sharkey had prompted the crisis by calling up militia companies in every county. Local military commanders disapproved, and Johnson at first sustained the army. Then, in a startling turn, Johnson reversed himself and authorized the militia. Why did Johnson change his mind? In part it was timing. When he first said no, he believed he was responding to a hypothetical question. When he learned that the governor had actually already created the militia, Johnson changed his stance. This was part of his management style; he gave forceful advice but disliked personally overriding provisional governments. Johnson may also have been swayed by his annoyance with Carl Schurz, a Radical Republican politician touring the South. While Schurz imagined he was giving advice to Johnson, Johnson punished him for meddling and forced him to deliver the order that permitted the formation of the militia. Shortly afterward, Johnson suggested that Governor Lewis Parsons raise a militia in

Alabama to show "your citizens would be committed to the cause of Law and Order." With the militia in place, the state governments seemed newly empowered and legitimate.[38]

What emerged from these indeterminate interactions were not restored states but a peculiar form of what the *Army & Navy Journal* called "duplex authority," in which provisional governors and military commanders each exerted control over the same space. Johnson's support for militias expanded civil authority but did not restore civil control. The state militia helped white Southerners assert their power, but it did not force the military into retreat, nor did Johnson lift martial law. Even as civilians drilled in squads, soldiers could break into jail cells and, in extreme cases, arrest local officers while disregarding warrants and writs of habeas corpus. This was not a policy but "a sort of hybrid rule, a 'miscegenation' of martial and civil sway," the *Army & Navy Journal* wrote. The question, the newspaper noted, was "Which is the final and sovereign power?" Despite frustrations in South Carolina, Mississippi, and elsewhere, Johnson still provided "a distinct ratification of the military sway under which the South now lives. . . . United States troops are all that are left to put down force with force." Johnson had empowered the civilian governments but without relieving the military ones. He seems to have been waiting to see what the states would do, in hopes they would act in a manner to bring Reconstruction to a close.[39]

Despite his retreats, Johnson did not capitulate to the new Southern state governments. Instead, he used his unusual powers ordering them to remake their constitutions, intervening in legislative debates, and deciding when to recognize elected governments. In the constitutional conventions across the rebel states, Johnson found himself trapped in a dilemma that would stymie government officials throughout Reconstruction: paths to peace required utilizing the tools of war. Although Johnson hoped the rebel states would adequately remake themselves, he could not trust them to do so. Therefore, to move toward peace, he issued what amounted to orders to them about how to set up their constitutions and their laws. Because he controlled the military that governed these states, his directives had far more power than the typical presidential suggestions. When Mississippi's convention became the first to meet in mid-August, Johnson urged the delegates without delay to end slavery and adopt the Thirteenth Amendment. Behind this lay a threat; his allies warned recalcitrant delegates that their readmission depended upon their obedience. At last, the convention settled on a compromise that acknowledged slavery had "been destroyed" and would not exist again. Johnson's intervention in Mississippi sent a clear message. Alabama's constitutional convention, which convened next, "wheeled into line" on the slavery issue to avoid being held under martial law. When South Carolina's convention did not reapportion delegates to his liking, Johnson had Secretary of State William Seward set them straight. So too with the South Carolina convention's reluctance to acknowledge the end of slavery. With the meeting of the North Carolina convention, Johnson began directing states to repudiate "every Dollar" of Confederate war debts "finally and forever." When Georgia's convention bristled against repudiation, Johnson warned them not to "hesitate one single moment." In Texas, which did not meet until February, delegates had to be brought around by the threat that they would not be restored unless they voided secession and eliminated slavery.[40]

More striking, if less successful, was Johnson's suggestion that Mississippi "extend the elective franchise to all persons of color who can read the constitution of the United States in English and write their names, and to all persons of color who own real estate" worth $250 or more. "As a consequence the Radicals, who are wild upon negro franchise, will be completely foiled in their attempts to keep the Southern States from renewing their relations to the Union." Having earlier stated that he could not interfere with state suffrage, Johnson now intervened in the form of a suggestion. Although the letter cannot reveal Johnson's intimate thoughts on black suffrage, it does illustrate his understanding of the restoration process. States would experiment with forms; Congress would judge some experiments worthy and some deficient. In the process, some states would act so foolishly as to remain under martial law until they corrected their statutes.[41] Extending suffrage to enough freedpeople to appease Congress—but not to so many as to give blacks real power—was simply good strategy.

Johnson's intervention through his army commanders helped remake the ultimate form of civilian law, the Constitution. The Thirteenth Amendment demonstrated that constitutional change depended on extra-constitutional powers. What was at stake was the survival of slavery. The Thirteenth Amendment established constitutional justification for ending slavery even when war powers concluded. Although the Senate passed the amendment in April 1864 and the House in January 1865, it required the approval of three-fourths of the state legislatures to be embedded in the Constitution. While some Republicans wished to count only loyal states, Johnson wanted the ex-Confederate states counted, too, in order to help establish their legitimacy. Therefore, he warned them—as he would not have warned a normal state—that they must ratify the amendment or risk not being seated by Congress. When South Carolina's legislature resisted, Johnson wailed, "I trust in God that the restoration of the Union will not be defeated and all that has so far been well done thrown away?" After some lobbying, the legislature acceded, but Mississippi resisted his importuning and did not ratify the amendment until 1995. With the ratification by South Carolina, Alabama, North Carolina, and Georgia, Johnson had secured crucial votes by using threats of continuing war powers. Other important votes came from the loyal, but in many ways fictional, governments of Arkansas, Virginia, and Louisiana, where tiny administrations relied heavily upon the army, and generals intervened in the amendment fight. On paper, the states had consented, but only if one overlooked the role of war powers in forcing them to. With these votes, the amendment became part of the Constitution in December 1865. Again and again, Johnson had demonstrated that he had, as the *New York Times* put it, the right and the duty to "impose conditions" upon the states. In his dealings with the Thirteenth Amendment, Johnson came up against a dilemma that would recur later in Reconstruction. Ending the war required changing the permanent law. But the only way to change the Constitution was to rely on the military. In former Confederate states, the fear of military power was doubly crucial in ending slavery, first in directly attacking it in the countryside, then in prodding the governments to pass the amendment.[42]

As politics resumed in the South, the scattered white insurgency coalesced into an organized political movement that frustrated Johnson's plans. Instead of electing loyalists or secession skeptics, white Southern voters chose proud rebels. Refashioning political alliances fractured by wartime, these insurgents resisted not just Congress but Johnson himself. One Alabama loyalist complained that "politically our State has gone wild." Candidates who accommodated themselves to Johnson's seemingly mild positions were "denounced as Traitors to the South." Rather than conforming to Johnson's policies, they asserted themselves in ways the president had not expected. In Louisiana, Johnson's efforts to appease whites by removing the commander and the state Freedmen's Bureau commissioner only hardened their resistance. As the previously loyalist Governor Wells switched sides and appealed to ex-rebels, Johnson in despair considered vacating the government and starting over. Ruefully, the *New York Times* concluded that white Southerners were "not loyal" but "only conquered." In Kentucky, conservatives, including large numbers of former rebels, carried the state in August. Even in Tennessee, where the government disenfranchised rebels and relied upon the army to sustain itself, Confederate service was the "best passport to position and power" in parts of the state. Clothed with the legitimacy that democracy conveyed, ex-rebels believed they would soon be rewarded with the resumption of civil authority. From the rebel states, governors complained vociferously about army commanders who overrode laws, and asked for the removal of black troops and the restoration of habeas corpus to prove that they would be treated as though the rebellion had ended.[43] Democracy had enflamed and organized the conflict between the United States and the former Confederates.

On the issue of civil rights, insurgents alienated Congress and frustrated Johnson's plans. While Republicans blamed Johnson for the outrageous developments in the Southern states, especially the creation of rigid Black Codes, Johnson in fact tried to stop Southern states from going as far as they did. But the politicians resisted him because white Southerners could not abide basic civil rights for black people, even ones so meager as to be acceptable to Johnson. Although Johnson was deeply racist, he was not the father of the Black Codes. Instead he reasserted war powers by allowing his commanders to override them. The first issue that arose was the right to testify in court, a basic right of free people elsewhere in the country. Freedpeople pressed this issue to local army commanders and to responsive Republicans in Washington, asking, "How will we Be protected" without "the full rightes and protections of the Government"? Many conservative Southerners likewise thought it savvy to extend basic civil rights in order to remove Freedmen's Bureau and provost court jurisdiction over freedpeople. But there was intense popular sentiment against extending rights in the white South. When Mississippi failed to extend the right to testify in court, Johnson and the state's military commander warned the governor that troops would remain in the state until Mississippi offered legal protection to freedpeople. Only after the governor issued a special message did the bill pass. In Tennessee, Johnson similarly wrote to express his disappointment, and the legislature acceded. After that, every state permitted some black testimony, although Tennessee was the only one to allow freedpeople to testify in cases between whites. When North Carolina's legislators tried to appease their constituents by making the right to testify contingent upon the withdrawal of the bureau's jurisdiction, Johnson urged legislators not to inflame Northern opinion.[44]

More broadly, Southern state legislators established harsh vagrancy laws, expanded the forced apprenticeship of black children, created separate punishments for black and white rapists, and increased penalties for crimes associated with rural blacks, especially theft and burglary. As in secession and in resistance to the Thirteenth Amendment, Mississippi and South Carolina took the first and most extreme stances. Mississippi's codes denied blacks the right to rent or lease land in rural areas, required every black man to have a written contract or license, banned blacks from carrying weapons, and imposed a head tax. In response freedpeople organized public meetings to draw Northern Republicans' attention to what they called a system of "warranteeism" that would "nullify the Proclamation of Emancipation" and lead to "practical reenslavement." Next, South Carolina passed a code that permitted whipping of blacks but not whites, fined blacks for selling farm produce, and practically barred blacks from working as artisans, mechanics, shopkeepers, and peddlers. "It is the old slave code minus the slave owners' responsibilities," Attorney General Speed wrote. Prodded by Johnson's administration, Alabama's governor vetoed three discriminatory bills in hopes of appeasing Congress; then, every state avoided the inflammatory licensing and property restrictions. Nevertheless, Florida permitted lashings and punished black workers for "impudence or disrespect."[45]

Irritated by their foolishness, President Johnson used his military power to undermine the legitimacy of the elected governments. While he did not accept Congress's power over the ex-Confederate states, Johnson also did not believe those governments were legitimate just because they were elected. Authority belonged neither to Congress nor to the Southern voters; it belonged to him, as a function of his war powers. With legislatures in session, virtually every governor expected "to be governed by law once more" and "relieved of military rule," but Johnson disappointed them. Beginning in South Carolina, Johnson ordered his provisional governors to remain in office even if their elected counterparts staged inaugurations. He, not Congress or the legislature, would determine when the elected governors took power. What this meant was that Johnson directed his generals to ignore the elected governors and to continue working through the provisional governors. Practically, the elected and inaugurated governors were merely pretenders; the states continued to function through the provisional governors because the commanding generals recognized their authority. The governments could not function without military cooperation, so the army's actions determined who actually filled the role of governor. When Mississippi elected an unpardoned rebel, Johnson refused to recognize him for two months. Against Georgia's "impracticable & refractory" legislature and North Carolina's election of Jonathan Worth over Holden, Johnson kept both elected governors from office. Of the six governors elected in the fall of 1865, Johnson made five of them wait more than a month after their inaugurations before he recognized them. Although the military hand had loosened, it had not let go.[46]

Recognizing that the strategy of inducing white Southern cooperation had failed, the army returned to its policy of coercion by the end of 1865. While Johnson spoke of restored states, his army sustained wartime military powers. In Florida, Colonel John Sprague simultaneously proclaimed the restoration of law and retained military control over a wide range of cases involving rape, murder, manslaughter, arson, assault and battery, riots, robbery, and burglary. Commanders in Virginia, Mississippi, and Georgia suspended discriminatory laws. Officers in North Carolina arrested editors and ordered the militia to obey army commands; military commissions continued to try cases involving Southern civilians. It all reflected, as one Southerner bitterly complained to Johnson, the "assumption by the *military* authorities, of the prerogative of expunging from our statute-book, whatever they may consider a discrimination." In the confusion over the power of civil government, Reuben Wilson's fate hung in the balance. Arrested by the U.S. Army in late April 1865 for his role in ordering his men to shoot two deserters, two white loyalists, and a black man in Forsyth County, North Carolina, Wilson finally came before a civilian court in December. But the judge, a provisional appointee, refused to hear the case on the grounds that he had no authority over crimes committed during the war. Instead he directed a county court to hear it in the next session when, presumably though not in fact, civilian law would be supreme. For the moment, the legal system hung between military and civilian control.[47]

In South Carolina, the army's enduring power over state governments was fully revealed. When Major General Daniel Sickles, a Democrat, replaced the ardent abolitionist Quincy Adams Gillmore as commander, white South Carolinians might have expected a smooth transition to home rule. Instead of retreating, Sickles voided discriminatory statutes and reaffirmed martial law. When the governor armed the militia, Sickles treated them as his deputized police force and ordered them to obey post commanders. On January 1, 1866, Sickles signaled that the new year was not quite so new for Southern states with an order that revoked most of the Black Codes.[48]

War powers had been too valuable to give up. At year's end, much had changed, but much abided. The rebel states established by Johnson's orders had some of the attributes of democratically elected, legitimate peacetime governments, but President Johnson did not actually treat them as states. In a real state, it would have been unthinkable for generals to convey instructions or even suggestions to constitutional conventions and legislatures, much less to refuse to recognize elected governors. Despite his racism and general conservatism, Johnson was not willing to turn over power in the South just yet, not while white Southerners acted so counterproductively, and not while they threatened to arrest U.S. soldiers still stationed there. Trapped between white Southern governments he mistrusted and Republican congressmen he came to hate, Johnson turned to the one tool he could partly control, the military. Johnson sustained an ongoing wartime occupation of the rebel states in late 1865 even as he claimed to be treating those states as equals. He was, one lawyer wrote, "contradicting his declarations by his acts." He presumed the Southern states were intact, yet "he still governs them by military force." More succinctly, another politician claimed that Johnson, "under a supposed necessity, seems to be trying the strange experiment of running a civil government by military law." It was a baffling situation, but occupations often produce these contradictory moments when efforts to wrap them up fall apart. Having created these Southern governments, and having watched them disregard his requests, Johnson could neither acknowledge nor dismiss them.[49]

- 4 -

AUTHORITY WITHOUT ARMS

A S WHITE SOUTHERNERS resisted federal power, it became clear that coercion depended upon control. The army's ability to regulate the South turned not just upon its legal authority but upon the force it possessed to make white Southerners obey. During the fall of 1865, those tools still remained relatively formidable; the occupation of the South dwindled but did not die. If seen from a satellite, soldiers in the South would appear to be moving rapidly in several directions in the spring, summer, and fall of 1865—hundreds of thousands north toward home, 50,000 southwest to the Mexican border, and tens of thousands west to the plains. But the South they left behind was not empty; there great clumps of armies spun into the countryside, flinging tens of thousands of soldiers into nearly 400 outposts. These two seemingly contradictory acts—demobilization and occupation—defined the dual nature of the postsurrender wartime in the fall of 1865. The nation simultaneously shifted toward peace and sustained the will to fight; its soldiers were sent both home and to duty. No one could look at the streams of men arriving home in the North and think the war continued as it had been, but no one could look at the hundred thousand men still on the ground in hundreds of outposts in the South and think the war was quite over. In the restored Northern household and in the occupied South, we see a nation drifting toward peace, a region still at war.

Although the army sustained broad authority throughout 1865, it also let loose large numbers of men. Soldiers stationed in the Confederacy dropped from roughly 1 million in April 1865 to 300,000 at the end of June, 190,000 at the end of September, 125,000 at the end of November, and fewer than 90,000 by the end of January 1866. If the large numbers stationed near the Mexican border in Texas are not included, the drops in the rest of the Confederate states are even more striking, from 180,000 in August, to 150,000 in September, to 99,000 in November, and to 61,000 at the end of January 1866. For these reasons, historians have often dismissed the army as nearly irrelevant by the end of 1865 and focused on the Freedmen's Bureau, even though the bureau possessed only a few hundred agents and depended almost entirely upon the army for its survival.[1]

Even as the army shed its soldiers like old skin, it also spread its arms widely across the South. To understand the paradox of an army both demobilizing and occupying, we have to see the enormous numbers of soldiers available in the late spring of 1865. For at least the first five months after surrender, the army chose both to send large numbers into the field and to send even larger numbers home. (See Appendix 2.) But around September, the demobilization caught up to the military, and the army started to become overstretched and undermanned. Although officers recognized the need for more forces by the fall of 1865, neither politicians nor policy makers in Washington were prepared to face these problems. Driven to cut costs and unable to anticipate the needs on the ground, they continued slashing the military after they should have kept men in arms. What remained was not—and would never again be—enough to fulfill the breadth of the army's mission. In the end, occupation was undone—to the degree that it was undone—by bad luck, bad timing, and bad judgment more than by bad intentions. In turn, white Southerners launched increasingly ambitious campaigns for control of the spaces the army could no longer reach. What emerged from the occupation of 1865 was a patchwork of sovereignties, with the military in firm command of some rail lines and coastal regions, planters and freedpeople in control of more distant upcountry and plantation belts, and near anarchy in the contested zones in between. The geographic shape of the government's power, the contours of its ability to enforce its will, had changed with the retraction of soldiers.

The occupation, therefore, both succeeded and failed in key ways in late 1865. Although the army could not create security throughout the South, its tenuous hold over some regions permitted the growth of defensible rights there, and also carried information northward about the violent outrages taking place in the South. The occupation's successes and its failures both emerged from its ambitions. Had the army maintained instead of undermined planter control, it would have preserved the peace more effectively. Instead, it was the occupation's very successes in creating space for freedpeople that fueled the violent insurgency that exposed the military's inability to secure the South.

Judging Reconstruction requires stepping out of the shadow of post–World War II occupations and understanding it within similarly short-staffed nineteenth-century military presences. Next to the 60,000 soldiers in the non-Texas rebel states in January 1866, or the roughly 25,000 soldiers the army deployed later in Reconstruction, the United States typically stationed fewer than 20,000 troops in the 1870s American West, 25,000 in the Philippines after the end of combat, 5,000 in Cuba, and fewer than that in Puerto Rico. Forceful U.S. occupations of Haiti and the Dominican Republic in the second decade of the twentieth century typically relied upon 2,000 to 3,000 American troops. Other than in the Philippines, these occupations did not face insurgencies on the vast scale of the U.S. South, but more ambitious imperial military presences were hardly better staffed. In India, British troops ranged from under 40,000 before the Mutiny of 1857 to 65,000 in 1877, supplemented by 125,000 to 230,000 Asians to regulate a region three times the size of the Confederacy and with twenty times its population; British troops in Ireland generally fluctuated between 20,000 and 30,000 over the century. Although the French in Algeria and the Habsburgs in rebellious cities after 1848–1849 utilized more forces and more sweeping powers, the United States' occupation of the Confederacy was thorough and well supported by historical standards, at least for the first year. What hampered Reconstruction was its historical context. Nations that confronted sticky problems of occupation in the mid-nineteenth century simply did not utilize the range of forces or possess the technological advantages over citizens that twentieth-century occupiers did. To judge Reconstruction as weak is therefore to judge it anachronistically, against standards of occupation that would not be clearly developed for another eighty years.[2]

The most important reason for the drawdown of soldiers in the South was financial. Only two things were "indispensable in war," economist Amasa Walker wrote in January 1865, echoing Julius Caesar: "men and money." Keeping men in service hinged on the government's capacity to raise funds to pay, clothe, and feed them. "You may, indeed, have money without men, but cannot have men without money."[3]

A brief but crucial financial panic in the spring of 1865 played a key, nearly forgotten role in speeding the discharge of the soldiers. Like almost every wartime nation, the United States depended upon being able to sell bonds and loans at low prices to meet its enormous bills, which totaled nearly $6 billion. The war machine that won the battles was the product not just of democratic fervor but also of an amazingly efficient transformation of the government into a vast employer and contractor, tying millions of people's self-interest to the nation's ultimate victory. To pay and equip an army of more than 1 million men, the United States raised tariffs, imposed an income tax, and issued paper money, but mostly it relied upon loans and bonds to manage the $3 billion difference between income and outflow. The most effective methods were the famous "5–20s," loans which paid 6 percent interest in gold for between five and twenty years. Philadelphia financier Jay Cooke's firm led the sale of more than $650 million in 5–20s by late 1865. After a failed experiment with ten-year loans at lower interest rates, the government turned back to Cooke to market new 7–30s that paid 7.3 percent interest until 1867 and then could be converted to gold-bearing 5–20s.[4]

These loans saved the nation, but they also tied the government's borrowing to the price of gold. More than half of the government's securities promised interest payments in coin rather than greenback dollars. As the government broke with the gold standard and flooded new money into circulation, and as faith in the United States' success faltered, the price of gold rose dramatically, from a 3 percent premium against the U.S. dollar in January 1862 to a 50 percent premium for most of 1863, and an incredible 160 percent premium in August 1864. Peculiarly, the high price of gold helped the Treasury Department by alchemically fusing patriotism and self-interest. Because one could buy bonds and loans with paper money and receive interest payments in gold, they became instruments for profiting off the gold premium. But this was a precarious balance. If gold rose too high, the government incurred huge interest payments. If it dropped too low, the loans and bonds lost their financial appeal.[5]

All these precarious positions threatened to collapse in a since forgotten panic in March 1865. As the government followed its usual spring practice of withdrawing money from circulation, confidence in the imminent U.S. victory spurred a drop in gold. Sellers drove down gold prices from a 101 percent premium on March 1 to a 48.5 percent premium on March 24. The fall in gold suddenly dried up the market for government loans and bonds. The best-established loans, the 5–20s, fell from a 10.5 percent to a 5 percent premium. The two newer securities fell more dramatically, with the 10–40s and 7–30s both selling below face value. It was now cheaper to buy the loans on resale markets than from the government. "We are in the midst of a panic which, though not entirely unlooked for, may, unless arrested be productive of most serious consequences to the public and to the government," Assistant Treasurer John A. Stewart wrote to Treasury Secretary Hugh McCulloch on March 21. Beyond government bonds, the fear drove down the price of railway shares, petroleum, pork, tobacco, and cotton by more than 20 percent.[6]

The slowdown threatened to dry up the Treasury Department just as the government faced a $100 million cash deficit in April and bills accumulating at nearly $4 million per day. Alarmed at the threat to the nation's finances and credit, the Treasury Department launched a secret program to stop the fall by buying tens of millions of dollars' worth of securities and gold, hoping to prop up prices. After a week of intervention, Cooke's agents and the assistant treasurer succeeded, and the 5–20s rose back to 8.5 percent above par. After spending another $20 million in mid-April, the government kept prices stable through Lee's surrender and Lincoln's assassination. Cooke's firm sold nearly $4 million a day in securities.[7]

The March crisis taught Treasury Secretary McCulloch to cut expenses dramatically, or there would be "more trouble ahead." The obvious place to slash was the military. Two days after Lee's surrender, a journalist wrote to Cooke that "the payroll of the army should be instantly subjected to unsparing scrutiny and unsparing hewing + chopping."[8]

Even before the Appomattox surrender, the War Department formulated plans for a speedy, massive demobilization. While the government had many reasons to send volunteers home, the leading military newspaper wrote that demobilization was driven "principally from the enormous drafts their maintenance each day made upon the Treasury." To his chagrin, Secretary McCulloch discovered that dispatching the men home could actually be costlier than keeping them in the army since many had six months of back wages due. The first wave of 120,000 returned soldiers carried $50 million in additional draws upon the Treasury. McCulloch "is poor, very poor," Cooke's brother wrote.[9]

Even if the panic altered only the velocity and timing of the demobilization, those elements played crucial roles in shaping the postsurrender South. At a period in March when the War Department might have focused upon confrontations with the large armies in Virginia and North Carolina and Texas, it instead crafted a blueprint for the mustering out. While the Confederacy still breathed, the army began to issue orders to send its men home. At Appomattox, with Johnston's large army still in the field, Grant skipped the laying down of arms ceremony so that he could travel by rail to Washington to finalize plans for demobilization. Had the army moved at a slower pace—perhaps three months behind its schedule—then 200,000 troops, the number actually available in September 1865, might still have been in the field in December when Congress returned to session and began to legislate on the occupation. That number, as it happens, represents roughly the level of forces needed to occupy a region with the South's population, according to some contemporary analysis.[10] At the least, the winter and spring contracting and planting seasons might have proceeded differently.

Faced with the need both to subdue the South and to reduce the growth of the debt, policy makers in April 1865 did not select one over the other. They elected to do both without recognizing the contradictions between the two policies. This simultaneous decision to expand the army's role and shrink its size may have appeared foolish in retrospect, but it was not an effort at sabotage. For the next five years, politicians—including the most radical—struggled to understand and fund the demands they placed on the army. While it is tempting to assume the occupation forces were deliberately undermined by ideological opponents, the challenges were deeper. Some supporters of Reconstruction could not fathom how many troops it would require. They assumed the government could accomplish its goals through laws or bureaucracies and were not prepared for the problem of enforcement. Others simply celebrated the return of soldiers home without thinking of the consequences. While army officers spotted the contradiction between their duties and their forces, few politicians did in 1865 or even after. The blind spot was just as wide for radicals as for conservatives. Even politicians like Charles Sumner and Benjamin Butler who wanted an extensive reconstruction of the South voted consistently to slash the army that would carry it out. As in many democracies, it was easier to call for an occupation than to pay its human and financial costs.

Deep-seated fears of standing armies, powerful evangelical currents of mercy, and a fundamental confusion about the conditions in the South reinforced the necessity of demobilization. From the beginning of the republic, Americans had invoked Caesar's Rome to warn against a strong standing army, the "old terror of an army a million strong, ready to be used by some ambitious, unscrupulous chief, military or political, to destroy liberty, and by a single coup d'état to reduce the Republic to an Empire." At the same time, many Republicans also began talking about the importance of mercy. While Lincoln's assassination sparked fury across the North, pastors and politicians quickly proclaimed the importance of putting vengeance aside. Drawing from evangelical views of grace and historically grounded fears that revenge would prompt more civil wars, they called for a return to peace defined not by legal status but by recognitions of shared humanity. In an echo of the sermons heard in many Northern churches, army chaplain George Carruthers quoted the Bible: "Vengeance is mine, saith the Lord." Carruthers was no conservative; an Oberlin-educated antislavery activist and chaplain to a black regiment, he worked in the Freedmen's Bureau and urged the army to extend its coverage into the countryside. Even for him, Christianity's language of mercy softened his sense of the army's role in the postwar South.[11]

Ever since Herman Melville compared the dissolution of the army to a "deep enforcing current" that drew soldiers home, writers and politicians have cast the army's reduction as both inevitable and uninteresting. The discharge was like the dew that "disappears before the morning sun," former major general Nathaniel Banks said in a July 4, 1865 speech. Or the army "melted quietly" as "the New England snow" under "vernal suns." These naturalistic metaphors both captured and obscured the confused status of the war during this transition period. At the same moment, people proclaimed the endurance of wartime in occupation and also celebrated the return of soldiers as proof of peace. In a single editorial, the *Army & Navy Journal*—generally careful about these matters—celebrated demobilization as the end of the war and also called for an indefinite occupation of 100,000 soldiers in the South. Like melting snow, the army—and by extension the nation—was no longer ice but not yet vapor. From Louisiana, Freedmen's Bureau officer Joseph Sumner celebrated the way soldiers "melted back into the many busy walks of life" even as he also called for a standing army in the South "till the crack of doom if necessary." Out of a mix of optimism and naiveté, supporters struggled conceptually to recognize the manpower needs of the occupation they endorsed.[12]

The army did not actually melt away; it was mustered out by a cumbersome but rigorously managed bureaucratic operation. Because of the March panic, the pieces were in place even before the fighting stopped. Four days after Lee's surrender, Secretary of War Edwin Stanton issued orders ending the draft, curtailing equipment purchases, and cutting staff. Two days after

Johnston's surrender to Sherman, the War Department unveiled its broader plan for an "immediate reduction of the forces in the field." Under the careful watch of Assistant Adjutant Generals E. D. Townsend and Thomas M. Vincent, the army discharged the sick, the newly enrolled, many cavalrymen, those volunteers whose terms ended in May, and most troops in the Army of the Potomac and in Sherman's army. Next it mustered out those three-year volunteers who had enrolled on or after July 1862, and then one-year volunteers who had enrolled between May and October 1864 and black troops who had been organized in Northern states. Under these orders the army sent home 279,000 men from the Army of the Potomac and from Sherman's army by August 1; a total of 640,806 by August 8; 719,338 by August 22; 741,107 by September 14; 785,205 by October 15; and 800,963 by November 15. Soldiers who participated in the Grand Review moved relatively smoothly through field rendezvous points, to depots in their home states, and to their families. For the vast majority of soldiers who did not march to Washington, however, the end was less organized. Money and forms were often slow in arriving from overwhelmed printing offices in Washington, and soldiers sat in camp for weeks waiting for clerks to complete their documents.[13]

In tandem with the sweeping discharges of infantry, the army also dismantled the vitally important cavalry by selling off its horses. As part of its overall sale of boats, railroad cars, and other equipment, the Quartermaster's Office auctioned 10,000 mules and horses in a single week. By the late fall, the army had dispatched 128,000 horses and mules for $7.5 million. Cavalry in some states disappeared. North Carolina's numbers fell from more than 10,000 cavalry in May to 854 by July, while Mississippi's dropped from 2,419 in August to fewer than 100 by October; Georgia's from 8,879 in July to 709 in August; and Alabama's from 4,619 in September to almost none. In regions with regular cavalry, such as Texas, Virginia, Arkansas, Tennessee, Louisiana, and Kentucky, commanders were still able to regulate the countryside. Elsewhere, however, officers begged for a "mounted force" to "enforce law and order" and "reach any point where disorder may be threatened." Around Bladen Springs, Alabama, "its no use to try to get [desperadoes] with infantry for they are on horse," another wrote. The geographic range of sovereignty shifted with the loss of horses. Rather than projecting power 30 or 50 miles from outposts, an occupation based on infantry could realistically reach five to ten miles. With the disappearance of cavalry, the federal government could not regulate whole regions of the South.[14]

Even more worrisome was the fact that the very soldiers who would have to staff a proper occupation were desperate to return home to their families, friends, and jobs. When news of Lee's surrender reached New Bern, North Carolina, on April 12, Theodore Edgar St. John wrote to his future bride, "Oh Janie you can't begin to think how happy every body is feeling this evening." After Daniel Sterling's wife wrote in May to say that she did "not know how to wait another day," Sterling responded that "going home is the uppermost in the soldiers mind. . . . In every tent it is the first thing in the morning and the last thing at night the first word after salutation is when are you going home."[15]

Using their political power, soldiers and their families lobbied congressmen and governors to spring them from the army. As in many democracies, war proved much more popular than occupation. One soldier complained that "we were mustered in to serve 3 years or during the war we now consider our time out, for the war is over." While lawyers and politicians learned to define war as a legal status, most soldiers—like nineteen seamen who wrote in June 1865—called upon commonsensical views that war meant fighting and the end of exigencies meant peace. The war had empowered the soldiers to assert what they saw as their rights. "We was promised To be sent home at the Close of the war and we Entend to go too you and No one else need make Any calculations of keeping us," one soldier wrote. "Soldiers has save[d] this nation and soldiers will run it."[16]

When politicians did not respond, some units took their fate in their own hands by deserting. Mutinies flared from North Carolina to Florida to Texas; desertion was so common after surrender that many officers did not bother to try to recapture the runaways. One-quarter of Ohio's 27,000 deserters fled in the period after Lee's surrender. When Ohio voters in 1867 considered an amendment to simultaneously enfranchise blacks and disfranchise deserters, Congress quickly clarified that soldiers who left after April 1865 should not be classed as deserters at all. In one report from Alabama, an inspector found "the general condition of the troops is poor, the discipline with few exceptions poorly inforced," and multiple regiments "defiant" or in a state of "perfect demoralization."[17]

Some soldiers wanted to return home because they fought solely for the Union, not for emancipation.[18] Unsympathetic men like Henry Gay hated their lingering time in the service precisely because they were helping freedpeople. "We are keeping the Niggars from killing the whites," Gay complained. "There is not eny fun in it." W. D. Latimer of Iowa blamed abolitionists for his time on occupation duty in May and June in Alabama and promised to vote against black enfranchisement whenever he could.[19]

But many other soldiers rejected the choice between union and emancipation. They wanted to go home not because they disliked fighting to end slavery; they wanted to go home because they believed the fight against slavery either was complete or could be conducted without them. This blind but understandable inconsistency ran through the letters of J. R. Rey, who swore that no "punishment cant bea to great for" Confederates while also wishing to "spend a Diffrent forth this forth coming then I did at the forth of 63 at gettysburgh." In Savannah in May 1865, George Putnam at once expressed fury at the "haughty and impudent" rebels, sympathy for freedpeople, and a determination to escape if not mustered out quickly. Likewise, Edward Reynolds of the 46th Illinois celebrated his regiment's efforts to block masters from reenslaving freedpeople and at the same time expressed frustration at his "very tiresome" time in the post.[20] Like politicians who simultaneously hoped to remake the South and reduce the army, these soldiers had not adequately reckoned with the need for force in the postsurrender Confederacy.

Even as it mustered out volunteers, the army staunchly defended its view that wartime continued. In an August 12, 1865, order, Major General Alfred Terry, commander of the Department of Virginia, acknowledged that "many of the men serving in the Volunteer regiments of his command suppose themselves to be legally entitled to their discharge, on the ground that they enlisted to serve for a fixed time, 'or during the war,' and that the war is ended." This, however, was "not true." The "plain and evident meaning of the words 'during the war,' in the contract of enlistment is 'while the necessity for a military force created by the present rebellion shall continue to exist;' that necessity still exists, and therefore those men whose terms of enlistment have not expired are as fully bound to service as if organized Rebel armies were still in the field." The war would not be "brought to a close" until "civil authority shall be fully restored" and the states "shall have returned to their former relations to the National Government." In response, the *Army & Navy Journal* wondered "how and when it may be known that the great Rebellion is over." It was only natural for soldiers to believe that "practically the war is over—for the purposes of business, of campaigning, of ordinary life." Only "constructively, and for the purposes of settling certain relations which it disturbed, the war is not over."[21]

Overly confident that Confederates had acquiesced, the War Department in July accelerated demobilization. Most white Southerners did not form open bands to fight the army, but officers were slow to see the ways that they still resisted federal authority. Although Southern state commanders retained the discretion to keep necessary troops, Virginia mustered out three additional cavalry and two infantry regiments and North Carolina discharged more than half its remaining regiments in July. On the single day of August 1, nine army corps were disbanded. By mid-August nearly half a million volunteers had been sent home, with 200,000 more waiting for paperwork.[22]

In Texas, the army began discharging the occupying force in August. Once Secretary of State Seward blocked efforts to extend the war to Mexico, Grant began preparing to muster out the cavalry in Texas, although he permitted discharged soldiers to stay there if they wished to volunteer to fight in Mexico. From almost 50,000 soldiers in August, the number shrank to 23,000 in December. Soon Texas was no longer mobilized for an open war but was, the *Army & Navy Journal* wrote, on a "peace basis." The peace basis in Texas in the fall and winter of 1865, however, was a far different peace than it had experienced before the war. There were about fifty percent more soldiers in Texas in late 1865 than had served in the entire U.S. army in 1860. Even though the number of troops fell by half between August and December, the army's coverage of Texas expanded from twenty-four posts in the summer to twenty-seven in fall and winter, and to forty-two in the spring of 1866. From a cluster of camps near the Rio Grande, with a few scattered forts along the border of Indian Territory, the army pushed deeper into both northeastern and central Texas, aiming to subdue the guerrillas who fled southward from Missouri and Arkansas and to enforce emancipation in the plantation districts up the Brazos and Colorado rivers.[23]

Despite their impressive numbers, these early discharges did not at first undermine the occupation of the South. Many of the early waves of demobilized troops had done little, if any, postsurrender duty. They simply moved men already in the field to their homes. The musters out did, however, draw down reserves and make it difficult to extend forces into regions unconquered by the army and unguarded in the weeks after surrender. When Florida's state commander asked for troops to establish control over the entire state, his superior refused because the pressure from the War Department "for the muster out of all troops" was "so great." In an unregulated region of northern Louisiana and eastern Texas, the July muster pulled away half the available cavalry, making it impossible for the commander to send detachments to "remote points."[24]

The early discharges played havoc with the Freedmen's Bureau. State bureaus found it "next to impossible" to staff the agencies. In August, Virginia lost forty agents to musters out in a single month, and the Fredericksburg office changed hands four times in twenty days. Half of North Carolina's offices were unstaffed, and one agent was attached to North Carolina's bureau and then mustered out on the same day. "What am I to do for men?" North Carolina's commissioner wrote. "I am crippled entirely." As the demobilization continued, state commanders refused to detach their officers to the bureau for fear of weakening discipline in already understaffed units. When Arkansas's commanding general declined in September to replace mustered-out agents, the bureau closed several offices. "Great confusion will prevail," the state commissioner complained. In response, bureaus turned to post commanders and provost marshals to do bureau duty as they fulfilled their normal army work.[25]

It is tempting to presume that the army reduced the force to appease the rebels, but conditions in the West show that the army was experiencing a systemic, not a Southern, reduction. In both regions, army commanders ran up against serious challenges of morale rooted in the commonsensical belief that the war had ended. Placing the South alongside the West allows us to see Reconstruction as one part of a broader story about the limits of national power. In both regions, the army was unable to fulfill the security demands of freedpeople, white settlers, Indians, or ex-Confederates. In this Greater Reconstruction of national authority, the federal government possessed newfound powers and ambitions, but not always the capacity to fulfill them. Instead of a salutary example of what the South might have been, the West suggested how hard it would be to reign over large, resistant regions.[26]

The Civil War exposed the nation's tenuous hold over its internal Western frontiers. Most concretely, the Civil War affected Indian Country (now Oklahoma) through the alliance between some Cherokee, Creek, Choctaw, and other slave-owning tribes and the Confederacy. Farther north, there was full scale war on the Plains. After white settlers encroached on eastern Sioux in Minnesota, and the federal government refused to pay its annuities, the Indians counter-attacked. In response, the government hanged thirty-eight Indians in 1862. Farther west, both regular army units and militias launched bloody campaigns against Sioux forces in the Dakota Territory and Colorado, killing 300 Sioux at Whitestone Hall in 1863 and 200 peaceful Cheyennes and Arapahos at the 1864 Sand Creek massacre. In California, volunteers slaughtered 250 Shoshone near the Utah-Idaho border in 1863. Along the Santa Fe trail, Comanches drove back white settlers. With Confederate surrender, the army began sending some soldiers from the Southeast to the West. After a series of Indian counterattacks in Colorado, Wyoming, and Montana, 1,000 cavalry marched through Wyoming and Montana in the extraordinarily expensive Powder River expedition, and others rushed to Colorado against Indian attacks at the Platte Bridge Station. Up north, conflict centered upon a series of new forts the government built in Lakota lands on the Bozeman Trail that brought miners to Montana. Tying Indian attacks to the United States' weakened condition, some Americans argued that the Civil War was a general threat to national sovereignty that would end only with peace on the plains. But if victory meant order, it turned out to be almost as hard to obtain in the West as in the South. No matter what it said on a map, the United States' practical sovereignty was geographically limited to towns and a few guarded roads in both regions.[27]

Rather than choosing to occupy the West at the expense of the South, the army was stretched thin everywhere. Officers in both areas frequently felt outnumbered, sought allies where they could, and pleaded for troops in strikingly similar terms. When former brigadier general Thomas Meagher requested a mounted escort and a "howitzer battery" to accompany an expedition from Saint Paul to Montana, the Western commander—like his colleagues in the South—explained that there were no excess men available. In New Mexico,

Anglos complained that the soldiers there were inadequate. Indians seized control over several Montana roads, while in the towns of Virginia City, Bannock, and Helena vigilance committees and road agents overpowered magistrates and enforced their own rough justice. Although it is disconcerting to imagine the U.S. Army at times helpless against, rather than in concert with, white settlers, many officers and soldiers saw white travelers as agents of lawlessness.[28]

Eager to stop fighting, the government tried to broker peace in the West. Now that the United States had proven "its stability and purpose," President Johnson ordered agents to convince Indians to make treaties, abandon lands on wagon trails, and begin farming. Delegations visited Indian Country and the Dakota, Idaho, Montana, and Colorado territories. What emerged from the nineteen treaties the U.S. government negotiated between March and November 1865 was a complex, segmented sovereignty. At once the treaties confirmed the ultimate power of the national government but also established zones of occupancy where tribes would theoretically be left alone. In exchange for title to some lands, and pledges to "submit to the authority" of the United States, tribes received money and assurances of protection from the federal government. In the resolution of most Western conflicts, except for the ongoing battles against some Sioux, Lakota, and Comanche, the United States both proclaimed and delegated its power. Meanwhile, in Indian Country, the United States required Confederate-sympathizing tribes to emancipate slaves and grant them basic civil rights.[29]

Like their compatriots stationed in the South, soldiers in the West demanded to be sent home. Instead of a regional reaction against emancipation, soldiers' desire to return home was part of a comprehensive crisis for the military. In July 1865, 190 members of the 6th West Virginia Cavalry at Fort Leavenworth refused orders to fight Indians. This was simply the most explosive of "instances by the dozen and score of similar conduct" among companies sent to the Indian wars. In three Illinois regiments, 300 men deserted when sent to the plains in early fall. Soldiers from Wisconsin in turn lobbied their governor to press for their discharge, and army commanders in the West faced the same challenges of morale, mutiny, and war weariness that their peers in the Southeast battled. By the fall, the United States began to withdraw volunteers from the West, and forces drew down methodically over the next year from about 27,000 to 15,000 in the western Division of the Mississippi. The War Department aimed for retrenchment for the same reasons as in the South: to save money and to save the trouble of regulating volunteers.[30]

Despite the demands that soldiers, financial markets, politicians, Western white settlers, and Indians put upon the army, the occupation of the South still seemed robust in September 1865. In reports, generals said they retained a force strong enough to secure the government's gains and to keep the peace. But they could not afford to lose more. After touring the Carolinas and Virginia in August and September 1865, Major General George Meade echoed this claim: "So long as the State is in its present disorganized condition, and the question of free labor is so unsettled, it will in my judgment be necessary for the Government to exercise a quasi military jurisdiction, and for this purpose and to enforce prompt acquiescence to its orders, the existing force will be required." The state commanders repeated Meade's judgment. Simply holding down cities and ports would require fewer troops, but the "abandonment of the country" would eliminate the "protection of the freedmen." These reports give us an unusually clear window into generals' expectations about the force necessary to subdue the South. Leaving aside the troops still in Texas, there were roughly 116,000 soldiers in the ten other Confederate states at the end of October, or roughly 11,600 per state. While Virginia held an unusually large number of soldiers—18,733—the Carolinas were each well below average, with 6,189 in North Carolina—the fewest in the ex-Confederacy—and 8,674 in South Carolina—the eighth-lowest figure in the Confederacy. Carl Schurz generally confirmed Meade's judgment about the late-summer troop levels in his tour of the South. Mississippi was "more perfectly garrisoned" than any other state, Schurz believed, with 15,000 troops spread over thirty-nine posts in August. But already there were signs that the army did not control the hinterlands, especially in Alabama, where soldiers were kept in central locations and the peripheries were in a "state of anarchy."[31]

These late-summer reports emphasized the importance of proximity in shaping federal power after the Civil War. Control depended not on orders but on enforcement. When the superintendent of the Richmond & Danville Railroad asked an army commander to stop marauders "by telegraph," the officer responded sarcastically that "it is impossible to stop stragglers and marauders by telegraph." Even with perfect communication, orders, to be meaningful, depended upon finding troops "with the will and force to prevent outrages." In parts of the South, rural people did not have to rely upon parchment guarantees; they could walk to an officer of the federal government and request aid. This revolutionary imposition into previously inaccessible areas of the South gave the government new powers where it could be seen. That force, however, extended only to a narrow radius around the station. In one violent county, "the withdrawal of the garrison was the signal for a fresh installment of murderous outbreaks." Across the states, Carl Schurz found pockets of order around posts and outbreaks of violence farther away. When a West Point, Georgia, freedman was tied up by his thumbs, a sergeant from ten miles away freed him, but when that detachment was removed, the nearest post would now be fifty miles away in Columbus, far too distant to have any influence. As soldiers withdrew from towns across middle Tennessee in the late summer, guerrillas launched a series of assaults, and teachers fled until the army posted troops to "enforce the laws and protect the schools."[32]

These August and September reports show an imperfect but effective occupation. During this period, some states were poorly regulated, and others wild with violence, but many generals seemed to have fashioned a tenuous equilibrium. An occupation stabilized at these levels might well have managed the new contract season in the winter more effectively and created more reliable frameworks for defensible rights. The army had the capacity to hold its volunteers for longer periods. Of the million volunteers available in April 1865, only about 200,000 had terms that would expire before the summer of 1866, and perhaps a half million had terms that would extend into or beyond the winter of 1866–1867.[33]

Rather than stabilizing, however, demobilization accelerated in the fall. Part of the reason was simply the weather; most Southern posts lacked permanent quarters to handle the winter. But the key reasons were political. Although Meade's reports swayed the *Army & Navy Journal* and Secretary of War Stanton, they did not convince President Johnson or General Grant. It seems reasonable, although it is impossible to say definitively, that Grant's skepticism about the need for troops was a result of his travel schedule. As men like Meade and Major General George Thomas confronted Southern violence in the summer, Grant spent ten weeks touring Midwestern cities. Without their practical knowledge, Grant remained trapped in a June mind-set as October approached. Although they had other reasons for resisting occupation, two major generals who spent the fall of 1865 in loyal states, William T. Sherman and Winfield Scott Hancock, were even stronger supporters of withdrawing troops from the South.[34]

When Grant returned from his tour on October 6, he pressed demobilization forward. The "collapse of the rebellion rendered a large part of our military force unnecessary," Grant reported. White Southerners simply wanted to "resume the ordinary pursuits of civil life." In short order Grant discharged all volunteer cavalry east of the Mississippi, shifted many black troops out of the countryside and into forts along the Atlantic coast, ordered quick sales of stores and animals, and sped demobilization for the remaining volunteers. It was "radical and sweeping," the *Army & Navy Journal* wrote, and turned the volunteer army into "but the shadow of its former self." In November, Grant visited several Southern cities to counter Carl Schurz's description of a violent, disloyal South. Puzzlingly, Grant's portrayal of white Southern acquiescence does not match notes taken by his aide Cyrus Comstock that described "much bitter feeling" and a need for federal "control over the south for a year to come." Despite Grant's appeasing tone, however, he ambiguously supported an enduring, small-scale occupation of the South, since the people were not yet willing to "yield that ready obedience to civil authority the American people have generally been in the habit of yielding." Grant wanted to hold onto the war powers but did not yet realize the extent of Southern resistance, or the way that authority depended upon force.[35]

Generals across the South resisted Grant's orders for demobilization. When Grant urged Major General Thomas to "discharge all or nearly all the White Volunteers" and reduce the "number of interior posts," Thomas argued that they needed to keep the men in service. A native Southerner, Thomas was no radical on racial issues, but he had come to see the need to subdue the former rebels. Along the seaboard, the conservative Major General George Meade emerged as an unlikely but clear-headed defender of occupation. When Grant pressed him on November 6 to discharge white volunteers and reduce the interior posts, Meade responded that it was not practicable. Repeating the findings of his September 20 report, which Grant possibly had not read, Meade said that state commanders unanimously believed that the withdrawal of all military force would very likely be followed by "a war of races." In the upcountry, blacks needed defense against violent whites; in the low country, where freedpeople were a majority, white landowners could not claim their plantations without military support. The army should retain its nearly sixty posts "for some time" to "protect the rights and liberties of the freedmen."[36]

Over the fall, Grant changed his mind. Lobbying by his officers and the continuing violence of white Southerners convinced him that more force was required. Grant personally apologized to Schurz for dismissing his report and asked his commanders to report all "known outrages." Armed with this new understanding of the situation in the South, he urged President Johnson not to withdraw troops "until there is full security for equitably maintaining the right[s] and safety of all classes of citizens in the states lately in rebellion." By January, fearful of white Southern violence and legal actions against soldiers, Grant traveled to Georgia to stop the demobilization of two regiments stationed there.[37]

Grant's December 1865 turnabout would save occupation in 1866, but considerable damage had already been done. For the ten ex-Confederate states outside of Texas, the number of soldiers fell from roughly 116,000 in October 1865 to 61,835 in January 1866, and the average number of troops per state from almost 11,600 to 6,180. (See Appendix 2.) By January almost 29 percent of all troops in the former Confederacy were stationed in Texas. Under Grant's orders all white volunteers in Alabama and Mississippi were mustered out in December, with Virginia following in early January, and Louisiana, Texas, Tennessee, and North Carolina in April and May 1866, although some volunteers were replaced by regulars. All together, 120,000 additional troops were sent home between November 15 and January 20, and another 30,000 by February 15.[38]

Under these fall discharges, the army began to shrink to the centralized plan that Sherman had suggested back in April. Instead of broad-based coverage of the countryside, the army fell back into rail lines and river ports. As troop levels plummeted, the number of posts dropped almost exactly at the same rate as the number of soldiers. (See Appendix 3.) Total posts declined by 40 percent, from 345 in the former Confederacy (counting twenty-one in Texas) in September 1865 to 207 (counting Texas's sixteen) in January 1866. (See Appendixes 4 and 5.) Some regions—the stops along the major rail lines, South

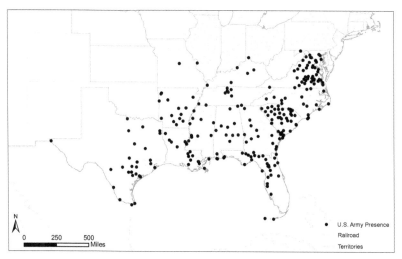

U.S. Army presence, December 1865–February 1866. University of Richmond Digital Scholarship Laboratory.

Carolina, Florida, North Carolina, and Tennessee—were hardly affected, South Carolina because it still remained heavily covered, Florida, North Carolina, and Tennessee because they had already experienced centralization. Other areas—especially southern Mississippi, western Alabama, northern and southwestern Georgia, and western and central Virginia—saw federal power mapped in a dramatically reduced way over the landscape. The most striking changes were in Georgia. The number of posts fell from seventy-five in September to sixty in November, forty-five in December, and then fourteen in January. Within months, the federal government's occupation shifted from an unusually geographically expansive effort to a much more restrained one. The line of practical sovereignty had been withdrawn; the federal government had concentrated its forces and left much of the countryside under the control of the residents.

As the army withdrew, planters rushed to fill the power vacuum in the countryside. While soldiers had never been able to regulate regions perfectly, their placement in county seats and crossroads towns created a counterweight to open warfare. The army's turn to a centralized occupation cut the communication networks that connected rural people to commanders. Assaults "increase just in proportion to their distance from United States authorities," one report stated. In northern Louisiana, the closing of posts at Monroe,

Minden, and Columbia sparked violence across the northern region of the state, now covered solely by Shreveport. Guerrillas controlled highways in Caddo and Bossier parishes, where local officials disarmed blacks and set free white assailants. In southeastern Bayou Sara, a "spirit of insubordination and ruffianism" surfaced as soon as a detachment of the 4th U.S. Colored Cavalry departed. In Mississippi, where posts fell from thirty-nine in August to eleven in December, white partisans attacked the soldiers who remained, and assaults on freedpeople were "of a daily occurrence." In Alabama, the closing of the post at Eufala left the eastern part of the state almost unprotected, and freedpeople were repeatedly murdered in the woods. In the largely ungoverned interior of Texas between the Nueces River and the Rio Grande, white and black loyalists fled, and those who remained behind could not even plant crops without fear of attack. In western South Carolina, updates read like coroners' reports, with descriptions of killings in Barnwell and knifings in Edgefield. As Georgia's posts were retracted, white men attacked at least four black men around Augusta; in the formerly occupied town of Washington, outlaws turned to "shooting and burning and beating negroes." Georgia Freedmen's Bureau commissioner Davis Tillson complained that "wherever our troops are withdrawn . . . fiendishness" reigned. Arkansas's U.S. attorney similarly wrote that "he who stands between the late master and the freedmen for their protection, must be backed by the power of the bayonet." As planters launched broader assaults, freedpeople in turn mobilized for self-defense, fled toward posts in cities, or—in regions where they outnumbered whites—directly claimed power through force. The army had lost its hold over large sections of the South.[39]

One surprising effect of the fall demobilizations was the dramatic increase in the proportion of black soldiers. As the army rushed home white volunteers, black soldiers made up 85,000 of the roughly 180,000 men who remained on duty across the country by November 1865. Although many of them had been moved to Texas or the West, tens of thousands remained east of the Mississippi. To white Southern politicians, nothing symbolized the endurance of the war more clearly than these black men in uniform. Peace, to many white

Southerners, could not return until black soldiers left. Black soldiers transformed life in the South by encouraging freedpeople to what white North Carolinians called "the most extravagant pretensions." Along the Savannah River, black soldiers urged workers to refuse contracts and to remain on lands the government wished to return to white property owners. Black soldiers often responded energetically to complaints of mistreatment; sometimes they took matters into their own hands and punished white assailants without waiting for orders. Although some black troops were unsympathetic, exhausted, or even predatory, in general their presence helped empower local black people to fight for their rights. Southern politicians campaigned relentlessly to remove black soldiers from their states. Beyond lobbying, whites assaulted black troops as the living symbols of the revolutionary age. When Elijah Marrs traveled to Shelbyville, Kentucky, three men rushed at him with knives, one hollering, "Yonder is a negro officer of the army."[40]

Although President Johnson sympathized with planters' complaints, the army generally did not send home black units. Generals kept black units in the South because they needed them. "It is undoubtedly true that the people of the South are very much prejudiced against these troops," Meade wrote, "but I could get no evidence to justify these fears and prejudices." Nevertheless, Meade considered it prudent to move them to the seaboard where they could garrison forts and be "measurably removed from contact with the whites." But Meade's statement did not dictate policy. While North Carolina's commander followed Meade's recommendation and moved virtually all black soldiers to coastal forts, in other states black units were still stationed in towns and cities. As late as March 1866, about two-thirds of South Carolina's black troops were in Charleston and Summerville, and about 85 percent of Mississippi's were based out of Vicksburg and Natchez. While some black troops in Georgia were at Fort Pulaski, more operated from Macon and Thomasville. Elsewhere, black troops occupied Huntsville, Bridgeport, and Mobile, Alabama; Little Rock, Helena, and De Valls Bluff, Arkansas; and New Orleans, Shreveport, Baton Rouge, and Alexandria, Louisiana. In Tennessee, Johnson intervened more directly to remove black soldiers. There, letters from friends, allies, and neighbors in his hometown of Greeneville primed him to be suspicious of black soldiers and Reconstruction. Although Major General Thomas defended the black troops, he sent two regiments from Greeneville to Georgia. Black troops remained on hand in part because, unlike their white counterparts, many wanted to stay in the army, and in part because they lacked the lobbying power to push for muster out.[41]

As winter approached, planters took advantage of the power vacuums by trying to force freedpeople into oppressive contracts. Beyond the noble, if unlikely, dream of land redistribution, the future of the South turned upon the extraordinarily complex question of how to maintain a cash crop economy through a contract labor system that would simultaneously create profits and help freedpeople establish family wealth, security, and leisure time. In the South, the end of the year was typically a time for negotiation of new contracts, and many freedpeople's terms expired around Christmas. As soldiers withdrew in November and December 1865, negotiations for the following year were just under way. Although Northern soldiers believed too widely in wage labor and embraced too many racial prejudices to support a complete overthrow of the Southern system, many supported simple fairness in contracts. Officers generally backed basic provisions of contracts, including the right of employees to switch jobs at the end of the term and some general guidelines about how proceeds would be allocated. After a change in companies around Cheraw, South Carolina, the commanding officer complained that freedpeople would only make contracts if they could verify the contents with trustworthy soldiers; any change could disrupt the negotiations.[42]

In the absence of reliable protection, some freedpeople claimed broader authority for themselves. During the negotiation season, rumors spread across the South that the ex-slaves, perhaps aided by black soldiers, planned to resist contract demands and perhaps even rise up and claim land of their own. From a distance it is difficult to tell if any of these plans for a Christmas insurrection had concrete form, but the loud talking helped freedpeople gain some much-needed elbow room; by undercutting planters' efforts to create order, they convinced whites that there might be some need for troops. In regions where black people were a majority, planters often panicked and called for help from the army. There were many ironies here. The people who had tried to defy occupation now helped save it. And the army that had aided freedpeople was now being called to restrain them. Although commanders dispatched men into the countryside to tell freedpeople there would be no distribution of land, most officers dismissed the rumors of insurrection as simply tales to "injure the colored people and to make pretended evil intention on their part, the pretext for severity and harshness." Some officers did crack down; in Louisiana, Major General Edward Canby refused to let black soldiers keep their weapons upon being mustered out. But in South Carolina, Major General Daniel Sickles did not dispatch troops to quiet freedpeople in the planation belt; instead he sent troops into the upcountry to put down violent whites. The rumors of a Christmas insurrection had struck fear into whites and demonstrated that they could not regulate society on their own. The South was not by any measure at peace.[43]

As 1865 ended, occupation had fallen, but it had not fallen apart. At crucial moments President Johnson and Grant had threatened its survival. Yet at other moments, Johnson and even Southern governors had stepped in to defend it. By December, Grant had become increasingly attuned to both generals' and congressmen's belief in the need for continued occupation. As Congress returned, the United States had lost much of its capacity to regulate the countryside, a capacity that it would never regain. Yet occupation survived. In the eight months after surrender, the army's occupation of the South had not quite died. The tool that congressmen would grasp as they returned to Washington had been dulled but not destroyed. The hopes for an easy path to peace had faded, but the opportunity to remake the South had not. The force that remained in the South was enough to do something but not enough to do everything.

- 5 -

THE WAR IN WASHINGTON

WHEN CONGRESS RETURNED in December 1865, the fight over rights and war powers shifted in part from the Southern countryside to the halls of the House and Senate. Congress's actions would determine whether the military could overturn oppressive local laws. If Congress seated representatives from the rebel states, the war would be over. But if they refused, many Republicans believed, the war continued. At first many Republicans hoped to extend the war briefly while they devised a lasting plan for peace by remaking the Constitution. But President Johnson's vetoes of their civil rights and Freedmen's Bureau bills made it difficult to create the peacetime powers congressional Republicans sought. There would be no easy exit. After months of scrambling, and after passing a landmark Fourteenth Amendment, congressional Republicans faced the key question of whether to end the war or to delay peace in hopes of making additional changes in the next session. They did not act lightly; many understood that they risked doing damage to the nation's constitutional structure by maintaining a state of war. But it was either a firm stance or surrender. To the surprise of many observers, Republicans committed themselves to a policy of delay. They refused to set any reliable peace terms for the South. They simply continued the war until they could build a firm foundation for the future. While we now pay more attention to the Fourteenth Amendment and the Civil Rights Act they passed during the session, the decision not to end the war would be Congress's crucial act, the basis for the eventual ratification of the Fourteenth and Fifteenth constitutional amendments, and the bridge to the enfranchisement of freedpeople in the South.

By extending the extraconstitutional time of war, Congress recognized that "the political revolution" that the Civil War provoked "has hardly yet been completed" even though "the Rebellion is ended." Republicans typically classed as moderates, such as the influential senator William Fessenden, did not run toward compromise, but instead solidified their determination not to "yield the fruits of war." While Republicans adored the Constitution and were committed to what one scholar calls the "constitutional plausibility" of their actions, they also utilized war powers to hold open the possibility of revolutionary change.[1]

On the surface, it seems strange to think of the 1865–1866 congressional session as wartime. When Congress returned to Washington, D.C., in December 1865, no one whispered about Confederate troops on the horizon; no one burst onto the floor with news from the battlefield; no one telegraphed stories of the day's victories or of the day's dead. For the first time in four and a half years, the nation's capital seemed to be at peace. But inside the Capitol, the Civil War continued. In heated arguments on the floor of Congress, Republicans and Democrats fought over the central question of whether peace had in fact returned. This was not mere semantics. Most of the session's major struggles turned in part on the question of whether the extraconstitutional war powers continued, and, if so, who controlled them. Congressional Republicans divided over what the war should accomplish but united around the idea that the country remained in a "time of war" controlled partly by the legislative branch. The "war powers" should "be continued and exercised until the civil authority of the Government can be established firmly and upon a sure foundation," Senator Lyman Trumbull said. "Peace has not yet come; the effects of the war are not yet ended; the people of the South . . . are yet subject to military control." Democrats furiously dismissed this broad, legalistic definition of war as "radically and wickedly wrong." If war did not mean "meeting in deadly array upon the field of battle," one asked, was it merely a "war of words?" The simple fact of peace "cannot be controverted," one senator said. "You might as well try to controvert the fact, in noon day, when the heavens are cloudless, that the sun is shining."[2]

From the time Congress gaveled into session in December 1865, congressional Republicans tried to seize control of President Johnson's war powers. They supported the ongoing wartime occupation of the South through the Freedmen's Bureau, habeas corpus, and army bills; threaded some powers of occupation into a newly conceived vision of peacetime in the Civil Rights Act and the Fourteenth Amendment; and, most crucially, staved off the coming of peacetime until at least December 1866 by refusing to offer any reliable terms to the Southern states. In the process of continuing the war, congressional Republicans fell into a grim struggle with the very man who had first extended wartime past Confederate surrender: President Andrew Johnson. Johnson argued that he alone controlled war powers and that the states had an inherent right to representation, positions the Republicans could not accept. More broadly, however, Johnson warned that wartime, once extended, would be impossible to control. By holding rebel states out, Congress risked overturning the constitutional order. Although many Republicans shared this fear, they feared the return of those states even more.

The session has long been a puzzle, even a disappointment, compared to the momentous changes that came later. The key question of the enfranchisement of freedpeople was left untouched. As a test of the American value of the expansion of democracy, the session was indeed a failure. Despite widespread support among Republicans for extending voting rights, Congress concluded without accomplishing this. Despite the inaction on the vote, an enormous transformation took place in the crucial realm of rights making. Republicans in this session began constructing, through the tools of occupation, a sense of defensible and accessible rights. Seeking to sustain the gains of war, they fought to create rights that were meaningful not just on paper but on the ground. This was a rare and bold effort in nineteenth-century America. Republican actions tested not national values but national force.

What shaped the session was the break between Congress and the White House. By the end of the session, Republicans simply could not trust President Johnson to run the occupation properly. Although hopes ran high at first that the president and Congress might cooperate, there were already signs in December 1865 that they would clash over who controlled the war powers. While congressional Republicans had tried to build an alliance with the president in the summer and fall, it was no simple task. Johnson, a former Democrat who had governed Tennessee for the previous three years, was more admired than understood by congressional Republicans. Some were angry that he had undermined the Freedmen's Bureau and failed to enfranchise freedpeople in his proclamations. Many more were concerned about his support for the Mississippi militia. Johnson compounded the problem by misjudging the Republican ranks. Mistaking the normal splits in any political community for hard and fast factions, Johnson wrongly believed that only an isolated handful of Radicals opposed him. In fact the beliefs that bound Republicans together were much stronger than the ideas that pulled them apart. They agreed that Congress would have the final say on the use of war powers. The incoming Speaker of the House, Schuyler Colfax, pledged in November that Congress would not restore Southern states until they had protected civil rights for freedpeople. Colfax also divided the president's "mission" as the commander in chief when Congress was out of session from Congress's "duties" once it returned. Immediately, the perceptive French journalist Georges Clemenceau predicted a schism. While the *Army & Navy Journal* believed that Johnson would probably approve a "systematic, moderate, just, and generally acceptable" congressional plan of reconstruction, this optimism was doubly misplaced: Johnson had no desire to yield his powers to Congress, and Republicans were not ready to submit a systematic plan to end the war.[3]

In his December message to Congress, President Johnson tried to prevent Congress from taking control of war powers. Instead of acknowledging his own reliance on war powers, he pretended war powers did not exist. Even as he governed through the army, he spoke as if the military played only a small role. Johnson both aimed to shield war powers from congressional oversight and to navigate a tricky political situation. Never a Republican, he—with the help of Secretary of State William Seward—would move toward a new political alliance with Northern Democrats, conservative Republicans, and Southern loyalists. Since Northern Democrats by and large did not approve of war powers, Johnson had to deny the very tools he utilized. Ideologically committed to presidential power, Johnson also rejected a draft from Seward that said that Congress had the final power to complete restoration by seating representatives. Instead, he shifted to the rhetorical high ground of state survival. With the help of a masterfully vague draft by the historian George Bancroft, Johnson turned the question from war powers to the issue of whether the states remained in the Union. To distract attention from the occupation he supervised, Johnson defined occupation as the absolute reign of a military governor and celebrated his actions, peculiarly, as a triumph of civilian rule. In another masterful ambiguity, Johnson suggested—but deliberately did not say—that the war had ended and that "resistance to the General Government appeared to have exhausted itself." Faced with an extremely delicate political situation,

Johnson aimed to concede nothing, appease as many people as he could, and disappear behind a thin but seemingly solid scrim of rhetoric about state survival. While the *Army & Navy Journal* recognized that Johnson's message was "obviously contradictory," it cheered the flexibility he had shown.[4]

Although Republicans disagreed about many things, most shared a general sense that Congress controlled some war powers, that emancipation had not been completed by the Thirteenth Amendment, that many white Southerners still violently resisted government authority, that some method must be devised for protecting rights, and that rebels could not immediately be trusted. The idea that Congress controls war powers seems peculiar after the increased executive authority in the twentieth and twenty-first centuries, but it was a commonplace among nineteenth-century Whigs and Republicans. Although the president directed the army, Congress regulated it through legislation; in the Civil War Congress, for example, it passed army policies toward fugitive slaves. Although Republican members of Congress argued about the precise way to restore Southern states or construct viable rights, most shared a sense that they should begin by refusing to seat anyone from a rebel state. By keeping rebel states from representation, they would continue the state of war until they settled on what to do next. These beliefs were hardened by a flood of letters from Southern loyalists and freedpeople in the autumn of 1865 about the "bitterness" of rebels and the thinness of freedpeople's rights.[5] More practically, Republicans understood that the end of slavery had the perverse effect of expanding the power of the South. Because the Constitution counted slaves as three-fifths of a person, emancipation would increase the number of fully counted free people in the South and thus the number of congressmen and the electoral votes from the region. No Republican was comfortable with this. Next to these shared commitments, disagreements about black voting were far less significant. By the fall of 1865, most Republican congressmen abstractly backed black voting rights. But many were also terrified of the political backlash, especially after Connecticut voters rejected enfranchisement in a statewide referendum. Sharing a general affinity for enfranchisement and a practical desire to protect the party, most Republicans supported wartime occupation as a way of deferring the extension of the vote but keeping alive the chance for future changes down the road.

Congressional Republicans therefore coalesced around a policy of delay. They celebrated the power not of legislation but of time. The way to maintain control of time was to refuse to seat the representatives and senators sent from the rebel states. "Be in no haste to get the seceded states back into the Union," former Republican congressman Amasa Walker wrote. "The great question is, not *how soon they shall be brought in,* but *how long they can be kept out.*" To avoid seating them, Republicans decided to simply pretend they weren't there. Instead of calling each Southern congressman and then initiating a debate about his qualifications—a process that might lead to some representatives being seated—House clerk Edward McPherson refused to read their names. It was, Democratic congressman James Brooks of New York said, "revolutionary." Brooks was not wrong. Keeping them out held parts of the United States under military rule. And governing sections of the country through the military raised serious questions about the republican system. If Congress could deny these states representation, could it do the same to others? Would this become a common tool for fighting political enemies? Once unholstered, the useful powers of war might be difficult to put away. While Republicans acknowledged the merits of those questions, they also believed that turning over power to the rebels was even worse.[6]

Congressional Republicans therefore unified around acting "gradually" by creating a Joint Committee on Reconstruction to slowly consider all issues relating to the South. This was the pet project of Thaddeus Stevens, a shrewd and sharp-tongued Pennsylvania lawyer and industrialist who combined high ideals, rugged practicality, and a deep understanding of procedure to a degree nearly unmatched in American history. Feared for his invective and admired for his beliefs, he forged House Republicans into an extraordinarily unified and coherent voting bloc by discovering and defending the principles that united the party. At Stevens's request, the entire House Republican caucus cut off debate and pledged not to act on any representative until the Joint Committee reported. Although senators insisted on retaining their right to consider candidates, they too endorsed the Joint Committee. Johnson rashly compared the committee to a French Revolution directory. "Let no man deceive himself," the *New York World* wrote. "The peace we have so fondly dreamed was won, recedes from us afresh into a darkening vista of sectional passions."[7]

Nevertheless, like other Americans, Republicans at first struggled to define exactly what wartime meant. They worried that calling a period without battles "war" made the term meaningless or made their own actions tyrannical. No one agonized more than Senator William Fessenden, a dyspeptic moderate who worked closely with Lincoln, oversaw the extraordinarily complex finance bills, and feared the political fallout of extending the vote to freedpeople. In wartime, Fessenden said, he was willing to go beyond the Constitution, but peace meant a return to normalcy, forgetting "any precedent" the war set. Although Fessenden initially defined December 1865 as peacetime, he shifted his position once he realized the necessity of holding on to war powers to protect freedpeople's rights. In early January 1866, he said, "These are so very near war times" and that "same doctrine" might "apply." By April, Fessenden worked with Stevens to make sure they did not "yield the fruits of war." Other Republicans also moved toward expansive definitions of wartime as the session advanced. Although some had supported other theories of control over the South—including the idea that the South was a conquered region or had reverted to territories—these distinctions mostly vanished once it became clear that Congress would not yield control to Johnson. The differences between Republicans had been "more in the theory than in the practical application," one congressman said. When he found himself disagreeing on an esoteric point about state status with another Republican, Congressman James Garfield waved away the distinctions to focus on their shared core principles: "The state of war did not terminate with the actual cessation of hostilities," and emancipation could not be "a mere negation; the bare privilege of not being chained, bought, and sold, branded and scourged."[8]

Having slowed the return of peace by refusing to seat representatives from the rebel states, Congress tried to take control of the occupation of the South. On January 8, Republican congressman Thomas Williams of Pennsylvania introduced a resolution stating that the military forces should not be withdrawn from the seceded states until Congress "shall have ascertained and declared their further presence there no longer necessary." Although one Democrat denounced "this attempt by the House to usurp the duties of the Executive," the resolution carried. While the Senate did not take up the resolution, its passage still slowed troop withdrawal. Upon receiving it, Secretary of War Stanton countermanded earlier orders to withdraw troops from Virginia and Georgia. The resolution "rebuked the evident haste with which the Administration sought to hurry the troops away from the South" and demonstrated that "the military occupation of the South was still necessary," the *Army & Navy Journal* editorialized.[9]

Inspired by Congress's firmness and by lobbying from worried generals, Lieutenant General Grant began to protect occupation. His General Orders Number 3, issued on January 12, 1866, directed military commanders in the former rebel states to shield soldiers, officers, and loyal citizens from predatory prosecution or lawsuits in the reconstituted civil courts. His order charged them with "protecting" freedpeople from discriminatory prosecutions. In February, Grant defended the retention of troops in the South to "protect the negro in his life, person and the few rights he has acquired." Grant also suspended newspapers and tallied outrages in the South, sending records of dozens of murders and hundreds of assaults by whites upon black people. Although Grant's orders contradicted Johnson's rhetoric, the president did not overrule them.[10]

Congress reaffirmed its strategy of delaying peace when it refused to admit Johnson's home state of Tennessee. If any state would be immediately recognized, it would undoubtedly have been Tennessee, where white loyalists had abolished slavery early in 1865. On its own terms, Tennessee probably deserved recognition since loyalists controlled the government and had ended slavery. One subcommittee actually voted for recognizing Tennessee. But bringing one state in might set a precedent that Congress could not contain. Additionally, Tennessee was plagued by violence. Many speakers told the joint committee that the state required ongoing military occupation to protect freedpeople. Lieutenant Colonel R. W. Barnard offered the most vivid explanation of why he did not favor "removing the military." A man told him, "I tell you what, if you take away the military from Tennessee, the buzzards can't eat up the niggers as fast as we'll kill 'em." Together, Fessenden and Stevens delayed the state's readmission by sending it to a new subcommittee stacked with radicals. Despite their ideological differences, the Radical Stevens and the moderate Fessenden were cohering around a plan of extending war powers. On the same day he supported delaying Tennessee, Fessenden wrote to a cousin that "though I will do something to keep peace, I will not vote away one inch of the safeguards necessary in this terrible condition of affairs." After the Joint Committee delayed Tennessee's readmission, President Johnson came undone, muttering to his cabinet that Congress meant to impeach him, and boorishly accusing black leader Frederick Douglass of wanting "just like any nigger" to "cut a white man's throat." Johnson had hoped to fight Radical Republicans on the issue of black suffrage, ideally in a bill that passed the House to give black men the vote in Washington, D.C. When the Senate let that bill die, however, Johnson lost his chance. Instead, he had to battle a united Republican Party on the issue of the extension of wartime. It was a fight he would lose.[11]

Next, congressional Republicans moved to construct defensible rights through legislation. The three signal achievements of the session—the Fourteenth Amendment, the Civil Rights Act, and the Freedmen's Bureau extension—all centered on the problem of creating practical freedom. These efforts simultaneously depended upon war powers and were meant as escapes from war powers. They could pass only while Congress held Southern states out, but their goal was to make war powers unnecessary by building protections into enduring peacetime law.

The first Freedmen's Bureau bill extended wartime to meet the crises on the ground. Although the previous Freedmen's Bureau bill, passed in the 1864–1865 session, had an expiration date, the first bureau bill in 1866 allowed the agency to run forever. Moved by reports circulating from freedpeople to agents, Republicans wrote an act that continued to permit the bureau to promote education, regulate contracts, and provide public health. It also authorized the president to set aside unoccupied public lands in the South to rent to loyal refugees and freedpeople, and gave freedpeople on coastal lands possession for three years. But its most striking characteristic was its reliance upon military power. It granted the bureau "military protection and jurisdiction" over discrimination and civil rights violations. The bill cleared a path to peacetime by normalizing military powers. Its lead author, the moderate Lyman Trumbull, called it preposterous to imagine that war powers expired the moment the rebel armies surrendered. Instead, Trumbull said, the bureau could exercise military powers "until peace shall be firmly established and the civil tribunals shall be restored with an assurance that they may peacefully enforce the laws without opposition." Fessenden, too, embraced the necessity. "Whether you call it the war power or some other power, the power must necessarily exist, from the nature of the case," he said. Against this broad definition of wartime, Democrats sought to narrow war into "that abnormal, convulsive condition of society," as one Democrat asserted. "Gentlemen must not undertake in this country to perpetuate a war upon paper."[12]

By relying upon military force, the Freedmen's Bureau bill created concrete federal protection for civil rights. Civil rights, to be meaningful, would have to have arms behind them. "The power to free them involved the duty to protect them," one Republican congressman said of ex-slaves. Ridiculing the idea that the Constitution was "mere verbiage" or a "grand abstract declaration, unenforced by the arm of authority," another Republican congressman celebrated the new "instrumentality which shall reach to every portion of the South and stand between the freedman and oppression." Outraged Democrats vociferously denied that the federal government could enforce its will in every crevice of the country. Freedom "does not mean protection," one Democratic senator warned.[13]

Although Johnson had supported temporary military policies to protect freedpeople, he surprised Republicans by vetoing the Freedmen's Bureau bill. In his message, Johnson ridiculed the idea that the country remained in a "time of war," even though his own policies had created that condition. To finesse the gap between his rhetoric and his own utilization of war powers, Johnson relied upon ambiguity. "The country has returned," he wrote, "or is returning, to a state of peace and industry, and the rebellion is in fact at an end." For Democrats, Johnson suggested peace had returned; for conservative Republicans who saw some dangers still ahead, Johnson stated that peacetime was still in the process of returning and that some war powers remained in his hands. Then Johnson struck at the heart of his complaint: Congress had no right "to shut out in time of peace any State from representation to which it is entitled." The very act of meeting without representatives from the rebel states was a dangerous continuation of war.[14]

Johnson's veto shattered his relations with Congress. Knowing of Johnson's own reliance upon military powers, many Republicans had expected him to sign the bill. Now, with the fight joined, Republicans did not know what to do. Johnson's plan of restoration might be flawed, the *Army & Navy Journal* wrote, but it was "simple and positive," while delay made it appear that Congress "dilly dallies." Three days after the veto, Johnson gave a spectacularly ill-advised speech to a Washington's Birthday crowd gathered outside the White House. Full of bravado, he denounced Thaddeus Stevens and Charles Sumner, among others, as traitors seeking to break up the country to destroy slavery. While Johnson allies like Secretary of State William Seward and publisher Thurlow Weed celebrated his "triumphant" speech, moderate Republicans were disgusted. Believing the Freedmen's Bureau a necessary measure to protect former slaves' freedom, moderates could not ally themselves with a man who seemed willing to kick freedmen aside so quickly. A Philadelphia newspaper opined that Johnson "has managed to make the term radical synonymous with the entire mass of the dominant party." To his cousin, Fessenden expressed sorrow but not shock. "He has broken faith, betrayed his trust, and must sink from detestation into contempt." Trumbull responded with "surprise and profound regret." "I do not hold that the consequences of the war are over," he told the Senate. "I do not understand that peace is restored."[15]

In response the Joint Committee pledged for the first time that neither the House nor the Senate would end the war by itself. Earlier, senators had maintained their right to act on their own judgment. Pressed by Johnson's actions, they were now ready to bind themselves to the House. They would readmit representatives only if both houses together declared them entitled. Tennessee therefore would be kept waiting. Still, over the next two months, as Republicans regrouped, publishers and moderates worked for reconciliation. Optimism thrived when nothing was at stake. But moderates had not moved toward Johnson's position. All they had done was soften their tone.[16]

Congressional Republicans next tried to construct defensible rights in peacetime through the Civil Rights Act. For the first time in American history, this bill defined who was a natural citizen and what citizenship meant. The bill was, in language Senator Lyman Trumbull possibly picked up from Freedmen's Bureau reports, an effort to fashion "practical freedom" by extending some military protection of civil rights into peacetime. This meant essentially undoing the Black Codes. Citizens were people born in the United States and not subject to a foreign power, except for Indians who were not taxed. The rights of free citizens, regardless of race, color, or previous condition, were—at least in theory, though not always in practice—to make contracts, to sue, to testify in court, to buy or inherit property, to travel, and to enjoy full and equal benefit of all laws. All citizens should be subject to similar punishments, even if states had discriminatory laws or customs. Although the 1866 Civil Rights Act sometimes disappears behind the Fourteenth Amendment, it was a signal moment in the creation of a set of citizens' rights, though some were much more available to men than to women. Just as crucially, it did not rely upon parchment guarantees but specified modes of enforcement, drawn in part from the system Southern congressmen put in place to enforce the 1850 Fugitive Slave Act. Like that act, it depended on federal commissioners and marshals to enforce its terms. Under the law, anyone who violated a civil right could be subjected to a fine and imprisonment. Cases could be removed to federal courts when state courts acted in discriminatory ways. Since the Civil Rights Act was a peacetime act, one that meant to forever reshape federal law (and through it, state common law), its boldness created some doubts among strict constitutionalist Republicans like the influential John Bingham.[17]

Like the 1850 Fugitive Slave Law, the Civil Rights Act of 1866 expanded the military's role in peacetime. While the 1850 law extended the military's role by implication when it gave federal marshals the authority to call out a posse to aid them, the 1866 law explicitly authorized the president to use the army or militia to enforce its provisions. This reflected both a sense that rights had to be defensible to be real and a recognition that local judges and sheriffs might not defer to federal laws or court rulings. It exposed both the role of force lodged behind all laws and the peculiarly tumultuous conditions that wartime and emancipation brought. Many Republicans feared that federal courts were too weak and too dispersed to provide any "remedy at all." Therefore the bill would have to rely upon force. "Southern legislators and people must learn, if they are compelled to learn by the bayonets of the Army of the United States, that the civil rights must and shall be respected," one senator said. Even more explicitly, Maine congressman James Wilson described the bill as simply the extension of army orders into peacetime. If military protection for freedpeople could not be rendered during peace, "a perpetual state of constructive war would be a great blessing to very many American citizens." Happily, Wilson believed law could provide "the same ample protection through the civil courts that now depends on the orders of our military commanders." Instead of a "paper guarantee," one congressman said, the bill would give emancipation "practical effect and force." Democrats attacked the reliance upon force as a sign that the "passion for arresting people" had become so "general, wide-spread, and universal, that now that peace is restored, at least when hostilities do not exist, we are not to get rid of that feeling." Calling his fellow congressmen "these military gentlemen," another senator complained that they "think they have a right to command control everywhere. . . . The military power is now rampant and triumphant, and all we have to do is to bow our heads."[18]

Although conservative Republicans and two cabinet members urged President Johnson to sign the Civil Rights Act, he vetoed it. "I know I am right, and I am damned if I do not adhere to it," he told his secretary. In his message he angrily dismissed the bill for continuing the powers of war. To Johnson, the balance between local and federal law was not simply a constitutional provision but also a method for sustaining peace. If the federal government stayed out of local affairs, there would be no need for force and no problem enforcing the few federal laws. But national intervention against the customs and laws of states or localities could not succeed by legislation; it would require force. Turning judges into "mere ministerial" officers and bureau agents into a "sort of police," it "seems to imply a permanent military force, that is to be always at hand, and whose only business is to be the enforcement of this measure over the vast region where it is intended to operate. . . . It is another step, or rather stride, toward centralization and the concentration of all legislative powers in the National Government." Johnson's determination to keep Congress away from war powers fueled his increasingly open racism. Denouncing the bill as a way of favoring black people over whites, he played upon white resentment. The bill, he claimed inaccurately, provided "for the security of the colored race safeguards which go infinitely beyond any that the General Government has ever provided for the white race." Johnson's ferocity illustrated the differences between himself and President Lincoln. While Lincoln lobbied against and even vetoed some congressional legislation, he never tried to split the party. Johnson's vehemence reflected not just his emotional state but also his party membership. Unlike Lincoln, Johnson simply was not a Republican.[19]

Then President Johnson seemed to trump Congress by issuing a proclamation of peace. In a surprise announcement on April 2, he seemed to proclaim the end of the war. Consulting only with Secretary of State William Seward, Johnson acted as if he had resolved the issue once and for all. "There now exists no organized armed resistance" outside of Texas, Johnson wrote. Since residents in the other states had "given satisfactory evidence that they acquiesce," the government should not rely upon "standing armies, military occupation, martial law, military tribunals, and the suspension of the privilege of the writ of *habeas corpus*" in what Johnson called a "time of peace."[20]

Despite those strong words, President Johnson did not lift the suspension of habeas corpus. A war that seemed close to its end instead dragged on, not because Congress intervened but because Johnson himself still relied upon war powers to protect his soldiers in the South. There were many reasons why Johnson could not let go of the war powers. Conservative navy secretary Gideon Welles worriedly asked whether Johnson's proclamation dismissed all volunteer officers who had enlisted for the duration of the war. Since the nation needed them, the answer turned out to be no. Others feared that soldiers would be arrested in the rebel states, as they already had been in Kentucky. But that was unacceptable. So the Freedmen's Bureau and the army then informed officers that the proclamation did not end martial law or restore habeas corpus, not even in Kentucky. Two days after Johnson's proclamation, Judge-Advocate General Joseph Holt said that military tribunals remained legal (as they were not in peacetime), although officers should treat the proclamation as a spur to minimize their usage. To make sense of a peace proclamation that did not seem to bring peace, and to provide guidance to his fellow federal judges, Chief Justice Salmon P. Chase asked Johnson to issue an order ending martial law and restoring habeas corpus, but Johnson refused. Even if he might have preferred to act consistently, Johnson had good reason to hold on to his authority. Unless he meant to withdraw all soldiers from the rebel states, Johnson needed war powers. Otherwise he would be sending soldiers into the arms of local jails. What he also needed was rhetorical high ground. The proclamation was a political document, not a legal order. Johnson told crowds that he thanked "God that peace is restored," but he did not actually restore peace.[21]

In response, congressional Republicans asserted their power over wartime. No president could declare "that peace was restored," Senator Jacob Howard said, since that power belonged to Congress. More broadly, talk of reconciliation with the president disappeared. With the veto of the Civil Rights Act, Fessenden completed his journey away from the White House. "I have tried hard to save Johnson," Fessenden wrote, "but I am afraid he is beyond hope." He pledged to "hold on" to what the war had accomplished at least until the fall midterm elections when Congress would take the issue "to the country." To protect those gains, Fessenden joined a group of Republican senators who expelled a New Jersey Democrat from his seat in order to increase the Republican majority. Then, the House and the Senate overrode the Civil Rights veto, the first override of a veto of a significant act of legislation in United States history. Aided by both the expulsion of the New Jersey senator and by the defection of previously Johnson-supporting Republicans, they fused Radicals, moderates, and some self-styled conservatives into a partnership to protect civil rights.[22] Hoping to shatter the Republican coalition, Johnson had instead cemented it.

Republican congressmen then tried to protect occupation by guarding soldiers from lawsuits in the Southern states. In a revision of the Habeas Corpus act, they approached a basic distinction between military rule and civilian law. In a period of peacetime, soldiers could be sued or arrested. During occupation, however, the military was supreme. First in Kentucky, and then in Virginia, civil courts had heard thousands of lawsuits against soldiers, threatening to dismantle occupation one ruling at a time. At the personal request of Virginia's commander, Republicans therefore wrote a Habeas Corpus bill to protect soldiers from lawsuits by letting them use orders as a defense and by allowing them to remove cases from unsympathetic local courts to federal courts. In a sign of fights to come, the House and Senate divided on whether the bill would apply to future actions or protected soldiers only for what had already transpired. An outraged Democratic congressman Andrew Jackson Rogers of New Jersey claimed that "the Queen of England could not exercise such power as this bill proposes to legalize." Although Johnson considered a veto, he eventually signed it. Like Congress, he too feared leaving the soldiers at the whim of courts and sheriffs. He disliked acknowledging that the war powers still existed, but he continued to rely on them.[23]

As the session moved deeper into spring, Congress struggled to devise a pathway to peace that still protected civil rights. No law alone could provide adequate protection. It would require a fourteenth constitutional amendment. Republicans faced the strange fact that emancipation empowered the Southern states. When determining how many congressmen a state merited, slaves counted for only three-fifths of a person. Abolition, then, effectively added almost a million and a half people to the former slave states' tally, giving them more than twenty additional congressional seats and electoral votes. Since freedpeople could not vote, rebels and white planters would exert more power in national politics than they had before secession. Only a constitutional amendment could rectify this situation. Beyond that, Republicans debated broadening the amendment to include civil rights for freedpeople to guard those rights from the Supreme Court or future congresses. Finally, they had to determine whether the amendment would actually signal the return of peace, or whether it too was just an intermediate step in an ongoing wartime. If the amendment led to Southern state representatives taking seats in Congress, then that would mean that peace had been restored. But if the amendment simply embedded rights into the Constitution and did not promise seats to Southern representatives, then it might not foretell the end of occupation.[24]

As they pondered those questions, news from the outside world changed Republicans' understanding of the conditions in the South. The most famous incident was the pogrom in Memphis in early May. As black troops were mustered out on April 30, white Memphians talked wildly of an uprising. In this tense climate, white police fired on a crowd of black people on May 1. Local business owners, policemen, and other whites then attacked black neighborhoods. Over the next two days, men broke into houses, raped at least six women, and burned more than one hundred homes, schools, and hospitals. By the time troops quieted the town, forty-six blacks and two whites had been killed. To reporters and politicians, local home rule seemed nothing more than mass violence against freedpeople. Within days Grant called Memphis a massacre, faulted the army for not responding more quickly, and defended the occupation of the South. The bloody scenes became a shorthand for the overall violence in the South and the need for federal intervention to protect freedpeople.[25]

Beyond Memphis, congressional Republicans heard 140 witnesses who testified before the Joint Committee on Reconstruction. These witnesses narrated an ongoing violent conflict in the South between planters and ex-slaves. Person after person described a South that remained disloyal, where rebels tore down U.S. flags, taught their children "to hate the government," voted only for secessionists, and drove white loyalists from towns. "There is a class of boys of nineteen or twenty years of age, who would put a bowie-knife or a bullet through a northern man as soon as they would through a mad dog," a minister claimed. But the most gruesome testimony was about the maniacal assaults upon freedpeople. When congressmen asked why landowners would murder their own labor force, a Virginia Unionist replied, "I cannot answer that in any other way than by supposing it owing to human depravity." Against this lawlessness, the witnesses asked for enduring force to quiet the South. Like the officers' and agents' reports that rolled in from the South, the witnesses tried to reconcile conflicting ideas: that the South was wildly violent, and that a small number of troops could regulate it. Whether driven by a fear that large-scale occupation was impossible, or by a typical midcentury overconfidence in the power of a small number of troops, these witnesses asked for immediate, but not necessarily large-scale, action. To teach white Northerners about the need for occupation, the Joint Committee distributed tens of thousands of copies of the testimony.[26]

Although Republicans agreed that they needed a Fourteenth Amendment, the details were daunting. Two first tries failed early in the session. One thorny issue revolved around gender. As Congress considered a wide range of approaches, women's suffragists led by Susan B. Anthony and Elizabeth Cady Stanton unsuccessfully petitioned to extend voting protections to women. Republicans beat back that challenge but were mired in indecision until Johnson proclaimed peacetime in April. Realizing that they must present some counter to the president's plan or risk losing popular support, Republicans in late March and early April considered two new plans. One offered both enfranchisement and amnesty; rebels would be pardoned, and all men could vote. Another option, advanced by reformer Robert Dale Owen, established civil rights immediately but delayed black suffrage (and the expansion of Southern representation in the House) until 1876. While part of the joint committee approved this plan, they retracted their support once other Republicans expressed concern that black suffrage would cost them the midterm elections. In place of black suffrage, the Joint Committee substituted the short-term disenfranchisement of rebels until 1870. If Thaddeus Stevens and other Radicals could not gain black voting rights, they wanted at least to slow the return of the ex-Confederate elite. While Stevens had hoped for a redistribution of property to give freedpeople "forty acres and a hut," he accepted the Fourteenth Amendment as "all that can be obtained in the present state of public opinion."[27]

Much of the debate in Congress turned on whether the national government had the capacity to enforce a ban on voting in peacetime. "How do you propose to carry its provisions into practical execution?" Republican Congressman James Garfield asked. "Will nine tenths of the population consent to stay at home and let one tenth do the voting?" A senator said that the only way to enforce a ban on voting was through a "military despotism by the

General Government." More broadly, they argued about whether disenfranchisement was unusually cruel. Looking to world history, Republicans compared their plan to Britain's suppression of a 1745 Jacobite rebellion or the Swiss Sonderbund War of 1847, both of which ended by excluding rebels from voting. Against these arguments Democrats compared the occupation of the South to Britain's rule over Ireland, Austria's over Hungary, and Russia's over Poland to prove that no country could "coerce friendly feeling on the part of a hostile people." After a monthlong debate, the Senate struck the disfranchisement clause and added new sections barring some rebels from federal office, making all people born in the United States citizens, guaranteeing the federal wartime loans, and forbidding the payment of rebel debt.[28]

Disappointed that the amendment did not disenfranchise rebels, Stevens and other Radical Republicans focused on making sure the amendment would not end the war. While some moderates expected to pass a resolution promising to seat states that ratified the amendment, Stevens wanted Congress to pledge only to readmit states once it was "consistent with the future peace and safety of the Union." By these vague terms, passing the amendment would be necessary but not sufficient for restoring representation and ending the state of war. In a now-famous speech where he ruefully accepted the Senate's version, Stevens declared his disappointment that they could not free institutions "from every vestige of human oppression" but instead were "patching up the worst portions of the ancient edifice." Why did he then accept so "imperfect a proposition?" "I answer because I live among men and not among angels." His equanimity arose not just from his pragmatism but also from his understanding that other Republicans, including moderates, had accepted his view that the amendment would not close wartime. The next Congress might well go farther. "You need feel no alarm about Congress," Fessenden wrote in May. "We will stand firm to the end."[29]

In the face of Republican unity, President Johnson launched his own Union party that promised a return to peace. All pretenses of working with moderate Republicans vanished. As Johnson's allies denounced the Fourteenth Amendment and the Civil Rights Act, the Radical-leaning members of the cabinet resigned, except for Secretary of War Edwin Stanton. But Johnson still remained trapped between his alleged allies. Conservative Republicans urged him to accept the amendment; Democrats wanted him to reject it. Once again the president turned to platitudes about peace and state survival to keep his fractious supporters aligned. To a Union party audience, Johnson emphasized the rhetorical significance of peacetime. "One view is of war, the other of peace—yes, peace."[30]

In the last months of the session, before the final fight over peace terms, Republicans worked to embed federal power in the Freedmen's Bureau and army bills. As Congress wrote a new Freedmen's Bureau bill to replace the one Johnson had vetoed in February, it asserted Congress's control over wartime. Instead of promising the permanent continuation of the bureau, as the earlier bill did, the revised version treated the bureau as a wartime agency. Crucially, however, it established Congress as the judge of when that wartime power would end by extending the bureau for two years, until July 1868. Although Reconstruction policy would twist and turn several times over the next two years, July 1868 would in fact be the end of the war in most rebel states. Partly by chance and partly by a recognition of the importance of establishing peace before the 1868 presidential election, Congressional Republicans had come upon a timetable for peace that would extend wartime for three years after Appomattox. The bill retained the military's power to intervene in civil courts until Congress readmitted the rebel states. Until then, "there is no jurisdiction anywhere except in the military," Republican congressman Thomas Eliot said. "No peace can come that will 'stay' until the Government which decreed freedom shall vindicate and enforce its rights by appropriate administration." By narrowing the bureau's power to wartime, Republicans had eased the fears of some moderates that they were permanently remaking American law, while also assuring Radicals that freedpeople would be protected until Congress deemed them safe.[31]

President Johnson and congressional Democrats once again denounced Republicans' definition of wartime and complained of "subjecting the civil authority in time of peace to the military authority." Johnson again vetoed the bill on the grounds that it relied upon a "war-making power" that would last until each "State shall be fully restored." Almost immediately, and with very little discussion, both the House and the Senate overrode the veto.[32]

While Republicans agreed upon a refashioned wartime Freedmen's Bureau, they divided over the size of the army that would staff the occupation. Here, debates exposed deep and troubling structural limitations to occupation.

Many Republicans, including Radicals, seemed unwilling to pay for the occupation that their bills demanded. For some, this was simple thriftiness; for others, an inability to understand the necessity of force and an overconfidence in the capacity of courts to remake society; and for yet others, a slowly growing fear of the army's power and of the constitutional costs of sustaining military authority. The issue turned on the size of the regular army that would be all that remained once the volunteers returned home. During the war, President Lincoln suggested a size of about 31,000 men, almost double the 16,000 men in the army before the start of the Civil War. But by 1866 it was clear that those numbers would not be sufficient.[33]

The discharge of volunteers during the summer and fall of 1865 made the issue pressing; without further legislation, the army would drop to its prewar maximum of fewer than 25,000 men, and thus empty troops from the South. Against this, Grant suggested 80,000 men to regulate the South, the West, and the coasts, but as the administration prepared reports for Congress, the request fell to 50,000 with the potential to add 20,000 more. While Johnson reduced Grant's request, he proved to be more supportive of military expansion than many Republicans. Although Republican floor leaders in both the House and the Senate tried to expand the army beyond the administration's request, and the House manager wished the nation could "preserve an Army of at least one hundred thousand men," Radicals joined with Democrats to thwart them. When an amendment to increase the size of the army reached the floor, many Radical politicians voted against it, from financial frugality or a confidence that no more forces were needed. Democrats meanwhile tried to cut the army to 40,000 or even to 15,000. "It was the wisdom of our fathers," Democratic congressman Andrew Jackson Rogers said, "that large standing armies in time of peace were not only dangerous to liberty, but they involved the country in heavy and enormous expenses." After four months of squabbling, and under intense pressure from Grant to act before the entire volunteer force evaporated, the House and Senate finally agreed to a bill that set the regular army at 54,302 men, three times the size of the 1860 army. The issues that had divided Republicans included not just the total number of soldiers but also the number of units reserved to black soldiers and to injured veterans. The final version preserved two of ten cavalry units and four of forty-five infantry units for black soldiers, and four infantry regiments for disabled veterans. It was a "hard fight," Senator Henry Wilson wrote to Grant. "Certain parties not in the Senate seemed determined to make a raid on the army, which I would not permit." As soon as the bill passed, Grant dispatched troops to the plains and began raising new companies for the South.[34]

Overconfident that symbolic numbers of troops could regulate large areas, Republicans already struggled to pay the human and financial costs of occupation. Popular support for cutting taxes and the budget reinforced this self-deception. Shortly after they had created the Joint Committee on Reconstruction, Republicans had established a Joint Select Committee on Retrenchment to "relieve the people at the earliest possible day from the burden of excessive taxation." To people who understood the military's duties, it looked like foolishness or hypocrisy. "The history of the world does not exhibit such carelessness as that of our own country at the present time," Major General Philip Sheridan complained. The *Army & Navy Journal* editorialized, "We are in danger of repeating the mistakes we have heretofore made at the close of our wars—forgetting too speedily the lessons of the conflict." The challenge of maintaining Republicans' support for the army would resurface several times before Reconstruction ended. This wariness of the military was stronger in the West, where several Republicans sought a peace policy to save money. Even as Republicans hung together against President Johnson, some of them were becoming wary of what Lyman Trumbull called "the concentration of power in the hands of the military." While Republicans were unified against Andrew Johnson, they disagreed about what they were for.[35]

In the session's final weeks, Congress turned at last to its most significant question. Would it offer a road map to restore the states and end the war? Some moderate Republicans feared extending the war, and Republican congressman Henry Dawes expected the party "to break to pieces" over the issue. If President Johnson had urged Southern states to pass the Fourteenth Amendment and then demanded that Congress seat their representatives, many moderate Republicans might well have buckled. But when Johnson refused to support the Fourteenth Amendment, Republicans cohered around the idea of admitting Tennessee but making no promises to other states. Democrats and the few remaining administration-supporting Republicans were outraged. Back in December "little remained to be done to complete the work of restoration," Congressman Henry Raymond said, but Republicans embarked on a utopian plan of "distant perfection" like Cromwell's England or Revolutionary France. As Democrats submitted bills to admit several or even all of the former Confederate states, Senator Charles Sumner derided this act of historical amnesia. Democrats "forgot that we had been in a war" and that 4 million slaves had been emancipated. If "I could forget this terrible war, with all the blood and treasure that it has cost us, I, too, could forget the guarantees."[36]

Although Stevens and other Republicans wanted to say no to peace, they feared being tarred as a war party during the midterm elections. Tennessee gave them a way to stand firm while also appearing to be flexible. When that state's legislature passed the Fourteenth Amendment, congressional Republicans faced a decision. They could reject Tennessee, accept Tennessee as a distinct case, or use the state as a model for future states. Rejecting Tennessee outright seemed politically unwise, but restoring it based solely upon its passage of the Fourteenth Amendment would establish a bad precedent. To solve the problem, Republicans crafted a long list of reasons why Tennessee was to be admitted that would not count as a precedent for any other state.[37]

In the final days, Republicans defeated one last effort to take up a bill to restore states that passed the Fourteenth Amendment. By a margin of nearly three to one, they said no to peace terms. On the final day, Stevens offered a symbolic amendment stating that Southern governments were provisional and under "military surveillance" until new constitutional conventions were elected by universal male suffrage. In the next session, this would indeed become part of Congress's plan. For this session, however, Stevens did not press his amendment for a vote. He was gesturing to the future.[38]

By refusing to set terms, Republicans had protected the crucial power of wartime to sustain civil rights. Prolonging wartime, they kept hold of the extraconstitutional authority they needed to protect freedpeople. Looking forward to the November election, they held open the possibility of even more significant change if the people supported them at the polls. By extending wartime long after surrender, congressional Republicans had entered a revolutionary phase. They did not seek guillotines; they remained liberal democrats, and they hoped to return to constitutional rule in the near future. By continuing wartime, however, they had shed some of their constitutional scruples to hold open the chance to build the type of liberal democracy they coveted. This decision would be momentous, for the better-known accomplishment of the session, the Fourteenth Amendment, would be a product of the government's wartime authority over the rebel states.

Far away from Washington, in the city of Chicago, Republican power broker Joseph Medill could not believe his eyes. In a judgment shared by some contemporaries, Medill thought Congress had done nothing at all. "It is surely not the intention of Congress to adjourn without giving the country some plan of reconstruction and of offering to the South some conditions of readmission," he wrote. Like many others, Medill did not recognize that congressional Republicans' failure to enact a plan had become a policy itself, one that extended military occupation and delayed the date of any final judgment. Everything Radicals hoped for—enfranchisement and new state governments—depended upon not acting. From early December 1865, when they gaveled their session to order, through the wintertime fights with Johnson and the vernal victories on civil rights, the Freedmen's Bureau, and the Fourteenth Amendment, and through the early summer disappointments of the army bill, congressional Republicans faced a dilemma. Could they hold to Fessenden's pledge not to "yield the fruits of war"? By gaveling out in late July without making any promises to the excluded states, they answered yes. Having kept at bay the resumption of peacetime and constitutional normalcy, Congress would now pass the question to the only judge Fessenden acknowledged, the voice of the people. Congress would hold to its plan "unless the people overrule me," he wrote, "and I don't think they will."[39]

- 6 -

A FALSE PEACE

BY JANUARY 1866, a passionate young Freedmen's Bureau agent in north-central Louisiana had lost faith in his power to protect freedpeople. His pessimism would have surprised people who knew George Carruthers well. Dedicated and clear-eyed, he seemed a perfect fit for a job that required both idealism and hard-headed pragmatism. While working with freedpeople during the war, he learned that emancipation required direct, continuous, and powerful assistance, not just legal pronouncements. As a chaplain for a black infantry regiment and then as a bureau agent for Caldwell and Franklin parishes, Carruthers dedicated himself to making those rights real. So he did not despair of freedpeople's capacity. His pessimism had other sources. Through the fall, a company of troops in Columbia, Louisiana, had provided him with the force necessary to make his orders felt. When those soldiers were sent home in November 1865, however, an exasperated Carruthers soon gave up on the region and on his job. "I could do but little good in so delicate a matter as 'acting next friend' to those who had no friends with military support," he wrote. Without soldiers to assist him, he could not aid freedpeople or even protect his own life "in a bitter, half conquered and half civilized community."[1]

Carruthers had not abandoned Reconstruction; he had only given up on the regions the army had left behind. He wanted to leave the bureau and return to his regiment sixty miles away in Alexandria, where the presence of more than 700 black troops and an additional company of cavalry acted "like an anchor to the ship in storm," he wrote in February 1866. Although the military no longer directly regulated everyday life, "its very presence is a power." The necessity of continued occupation "is a fact so obvious to every military man who is in circumstances which enable him to judge that it needs no arguments."[2]

As Carruthers found, the status of occupation was shifting in 1866. Early in the year, the occupying army had maintained war powers—but not always sufficient power—to regulate their regions. In the last half of the year, President Johnson attacked those war powers, leaving freedpeople to the mercies of planters in many regions of the South. By the end of 1866, much of the South looked like Carruthers's Caldwell Parish, nearly bereft of military support. It was possible to think that the nation was finally at peace. But the legal peacetime of late 1866 was a false peace. It was false partly because of violent clashes between a growing white insurgency and organized freedpeople. Unrestrained by direct military force, ex-Confederates launched campaigns of terror to coerce freedpeople into oppressive labor conditions, to limit their mobility, and to try to frighten them into acquiescence. The peace was also false because freedpeople's resistance, backed at times by the assistance of the army, exposed the thinness of planter-led state governments. If planters at times could achieve dominance, they could not create hegemony. They had to rely upon open and brutal violence, and their continued turn to bloodshed came at a grave cost.

Finally, the peace was false because the army did not let go of all the powers of war, despite Johnson's orders. In the face of these ongoing campaigns of violence, it might be easy to think that the retreating army did not matter at all. But George Carruthers's rueful story suggests that the army—where it remained—still played a central role in shaping both the methods and outcomes of these struggles on the ground. At one hundred outposts in the former Confederate states in December 1866, more than 25,000 soldiers exerted unusual influence over the surrounding regions. Even as the legal support for occupation crumbled around them, commanders kept slivers of military rule alive. A patchwork occupation produced patchwork rights. As freedpeople appealed to local officers, the army sporadically displaced sheriffs by arresting criminals, magistrates by settling small suits, judges by hearing serious crimes, and even appellate courts by denying rights of appeal. As white Southerners sought to rebuild antebellum masters' powers through the legal system, soldiers gummed up the works, and at times they did quite a bit more.[3]

Even where the military lacked the force to stop the violence, its presence made it a conduit of information back to the North. This news in turn helped to move Northern public opinion against reconciliation and reunion, and toward the reimposition of military rule. It was enough to convince Ulysses Grant that parts of the South remained in late 1866 "practically" in a "state of insurrection." When a questioner in February 1867 contrasted wartime and postwar policies, Grant rejected the distinction. "The work is not all done," he answered. Although the occupation of 1866 was not a brilliant one or a success on conventional grounds, the endurance of the military created useful pockets of governance, stabilized some gains of emancipation, and provided the institutional framework for Congress's sweeping reconstruction of the rebel states in the winter of 1866–1867.[4]

Occupation and the protection of freedpeople's rights seemed to be on the verge of disappearing even before 1866 began. In December 1865, as President Johnson sped the mustering out of volunteers and urged Congress to seat some Southern congressmen, military rule seemed close to its conclusion. But thousands of civil and criminal court filings against soldiers in Kentucky and a campaign of terror against freedpeople in South Carolina persuaded Grant that he could not let loose of occupation's power over civil governments. The Black Codes likewise convinced agents that it was "impossible to secure to freedmen their just rights without the aid of a military force." After Major General Daniel Sickles aggressively sparked a crisis on January 1, 1866 by rejecting nearly all of South Carolina's Black Code, Grant was nudged to a decision.[5]

Awakened to the problems his men faced on the ground, pressured by Republican legislators, and chagrined by his earlier, optimistic report on the South, Grant reasserted the power of occupation to protect freedpeople's rights in January 1866. On the same day that Senator Lyman Trumbull's committee reported out the Freedmen's Bureau and civil rights bills, Grant issued his General Orders Number 3. This order primarily shielded soldiers from lawsuits but it also empowered the military to protect freedpeople from discriminatory state laws or courts. By joining the power to defend freedpeople to the authority to defend his own troops, Grant saved the occupation of the South. Still, no one was sure whether Grant's order created procedural or substantive justice, whether it only barred explicit discrimination in the Black Codes or overrode all unfair rulings. In some states, especially Mississippi and Florida, commanders treated Grant's ruling narrowly. There freedpeople tried to use Grant's orders to their own ends, asking him in petitions to "give us Protection."[6]

In many states, however, generals intervened forcefully in Southern life to create pockets of defensible rights for freedpeople in early 1866. In Virginia, Major General Alfred Terry overturned the state's vagrancy law even though its language was racially neutral. Terry barred magistrates from applying the law to freedpeople because it would inevitably be enforced in a discriminatory way to "reduce the freedmen" to a "condition which will be slavery in all but its name." In Georgia, commanders voided parts of the Black Code and stripped judges of jurisdiction, leading the state's governor to bemoan the imposition of military authority over state law to end discriminatory practices. Although Virginia and Georgia turned over all criminal cases to state courts in April or May, North Carolina and Florida continued Freedmen's Bureau and provost courts throughout the summer, and South Carolina's commander kept control of freedpeople's cases until October 1866. In those military- and bureau-run courts, agents and officers ruled on civil and criminal cases involving freedpeople, acting under a combination of military-corrected local law, military law, and personal judgment. In South Carolina, Sickles ignored state writs of habeas corpus, banned concealed weapons, regulated liquor licenses, and threatened to remove all freedpeople from two upcountry districts if whites did not curtail their violence. In provost courts that took petty cases, officers, who were usually not lawyers, rendered judgments that one agent claimed offered "substantial," if "not strictly legal," justice. In the spring, an Arkansas man complained that army officers "seem inclined to take advantage of the *fact* that the President has never issued a Proclamation, affirming that 'Peace' *existed* in the Country; and until that was done they had a right to presume that *war* existed still, and of course *War remedies*."[7]

In Virginia, there was more proof of the military's authority as Grant suppressed a Richmond newspaper for discouraging social interactions between local women and U.S. soldiers. "The power certainly does exist when martial law prevails, and will be exercised," Grant wrote. Although President Johnson eventually convinced Grant to lift the suspension, Grant continued to hold on to the authority to suspend newspapers and asked his commanders to forward copies of disloyal articles to him. The suspension proved that the "condition of affairs in southern States" had changed in "degree" but "not in na-

ture" since the army closed newspapers in the summer of 1865, the *Army &
Navy Journal* wrote. Although the troops had been "greatly decreased," nevertheless "there is an army of occupation now in the South." In Texas, Captain Samuel Craig fined and then jailed the editor of the Brenham *Banner*
for denouncing his work as bureau agent.[8]

Aware of the perilous conditions on the ground, Grant lobbied to maintain soldiers in the South. Although politicians from both Georgia and Alabama asked him to remove troops, Grant on January 15 urged the president
not to. Seeking more information, Grant sent two aides to the South. They
reported back that if martial law were withdrawn, "a second Kansas war
would extend over the south." As the "black race have become as it were the
wards of the Government," it was "an act of humanity to retain troops in the
late slaveholding states in order to protect the negro" from violence, oppression, and discrimination, one of Grant's aides wrote. Armed with these reports, Grant dismissed the Mississippi legislature's request to withdraw troops
because the state would not "fairly and justly execute the laws among all her
citizens." Although President Johnson forwarded a complaint about black soldiers in Columbus, Georgia, Grant dismissed it, telling the commander that
he should not transfer troops if it would endanger the rights of "loyal Whites
and Freedmen."[9]

The military's influence depended on the force that lies behind all effective governance. Occupation had to be asserted and reasserted as white Southerners
both ignored and resisted it. Some of the challenges were symbolic. Local
judges often tested military rules, ignoring army commanders and protesting
their "unjustifiable interference with the civil authority." To counter resistance
in towns like Darlington, South Carolina, and Ocala, Florida, commanders
sustained very public occupations with patrols through town to arrest disorderly
civilians and demonstrate the "presence of the power of the Government."[10]

But the army's ability to exert that force diminished over 1866. Between
January and March, the army mustered out 56,000 soldiers, almost half of its
remaining volunteers. By the end of April, only 17,000 white volunteers remained, and they soon were ordered out, leaving a force of 30,000 black volunteers to supplement the regular army. (See Appendix 6.) At a slower rate,

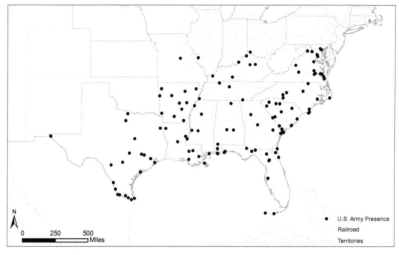

U.S. Army presence, September–November 1866. University of Richmond Digital
Scholarship Laboratory.

commanders ordered out black troops, dropping their numbers to two regiments in Kentucky, four in Tennessee, one in Georgia, two in Alabama, four
in Mississippi, one in South Carolina, and one in Florida. From almost 87,000
total troops in the former Confederacy in January (with about 25,000 of those
in Texas), the numbers fell to roughly 28,000 (with more than 8,700 of those
in Texas) by the end of July 1866. In some states the declines were staggering;
Alabama dropped from 7,800 to 832 and Mississippi from 9,119 to 439 between January and July 1866.

    With fewer soldiers to call upon, army commanders drew their men into
central towns and cities. (See Appendix 7.) Officers were "rapidly reducing
the number of districts within their commands to the smallest number consistent with the interest of the service," the *Army & Navy Journal* wrote. From
the already much-reduced 200 outposts in January 1866, the number fell
steadily to 103 at the end of August and remained there throughout the winter.
As soldiers mustered out, Mississippi commander Thomas J. Wood reduced
the posts from eleven in December to seven, then to six in March and to five
in April.

    The withdrawal of cavalry weakened the army's ability to regulate the
countryside. Without horses, the military's authority shriveled to a small ra-

dius around its tents. When a group of robbers began attacking Nanafalia, Alabama, the nearest post commander found it a "hard matter to catch these fellows" since they "laugh defiance at our Infantry. . . . They are all mounted and can very easily escape our soldiers sent on foot." "Mounted men" who could reach "any portion of the state" were indispensable "to prevent the constant occurrence of such outrages," a bureau commissioner reported. In Florida, cattle thieves on horseback essentially controlled a wide band from Enterprise to Tampa. Where cavalry was available, it made an enormous difference. Alabama's Freedmen's Bureau commissioner thought that "a few companies of cavalry, so stationed that the radii of their operations would reach the whole State, would be of great service both as a police force and for the moral effect."[11]

As the army sent home its white volunteers, black troops continued to play an outsize role in shaping life on the ground in the South. Black soldiers' presence tested the endurance of the war, both to protesting white Southerners and to the soldiers themselves, who were retained as volunteers even though direct military combat had long since faded. In response to furious white complaints, Grant famously directed his commanders to withdraw black troops from the interior of states to "avoid giving unnecessary annoyance." But Grant left much to their discretion. "How far it is practicable to carry out" those orders, commanders on the ground would have to judge. "It is a greater duty to protect troops acting under Military authority and also all loyally disposed persons." In 1866, as in 1865, black troops in North Carolina were kept at coastal forts beyond the sight of white and black civilians, but soldiers in many other states remained stationed in central towns and cities. Major General George Thomas dismissed white Southerners' complaints since the army "must use such as we have, be they white or black, without regard to their feelings on the subject."[12]

If the army was the eyes of the federal government, its departure from some regions suggested that the government had stopped paying attention. In Texas a Freedmen's Bureau commissioner described a direct relationship between the distance from a military post and the violence of the white population. The people of Texas, like the people across the South, needed to "become familiarized with the idea of law as an irresistible power to which all must bow." From Jackson County, Florida, another bureau agent wrote that whites were wild and violent when out of the government's sight but "stand in awe of the power of the triumphant Government, and become meek as

Christians in their manner, at the suggestion of military persuasion." What government presence produced was not a permanent terror but a "constrained submission," another wrote. One agent said, "It is useless to say that the laws are enforced—wherever there are bayonets there the people respect the laws, but nowhere else." At its essence, they saw that the law was not a series of rules but an expression of force. From the towns of Anderson and Aiken, South Carolina, a minister's son from Maine provided some of the clearest descriptions of the military's declining but still important role. William Stone, who had fought with the 19th Massachusetts Infantry before his assignment to the bureau, found himself "dependent on the military forces for assistance." When he could call upon detachments at nearly every courthouse town, Stone was confident he could teach "correct notions of government and liberty," but once the military withdrew, he lost faith in his power. His authority depended not on his title but on the force he could command.[13]

The limited reach of government was not peculiar to the postwar South. Rather than a counterpoint, the West remained a complement to the South; both regions faced deep challenges to the federal government's claims of authority and had pockets of defensible national sovereignty as well as large areas that were nearly ungoverned. Out West, the crisis of authority seemed worse in 1866, as demobilization reduced the numbers of cavalry and let loose floods of veterans who disrupted the very lands the army hoped to pacify. In turn, Indians probed at the nation's weak spots and fought back against encroachments. Instead of a pacified region, the West appeared to be anarchic. "Why does not the Government hold the Indians in control?" the *Army & Navy Journal* asked. "Why is it that all our power, which they understand as well as we do ourselves, weighs so little with them?" In places like New Mexico, where fewer than 1,500 troops covered extended routes, citizens complained that the government failed to deliver the protection it guaranteed, while officers argued that they could barely defend their own men. On the Bozeman Trail, tribes successfully fought back against an overextended military line. In Arkansas and Texas, Southern and Western crises intertwined, as commanders struggled to deploy their limited forces simultaneously against planters and Indians. For the moment, the army's focus was upon the Southern problem of emancipation; Grant denied the Arkansas commander's request to move headquarters to Fort Smith to regulate Indian Territory and required him to stay in Little Rock and oversee the legislature and eastern planters. In Texas, western settlers asked for soldiers against the Comanche, and eastern freedpeople for troops against the reimposition of planter power. For the summer, the army maintained a tense balance, moving troops both to frontier belts and to the interior.[14]

As the army retracted its hold over the countryside, white Southerners exposed the limits of the law as they fought to reassert their control. Where the government would not use force, locals would. They sought to drive away white loyalists in order to cut ties of communication with the North. One Virginia loyalist wrote that ex-Confederates threatened that he was "outside the protection of the damned theaving sons of bitches now," and a telegraph operator refused to send his message because it included the word "Grant." They also attempted to frighten freedpeople into acquiescence, to create the hegemony they had failed to fashion in the fall of 1865. Therefore, their actions were notoriously, deliberately public. Whites patrolled roads, killed hundreds of freedpeople, confiscated their property, burned churches, and shot soldiers. In Morgan County, Alabama, a former rebel colonel fired at black soldiers and promised to make the streets "run with Yankee Blood." As soon as the soldiers departed, he threatened, the "negroes will be gutted or made slaves as of old." Rebels acted as if "theay have eveary thing in thir owne power," a Tallahassee loyalist complained. "It donte appear that the united states has any power ovear them." In Prince William County, Virginia, a white man named John Cornwell shot a black U.S. veteran named James Cook and left him at the door of the jail as a "good lesson to the niggers." After a local Freedmen's Bureau agent complained, a physician told him that the white people did not intend to permit "niggers to come among us and brag about having been in the Yankee Army."[15]

Black Southerners mobilized in increasingly organized efforts to defend themselves against a growing white Southern insurgency. In black belt counties, and in regions where there were large concentrations of former soldiers, they came together to assert control. In Norfolk, Virginia, and in parts of Texas, freedpeople marched through towns, brandishing weapons to claim their right to public space. In Saint Augustine, Florida, hearing rumors that whites aimed to "clear them out," black dockworkers armed themselves and created what one fearful white man called a "secret military organization." In Jackson County, Florida, forty armed freedmen gathered together to protect a threatened school. Although the local agent "discountenanced the movement," he also found solace in the fact that it inspired terror among whites. In parts of the South, Union and Loyal leagues that began among white Northerners took on new forms as freedpeople turned them into military-style self-defense organizations.[16]

Many white Southerners cheered when Johnson began to issue peace proclamations in 1866. They hoped the proclamations would allow local civilian courts to rule without fear of military intervention; that path, they believed, would lead to hegemony and the eventual acquiescence of the freedpeople to planter power. With more money, more guns, better communications systems, and, in most of the South, more people, many white Southerners believed that they would inevitably prevail as long as the army did not intervene. At first, Johnson's April 2 peace proclamation seemed to satisfy their hopes. A Claiborne County, Mississippi, man celebrated what he believed was the war's end and the restoration of civilian control. "Thank God for it. We are tired of Military. We are tired of War, and wish to be again as we were before." Many Northerners also took Johnson's proclamation as proof of peace. The *Army & Navy Journal* claimed that Johnson "abdicates the 'war' power by which he has governed the South. . . . He will withdraw all troops, except the customary garrisons, from Southern States. He will restore the *habeas corpus*. He will abolish martial law. He will cease to permit military tribunals." In response, some generals withdrew military commissions. Alabama's commanding general was uncertain if he should respect state judges' writs of habeas corpus. Georgia's Freedmen's Bureau commissioner and army commander were unsure whether the army could still arrest outlaws.[17]

But they had all misunderstood Johnson's actions. If peace meant the civil government's supremacy over the military, however, Johnson's April proclamation had not in fact ended the war. It was a political, not a legal, strike. The war powers, nebulous and weak as they might seem, were too necessary to let go. Instead of ending martial law, Johnson continued it; instead of restoring habeas corpus, he maintained the suspension; instead of withdrawing all the troops, he kept many thousands in place. Within days Grant wrote to Virginia officers to assure them that he did not believe martial law removed or the writ of habeas corpus restored. Soon, and "with the approval of the

President," orders went out to all Freedmen's Bureau commissioners and army commanders stating that the proclamation "does not remove martial law, or operate in any way upon the Freedmen's Bureau in the exercise of its legitimate jurisdiction." When Kentucky commanders refused to obey a writ of habeas corpus for a contractor held in military prison, a judge was baffled. "If the effect of this proclamation be not to restore the right of the citizen to the writ of *habeas corpus* and to resort to the civil courts for protection it is impossible to conceive what its effect is," he wrote. "Have we a Government not of law but of arbitrary power?" A New Orleans man experienced similar confusion after a civilian remained in military prison. "*The existing condition of things is perfectly anomalous,*" he wrote to the president. People "hailed the coming of your peace proclamation" because "they supposed it was to be the knell of martial law." But it wasn't. Instead, Louisiana's bureau commissioner decided, the proclamation was an effort to make the army cautious of using powers it continued to hold.[18]

Throughout the spring, Johnson edged closer to ending the war powers. In May, he lifted the suspension of the writ of habeas corpus in most states. The War Department also issued General Orders Number 26 directing that civilians be turned over to civil authorities for trial wherever courts existed. By the summer, Grant retracted his orders on monitoring newspapers, and state commanders had to seek prior approval before suspending judges. Yet the army still retained a good deal of power. To salvage military authority, Grant in his General Orders Number 44 relied upon peacetime legislation in the Freedmen's Bureau Act and the Civil Rights Act to authorize his men to arrest criminals. No longer judge and jury, the army might still function as a national police. Bureau commissioner O. O. Howard also reminded bureau agents that President Johnson had never countermanded earlier orders that permitted them to intervene on behalf of freedpeople; therefore, they should act with "unusual vigilance." The army therefore continued to hold people and intervene in trials to protect the peace. In Florida, the state commander directed officers in several counties to arrest civilians until local authorities took action, and an officer sent fifteen artillerymen to Milton to show that the government's military power was "still supreme." Commanders elsewhere continued to set aside laws, dismiss lawsuits, send troops to quell disorder, and forbid Confederate gatherings.[19]

The massacre in Memphis in May 1866 altered not just political debates but also army policy. When the local sheriff did not arrest the offenders, Grant suggested that the army seize them. But Attorney General James Speed denied that the army had such powers in a state where courts were open. Those courts signaled that "there is no war." Speed's emphasis upon open courts, not order or lawfulness, as the signal of the return of peacetime echoed the Supreme Court's evolving response to military intervention. In *In re Egan* in June 1866, Supreme Court Justice Samuel Nelson claimed that civilian rule returned even earlier, the "moment the rebellion was suppressed." At the Supreme Court, a recent order in *Ex Parte Milligan* seemed to confirm the idea that the mere existence of courts separated peacetime from wartime. Although the Court had not yet issued its opinion in the summer of 1866, it had released an Indianan named Lambdin Milligan, who had been sentenced to death by a military commission for stirring up dissent against the war. Without knowing the reasoning, however, no one could be quite sure of the legal status of military commissions in the South. In practice, military commissions diminished but did not die in 1866, as the number of cases fell from 921 in 1865 to a still-substantial 229.[20]

As Johnson and the Supreme Court looked toward peacetime, Grant for the first time defended the powers of occupation secretly. Instead of using the attorney general's Memphis opinion as a general guideline, Grant decided unilaterally that it applied only to the specific question of the Memphis riot. Rather than a distinction between wartime and peacetime, the opinion defined the peculiar conditions of Tennessee. At last Grant had learned a lesson: he should stop asking for approval. His silence empowered his generals on the ground to continue to use war powers to protect freedpeople's rights elsewhere. Commanders in Florida invoked Grant's earlier orders to protect loyal people as "the best friends of the United States, and fully entitled to the fostering care of the Government, and to the protection of its officers." If "truly loyal citizens of whatever color" were not treated equally, officers should help transfer cases to federal courts. In Virginia and South Carolina, commanding generals continued to make arrests and ignore writs of habeas corpus in an effort at "overawing any who may [be] disposed to create further disturbances."[21]

The infamous New Orleans massacres in July 1866 showed Northern whites how far ex-rebels would go to reclaim their authority. As former Confederates gained power, Governor J. Madison Wells desperately turned back to the Republicans he had abandoned and tried to reconvene the 1864 convention and write a new constitution. With commanding major general Philip Sheridan off in Texas, the responsibility for managing the situation fell to the timid brigadier general Absalom Baird, who kept his soldiers in their barracks during fiery public meetings. When 200 black veterans paraded across the French Quarter to show their support for the convention, a crowd of roughly 1,500 whites attacked first the paraders and then the delegates inside the Mechanics Institute. As convention leaders tried to surrender, police dragged a former governor from the hall and beat him senseless. In short order, the crowd killed about thirty-four black men and four whites. After an inexplicable delay, Baird finally declared martial law and mobilized his forces. Sheridan, returning from Texas, wrote bitterly that "there is now a test of what shall be the status of Northern men." Although the military was able to restore quiet to the city, it had to call on the same murderous police force for assistance.[22]

Many Northerners interpreted the riot as proof of white Southern intransigence. In vivid descriptions, Republicans made white Louisianans out to be barbaric and incapable of self-control, much less self-rule. The massacre, along with the one in Memphis, taught the North the "necessity of strongly garrisoning the subjected portions of the Union" for two or three years, the *Army & Navy Journal* wrote. In letters from New Orleans, Republicans called it "heartsickening," a "butchery not a combat." In a missive passed along to legal thinker Francis Lieber, a New Orleans–based Northerner described a three-foot-wide path of coagulated blood leading to a stack of forty dead bodies. As a wagon carried away corpses, one of the seemingly dead black men suddenly sat up. Then a policeman shot him through the head. "And these men are to take the reins of Govt!" the writer exclaimed.[23] Although ongoing, geographically scattered attacks in the Southern countryside were more widespread than urban massacres, New Orleans and Memphis provided an accessible way to picture the lawlessness in the South.

While Republicans interpreted the massacre as evidence of the need for ongoing occupation, President Johnson saw it as proof that he should unwind war powers as quickly as possible. In his view, the problem in New Orleans was the presence of the army, which he believed had encouraged Republicans and freedpeople to assert themselves. To stabilize the South, the simplest method was to remove the army's power. Now that Congress had finally adjourned, Johnson thought he could do so with impunity.

On August 20, 1866, Johnson at last seemed to end the war. In a proclamation that extended his April order to Texas, Johnson wrote that the "insurrection is at an end, and peace, order, tranquillity, and civil authority now exist in and throughout the whole of the United States of America." As Johnson moved toward peace, he acknowledged that peace powers had been expanded by Congress. He could end the war, he argued, because "adequate provision has been made by military orders to enforce the execution of the acts of Congress, aid the civil authorities, and secure obedience to the Constitution and laws of the United States within the State of Texas if a resort to military force for such purpose should at any time become necessary."[24]

Unlike Johnson's April proclamation, his August announcement had military, not just political, consequences. No longer would the executive branch be the source of extraconstitutional war powers to occupy the South or intervene to defend freedpeople. Viewed from the White House, the war indeed almost seemed to end on August 20, 1866. Judges used that date as the clear designation between wartime and peacetime. After puzzling over the meaning of Johnson's April proclamation, Chief Justice Salmon Chase accepted the August one as final, not because its language was different but because there were, to his eyes, no more orders "asserting the continuance of Military government." Therefore, "it seems fair to conclude that martial law & Military government are permanently abrogated & the writ of habeas corpus fully restored." Later that year, Johnson's new attorney general also pointed to the proclamation as the "restoration of civil order." Although Congress reasserted the endurance of war powers in February and March 1867, it also confusingly acknowledged August 1866 as the war's end for the purpose of determining soldiers' combat pay. The Supreme Court over time came to use August 20, 1866, as the war's end, while settling on April 1866 for some issues that affected only individual states. For all of these reasons, the August date is often cited as the technical, legal end of the war. Legally, however, the issue remained murky. Later Supreme Court justices admitted that April or August 1866 were essentially legal fictions that allowed them to resolve particular cases;

they could not or would not settle the political question of when war powers actually ceased. In 1869, Justice David Davis wrote that the war might be "considered as suppressed for one purpose and not for another." Therefore, Davis separated the "actual termination of the war" from "the political question of the continuance of the rights of war, after the termination in fact of hostilities." Later courts similarly used August 1866 for individual cases but acknowledged that war powers endured. Despite Johnson's actions, ending the war would be a political question, determined not by justices but by a fight between the president and Congress.[25]

The army still continued to exercise certain war powers after the August 1866 proclamation. Surprisingly, this seems to have been Johnson's intention. In an early draft, Johnson stated that orders for the Freedmen's Bureau and the military to sustain the authority of the federal government "are not affected by this proclamation" and would remain in force until revoked. He struck out those words in his final draft, but the proclamation's impact on the military was still mixed. While Johnson immediately released his proclamation to the newspapers, he did not disseminate it as a military order until October. After Arkansas commander Major General Edward Ord asked what he should do when planters or local courts were in "violation of the civil rights bill," Grant's aide responded that he should "exercise a wise discretion" because it was impossible to give instructions. Grant wrote blandly that generals should avoid interfering with legal cases "when the laws of the State are not in conflict with the laws of the United States." This made officers adjudicators of whether state laws met the requirements of the Civil Rights Act. Grant's order also advised them not to permit the arrest of soldiers in unrestored states. In Texas, Sheridan interpreted Johnson's reluctance to promulgate the proclamation as proof that it was not a military order and did not affect the "military status" at all. Sheridan therefore used his discretion broadly, issuing a circular that included the texts of the 1866 Habeas Corpus Act and the Civil Rights Act but leaving it to officers to determine the precise powers those laws gave them. When local officials in Florida began arresting soldiers under the belief that the proclamation restored the "supremacy of the civil law," the state commander sent troops to the capital to prove that "martial law is still supreme." In South Carolina, site of the most intrusive occupation, Major General Daniel Sickles ended military courts in most counties and turned over civilian prisoners, but also continued to overrule the state's vagrancy and corporal punishment laws and threatened to act against recalcitrant judges.[26]

The army's orders, designed to protect soldiers, could still empower the military to assist freedpeople. In November, Grant instructed his generals to "protect the law-abiding against the acts of the lawless" as long as troops remained. In turn troops required planters to pay wages, patrolled highways, and treated vigilante "regulators" not as outlaws but as guerrillas. "Although the appeal to force" was "objectionable" where the courts had been restored, Georgia's Freedmen's Bureau commissioner wrote, "experience has shown it to be" the only way to keep the government's promise to regulate contracts. By giving the army enough discretion to help, however, Grant also gave it enough to hinder. When freedpeople protested working conditions around the North Santee River in South Carolina, the nearest post commander broke up armed organizations among the freedpeople and sent troops to put down complaints among the field hands.[27]

No place illustrated the proclamation's impact and its limitations more vividly than Texas. Commanders there immediately ended military commissions, but great reservoirs of power remained. In the town of Brenham, months of strife between army officers and local officials exploded on September 7 when local citizens shot soldiers out socializing in town. In response, other army men raided the town and set it on fire. As troops rushed from Seguin to Brenham, a posse of townsmen barred them from entering. Back in Seguin, a judge used their absence to arrest Freedmen's Bureau agent Samuel Craig. Upon returning to Seguin, the soldiers broke into the jail and freed him. Although the state's governor protested, Sheridan refused to let sheriffs arrest soldiers, and Johnson's cabinet declined to support the governor. Even conservative Gideon Welles "concluded to temporize" on the legal situation in order to maintain some "military force." When Brenham authorities finally charged the shooter, this particular crisis passed, but the general condition of affairs remained chaotic. In the plantation belt, over the outraged complaints of white Texans, soldiers continued chasing down criminals, forcibly releasing freedpeople from jail, and ignoring writs of habeas corpus. Did the military respect the proclamation or would it "continue to disregard and over-ride the rights of the loyal citizens of the United States, leaving them powerless and at the mercy of every petty military upstart who may choose to have bayonets to enforce the edicts?" the state's governor asked.[28]

As the army's legal powers waned, so too did the number of troops it could call upon to enforce its orders. Over the fall and winter of 1866, the army's actual presence in the South dropped to its lowest levels. By the end of No-

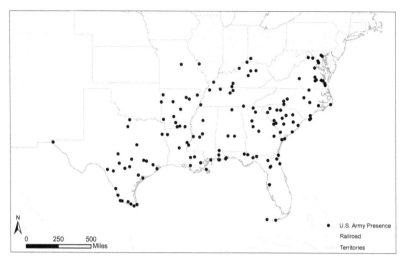

U.S. Army presence, December 1866–February 1867. University of Richmond Digital Scholarship Laboratory.

vember 1866, the volunteer army had all but disappeared, with only 11,000 men, mostly African Americans, left of the more than 1 million volunteers in service at surrender. Although the last companies would not be mustered out until the end of 1867 and the final detached individual volunteer until 1869, the army would be left primarily to its regular forces in late 1866. By recruiting to fill the numbers authorized by the army bill, the military sustained similar and at times even increased levels of occupation, with about 7,300 troops in Texas and 17,500 in the other former rebel states. From 122 outposts in December 1866, the army influenced some regions by its mere visibility. Where they could, commanders in the Department of the Gulf continued to spread troops into towns and port cities to prevent "excitement" and remain accessible to freedpeople. Regular troops in Florida still covered thirteen towns in the northern and central part of the state, and Louisiana's troops still held down Carruthers's Alexandria post as a point of access for freedpeople. There remained fifteen posts in South Carolina and thirteen in Virginia. In other states, however, the army held only a core of railroad towns. Even so, the tide of centralization had been slowed. The occupation had survived the transition to a regular army, diminished but not destroyed.[29]

Constrained in numbers and in authority, the army was unable to regulate much of the South as the winter of 1866 approached. In large pockets away from those posts, much of the South had fallen into a condition of near-statelessness. What had emerged there was not a bad government but a failure of government altogether. Accustomed to delegating surveillance to patrols and passersby, and beset by a lack of funding, planters' governments could not stabilize the South. Unable to rely upon law, white Southerners turned increasingly to organized, violent bands of regulators. Emerging from antebellum patrols and wartime Confederate or guerrilla organizations, these bands increasingly coordinated acts of private violence and sought not just revenge but outright control over sections of the South. While the Ku Klux Klan had not yet cohered into an effective force in 1866, many paramilitary organizations sprang up across the South long before black people could vote. In Columbia and Winnsboro, Louisiana, the very region George Carruthers had left behind in January 1866, a group called the Black Horse Cavalry killed freedpeople systematically. After they murdered a military officer in Franklin Parish, neither the state judge nor the nearest army officer would visit the parish alone. When freedmen began organizing in self-defense, the Black Horse Cavalry killed two men and kidnapped six other organizers. In south-central Texas's Caldwell County, whites chased blacks on horseback, shot them, and whipped them for calling whites by their first names, leaving the legal system powerless.[30]

The peace that had settled upon the South looked to officers like anarchy. Grant collected reports of at least 440 black people murdered by whites in 1866 and 1867. "We have no Government or Law," thieves taunted a Florida magistrate. "Where is the law or authority to punish?" Colonel John Sprague wrote that "every day brings evidences" that "the Civil Law has no force." One Florida man wrote plaintively, "I know we have had a Peace Proclamation, but I have not seen the Peace." Brevard County, Florida, was in a "state of revolution," as the sheriff and judge refused to obey each other's orders, and in Pensacola, "the pistol and the bowie knife" had "become the common law of the State." In Texas, armed organizations burned black homes in Brenham and displaced the government over large sections of the state. "It is a fatal mistake, nay a wicked misery to talk of peace or the institutions of peace," a U.S. attorney wrote. "We are in the very vortex of war."[31]

In Tennessee, the restoration of civil government did not bring peace but instead led to the near-complete militarization of electoral politics. Founded as a social club in the spring of 1866 in Pulaski, Tennessee, the Ku Klux Klan soon morphed into a statewide organization to combat the Republican Party and also a cultural language for describing an organized Southern counterrevolution. Desperate to prevent conservatives from prevailing, Governor William Brownlow's allies barred rebels from voting. In turn conservatives plotted to overthrow the government through a new constitutional convention. To stop them, Brownlow called on the military. Although commanders tried to keep out of electoral politics, their mere presence was political. If Brownlow survived solely by dint of military support, conservatives claimed, his government could not be legitimate. Soon the entire state seemed on the verge of "civil war," a military reporter wrote back to President Johnson.[32]

By the end of 1866, it was easy to feel that occupation had crumbled upon itself. When the army suspended a North Carolina law inflicting corporal punishment in November, the state's governor protested vigorously. "These Orders seem to rest on the assumption that the Military Commandant of the Department, has a right to suspend or annul such laws of the States within his Command as he may deem inhumane or unwise," Governor Jonathan Worth complained to President Johnson. Weren't orders like these "essentially modified by your proclamation?" Unlike most people, Worth had access to the president, and he used it. After meeting twice with the governor in December, the president directed the army to suspend the order. Loyalists, shut out from access to the administration, complained but received no response. Without allies in the White House or support from local commanders, a federal judge in Georgia watched helplessly as the state enforced a "barbarous" vagrancy law to suppress organizing among freedpeople, and the mayor of Savannah used corporal punishment almost exclusively against blacks. Where freedpeople could not overpower planters, and where the army would not intervene, white Southerners were imposing a deeply coercive labor system in the South, enforced by violence.[33]

The changes the year had wrought upon military power were especially evident in South Carolina. There, Freedmen's Bureau agent William Stone had run provost courts and aimed to establish some sort of substantive justice.

On October 1, however, Major General Sickles ordered agents and officers to transfer all cases to civilian courts. For six months, until Congress authorized agents to once again take control of cases, Stone was "powerless to punish offences by or upon negroes or to secure to them their rights." Months after Carruthers, Stone fell into the same type of despair. Since a bureau agent could not "do anything for the freedmen" and the civil authorities were "independent of military control," he "urged in two or three reports the withdrawal of officers doing Bureau duty at military posts." Like Carruthers, Stone saw the only hope in the military. He hoped the army would go beyond its orders and reinstate some form of martial law out of necessity. To Stone's relief, this is exactly what began to happen. When at least ten freedpeople were murdered in Edgefield, Sickles sent cavalry to the region. Although they arrested few outlaws, they aimed at something broader. "Without any particular authority," the cavalry began to administer justice.[34]

Despite those glimmers of power, occupation seemed about to disappear when the Supreme Court finally released its written decision in the *Milligan* case in December 1866. What was at stake in this opinion was the federal government's power to run military commissions in areas where courts existed. At one level *Milligan* said nothing about the occupied South, since it covered the loyal state of Indiana, and the justices did not directly comment upon the legality of using military justice in the former Confederacy. But there were worrying signs. The majority argued that Congress did not have the right to establish military commissions where legal systems existed. The writ of habeas corpus was "the very framework of the government" and the "birthright of every American citizen." If military commanders could substitute their will for law, "republican government is a failure, and there is an end of liberty regulated by law. Martial law established on such a basis destroys every guarantee of the Constitution." Although the majority opinion did not directly address martial law in the South, it stated that military justice could be used only where "the courts are actually closed, and it is impossible to administer criminal justice." In dissent, Chase and three other justices tried unsuccessfully to narrow the ruling.[35]

Emboldened, Johnson turned the *Milligan* decision into a weapon against military power. As the decision was announced in December, Johnson ordered Freedmen's Bureau agents to stop bringing cases before military tribunals and dissolved military commissions in Virginia and Georgia. As late as October, the bureau had been the law of first recourse for freedpeople in South Carolina; then, it became the law of last resort when the courts refused to act; now the bureau was barely a bystander. In coastal Georgia, the president's orders to return land to planters finally ground to their grim conclusion. Tunis Campbell, the fiery leader of black settlements there, had been pushed out of office by Georgia's new bureau commissioner, but he stayed influential in the region. When the bureau asked freedpeople to give up their land grants, Campbell urged them to fight for the right to their crop. In early 1867, when the bureau ruled against them, soldiers forced freedpeople to leave the tracts that planters claimed. The Sea Islands in South Carolina and Georgia, once the site of extraordinary experimentation, now seemed to be an example of the war's fleeting gains.[36]

Even as the army lost the ability to regulate the South, it retained its role as the nation's eyes on the ground. Without the army's reports, it would have been easy for the upheaval in the South to be classed, as white Southerners dearly wished, as simply part of the normal everyday nature of nineteenth-century life, what Johnson ally Major General Gordon Granger called mere "local or specific issues." The problem was, Granger said, that "accounts of these isolated disorders have been collected and grouped together and sown broadcast over the north, so as to give to the public mind an utterly erroneous impression as to the condition of Southern society."[37] The crucial people collecting that information and broadcasting it back were army officers and freedpeople.

Through these reports from the field, soldiers helped prepare the way for the rebirth of occupation by showing Northerners the crucial, but easily misunderstood, role that force played in stabilizing society. Although legal orders typically operate through veneers of consent, defending individual rights in the end relies upon a threat of quick response. "Brute force is very close beneath the surface, even of the most quiet and civilized society," the *Army & Navy Journal* wrote. "There has never been any people yet so enlightened, self-controlled and Christian to be able to dispense with violence and blood. Close behind the majestic form of the judge, stands the broad-shouldered and rough-handed sheriff's office, to seize by brute force the chattels of the party in execution, and promptly to knock down the luckless owner, should he attempt to retain his goods." Freedmen's Bureau agent John William De Forest, who would go on to write popular novels about his time in the South, believed that "many of the planters seemed to be unable to understand that work could be other than a form of slavery." Reconstruction meant "educating the entire population around me to settle their difficulties by the civil law."[38] But paradoxically, requiring people to settle their difficulties under civilian law required the threat of coercion.

Their continued presence in the South radicalized army commanders and prepared them to continue the occupation. From the occupied South, new justifications for the reassertion of military power emerged from previously moderate generals. Some, like Major General Edward O. C. Ord in Arkansas, had come to believe in nothing but force. He wanted a long-term, intensive colonization of the region with about 100,000 troops scattered throughout the former rebel states. Without an increased military intervention, "all the laws which congress can pass are not worth the ink it takes to write them. . . . Agents of the government sent to execute odious laws, (without soldiers), among a well armed and fighting community—become laughing stocks." To keep this force at hand, Ord reached back to a Roman plan of settling retired soldiers on the frontier as a first line of defense. If the army could convince these soldiers to stay in the South for a year after discharge, then "the reconstruction would be Complete—lives and property would have safety where every company settled."[39]

Appalled by white Southern violence, other generals came to believe that the better solution to the problems in the South was to extend the vote to freedpeople. Through this method, they could call upon the powers of occupation one more time to create new conditions and then turn over government to freedmen and white Republicans. Foremost among the converts to this idea was General Ulysses S. Grant. Like Ord, Grant believed that a "sufficiently formidable" number of white Southerners acknowledged "no law but force." Unlike Ord, he saw a solution in enfranchisement, if backed with sufficient military power. It was part of a remarkable series of transitions that showed not only Grant's flexibility but also the way the world had changed. After celebrating peace in April 1865, Grant now proclaimed that the war continued. No longer defining peace by the absence of fighting, Grant now made peace the presence of order. And from expressing grave doubts about suffrage, Grant now came to believe that black voting rights were the best way to remake the South.[40]

Occupation had failed to remake the South in 1866. Buffeted by President Johnson, by the Supreme Court, and by the persistent violent resistance of ex-rebels, the army's powers over the region dwindled. What replaced military authority might look at one level like peace, like the natural reassertion of the civil power of local elites. That is how many white Southerners portrayed their efforts to construct hegemony in the fall and winter of 1866. Through the military's reports, through the petitions and pleas of freedpeople, and through the press coverage of massacres in Memphis and New Orleans, however, white Northerners had come to doubt whether the peace in the South was in fact peace at all, or whether in fact it was simply another stage of the Civil War.

In the South, ex-rebels seemed in command, but the final authority would not be theirs, or even President Johnson's. Instead it would belong to the voters who would go to the polls at the end of the fall of 1866, and upon the Congress that returned in December. Before peace could dawn, they would have to weigh in. As the end of 1866 approached, the occupation on the ground was nearly dead, but the fight to revive war powers was just beginning.

- 7 -

ENFRANCHISEMENT BY MARTIAL LAW

A S HUNDREDS OF congressmen descended from their trains and carriages in Washington, D.C., in December 1866, they stepped back into the fight over ending the Civil War. The president's August proclamation had made it seem as though the war was over. But the president would not have the final say. If peacetime and the supremacy of civilian law depended on the return of the rebel states to Congress, then the House and the Senate would have to be heard before wartime closed. The implications of ending the war remained grave. With the Fourteenth Amendment not yet law, there was no constitutional protection for freedpeople's civil rights; Republicans well knew that ex-slaves depended on military intervention to protect them from discriminatory laws or to safeguard the most basic, concrete rights. Facing these conditions on the ground, Republicans abandoned their strategy of delay; that tactic had evaporated with the president's August proclamation. If Congress held its tongue, the president would withdraw the army; the Supreme Court might recognize the existence of the provisional elected governments; the whole struggle might be lost. Republican congressmen therefore seized their chance to raise the ghost of war. It was the beginning of a new phase, what has been called variously Military, Congressional, or Radical Reconstruction.

Although Republicans quickly coalesced around sustaining the occupation of the South, they disagreed about what would follow. There were several possibilities: a long-term, indefinite occupation that would protect freedpeople's rights with military power but that might risk a Northern backlash at the polls and perhaps damage the country's constitutional order; a short-term use of the military to create new state governments by enfranchising freedpeople; or a decision to let white Southerners choose between occupation and black enfranchisement. At one level, these were marginal differences; almost all Republicans by this point agreed that both black enfranchisement and military enforcement of civil rights were useful. In prioritizing between the two, however, they confronted grave strategic and philosophical questions about the relationship of democracy and liberal rights. They asked whether the vote could protect the civil rights that defined freedom, or whether protection emerged from force. They also asked how long they could remain in the exceptional state of war before it became the new norm. Finally, they asked how much Northern voters could endure. If Congress went too far and alienated Northern voters, a Democratic victory in 1868 would destroy Reconstruction.

In these fights, old divisions between Radicals and moderates no longer mattered as much as they had between 1863 and 1865. The problem of occupation divided the party in new ways. From the summer of 1866 to the summer of 1870, loosely affiliated groups of wartime and peacetime Republicans fought over the best way to secure freedpeople's rights. For peacetime Republicans—a group that included Radicals who believed in the power of democracy to remake society and also constitutionalists like John Bingham who feared undermining the normal processes of law—voting rights became the ultimate prize, and the crucial way to remake the South. If secured, then peace and constitutional normalcy could and indeed must follow, since voting was truly significant only when the elected officials were supreme over military law. In these transformed circumstances, voting shifted from a radical policy in 1864 to a moderate alternative in 1867. It was the safest way to avoid undermining the Constitution any further. Against them, a surprising wartime coalition fused together the ultra-Radical Thaddeus Stevens and the cautiously moderate William Fessenden. What allied them was their shared sense that even after enfranchisement, rights would continue to depend upon force. They were willing to hold peace at the door so that they could continue to use the powers of war until they had secured freedom's gains. They had faith they could sustain war temporarily and then restore the Constitution.

From these struggles, Congress settled on a strange compromise that both temporarily extended war powers and pointed toward peace. For the wartime faction, there would be an explicit reaffirmation of the army's power over military districts in the former Confederate states; civilian law was not yet triumphant, and military safeguards remained. For the peacetime Republicans, there was a path to constitutional normalcy; Congress promised terms to end the war. If the states passed new constitutions that enfranchised black men and also endorsed the Fourteenth Amendment, Congress would seat their representatives, and normal law would resume. To create this path to peace, however, Congress expanded the military's power in a dramatic new way by authorizing it to register voters and oversee constitutional convention elections. Occupation endured, even expanded, but the end point was in sight.

Congress therefore wrested the powers of war from the president. Military Reconstruction, one furious Johnson ally complained, was "nothing less" than a "declaration of war against ten States of this Union." Republicans responded by arguing that the war had never ended. Military Reconstruction was not a declaration of war but merely a new "article of war," a modification of the "action of the military authority which has been exercised since the war began," one congressman said. "We have had no declaration of peace, and have had no peace in fact. . . . We have suspended active hostilities, but we have never given up our occupation of that country by military force."[1]

Because they relied upon military force to make rights meaningful, Republicans made Military Reconstruction with the tools that the 1865–1866 occupation provided them. Congressional Republicans understood—because the events of 1866 taught them—that civil rights depended upon access to a power that could override local law. They also believed that the military constituted the best access point for Southern freedpeople; many Republicans could not see any other mechanism for protection. Therefore, they did not start afresh but renewed the authority the army had held under Presidential Reconstruction, this time with guides in place to try to keep the president from undoing their work.[2]

Republican victories in the fall 1866 midterm elections spurred the party toward action. President Johnson had made the votes a referendum on his policies; he dragged his supporters through a notorious "swing around the circle" and denounced Radical Republicans as traitors. In return, audiences booed and heckled him. "Never was a political campaign so poorly managed," Navy

Secretary Gideon Welles lamented. The election results told the tale of Johnson's miscalculations. The Republican Party, a coalition only a dozen years old,
gained a handful of seats and a veto-proof majority in both the House and the
Senate. "No day's work of recent date will more decisively shape the destinies
of the Republic," the *Army & Navy Journal* editorialized. Although the newly
elected congressmen would not be seated until the next session in March 1867,
their presence shadowed the debates in the lame duck session that began in
December 1866.[3]

Congressmen also responded to the flood of complaints they received about
the violence in the South. Freedpeople and white loyalists bombarded congressmen with pleas and petitions for a "military protectorate" strong enough
to "break in a lawless rebel population." As these letters reached congressmen
like Charles Sumner, Thaddeus Stevens, William Fessenden, and the newly
elected Benjamin Butler, they read from the descriptions on the floor and circulated them among their colleagues to prove the state of war on the ground.
"We need the strong arm of the Govt to restore us to order," a Texas loyalist
wrote to Fessenden. "Troops should be quartered in every county." This led
one congressman to state that there was "war *flagrante* on the part of the rebellious people" of the former Confederate states, "for they give neither justice nor safety to the friends of the Union." "They slay them by night and by
day. . . . If the present condition of the Union men of the South be peace, may
God pity the most courageous and hardy of those whose country is at war!"[4]
The Supreme Court's ruling in the *Milligan* case also raised the dire possibility that the judiciary would end the occupation and leave freedpeople without
protection unless Congress acted. If the court next declared the Southern state
governments legitimate and voided military trials, Congress would be trapped.[5]

The final spur to Republican unity was the ham-handed behavior of
Southern states. Had former rebel states passed the Fourteenth Amendment,
Republicans probably would have divided over reinstating them. Despite the
party's refusal to set peace terms in July 1866, the Tennessee example still mattered. But rebel states saved them the trouble. In the fall elections, white voters
in the former Confederacy elected former secessionists to office. By February
1867, every state rejected the amendment, many by unanimous votes. "Worse
terms may be imposed by Congress," the defiant South Carolina governor Benjamin Perry wrote, "but they will be *imposed* & not *voluntarily accepted*." When
wavering legislatures in Alabama and Virginia considered supporting the
amendment, President Johnson intervened to say that no "possible good can

be attained" by passing it.[6] With the final rejections, Republicans seemed to face a simple choice: either surrender to rebel politicians or fight until they could place different leaders in charge in the region.

As Congress returned, President Johnson used his annual message to stake out the rhetorical ground that the war had come to an end: "Peace, order, tranquillity, and civil authority have been formally declared to exist," he wrote. But most congressmen could not accept Johnson's claim that they lived in a time of peace. In the opening prayer, Reverend Charles B. Boynton pleaded that peace would "be produced by the yielding of those who are wrong." Congressmen themselves openly asserted that wartime continued. "As war against our institutions existed before the firing upon Fort Sumter, so it has existed since the surrender," Republican congressman Ulysses Mercur declared. By dismissing the Fourteenth Amendment, Southern states were "still in rebellion. They have changed their weapons, but their object is the same."[7]

Voting rights emerged early in the session but were no longer a divisive issue for Republicans. Although Republican senators had been afraid to take up this subject in the summer of 1866, the fall elections taught the party that they would not be punished for enfranchising black men. The long grassroots and elite effort to embolden the party on this issue had at last paid off. In a first round of debates about extending the franchise in Washington, D.C., Republicans defended the vote as a method to "give these people the right to protect themselves," as Senator Henry Wilson said. Hoping to unravel support for enfranchisement, President Johnson's allies tried to extend the vote in Washington to women, but Republicans dismissed these efforts as a trick. Suffrage, they claimed, had its roots not in an individual right to be heard but in society's methods for providing protection. The right to vote trickled down from family structures, the "true base or foundation upon which to rest suffrage in any republican community. . . . While every man is king, every woman is queen; but upon him devolves the responsibility of controlling the external relations of his family." Seeing the ballot not as an individual right but as a method for exerting force over society, Republicans tied it also to military service. "The bullet is the inseparable concomitant of the ballot. Those who practice the one must be prepared to practice the other." Overwhelmingly,

Republicans beat back both the women's franchise and a literacy test, and then overrode Johnson's expected veto.[8]

In the rebel states, however, simply extending the vote would not be enough. Instead, the conditions of peace required additional terms. To set the debate on this issue, Thaddeus Stevens added two crucial planks to his initial plan for peace: the disfranchisement of rebels and a permanent federal role in regulating the ex-Confederate states. Under his plan, only men who had not served the Confederacy could vote for delegates to constitutional conventions to remake their states; this provision excluded more than a million white men from voting. Even upon readmission, the states would remain under the federal thumb; if they ever altered their constitutions to discriminate based upon race, they would lose their seats in Congress. It was not the quality of laws but power that determined the meaning of freedom, Stevens said. After another Republican worried that white Southerners would murder black men who tried to vote in these elections, Stevens added an explicit suspension of habeas corpus until Congress readmitted the states. Democrats charged that Stevens's bill was both revolutionary and unjust since it imposed war powers over a peaceful people. Rather than refuting Democratic charges, Republicans embraced the idea that the country remained at war. Treating surrender as a peace treaty was "too absurd for serious consideration," one said. If "submission is not given to the Constitution and laws of the country voluntarily, it should be compelled by the power of the bayonet," another argued.[9]

While most Republicans embraced the extension of war powers, many disliked Stevens's plan to put those states under perpetual supervision. That seemed to change the nature of the peacetime powers forever. Here, Republicans faced a quandary. They wanted to remake the former rebel states but not necessarily the nation. Generally they admired the North's legal and political system and feared that their actions would destroy it. For a month, Republicans considered other plans for peace, including one that would have made the states territories. Peacetime Republicans increasingly coalesced around Ohio's John Bingham, a careful constitutionalist who sought to end occupation quickly and preserve the nation's basic system of government. To push Stevens's bill off the floor, Bingham and his ally James Blaine moved to have the Joint Committee on Reconstruction replace it with one that enfranchised freedpeople and restored Southern states. After weeks of bitter debate, Bingham mustered up an alliance of peacetime Republicans and three dozen Democrats to send Stevens's bill back to the Joint Committee. Occupation seemed near an end.[10]

In the confusion, another plan for peace emerged in a separate bill for Louisiana. Irritated by the House's failure to agree on a Reconstruction bill, the chairman of a select committee to investigate the New Orleans riot introduced a brand-new act that would dismiss the standing government of Louisiana, appoint a loyal provisional council, and call for fall elections where loyal men of both races and some low-ranking Confederate soldiers could vote. Most Republicans (although not peacetime leader John Bingham) unified behind it since it balanced occupation and enfranchisement. In James Garfield's terms, it "shall place civil Governments before these people of the rebel States, and a cordon of bayonets behind them."[11] With its passage, it became clear that many Republicans were willing both to extend military rule and to enfranchise freedpeople; the question was going to be which took precedence.

When the Joint Committee met, it thwarted Bingham and dismissed the idea of peace terms. To Bingham's shock, it did not soften Stevens's bill but instead extended the occupation of the South. Rather than Bingham and Blaine's proposal to restore states in exchange for extending votes to black men, the Joint Committee passed an occupation bill that reinstated war without setting any terms of peace at all. The proposal declared martial law over the rebel states, divvied those states into five districts controlled by commanders appointed by General Grant, and empowered the military to enforce federal laws. It did not set terms for what would follow but left that for future congresses. In the meantime, there would be ongoing occupation. "This is a bill for the purpose of putting under government ten States without governments," Stevens said. "For two years they have been in a state of anarchy. . . . Persecution, exile, murder, have been the order of the day." Under the act, commanders had "the general supervision of the peace, quiet, and the protection of the people." Although the military bill sustained existing local governments for convenience, "they are to be considered of no validity *per se*, of no intrinsic force, no force in consequence of their origins, the question being wholly within the power of the conqueror." Once again Stevens had triumphed by working with his unlikely ally Fessenden, who differed from Stevens in temperament and ideology but shared his wariness for giving up the war powers. Fearful that the government would lose its capacity to intervene in the South once it restored states and ended wartime, Fessenden favored delay because he saw no advantage in rushing toward peace and much to be gained by "military government." Fessenden's coldness led him to the same insight that Stevens found through his passions. They could simply assert the powers of war and then do nothing more, perhaps until after the 1868 presidential election. "It may be as well to wait patiently until they grow wiser," Fessenden wrote to his father.[12]

The Joint Committee's new occupation bill tried to ease the differences in the party by deferring the hard question of the terms of peace until later. From one vantage point, the occupation bill could seem the essence of moderation, a simple extension of the 1866 powers into 1867. "There is no doubt in the world that this military control was too soon relaxed," the *Army & Navy Journal* editorialized. To Garfield, the "time has come when we must lay the heavy hand of military authority upon these rebel communities, and hold them in its grasp till their madness is past." In the House, Republicans took pains to portray the bill not as a new effort but as a simple continuation of Andrew Johnson's pre-August 1866 policies. The most elaborate theorist of war, Samuel Shellabarger, described the condition in the South as war *cessante,* when soldiers no longer fought but the rebellion remained strong enough to "overthrow and defy the courts."[13]

Some Republicans further defended occupation as the best way to protect minority rights. Although everyone acknowledged that normal, peacetime law would have to return someday, more than a few Republicans began to openly praise military rule. They looked to the army as the last, best means of defense, the only available counterweight in a hostile rural land. By maintaining itself as "an appellate power, strong and irresistible, to which the downtrodden and persecuted Union men of the South may appeal from the injustice and the outrage of their enemies and persecutors," the military could recalibrate power relations on the ground, change white Southerners' habits, and "enforce everywhere in the southern States the authority of the United States," one said.[14] If the test of emancipation and Reconstruction was the capacity of the federal government to defend freedpeople in the South, the military might be the best solution.

To Democrats, this celebration of army authority over law threatened the nation's survival. From the time of the American Revolution, U.S. politicians had warned of the dangers of military rule; classical history suggested that republics died at the hands of their armies. Once begun, they argued, an occupation would take on a life of its own until it became "nothing more and nothing less than a military despotism." By extending the occupation after battles, the Republicans had deformed the laws of war. "Theorize as we may, the common sense of mankind will pronounce that when one army totally and unconditionally surrenders to the other the war is at an end," one Indiana Democrat proclaimed.[15]

On the floor of the House, John Bingham and peacetime Republicans once more intervened to use enfranchisement to bring an end to war powers. They moved toward a compromise position that would rely upon the army as a "temporary expedient" to enfranchise freedpeople and create a path to peace. Once the nation crossed the threshold of peace, the war powers would be gone forever. The nation's legal order would resume; the compromises worked out eighty years earlier at the constitutional convention would not be put in jeopardy. "Military authority is not to be exercised an hour after those States shall have been restored to their constitutional relations," Bingham declared. To point a path to peace, Bingham's ally James Blaine offered a bill to restore states that passed the Fourteenth Amendment and enfranchised freedpeople. They would accept the "necessity of martial law," one Bingham ally said, but only if it were tied to a "system, to indicate to them what we require them to do" in "order that they may be rid of the bayonet."[16]

The fight between the occupation and enfranchisement bills tested Republicans' faith in the power of democracy. Some Republicans celebrated the vote as the ultimate line of self-defense. The government should arm black men with the "ballot, that he may not be compelled to arm himself with the pistol and the knife," one congressman said. Drawing from their experiences with relatively peaceful democracies in New England and the upper Midwest, they treated democracy as a force for stability, not as an instigation to further violence. At the extremes, peacetime Republicans argued that democracy made other forms of governance almost irrelevant; it could magically quiet societies. For peacetime Republicans, democracy and liberal rights could be self-reinforcing; people protected rights by voting. By their interpretation, the army had been necessary in the rebel states only because black men could not vote. Posing the choice between ballots and bullets, the influential *Nation* suggested that protection could be gained either by "a good police or by the admission of the blacks to such a share in the management of state affairs that they can provide a police for themselves." Suffrage was "the most far-sighted provision against social disorder, the surest guaranty for peace, prosperity, and public justice," one congressman said. Extending the vote, another congressman said, was the only way to "finish the work which was not completed by warfare."[17]

Although Thaddeus Stevens and other wartime Republicans supported enfranchisement, they were less confident that votes would protect civil rights. Only military force and permanent disenfranchisement of rebels would save freedpeople from the power that planters were already asserting in the South. Therefore it was worth withholding legal normalcy until a method for defending rights was established. Occupation was the only "practicable way of furnishing protection to life, liberty, and property in these ten States," Stevens's ally George Boutwell said. Blaine's bill was an "entire surrender of those States into the hands of the rebels," Stevens said. Peace under those terms would be resignation, an abject submission to the social power that planters exerted in the South. Angling to find allies, Stevens modified the occupation bill by accepting federal (although not state) courts' power to issue writs of habeas corpus for people arrested by the military. He also softened his language on the existing state governments. But he would not accept Bingham and Blaine's peace terms, even though he personally supported black suffrage. If he could not disfranchise leading Confederates, Stevens would prefer military rule.[18]

The fight between peace terms and an indefinite occupation came down to a procedural vote to send Stevens's occupation bill back to committee. There, it might be rewritten to fit Bingham and Blaine's plan for peace and enfranchisement. Pressed to decide between two important values—the extension of the vote and the use of the military to protect civil rights—Republicans divided almost evenly on February 13. The balance of power, then, lay with the small group of Democrats, who hated both options. What Democrats hoped to create was chaos by heightening Republican divisions. They wanted to prevent Republicans from agreeing on a peace plan before the end of the session in early March. Twenty-three Democrats therefore voted to keep Stevens's occupation bill on the floor. Bingham and Blaine's plan for peace was, for the moment, swept aside. As the House then voted on Stevens's occupation bill, the Democrats voted in lockstep against it. Perhaps they hoped that Bingham and his allies would join them in blocking passage; if so, the House would be stymied. But the Republican coalition, despite its internal differences, did not fracture. Having lost the fight to remake the Stevens bill into a peace plan, Bingham, Blaine, and their allies voted for the occupation bill. After it carried overwhelmingly, Stevens crowed, "Heaven rules as yet and there are gods above."[19] For the second time in less than a year, Stevens had defeated peace terms and extended the occupation of the South.

The questions of war and peace, of voting rights and civil rights, now depended upon the Senate. Once again parliamentary maneuvering helped shape the final outcome. When the Senate met, both the Louisiana bill and Stevens's broader occupation act were up for consideration. If the Senate had passed the Louisiana legislation first and remade that state's government, it is possible that the Senate might then have used the occupation bill as a warning to other rebel states: take action or your government, like Louisiana's, will be completely set aside. Or it is possible, if less likely, that the Louisiana bill might have been extended to the entire South; this would have swept away the existing governments and disfranchised some rebels. "Each is excellent," Charles Sumner said. "One is the beginning of a true reconstruction; the other is the beginning of a true protection."[20] Mistakenly confident that the occupation bill would pass quickly, the Louisiana bill's sponsor deferred his act's place in line to let the Senate take up occupation first.

The Senate then agonized over the same question that divided the House: Should a bill extending the war include terms of peace? Under intense pressure from other Republicans, the bill's sponsor, George Williams of Oregon, urged the Senate to extend occupation indefinitely and leave the peace terms for the next Congress. At this crucial juncture, the crusty, sometimes-brilliant Democratic senator Reverdy Johnson intervened. Fearing that the occupation bill would lead either to indefinite military rule or to a new wave of demands on the rebel states, Reverdy Johnson changed the debate by adding peace terms. With peace terms on the table, Republicans now fell to arguing with each other. Some Republicans defended an indefinite occupation. "Are we, who have stood here for five long bloody years and witnessed the exercise of military power over these rebel States, to be frightened now by a declaration" that they would "institute military rule?" Senator Lot Morrill asked. The bill was simply an "article of war" to "preserve order throughout a country where there is no civil authority. That is all." Although Fessenden mostly stayed quiet during this debate, he rejected any "express condition" in peace terms; Congress should not be bound by any promises to restore peace. Peacetime Republicans in the

Senate, however, echoed Bingham's and Blaine's arguments in the House that military rule must be a means, not an end. Every month spent in wartime risked undermining the nation's legal order.[21]

After hours of debate, many Republicans agreed to pass peace terms that included black suffrage. Military government would in fact be not an end but a means. They would intervene, but only briefly and only to restore normal law. They based their bill upon Congressman James Blaine's failed House amendment that both declared a time of war and cleared a path for peace. Stating that there were "no legal State governments" in the rebel states, the bill divided them into five military districts under commanders and granted those commanders power to use military commissions; to return, the states would need to form new constitutions through biracial suffrage. One crucial difference from the House bill was that it gave the president, not Grant, the power to name the district commanders. The act, California Democrat James McDougall complained, would make the commanding generals "pro-consuls here as emperors were made in Rome." But at 6:20 a.m. on Sunday morning, February 17, 1867, Republicans unified to pass it.[22]

Both houses had endorsed war powers; only one had pointed toward peace. Now the question moved back to the House of Representatives, where Stevens and his wartime allies fought against the Senate bill on the grounds that it offered peace without protection. The Senate bill was "fraught with great and permanent danger," George Boutwell argued, because it would give too much power to former rebels. The bill relied upon paper guarantees, a New York Republican complained. "We say to the black man, Go and vote. But it is a mere mockery to say so to him, for he cannot get within half a mile of the polls." Republicans needed to use "the bayonet there to enforce obedience." The Senate had, Pennsylvania's Thomas Williams complained, displaced the House's "protection without reconstruction" for a bill of "reconstruction without protection." Desperately, peacetime Republicans led by James Blaine and John Bingham tried to save the Senate's terms. Although it was important to put the rebel states "under martial law," James Garfield said, it was "equally important to announce to them" the "terms which we require of them." In a sign of the stakes, Senator William Fessenden violated traditional norms by coming on to the House floor to join Thaddeus Stevens in lobbying Republicans to reject the Senate bill. Both Stevens and Fessenden feared that suffrage alone would not be enough to protect freedpeople or remake the South. Better to turn the bill over to a conference committee than surrender the powers of war too lightly. As Republicans split, House Democrats once again held the balance of power. Along with their desire to divide the Republicans, they also saw the benefit of delay; if they could push the settlement into the session's last ten days, then President Johnson would not have to veto the bill formally but could let it die without his signature, a pocket veto that Congress could not override. With the Democrats' support, the Stevens wartime faction rejected the Senate bill and called for a conference committee. Because a conference committee could force both houses to vote on a new bill, it would give the wily Stevens a chance to prevail. [23]

Speaking in support of the conference committee, Fessenden vigorously defended war powers. Sick from dysentery, Fessenden had missed much of the earlier debate, but now he said he preferred the military bill, "pure and simple," over any terms of peace. Therefore, the conference committee gave him the best chance of salvaging war powers. Fessenden's position scrambled the usual Senate alliances. Noted Radical Republican Ben Wade criticized him, but Radical icon—and longtime rival—Charles Sumner leapt to Fessenden's defense. While Sumner and Fessenden disagreed on the precise terms of peace they might accept, they for the moment shared the belief that force, not the franchise, made authority in the South. Drily, Fessenden noted that Wade and others who gloried "in the name of radical" were "not quite so radical on that subject as I am." But the draw of the vote was too alluring for peacetime Republicans. The Senate rejected a conference committee and called the House's bluff. [24]

Once again the House faced the choice between accepting the Senate's peace terms or risking the end of war powers altogether. Democrats in turn used House rules to press for delay in order to push the bill into the last nine days of the session, thus saving President Johnson from having to veto it. Under pressure, House Republicans abandoned an indefinite occupation but made a few key revisions to the Senate bill: they empowered generals to overturn rebel state governments and temporarily excluded from the constitutional convention vote anyone barred from office by the Fourteenth Amendment. They could not, however, muster votes to put the authority to appoint district commanders in Grant's hands. In the Senate, some Republicans disliked disenfranchisement but were relieved to find a pathway to peace. Even Democrat Reverdy Johnson, a staunch opponent of black suffrage, supported the bill because it would show Americans "as a people capable of being in the end, the war terminated, as great in peace."[25] What emerged was a strange compromise. A bill to continue occupation had become a bill to end the occupation. Peace terms, offered as a way to avoid disfranchising rebels, then were altered to include partial disfranchisement.

To the astonishment of many congressmen, President Johnson chose to veto the Military Reconstruction Act even though he could have simply let it die. It is possible that Johnson actually wanted Congress to override his veto; if he pocket vetoed it, he would push the matter to the incoming, even more Republican-dominated Congress. Stevens might then be able to pass an even stricter bill. Johnson also probably relished the chance to denounce the Military Reconstruction Act as a double revolution, of black over white, and of military force over law. The bill "asserts a power in Congress in time of peace to set aside the laws of peace and substitute the laws of war. . . . This bill, in time of peace, makes martial law operate as though we were in actual war, and become the *cause*, instead of the *consequence* of the abrogation of civil authority." The "absolute despotism" the bill granted to officers was to be used, Johnson complained, solely to advance the cause of "Africanizing" the South. In the Senate, as he joined Republicans in overriding the veto, Democrat Reverdy Johnson acknowledged that the bill was "revolutionary" but argued that it presented the only opportunity to forestall permanent military rule. The Senate and House overrode the veto by massive margins.[26]

In other legislation, Congress also moved to undermine President Johnson's control of occupation. Republicans—at the request of Secretary of War Edwin Stanton—required Johnson to issue his orders to the army through General Grant. They hoped this would sustain Grant's power over the occupation. The army appropriations act also affirmed the occupation by disbanding rebel state militias like the one in Mississippi and by empowering the Freedmen's Bureau once again to block whipping. Although Johnson disliked these restrictions, he decided not to veto the bill since the army needed to be paid. In an action that would have an enormous impact on the impeachment trial in 1868,

Congress also protected one of the men responsible for running the occupation, Secretary of War Stanton. Republicans passed a confusingly worded Tenure of Office Act that prevented the president from removing officials without Senate approval. The final wording was ambiguous since it was unclear if it applied to cabinet members, like Stanton, who had been appointed in the prior presidential term. Still it was a warning to Johnson. Congress also passed two bills that extended federal courts' rights to hear habeas corpus petitions and an indemnity bill meant to foreclose lawsuits against the occupying army by legalizing all military commissions, trials, and arrests done under the president's authority up to July 1866.[27]

In a sign of the increasing power of the military within the government, Congress debated extending the army's authority over the West. In a partial echo of Military Reconstruction, some senators hoped to extend army rule there by stripping authority from the Interior Department. Military Reconstruction and the expansion of War Department control over Indian affairs were "the same kind of legislation" that aimed to use the army to create "law and order and justice" in both the South and the West, senators said. But war powers were controversial in the West, as in the South. In the end, Congress refused to place Indian affairs under the War Department; the military had a broadened, temporary control of the South, but there was no permanent expansion of its role across the country.[28]

The powers of occupation continued to expand in March simply because Congress did not go home. Rather than adjourning for nine months and leaving government to the president, the newly elected Congress swore in its members and gaveled into session to regulate the occupation. "We are living in a revolutionary period," Navy Secretary Gideon Welles grumbled. The first, crucial decision was the election of a Senate president pro tempore, to be the next in line if President Johnson died. Although William Fessenden's friends put him forward, firebrand Ben Wade defeated him handily in the Republican caucus, an outcome that would also help shape the impeachment crisis in 1868.[29]

Congress spent the session increasing the powers of occupation in the South by spelling out the army's new—and unprecedented—role in politics there. Although the first Military Reconstruction Act set peace terms, it did not start the process of registering new voters or calling constitutional conventions. Rebel states could delay simply by doing nothing; it was possible, in fact, that the rebel state governments were prohibited from taking any action at all. Although Senator Charles Sumner tried to reopen all the questions of Reconstruction, and some congressmen attempted to use the Louisiana bill as the model for all rebel states, Congress quickly turned toward modifying, not toppling, the just-passed Military Reconstruction Act. The House Judiciary Committee bill gave the commanding general the power to empanel registration boards, require voters to swear oaths that they had had not been disfranchised by the Fourteenth Amendment, and then order an election for delegates to the constitutional convention. Rather than relying upon local governments to steer the path to peace, the army would be in charge of creating new allies. It was a vigorous vision of the army's role in occupation. The army would now be charged with the duty of directing politics. Temporarily, the old division between the military and democratic processes had been erased; it was a bolder occupation than anyone had imagined, even if it was also to be a shorter one.[30]

Once again, the timing of the end of war powers divided Republicans in Congress. The issue turned on esoteric-seeming arguments about the process for passing state constitutions. Congress could either require a majority of all qualified voters or just a majority of those who cast ballots to support the new constitutions. If it held to the higher standard, white Southerners could block the constitutions just by staying home. Peacetime Republicans led by John Bingham feared that higher requirements would lead to an indefinite occupation. Now that the Fourteenth Amendment made it "utterly impossible" that "any advantages shall be taken in all the years to come of these men called freedmen," Bingham wanted to speed to normalcy before any more damage was done. Despite Bingham's arguments, House Republicans held to the higher standard. In the Senate, Sumner and Fessenden united to protect the House's high standard. "We sent to these people a military government" to "protect the loyal people of those States against oppression, the minority from being oppressed by the majority. That was the idea, and the only idea," Fessenden said. Therefore, "we should leave them to work out their own salvation in their own way." But peacetime Republicans led by Senator Lyman Trumbull successfully beat back Fessenden and Sumner and required only a majority to participate. Additionally, in the Senate, William Fessenden tried to slow the arrival of peace by adding another layer of voting at the beginning of the process, asking if electors endorsed calling a convention at all. If they said no, they would remain under military rule. Fearful of extending military government "one day longer than necessary," Republicans rejected Fessenden's amendment.[31]

At the end of their March session, Republicans divided on an issue that had been brewing since the new year, the possibility of impeaching the deeply unpopular President Johnson. Back in January 1867, a few House Republicans had introduced resolutions to impeach Johnson for usurping Congress's control over the war powers. The House agreed on mostly partisan lines to permit the Judiciary Committee to investigate Johnson's conduct. But the resolution's sponsor, James Ashley, failed to produce evidence for his charges. At the end of that session, the Judiciary Committee denied that there was a reason for impeachment. When the new Congress met in early March, Ashley pushed for further investigation. The issue turned on whether Congress adjourned or not. If Congress simply went into recess but retained the right to return in the summer, Ashley hoped the Judiciary Committee might continue to investigate. But several senators—including William Fessenden—wanted to prevent any work on impeachment over the summer because they believed impeachment would alienate the voters. After maneuvering between the House and the Senate, they agreed to adjourn until July. Then the houses would meet only if there was a quorum present, something highly unlikely unless Johnson took dramatic action.[32]

Before they left, Thaddeus Stevens described the revolution that might still come if the war continued. Part wishful thinking and part warning to the South, Stevens's vision was improbable but not impossible. If the rebel states were not readmitted, he argued, the government could seize property under the 1862 confiscation act, apportion forty acres and $50 to each ex-slave head of household, distribute other money to widows, and pay down the national debt. "Where there is no government capable of making terms of peace, the law-making power of the conqueror must fix the terms," his speech read. "The power to dispose of the property of a conquered people is vested in the sovereign law-making power of the nation, which in this Republic is Congress."[33] Because ex-Confederate governments did not accept the terms of peace, the decisions made in Washington in 1866 had not been binding; therefore Congress made new terms. Now, the question was whether the rebel states would accept these new terms or fall back into an extralegal state that would hold open the possibility of revolution.

As congressmen rushed to their trains in April 1867, they had succeeded in grabbing hold of the war powers and taking command of occupation from the president. It had taken two different sessions and two different defenses of wartime, but peace had been kept at bay. With these powers, the army could once again intervene in defense of freedpeople's rights and overturn the oppressive acts of courts and legislatures. It also was charged with protecting freedpeople's entrance into the political system. But the key questions were practical ones about the nature of authority and of rights in the South. Congress's intervention opened up these questions; the answers, however, would come not in Washington, D.C., but back in the ten unrestored states, states held under military law but now promised a path to peace.

– 8 –

BETWEEN BULLETS AND BALLOTS

I N MAY 1867, Republican congressman William Kelley headed south
to offer rebels a compromise: under Military Reconstruction, occupation
would last only until white Southerners accepted freedpeople's voting and
civil rights. If Southern states would protect those rights, then Congress would
offer peace, reconciliation, and a return to local home rule. But compromise
was not on the table. When Kelley reached Mobile, he found a mobilized
and anxious population, as black and white Alabamans organized to gain control of the state constitutional convention. When white hecklers interrupted
Kelley's speech in Mobile, the flustered congressman shifted from talk of compromise to force. Waving at the army band behind him, he said he "had the
Fifteenth Regiment at his back," a *New York Times* correspondent wrote, and
"if they proved inadequate, he would have the whole United States Army."
Undaunted, some white Alabamans charged the stage, and a ruffian fired a
gun. With that shot, the fundamental role of violence in Southern politics
was revealed. In the street both black and white men unholstered their guns
and began firing shots into the air to signal their willingness to defend themselves, while Kelley crouched "under the table." At that moment, the federal
government seemed as irrelevant as the cowering Kelley, but soon its power
re-emerged. Within hours, the local army post commander dispatched his
men to disperse crowds and investigate the shooting. As reports moved up
through the military hierarchy, the military district commander seized control of the Mobile police force, dismissed the mayor, and ordered soldiers to
keep the peace.[1]

As Military Reconstruction shifted from congressional debates to the rebel states, white and black Southerners became once again principal players in the story. Rather than waiting for Congress's guidance, they seized the chance to remake their world. Although Kelley may have expected to deliver news to white and black Southerners, he learned instead that they were already acting on their beliefs. The next step of Military Reconstruction would depend in large part upon those efforts that black and white Southerners took to make and unmake new governments in the South. Military Reconstruction therefore exposed the necessary interdependence of democracy and coercion. When white Southerners in partisan bands blocked voting and stymied the new governments, the army had to act; by acting, it revealed that the states could not stabilize themselves. Under pressure, the occupation became not just a vehicle to oversee elections but, once more, a force to protect rights. Despite these challenges, Military Reconstruction was in a basic way a success. Organized black Southerners allied with some military commanders to try to create new, loyal governments with biracial electorates and protections for civil rights in several states. These governments were, in many ways, the fruits of occupation.

But the fight begun on the ground could not be settled there. In Washington, as complaints and demands trickled up, the conflicts sparked the nation's first ever impeachment of a president. The reverberations of those struggles in Washington would in turn be felt in the South. Military Reconstruction revealed the necessary interdependence of national policy and life on the ground. Back in Mobile, Alabamans' complaints to President Johnson changed conditions once again. In response, Johnson replaced the district commander, and then moved against other generals and Secretary of War Stanton. Then, congressional Republicans faced the choice between abandoning the occupation and fighting back. In a sweeping set of actions, the House impeached Johnson, and both the House and the Senate stripped the Supreme Court of its power to regulate the occupation. Although the Senate failed by one vote to convict and remove Johnson, the effort frightened him and sped the return of newly made, fragile states.

As the November 1868 presidential election approached, Military Reconstruction had proved in many ways a success, as six new states with biracial electorates entered Congress, and the leader of the occupation, Ulysses S. Grant, prepared to assume the presidency. By those lights, the war seemed nearly at an end. But the process of making new states had also exposed their ongoing dependence upon military assistance. As many white Southerners cohered into an organized, violent insurgency to delegitimize these governments, the dangers of returning to civil law were also evident. By November 1868, four states had failed to reconstruct themselves and remained under martial law; even in several of the restored states, governments were nearly helpless to suppress white violence. Already people saw that the normal powers of peace would not be sufficient. Instead of quiet, the South was in a state of near anarchy.

To create democratic state governments and protect freedpeople's rights, the army turned to its old war powers. Once again, it did violence to the law in order to improve it. Taking up the tools of 1865, officers overturned statutes, displaced public officials, refused writs of habeas corpus, and hauled civilians into military courts. The "military law" that prevailed after March 1867 was the same "which existed at the time of Lee's surrender," the *Army & Navy Journal* wrote, because the "state of war" that existed was "the same state of war which prevailed at Lee's surrender." Acting as if the period between August 1866 and March 1867 was simply an aberration, several commanders reissued 1866 general orders empowering officers to intervene to protect freedpeople's rights.[2]

The commanders of these new military districts knew what to do because they had already directed occupations, often in the same states. "They have long partially exercised exactly the same functions, in substantially the same region, and over the same people, as they are now exercising again," the *Army & Navy Journal* wrote. Although President Johnson had the authority to name them, he accepted Grant's recommendations. The first five commanders—John Schofield, Daniel Sickles, John Pope, Edward Ord, and Philip Sheridan—had pre- and postsurrender experience overseeing violent areas in Missouri, Tennessee, the Carolinas, Virginia, Arkansas, Louisiana, and Texas. Some, like Ord, were conservatives who had become radicalized as they tried to occupy insurgent states in 1866; others, like Sickles and Sheridan, were already famously rugged occupiers.[3] In the Department of the Cumberland, Major General George Thomas continued to wield a firm hand over the restored states of Tennessee and Kentucky.

This *Harper's Weekly* sketch of the new military commanders shows Grant in the center, flanked by Sickles, Pope, and Thomas to the left. To the right, Schofield and Ord sit on horseback in the distance while the mustached Sheridan dominates the frame, as he dominated the early political fights over Military Reconstruction. *Harper's Weekly*, April 6, 1867, 216–217. Library of Congress.

In Louisiana and Texas, the bold and fearless Sheridan was Grant's particular favorite. They had, one of Grant's aides later wrote, "the friendship of chieftains." Their relationship was "like a story from Homer." Describing Sheridan's boldness and bravery, Grant had earlier written approvingly, "I saw there were but two words of instruction necessary—go in!" In 1867, Sheridan indeed dove in. Almost immediately, he dismissed people he blamed for the New Orleans massacre of 1866, including the mayor, a local judge, and the state attorney general. His officers followed suit by removing magistrates, judges, and deputy sheriffs in Louisiana and Texas and then the governor of Texas. "It is just the thing," Grant responded. Sheridan also took personal control over registration rules and barred lower-level rebel officeholders from registering even if they wished to take the oath.[4]

Sheridan's moves inspired President Johnson to launch a yearlong counterattack against occupation. At Johnson's behest, Attorney General Henry

Stanbery drew up a memorandum that dismissed the idea that war powers remained. Noting that Congress itself—in one of the maddening ambiguities of the period—had passed a payroll act that seemed to accept the August 1866 proclamation as the end of the war for the purposes of setting soldiers' pay, Stanbery declared that it was a "time of peace." Therefore, commanders only had the "power to preserve, not to abrogate; to sustain the existing frame of social order and civil rule, and not a power to introduce military rule in its place." In peacetime, the army could not remove state officers, convene military commissions, or judge voters' eligibility, but could solely assist the governments in place. "Where peace exists the laws of peace must prevail," he wrote. On June 20, Johnson sent the opinion to the five district commanders with the closing line "by order of the president."[5]

But Johnson could no longer regulate the army or occupation. The *Army & Navy Journal* immediately suggested that officers disregard Stanbery's "illogical, superfluous, unrepublican, and dangerous theory." As Congress once more prepared to reconvene, Grant told his commanders to treat the memorandum as an advisory opinion, not an order, and suggested they ignore it. In its earlier legislation, Congress gave commanders power to be "their own judges" of the Military Reconstruction Acts. Grant and Secretary of War Stanton then developed the novel claim that these laws created an army in the South that received its authority directly from Congress. Therefore Grant provided his commanders with unusually wide discretion and, at times, claimed that in "civil matters I cannot give them an order."[6]

Soon, Congress returned in a special session called to preserve the powers of occupation. Under the threat of losing control of the war, Republicans declared that the rebel state governments were "not legal," that district commanders could—with Grant's approval—suspend or remove officeholders, and that registration boards could exclude ineligible voters. The House tried one more time to prevent the president from removing commanders without Senate consent and to make interference a misdemeanor, but Republican senators would not go along. It seemed too great a change from the country's historical practice of deferring to presidential control of the army. So, too, did the misdemeanor provision raise fears that House Republicans were laying the groundwork for impeachment. Despite these compromises, Andrew Johnson denounced the revised Military Reconstruction bill for plunging a peaceful civil society into a horrific revolution. "Of what avail to demand a trial by jury, process for witnesses, a copy of the indictment, the privilege of counsel, or that greater privilege, the writ of *habeas corpus?*" Johnson wrote in his veto message. Immediately the House and Senate overturned the veto by huge margins. Once again, Republican unity dissolved over the question of impeachment. Charles Sumner and other pro-impeachment Republicans wished to stay in session to "remain as a guard to the Constitution," but Fessenden and other anti-impeachment senators succeeded in forcing Congress to adjourn until the fall.[7]

Backed by Congress, Sheridan now struck again. He removed the entire New Orleans levee board. When Louisiana governor J. Madison Wells protested, President Johnson overruled Sheridan, but Sheridan in turn dismissed the entire city council, the police chief, and Governor Wells himself in an act the *Army & Navy Journal* called "Sheridan's Raid." Fearful that wartime would be decided not by law but by political power, a nervous Grant wrote to Sheridan that the removal "will do great good in your command if you are sustained, but great harm if you are not sustained." He continued, "I shall do all I can to sustain you in it."[8]

The next test of war powers emerged from judges in the Carolinas. Supreme Court Justice Salmon Chase, in a speech at Raleigh, had urged lawyers to act as if peace had returned. The military's role was now "only to prevent illegal violence," not to overrule the federal courts. But the military disagreed. After a New Bern post commander blocked a U.S. marshal from carrying out a judge's order, and Wilmington's commander dismissed a writ of habeas corpus from another federal judge, Major General Daniel Sickles defended his power over the courts. Against mounting criticism, Sickles wrote that allowing federal courts to "disregard military regulations" would "soon nullify all military authority." The army was "paramount to all civil authority except that of Congress.—A great revolution is going on. Order must be maintained."[9]

Once Congress adjourned its special session in July 1867, Johnson moved against the occupation. He began with Secretary of War Stanton, the last Radical holdout in the cabinet. When Stanton refused to resign, Johnson—in a step that would have major implications in his impeachment trial—used the process outlined in the new Tenure of Office Act to suspend him and make Grant the interim secretary. After Sheridan approved the ouster of the Texas state treasurer, attorney general, land commissioner, and comptroller, and Sickles defended his authority over the courts, Johnson removed both of them. Angry and hurt, Grant severed his relationship with the president. No longer would Grant regularly attend cabinet meetings or consult with Johnson. Then, in September, Johnson once more proclaimed that civilian law had been restored and that officers should obey federal courts. Four days later, Johnson extended pardons to everyone except a handful of Confederate department heads, agents, and generals.[10]

In the four months since Sickles's and Sheridan's orders reached Washington, Johnson had promulgated new guidelines for the army, removed two of five commanders, pardoned hundreds of rebels, and proclaimed once again the triumph of civil law. Still, it was not enough to end the state of war. The proclamation had "fallen dead, nobody paying much attention to it," the *Army & Navy Journal* wrote. Inside the army, Major General George Thomas, a Virginia-born conservative, flatly refused Johnson's request that he succeed Sheridan in Louisiana and Texas. Johnson's actions were a "heavy blow" that "will encourage opposition" and make it impossible for the next commander to exert control, Thomas wrote. When Johnson turned instead to conservative major general Winfield Scott Hancock, Grant ignored his prior claim that he could not issue orders and directed Hancock not to reappoint the officials Sheridan had removed.[11]

Once he reached Louisiana and Texas, however, Hancock aggressively resisted the continuation of war powers. "Peace and quiet reign in this department," he proclaimed. "In war it is indispensable to repel force by force, and overthrow and destroy opposition to lawful authority. But when insurrectionary forces have been overthrown, and peace established, and the civil authorities are ready and willing to perform their duties, the military power should cease to lead." Hancock then retracted Sheridan's orders that extended jury service to Louisiana blacks, regulated civil courts, and governed voter registration. Hancock mocked the idea that the "rights of citizens" depended "on the views of the general" and moved soldiers from Texas's plantation belt to its frontiers. When Hancock tried to remove two white and seven black members from Sheridan's New Orleans city council, however, Grant ordered him to stop. Angrily, Hancock asked to be relieved. Hancock had lasted only four months.[12]

Elsewhere, Johnson found it even more difficult to remake the occupation by changing personnel. Johnson could not appoint conservative replacements because the "rebellious and barbarous condition of the south" had hardened generals' attitudes toward ex-Confederates. After touring the rebel states, one

Republican wrote that "every army officer" in the Gulf states was "intensely radical" because of the wild behavior of insurgent ex-Confederates. In the Carolinas, Johnson had appointed the seemingly more-cautious major general Edward Canby in place of Sickles, but Canby was "even worse" than Sickles, the governors of North and South Carolina wrote. Canby followed most of Sickles's practices, including sustaining provost courts, extending jury service to blacks, deposing local officeholders, and refusing to obey federal court rulings. With Grant's encouragement, the relatively moderate Ord and Schofield both empowered registrars to bar disfranchised rebels, despite the attorney general's memo.[13]

To occupy the South, the army constructed a "Military Supervisory Government." Because commanders lacked the capacity to regulate every county in the South, they worked through both accommodation and coercion. By retaining many local officials but threatening to remove recalcitrant ones, officers hoped to keep them in line. Alabama's governor, for example, immediately began conforming to Pope's wishes after the general removed Mobile's leaders. This fit Pope's belief that it was better to sustain officials "where they are (silenced) than by displacing them, make martyrs of them."[14]

More boldly, commanders used war powers to remake laws. Once again, the army ordered its officers to prohibit "whipping or maiming." Pressed by local activists, commanders desegregated New Orleans trolley cars and Carolina steamboats, and ordered equal treatment of black and white paupers. In the Fourth Military District, Ord regulated labor by staying land sales to protect tenants, establishing arbitration boards, and defending workers' rights to remain on the land. More broadly, the generals aimed to induce loyalty by providing services, suspending debt collections, changing licensing laws, voiding fraudulent contracts, setting times for markets, stopping unjust taxes, and rebuilding roads and bridges. Freedmen's Bureau agents also distributed food in 1867 but complained that it bought them little loyalty from whites who "received food one day from the Government or the 'Yankees' and cursed both the next." Other actions aimed to create public safety, such as bans on pistols and other weapons in Florida, South Carolina, Arkansas, and Mississippi, and widespread military regulation of alcohol. To create an atmosphere of obedience, officers ordered local leaders to salute the national flag, arrested men for trampling the flag, and told newspaper editors not to insult soldiers. Pope distributed all state and county public document contracts to the small number of newspapers that favored Reconstruction. When Ord directed the arrest of Vicksburg, Mississippi, editor William McCardle for calling the commander a "contemptible liar and braggart," the editor responded by suing, and his lawsuit eventually prompted Republicans' most revolutionary effort to preserve occupation.[15]

During Military Reconstruction, the army turned itself once again into a police and prison system. They made arrests and carted men back to military posts. In Selma, outlaw Milton Malone had been arrested twenty times by local police over 1866 and 1867 but never convicted. When Malone once again fired on soldiers and local magistrates refused to prosecute him, the local commander arrested and held him in prison to send a message to other whites. After the post commander in Huntsville, Alabama, heard that young boys blacked the face of a Republican in Athens, he sent a squad of soldiers to hold them until they had learned their lesson. While the army generally let criminal courts handle cases between white people, it took control of many crimes charged against black men. This meant, curiously, that the increase in military power led to more black people in military jails, kept there to keep them out of local jails and courts until their cases were judged.[16]

The army once again turned to its shadow legal system of military commissions. This was the clearest proof of wartime; the Supreme Court had already ruled in the *Milligan* case that military courts could not try civilians during peace, but the military commanders showed it was not a time of peace. In the seven states where commanders desegregated juries, generals mostly supplemented local law. But where the army did not rewrite the rules of jury service—in Virginia, Arkansas, and Mississippi—military justice came close to replacing civil law altogether. In Virginia, General Schofield established one of the most far-reaching military justice systems, creating thirty military divisions where officers commanded judges, police, and sheriffs. In Arkansas and Mississippi, Ord moved almost all aggravated cases to military commissions. But commanders struggled to staff a legal system that tripled their workload, as one complained, without any additional manpower. "Justice is unknown here," Pope wrote. "I have neither the officers nor the means" to take "all criminal cases." Some commanders sent most cases to civilian courts but pulled out troubling ones on appeal. In others, especially Arkansas, officers—in clear violation of military regulations—added trials to the bustling courts-martial system they used to discipline their own men. Meanwhile, North Carolina officers reinstated the provost courts. Of the nearly 500 civilians tried in the Carolinas between May 1867 and August 1868, some were tried before military commissions, others before the provost courts, and yet others before post courts-martial. In all, there were 285 military commission trials in 1867 and 1868, though these numbers do not include civilians tried under other military courts.[17]

This new legal authority opened up avenues of access for freedpeople and poorer whites. An Arkansas woman discovered this when a sheriff raped her and then threatened to charge her with a crime. Normally she would have been unable to find any justice, but after she complained to an army officer, a military commission tried the sheriff. When a Jasper County, Georgia, man killed a black woman who would not leave her husband, the local sheriff refused to arrest him, but a military commission intervened. In Texas in the summer of 1867, the army stripped ten cases away from local courts because it believed the white men would not be convicted of assaulting U.S. soldiers, murdering freedpeople, blocking black men from registering to vote, and shooting registrars. These men, like the Arkansas sheriff, faced a transformed society. Instead of acting with impunity, they could be held to account. Yet cases like these also illustrate one of the limitations of occupation, for they required enormous expenditures of force to prosecute a handful of people. Military commissions could not easily replace everyday law everywhere in the former Confederacy. They were also ineffective at regulating the South because they aimed to provide substantive justice, not prosecute the war. Georgia commissions acquitted sheriffs for neglect of duty and civilians for lynching. Arkansas and Mississippi commissions acquitted ten of fourteen whites charged with murder and fifteen of twenty-three people charged with property crimes. This spoke well of the commissions' procedures but not of their capacity to subdue the South.[18]

Unable to regulate the rebel states through top-down policies or substitute legal systems, the military had to rely upon a sense of awe. Therefore, occupation turned upon the size and spread of the army. Despite the period's name, the size of the military did not increase during Military Reconstruction. The number of soldiers in the South in fact fell slowly but steadily over the period, from 23,000 in February 1867 to 20,000 by October. In both the South and the West, the army faced expanding duties with shrinking forces. In part this was the result of Andrew Johnson's determination to force peace. Secretary of War Stanton had urged the president in March 1867 to use his discretionary power to expand the military to nearly 100,000 men, but Johnson flatly refused. Therefore, numbers drifted downward. Virginia lost 800 soldiers during this period, Louisiana almost 1,400, the reconstructed state of Tennessee another 1,000. In Mississippi and Arkansas, Ord lobbied for eight to ten additional regiments in each state but received only one for Arkansas and two for Mississippi. If Reconstruction failed for lack of force, Grant's aide wrote to Ord, "the responsibility will not rest upon you" but upon the president and Congress. Nevertheless, the South remained the focus of the army and was better staffed than the West. Over the winter of 1867–1868, almost 270 companies—more than 40 percent of all available—were stationed in the former Confederacy. Counting the border states and the District of Columbia, there were nearly 100 more companies in the Southeast than in the entire West. Leaving aside Texas, where seventy-five companies were spread across the plantation belt and the frontier, the other Confederate states held another 190 companies, more than 30 percent of all companies in the army. By contrast, the Great Plains had 144 companies, or about 22 percent of the total; the Southwest 63, or 10 percent; and the Pacific coast about 35, or 5 percent of the total.[19] (See Appendix 8.)

Despite these declining numbers, the army expanded its reach across the countryside to recreate a geographically expansive sense of national sovereignty. From seventy-nine posts in the non-Texas rebel states in February, the total expanded to ninety-three in May. The most dramatic change was in Mississippi, which increased from five posts in February to nine in May and fifteen in October, covering places like Meridian, Columbus, Corinth, Holly Springs, and Lauderdale. In Florida, commanders spread soldiers to interior posts at Lake City, Tallahassee, Gainesville, and at least eight additional spots. In other states, especially Arkansas, commanders retracted their posts because they feared being overwhelmed by outlaws.[20] While generals reversed the centripetal forces that drew in army posts in 1866, they could not match the sweeping coverage of the fall of 1865.

Although these posts had limited manpower, freedpeople and white loyalists gave evidence of their effectiveness as they streamed in from the countryside, carrying complaints and information to post commanders. People shut out from civil law suddenly found avenues of appeal and potential allies. Where

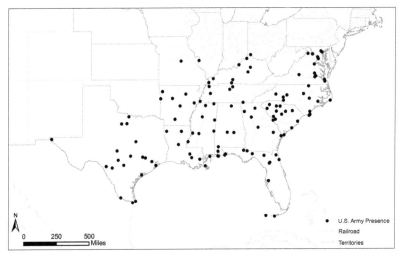

U.S. Army presence, March–May 1867. University of Richmond Digital Scholarship
Laboratory.

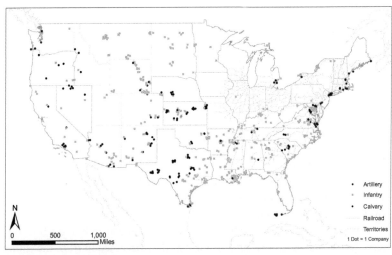

U.S. Army presence, 1868. University of Richmond Digital Scholarship Laboratory.

post commanders conducted regular low-level courts, especially in the Carolinas, the post became a center of activity all day and night, as crowds gathered for a chance to be heard. Zenas Bliss, stationed in South Carolina, opened court each morning and saw twenty to one hundred freedpeople per day in four-hour sessions where he slung "law and decisions around with a rapidity and recklessness that would have astonished a Webster or a Choate." Despite their haphazard nature, these courts were crucial ways for freedpeople to engage with the legal system. They helped sustain freedpeople's faith that the federal government might be turned to their ends. They also gave women access to powers beyond the household. This was most striking for women who complained about rape and harassment at the hands of white men, crimes for which there would have been no recourse prior to emancipation. But the presence of these courts also reshaped gender relations within black families, as women complained, with varying degrees of effectiveness, about their husbands.[21]

As physical spaces, the posts were unimpressive but important circles of safety for freedpeople and white loyalists. Some posts were formal barracks, often constructed just beyond the edge of town where soldiers would be accessible but not intrusive. Others were haphazard reconstructions of abandoned buildings, "mere hovels" where "day light can be seen through nearly every square foot of the roof." Many soldiers camped in tents—sweltering in the summer, freezing in the winter—either on the courthouse square or in swamps and fields beyond the edge of town. A great deal of the work at such posts was mundane. Before they could function as disruptive courts or alternative power sources, they had to sustain themselves. Soldiers spent long hours drilling and taking roll calls, as their officers struggled to sustain morale and discipline. The long list of courts-martial and the occasional suicide testified to the challenge this posed. Some soldiers spent almost all their time managing supply warehouses or guarding military jails. But others did quite a bit more. Perhaps the most poignant vision of posts as islands of refuge came from Baton Rouge, Louisiana, where a group of freedpeople moved inside the barrack grounds in the spring of 1867 and began farming small plots of land there. Although they did not leave direct evidence of their motives, presumably they were fleeing from the violence that engulfed the countryside. When a general tried to evict them, the local post commander fought to keep them in place until they harvested their crops.[22]

For white rebels, the posts were often hated and dangerous places, the site not of romances but of grudges. Near Mobile, Alabama, Captain Morris

Schaff feuded with and then killed ex-Confederate colonel Frederic Shepard. Soldiers in Camden, Arkansas, broke into the office of the *Constitutional Eagle* and threw the newspaper's press into the river; other soldiers fought with local law enforcement. To forestall conflict, commanders tried to limit contact by setting up across the river from town or on its outskirts. Where they camped on the courthouse square, as in Marksville, Louisiana, they were allowed an hour of free time during daylight. More prosaically, the court-martial records indicated that soldiers fell less into sympathy than into lassitude, as hundreds were brought up for sleeping on guard duty, drinking, going absent without leave, stealing supplies, deserting, and committing petty crimes.[23]

The posts were also staging grounds for excursions into the surrounding countryside to enforce rights and to "preserve the peace." When complaints reached them of crimes and unruly gatherings, soldiers often set out in detachments of five to fifteen men. Tangibly, they were charged with making arrests, running night patrols, resolving disputes, and transporting prisoners. Their goal was to restore that stability they called peace. But they were often outnumbered. In Columbus, Georgia, a company of roughly sixty men monitored a sixteen-county region without reliable communication. Once the post of Hilton Head returned its horses in the summer of 1867, the region it covered largely was beyond its control. "We are now without law," a local man wrote. Although the Hilton Head post commander was "indefatigable," he was also "powerless." Beyond those zones of control, white insurgents launched partisan attacks against freedpeople and other enemies. Outlawry and an organizing insurgency fed on each other. Around Kinston, North Carolina, a "gang of desperadoes" overpowered local law enforcement, broke into jails, murdered more than a dozen men, and created a general sense of anarchy. In Texas, whites at Fort Mason killed an army officer, and outlaws attacked the town of Bonham in hopes of capturing the Freedmen's Bureau agent there. There was a "war upon Union men by a desperate faction."[24] In the midst of all this fighting, army posts were sometimes forces of stability, sometimes just small islands of peace in a sea of conflict.

The army's most complicated work was preparing the way for constitutional conventions. The military did not have to teach people to value the elections.

Across the South, freedpeople convened large assemblies to prepare for the votes to come. Union Leagues became natural vehicles for black and white Republican organizing. But translating that enthusiasm into power required military assistance. Major General John Pope appointed mixed-race registration boards to ensure that blacks could sign up; one of those new registrars in Georgia was Sea Island leader Tunis Campbell. During registration, the army was largely able to keep the peace around registration books. More than 600,000 black men registered to vote in the rebel states. But as convention elections approached, the challenges were greater. In votes for constitutional conventions between September and November, each state but Texas (which lagged until February 1868) selected delegates. Scattered efforts to intimidate voters began almost immediately. In Asheville, North Carolina, a "premeditated conspiracy" launched simultaneous assaults on leading Republicans just before registration to frighten people into staying home. In Black Bayou in Caddo Parish, Louisiana, white men on horseback attacked an evening Republican meeting and shot a white Republican dead on the highway. Assaults like these aimed to disrupt the formation of a civil society that democracy depended upon, to make democracy itself a wartime act, to turn the vote into a pledge to fight. Against this, the army arrested offenders, positioned soldiers near the polls to "pursue and punish rioters," seized firearms, and closed barrooms. The army succeeded in creating enough stability for the constitutional conventions to begin; in every state more than half the registered voters turned out. The sight of black people voting for the first time in places like Palestine, Texas, was a remarkable symbol of the transformation of society, even though the presence of U.S. soldiers was a grim reminder of the tenuousness of the change. The results, while bold, were easy to overstate. There were worrying signs. Only in North Carolina and Virginia did a majority of white registered voters appear, and in South Carolina and Florida only 10 percent of white registered voters showed up. If elections were meant to provide emblems of consent that could end the war, they were not fulfilling the task. The army could run elections, but it could not compel people to participate.[25]

Between November 1867 and February 1868, each Southern state (except Texas, which was delayed until June 1868) convened a constitutional convention to create a new state capable of making peace and returning to Congress. These new conventions illustrated the transformation Reconstruction had wrought; they were the offspring of occupation. Of the roughly 1,000 delegates across the Southern states, there were about 265 black men, coming most

Freedpeople vote for the first time in 1868 at Anderson County Courthouse, Texas. U.S. soldiers stand guard to protect them. Palestine Public Library, Texas.

significantly from plantation belts in states where there were few native-born Republicans and in regions of South Carolina, Louisiana, and Florida held under long-term occupation. In South Carolina, 76 of the 124 delegates were black. In these conventions, men like South Carolina's Robert Smalls and Georgia's Tunis Campbell once more emerged as leaders. Smalls, a slave who had become a celebrity by piloting a Confederate ship out of Charleston Harbor and turning it over to the U.S. Navy, had returned to his native Beaufort and purchased his master's home. Less than six years after his escape, Smalls joined the South Carolina constitutional convention that enfranchised black men, extended civil rights, and created the public school system. In Georgia, Tunis Campbell—the deposed Freedmen's Bureau agent in the Sea Islands—also flourished in the new elections, becoming a delegate to the state's constitutional convention. Both would be elected to the state legislature too. These conventions overturned the political world of the South. They not only enfranchised freedmen and expanded public schooling but outlawed whipping, imprisonment for debt, and property qualifications for voting. They were signal locations for the expansion of the meaning of rights; some even considered extending the vote to women. All together, the constitutions they produced were hallmarks of democracy and economic development, efforts to construct new, modern governments in place of nearly aristocratic regimes. But they divided over the crucial question of whether ex-Confederates should be able to vote. In Alabama, Arkansas, Mississippi, Louisiana, and Virginia, conventions barred significant numbers of rebels from voting; Georgia, Florida, Texas, North Carolina, and South Carolina placed few restrictions.[26]

Instead of pacifying the region, the expansion of democracy accelerated the violence. While delegates debated legal forms inside convention halls over the winter of 1867–1868, partisans and freedpeople fought openly for control of space. Looking forward to springtime elections, both white and black Southerners mobilized into increasingly organized paramilitary forces. Most famously, white partisans bound themselves together in Tennessee under the mantle of the Ku Klux Klan, which spread from there to Georgia and the Carolinas. Other white partisan organizations, such as the Knights of the White Camellia, originated prior to or synchronous with the Klan in intensely violent southwestern states. In Texas, there were more than 300 homicides in 1867 and another 300 in the first six months of 1868. In Louisiana, a band of 3,000 "knights" patrolled Opelousas, murdered a parish leader, and destroyed the Republican newspaper. Some white men fought for their old sense of their rights, the view that "every master was a magistrate, and every overseer a sheriff," as some South Carolinians wrote. They had been the civil authority and did not intend to let federal regulations displace them.[27]

Freedpeople organized themselves into paramilitary organizations by remaking Northern-founded Union and Loyal leagues. In their meetings, freedmen assumed military titles, debated political issues, swore loyalty to the Republican Party, and pledged to defend themselves against white attacks. The line between self-defense and aggressive claims of space was in the eye of the beholder. Union and Loyal leagues did not simply wait to repulse white attacks but instead demonstrated their force to frighten off partisans and to intimidate black Democrats into silence. Around Black Bayou and Benton and Amite, Louisiana, black Republican clubs formed lines of battle and marched in formation. Local whites claimed that freedmen "believe that they are militia acting under the authority of the Government." These public displays sent the message that freedpeople intended to create a new "public order" and enforce justice as they "commenced patrolling the neighborhood," a Freedmen's Bureau agent wrote from South Carolina. Inspired both by long-standing dreams of acquiring farms and rumors that Republicans might confiscate land during Military Reconstruction, fiery organizers like Aaron Bradley and Solomon Talley drilled companies almost nightly in the plantation belts south of Savannah. Around Portsmouth, Virginia, freedpeople forcibly blocked a planter from reclaiming land they had settled during the war. In heavily black parishes in Louisiana and South Carolina, fearful whites asked for military troops to put down these organizations, in some cases even expressing a willingness for black soldiers. While officers sometimes intervened to stop black bands from counterattacking, some commanders, like Pope, actually wished freedpeople were more violent. Nothing else, he believed, could frighten white Southerners into submission.[28]

During the constitutional ratification elections between February and May 1868, partisan insurgencies spread over the rest of the South. Rebels helped mobilize opposition to the constitutions in Arkansas, Georgia, North Carolina, and Louisiana, and defeated the constitution in Mississippi. Klansman themselves seem to have carried organizing tactics to Georgia and North Carolina, while in Louisiana and Arkansas partisans drew on their own local organizations. One of the most startling attacks occurred in Georgia, where fifty white men in disguise shot constitutional convention leader George Ashburn to death in his home at the end of March. When the local authorities would not respond, the commander took possession of the town government, banned threatening notices, and arrested twenty-nine citizens, including two policemen, a doctor, and a lawyer. After ordering a military commission to try them, the commanding general asked for additional troops to subdue the state and received eight extra companies to place at voting precincts. Still, partisans held sway in a "reign of terror" around Columbus and killed at least eight people near Albany. Across the South, Klansmen attacked Freedmen's Bureau agents as well as politicians and leading freedmen, aiming to destroy the Republican Party. By invading homes, raping wives, and attacking children, white vigilantes hoped to emasculate male leaders and demoralize black people. In turn, freedpeople responded by public demonstrations of their force and their bravery, countering the narrative of emasculation with a hypermasculine politics of performance. Democracy had become a pitched battle between opponents, one that engulfed not only the public arena of speeches and precincts but also the private realm of home and family. Against this escalating conflict, the army turned once again to martial law.[29]

As the president, the army, Congress, white rebels, and freedpeople scrambled to determine the shape of the war, the elections of 1867 reminded them that public opinion in the North would also have its say. In one of the most disheartening moments for Republicans, Northern states turned against them in a series of 1867 votes. In the twenty states that cast ballots between March and November, Republican support dwindled almost everywhere. Early in the year, Connecticut displaced a Republican governor for a Democrat; Democrats swept California and won victories in New Jersey, Ohio, Pennsylvania, and New York. Minnesota and Kansas voters rejected black suffrage. Even in stalwart Massachusetts, the Republican share of the vote fell from 77 to 58 percent. The biggest blow was in Ohio, where the Democratic victory in the legislature denied Senator Ben Wade's bid for reelection. In Ohio and New Jersey, new legislatures tried to rescind the earlier approval of the Fourteenth Amendment. Although some of the defeats were narrow, the losses devastated Republican morale in the fall of 1867. "The chief trouble no doubt, is the suffrage question," Republican senator John Sherman wrote. "We will have to carry it because it is right but it will be a burden in every election." A cheered President Johnson wrote, "God bless Ohio!"[30]

Believing that he had the public behind him, President Johnson late in the fall once more moved to force the war's end. In a virulently racist message to Congress, Johnson denounced Military Reconstruction as tyranny that bound Southern whites "hand and foot in absolute slavery." When a Mobile editor wrote to complain that the new state constitution "simply Africanizes Alabama," Johnson removed Major General Pope and state Freedmen's Bureau commissioner Wager Swayne. At the same time he accepted Major General Ord's request to be relieved on medical grounds. Pope himself doubted the removals would make much difference. His replacement, Major General George Meade, would be "warred upon as I have been" by white partisans. "It is a misnomer to call this question in the South a political question—It is *War* pure & simple." Although Meade initially promised to defer to civilian authorities, Pope's judgment was borne out. After Georgia's governor and treasurer refused to pay the constitutional convention's expenses, Meade summarily removed them and also refused to obey a federal writ of habeas corpus.[31]

In response to Johnson's attacks, congressional Republicans simultaneously defended the powers of war and began to speed the return of peace. Once again, the House voted to strip Johnson of the authority to remove district commanders, though the bill died again in the Senate. Republicans also started to soften the terms they had set for rebel states. A year earlier, they had required half of all voters to participate in the ratification elections. When an Alabama boycott kept turnout below 50 percent, however, Republicans no longer had the heart for delay, and they retracted the requirement. Congress's revision ended the partisan strategy of boycotting elections; Arkansas, Georgia, Louisiana, North Carolina, and South Carolina passed their constitutions with sufficient turnout in March and April of 1868.[32]

Over the winter, Congress also went to great lengths to protect occupation from the Supreme Court. The Court considered a case from Mississippi that threatened to end the military's power over civil law in the rebel states. Mississippi editor William McCardle had been arrested and charged by a military commission for cheerfully predicting the lynching of Major General Ord. McCardle sued on the grounds that he could not be tried by a military court in peacetime. At stake was the army's right to take control of the courts in the South. Although a lower court refused to hear the case, since Congress made the courts "subject to the military commander," the Supreme Court accepted it. Immediately, Republicans realized they would have to act quickly or risk losing the occupation of the South; without army control over civilian law, Southern courts would demand the release of all military prisoners and would begin indicting soldiers. Republicans therefore stripped away the Court's jurisdiction by repealing a section of the 1867 Habeas Corpus Act that had permitted appeals from the rebel states. Democrats complained that the Republicans ignored the fact that the "war ended in April 1865" and cast aside the protections of law for force. Nevertheless, Republicans united to override Johnson's veto. By limiting Supreme Court jurisdiction, Republicans once again demonstrated their peculiar stance as republican revolutionaries. Unlike other revolutionaries, they approached problems cautiously, but once they settled on a course of action, they were willing to go beyond law and the Constitution to preserve it. If the normal legal order would not protect the war powers they needed, they would alter or bypass that legal order. It was, one of President Johnson's correspondents wrote, "a Jacobinical attack." It was also a measure to restrain more comprehensive change. Some fed-up Republicans were ready to strip the Supreme Court of its jurisdiction over any political case or to require super majority votes on the court. Removing this case temporarily protected both the occupation and the constitutional balance.[33]

The Republicans' most grueling fight to save occupation was their defense of Secretary of War Edwin Stanton. From the first days of Johnson's administration, Stanton had been the key defender of occupation and the crucial conduit between the cabinet and congressional Republicans. Although Johnson had shied away from direct conflict in hopes that Stanton would resign, by the late summer of 1867 the president had had enough. Johnson suspended Stanton under the Tenure of Office Act. When Congress returned in the winter, Johnson asked the Senate to approve his permanent removal, as the Tenure of Office Act required. Instead, Republican senators defended the secretary of war in hopes of saving the occupation of the South. Increasingly desperate to rein in the army, Johnson ignored the Senate and fired Stanton. When the president appointed a new interim secretary, Stanton refused to leave his post, and the competing secretaries of war occupied separate offices, while war veterans posted guards outside Stanton's door to prevent the president from removing him by force.[34] It was the ultimate test of the president's power over the war.

House Republicans defended both Stanton and the occupation by impeaching Andrew Johnson. When the news of Stanton's removal reached the House floor, a congressman called out that all in favor of impeachment should stand up, and every single Republican rose to his feet. The same day, the Senate, by a vote of 28–6, passed a resolution denying that Johnson had a right to dismiss Stanton, although it was notable that Fessenden and a few other Republicans abstained from the vote. The House impeached Johnson anyway by a tally of 126–47. For more than a year, peacetime Republicans such as John Bingham and James Blaine had resisted impeachment, but Johnson's attack on Stanton, and Major General Winfield Scott Hancock's efforts to stymie occupation in Louisiana, had turned the tide. In a sign of Republicans' consensus, Bingham squired his nemesis Thaddeus Stevens through the hall as the faltering old Radical chided his colleagues. "What good did your moderation do you?" he asked. "If you don't kill the beast, it will kill you."[35]

Now, the power to remove the president lay in the hands of the Senate. At first a conviction seemed likely, as Republicans held a 45–9 advantage, well over the Constitution's requirement of a two-thirds majority. But three Republicans almost always voted with the Democrats, and others indicated early on that they would not favor impeachment. For the remainder, the crucial question was whether a president could be removed for political reasons or only for a criminal act. William Fessenden, Lyman Trumbull, and two other Republicans came to believe that impeachment could only be criminal. Their votes turned on whether Stanton was actually covered by the Tenure of Office Act's ambiguous language. Believing not, they did not think Johnson had committed a crime and so would not vote to convict. Senators could not judge the entirety of Johnson's "deeds and acts," Lyman Trumbull said, only whether the president committed a crime. To Fessenden, impeachment set a terrible precedent for the future, a precedent that war powers by their nature avoided. Going beyond the Constitution temporarily did not risk the republican balance, but removing a president might "shake the faith of friends of constitutional liberty in the permanency of our free institutions," Fessenden worried.[36] Beyond these issues, Fessenden, Trumbull, and others disliked and distrusted Senate president pro tempore Ben Wade, who would become president upon Johnson's removal.

House Republicans argued that impeachment was not a criminal trial but a fight to save occupation. While the legalistic John Bingham wished to focus on the technical violation of the Tenure of Office Act, Thaddeus Stevens and Benjamin Butler emphasized Johnson's political efforts to undermine the legitimacy of both Congress and Military Reconstruction. These political charges commanded the strongest support among Republican senators like John Sherman. To protect occupation, Congress had altered the basic structure of government and stripped the presidency of its normal powers. Instead of further changing the government to rein in this president, many thought the Senate should simply replace the president and put the old structure back in place. It would be "wrong to exonerate" Johnson "upon a mere technicality" when his "animus" was "offensively conspicuous in his assignments and changes of the commanders of the several military departments, and especially by the removal of General Sheridan and the appointment of General Hancock," Republican senator Justin Morrill said. To Senator Samuel Pomeroy, removing the president was the only way to reach "peace."[37]

Had the impeachment trial moved quickly, Johnson might have been convicted. Instead, it dragged deep into April and May. During that time, events in the South shifted the relationship between the impeachment and the occupation by bringing several states to the verge of readmission. This would reduce the army's role and therefore Johnson's potential for making mischief. Between February and mid-May, seven states voted on their constitutions and stood at the doorstep of peace. The House passed bills in May to readmit the Carolinas, Louisiana, Georgia, Alabama, and Arkansas. Although the Senate did not take up those bills during the impeachment trial, it was clear that occupation was close to its end in some places. This lowered the stakes of Johnson's survival.[38]

Johnson also undercut support for impeachment by leaving the occupation alone. Under orders from his lawyers, Johnson kept his hands off the army in the rebel states and let a supplementary Reconstruction act become law. To quiet Trumbull's and Fessenden's fears, he promised to select an acceptable military man as the new secretary of war, Major General John Schofield. "Andrew Johnson has been a changed man," the Republican Chicago *Tribune* wrote. "The country has been at peace." The impeachment trial saved occupation by handcuffing Johnson; in turn Johnson's restraint undermined impeachment.[39]

Practically, conviction turned upon the question of whether Johnson could gain a few more Republican votes. As late as mid-April, Fessenden and many others expected Johnson to be convicted, but by May the vote looked very close. Rather than beginning with the violation of the Tenure of Office Act, the Senate opened with the article that seemed weakest legally but strongest politically, the catchall resolution that charged Johnson with undermining occupation and Congress's legitimacy. Although the vast majority of Republicans voted to convict, they came up one vote short. Talk quickly swirled that Missouri's senators had been bribed. Bingham sank his head in his hands. Someone in the crowd called Fessenden a "villainous traitor" for voting no. A furious Thaddeus Stevens said, "The country is going to the devil." Disheartened Republicans adjourned the Senate for more than a week. When they returned, they fared no better on the other impeachment counts. Stanton abandoned his War Department office and retired to private life.[40] The House Republicans had failed to remove Johnson. Nevertheless, impeachment had not been itself a failure. It bought crucial time between March and May for the army to complete its work in several Southern states without Johnson's interference, and it also prevented Johnson from undermining occupation by naming a conciliatory secretary of war.

After the failure of impeachment, congressional Republicans pivoted sharply toward peacetime. Although there were technical problems in Alabama and Arkansas, Republicans were in no mood to delay now that there were state constitutions that protected black voting rights. Those states, as well as the Carolinas, Georgia, Alabama, and Florida, would be represented in Congress, the occupation there curtailed, peacetime restored. The remaining challenge was once again the terms of readmission. Did wartime create permanent or merely temporary changes in the power of the federal government over the states? Would peacetime place the readmitted states on the same footing as every other state, or would the federal government claim the ongoing right to intervene? In a desperate effort to preserve national power, Thaddeus Stevens tried to block the readmitted states from depriving any male citizen of the vote, but peacetime Republicans such as John Bingham and Lyman Trumbull believed the United States had no power to enforce those conditions once wartime ended. "The real protection is to be found in the freedom we have given them, and the ballot we have given them," Trumbull said. "They will protect themselves." Senators passed token conditions requiring that the readmitted states not exclude voters based on race, but they did not include a practical mechanism for penalizing states that violated the terms.[41]

Admitting the states also helped pave the way to peacetime by leading to the ratification of the Fourteenth Amendment. Passed by Congress in the summer of 1866, the Fourteenth Amendment established birthright citizenship, the bundle of rights that citizens possessed, and the method for reducing the representation of Southern states that excluded black voters. Over 1866 and 1867, most Northern states ratified it. But there were several problems with getting the approval of the necessary three-fourths of the states that would place the amendment in the Constitution. The rebel states had rejected the amendment in 1866–1867, along with Kentucky, Delaware, and Maryland. Democrats who won victories in New Jersey and Ohio retracted their states' approval in early 1868. Although no one quite knew what retraction meant, it increased the pressure to get the amendment into the Constitution before

Democrats pulled any more states back. Finally, there remained the puzzling question of whether the rebel states not represented in Congress could in fact be counted as having approved the amendment. By seating the ex-Confederate states that passed the amendment, Republicans safeguarded it.[42] One of the great foundations of American law therefore depended on military rule to become part of the permanent Constitution. With the amendment, and with several states seated in Congress, in much of the South the state of war was over.

Despite their bold plans, Republicans continued to struggle over the ongoing need for force. Although they expanded the military's role, many Republicans still wanted to shrink the actual army. To try to appease budget cutters without slashing the military too quickly, both Congressman James Garfield and Senator Henry Wilson offered bills that let the army drift downward by a process of attrition. In the meantime, the army could sustain occupations in the South and the West. But Republican Benjamin Butler, a radical icon who nursed a bitter grudge against the army from his own wartime service, led an alliance of Democrats and some Radical Republicans to force immediate reductions. While Democrats opposed the army for ideological reasons, the Radicals who followed Butler seemed to exemplify Reconstruction leader and novelist Albion Tourgée's complaint that the North foolishly would not "perform the duty laid upon it as a conqueror." Under pressure, Garfield buried the issue in committee, believing it better to do nothing than to cut the army too far. Republicans also wrestled with the nature of force as they assessed the need for militias in the restored Southern states. Fearful of the rise of Ku Klux Klan violence in the South, they tried to send weapons to those new militias. If rebels "want war," one Republican senator said, "they have it." But this bill foundered in the struggle over the army bill and under increasingly sharp attacks by fearmongering Northern Democrats. Although each house passed a version, no combined bill was enacted.[43]

As they worriedly considered the public's response to occupation, Republicans rhetorically shifted to the high ground of peace. If Northern whites were tiring of the political controversy, it did not make sense to run as the war party in the November elections. In General Grant's letter of acceptance of the Republican nomination for president, he closed with the phrase "Let us have peace." Republican congressmen contrasted Grant's words with the increasingly belligerent language of Democratic vice presidential nominee Frank Blair, who suggested that the Democrats would use the army to undo Reconstruction. It was, Republicans charged, a "new declaration of war." The Democratic slogan should be "Let us have war; there shall be no peace." It was a bewildering but logical transformation. Having acquired what they believed could be gained from Reconstruction, Republicans now sought to normalize and preserve it by posing as a peace party before a war-weary nation. Democrats, one Republican charged, wanted to fight a "war for the destruction of the Union," while Republicans aimed for "peace and restoration."[44]

Although many Southern states were now legally in peacetime, they did not seem to be at peace. In Tennessee, readmission to Congress in 1866 had brought a steadily escalating conflict between Republicans and the newly formed Ku Klux Klan. By the spring of 1868, organized bodies of men "seemingly desperate in purpose are scouring the country by night" and "our civil authorities [who] are powerless & terror struck themselves not only fail to arrest, but are silent & inactive," a legislator complained. To Major General George Thomas, who oversaw Kentucky and Tennessee, this "resistance to the laws" was clearly an "outgrowth of the rebellion." But Thomas wondered what powers the military had in a "fully constructed state." During wartime Thomas could respond, but he was not sure of his authority after restoration. President Johnson directed him to follow the prewar guidelines of waiting for an application from the legislature. Dutifully, Tennessee governor Brownlow called the legislature back into session, where it passed a militia law to arm both black and white loyalists. As Klansmen openly fought against sheriffs and militia, places like southcentral Wayne County were in what one Tennessean called "a State of civil war." Once the legislature properly petitioned President Johnson for help, he authorized the War Department to send seven companies to quiet twenty different towns.[45] Tennessee seemed to prove that the end of war powers did not mean the end of the army's intervention in Southern life, but there would be a change in the mechanism. In peacetime, officers waited upon governors and the president instead of acting on their own authority.

In seven other Southern states, the army shifted toward a peace footing even as the conflict raged around it. After the ratification of the Fourteenth

Amendment, Grant dissolved the Second Military District and returned the Carolinas to civil rule around July 21. Peace spread soon over most of the rebel states. Instead of the military districts, five ex-rebel states were in the Department of the South, which oversaw the Carolinas, Georgia, Alabama, and Florida; Arkansas and Louisiana were in a separate Department of Louisiana, another peacetime military unit. Still, the precise meaning of peacetime was murky. For Major General George Meade, who commanded the Department of the South, peace meant the withdrawal of the army from the countryside. Over the summer the troops in the seven restored states fell from 9,500 to 8,000. Meade concentrated his soldiers at central cities and railroad hubs in hopes of breaking county officials from their habit of calling upon the army for help. In August there were only three posts each in Georgia, Florida, and South Carolina; he hoped to cut Alabama from eleven to two but was stymied when local protests led Grant to order him to sustain a third post at Montgomery. "The people seem to be ignorant of the fact that the reconstruction laws no longer existing, the military cannot do police duty," Meade complained. By October 1868, there were only thirty-nine posts in the seven newly readmitted states, down from fifty-nine a year earlier. Beyond the withdrawal of the army from the countryside, peace also meant restraint as commanders directed their men not to interfere with the "civil law" or "exercise control over the civil authorities." Generals closed military commissions, turned over prisoners to civil courts, obeyed federal writs, gave consideration to state court orders, stopped arresting civil authorities, and avoided issuing rulings on state laws. When Colonel Nelson Miles urged intervention against the Klan in North Carolina, Meade ordered him to simply aid civil authorities, not take matters into his own hands.[46] Even if peace did not mean quiet, it meant a new set of restraints on the military; it should arm, not overpower, local officials.

But the habits of wartime died hard. Conditioned to the "state of war," many officers needed guidance in managing a "time of peace," Louisiana's commanding general wrote. Seven years' training in using posts as a police force could not be immediately undone. Even more profoundly, Southern Republicans would not give up on the military; it was too useful, too proximate, and too necessary. Civil officers frequently turned to the army for help in resolving political conflicts. Within weeks, Louisiana legislators petitioned for assistance, and Florida's governor asked that the army be placed "at my disposal" for the "peace & security of society." By September, governors in North Carolina, South Carolina, Georgia, Florida, and Alabama also called on

Meade because they were "powerless and unable to enforce the laws." Although Meade recognized that the "present State Governments are powerless," he resisted these appeals. His "sole and exclusive duty was to preserve the peace" after the civil power tried and failed to do so. In Florida, Meade ordered the state commander not to heed the governor's pleas to arrest offenders. "However lamentable may be the state of affairs as reported, you have no power to remedy it," Meade wrote.[47]

At this point, the Army looked back to the 1850s for an expansive view of its peacetime powers. A dormant 1854 opinion by the attorney general had used the Fugitive Slave Law of 1850 to justify an increased military role. U.S. marshals or sheriffs could directly call upon soldiers or civilians to form a posse to execute the law, and commanders could respond to their appeals without waiting for authorization from the president or the state government. Compared to wartime, this was a limited power to be used only in "rare cases of necessity," not to suppress common disorders or preserve the peace. But it also represented an expansion of the military's authority in peacetime.[48]

Events in Georgia soon destroyed any illusion that democracy would bring peace. When the legislature first met in July, Meade tried to leave it to govern itself. But in September, white legislators expelled all the black elected members, including the just-elected Tunis Campbell. Meanwhile in the south Georgia town of Camilla, whites launched a brutal assault on freedpeople. As about 200 freedpeople marched in a political parade, the county sheriff and a posse of 400 men shot them down, killing more than 20 freedmen and chasing the rest deep into the woods. The legislature, now firmly under conservative control, refused to permit Governor Rufus Bullock to call for assistance. By its own rules, the army therefore was handcuffed; all it could do was prepare a report. The civil authorities meanwhile did nothing at all. Camilla, like New Orleans and Memphis two years earlier, served as a harbinger of a continuing Southern insurgency. In Louisiana, the Knights of the White Camellia and other vigilante groups killed perhaps 1,500 men in the late summer and early fall, including as many as 200 near St. Landry Parish alone.[49]

Desperate to avoid a violent Democratic takeover in the November elections, the army rediscovered some of its authority. Finding authorization in an 1865

act that barred the military from intervening in peacetime elections but seemed to authorize it to protect polling places, Meade sent troops to "preserve the peace" by once again making military power visible. In the Carolinas, Georgia, Florida, and Alabama, Meade expanded posts from fifteen to forty, far too few to regulate every precinct but enough to be accessible. In North Carolina he scattered troops to Fayetteville, Charlotte, Salisbury, Greensboro, Weldon, Plymouth, Goldsboro, and Raleigh, and he covered many towns in South Carolina, Georgia, Alabama, and Florida. These soldiers should not "let mobs or political clubs, or other irresponsible bodies" obstruct the law, Meade ordered. In Tennessee, Major General George Thomas spread the 29th Infantry across the state and dispatched the 2nd Infantry to Memphis. When South Carolina's governor complained that there was "practically no government" in the western counties, Meade agreed to place troops there. But these actions were temporary maneuvers, not permanent reversals. After the election, Meade intended to "re-concentrate the troops," and the 29th Infantry left Tennessee altogether for Texas.[50]

With the army in place to protect the polls in the South, General Grant carried the presidential election in 1868. By some measures, his election represented, as he claimed, the triumph of peace. With the strong support of freedpeople, he won the Carolinas, Tennessee, Alabama, Florida, and Arkansas, a remarkable transformation that the war had wrought. But there were also signs of the conflict that still lay ahead. Democrat Horatio Seymour had probably won a majority of the white voters across the country. In Florida, the fearful legislature canceled the presidential election and assigned the state's electoral votes to Grant. Even in states where Republicans prevailed, there were signs that the Klan had depressed turnout. In states where the Republicans lost, the news was bleaker. In Georgia, political terrorists frightened freedpeople and white Republicans from the precincts. In eleven black majority counties in Georgia, Republicans received no votes at all. Then there was Louisiana, where the election became an open battle fought by "secret political clubs, semi-military in their character." In New Orleans the city police and white partisans drove the state-created biracial metropolitan police from their beats, and in Gretna bands of armed whites expelled the police and a company of U.S. infantry. In response, the conservative army commander, Brigadier General Lovell Rousseau, persuaded the governor to urge black voters to stay home. Vigilantes nevertheless killed at least 63 men in New Orleans; a congressional committee estimated that 1,081 had been killed in the state between April and November 1868. Without military

A bandwagon of musicians campaigns for a state senate candidate in a late 1860s election in Baton Rouge, Louisiana. Andrew D. Lytle Collection, MSS 893, 1254, Louisiana and Lower Mississippi Valley Collections, Louisiana State University Library, Baton Rouge, Louisiana.

support, freedpeople's access to the ballot disappeared; perhaps only ten black men in all of New Orleans voted, and seven parishes with large black populations recorded not a single Republican ballot. In his final report as general of the army, Grant argued that "troops are still needed in the Southern states" to prevent more attacks like the ones in Camilla and New Orleans.[51]

If conflict stretched into peacetime in parts of the South, the state of war endured in Virginia, Mississippi, and Texas because they had not approved constitutions or been seated in Congress. There martial law still reigned, and the states remained under Reconstruction military districts. In Mississippi, conservative governor Benjamin Humphreys helped defeat the constitution with the support of what a Panola man called "gangs of white men" who attacked leading freedmen and frightened "hundreds and thousands" from voting. The state's military commander therefore forcibly expelled Humphreys from his office and replaced him with Brigadier General Adelbert Ames, a New Englander. In Virginia, Major General John Schofield disliked the proposed state constitution's clause disfranchising rebels and feared conservatives would prevail at the polls, so he refused to call an election to ratify it. In April 1868, Schofield replaced Governor Francis Pierpont with former U.S. brigadier general Henry Wells. In Texas the constitutional convention still remained in session in November 1868, riven by battles between radicals and conservatives. In these three states, war powers continued, and the army remained visible. As other states declined to about five posts each, Mississippi and Virginia retained twelve each and Texas thirty-one. Even defined on narrow legal terms, peacetime had not yet come to the entire South.[52]

By the end of 1868, the occupation of the South had birthed some extraordinary changes. In several Southern states, biracial Republican governments were seated, with black legislators beginning the process of writing new laws to remake labor relations and local democracy. Among those new legislators were black leaders like Robert Smalls, who utilized the spaces available in Military Reconstruction to build powerful political machines. Those new states in turn had completed the ratification of the Fourteenth Amendment with its protections of citizens' rights. Black votes in the South had also helped elect a new president in Ulysses S. Grant. Although President Johnson had tried to destroy the war powers, Congress had fought him back long enough to make these changes bear fruit. Even though Johnson had saved his office, Republicans had saved occupation. But saving it had come at a cost, as some of the states rushed back into Congress were clearly not capable of defending themselves on their own. And it was not apparent what powers the army would be able to use to protect them now that they were restored.

In November, standing in Huntsville or Raleigh or one of the other occupied cities of the reconstructed South, peace once again might seem alluringly close. No more could President Johnson thwart Reconstruction. Since the spring of 1866, President Johnson had done almost everything he could to impede black legal and political power. But his actions had peculiar consequences. Unified against him, congressional Republicans who might have accepted civil rights without voting rights for black people in 1866 had instead pushed forward to extend both wartime and voting rights. And now Grant, the very man who had helped save the occupation, would soon direct it from the White House, backed by the votes of hundreds of thousands of freedpeople. With amity between the White House and Congress, and with the weapon of the vote for self-defense, it was now possible to imagine peace dawning, spreading evenly from cities over the countryside. But peace had not yet arrived, and there were reasons to fear that it might still be a long way off. From the war-torn states of Mississippi or Texas or Virginia, or from the Klan-infested counties of Tennessee, Georgia, and the Carolinas, where terrorists attacked black families and claimed power over the land, posts like Raleigh and Huntsville might seem like specks in a drowning sea of blood.

- 9 -

THE PERILS OF PEACE

ALMOST EVERY DAY between June 10 and July 14, 1869, a half-dozen soldiers "with fixed bayonets" marched a "hand-cuffed and man-acled" Mississippi white man from his cell in the military barracks at Jackson, Mississippi. In a makeshift courtroom on the army post, he faced not a jury of his peers but a military commission of active-duty officers. That Mississippi man, Edward Yerger, was on trial for stabbing to death the U.S. Army officer who served as Jackson's mayor. Although the details were colorful—they had argued over tax payments Yerger owed for a piano—the military commission trial turned on grave questions about the status of the Civil War in the unrestored states. Reading from a recent opinion by President Grant's new attorney general, the army's lawyer argued that the country held Mississippi and the remaining unreconstructed rebel states in the "grasp of war" since the "power to declare war undoubtedly includes" the right to determine "how long the war shall continue." But Yerger's lawyer argued that the attorney general had confused the "*effects* or consequences entailed on the country by a *past war* with a *condition of war.*" If it was a war, he asked, how could it be fought solely in a Mississippi courtroom, not on a battlefield? Could the United States make "war judicially"? After the Supreme Court took the case, congressional Republicans once more moved to save war powers by stripping the court of jurisdiction. But the fight was in some way already academic; peacetime was imminent. In a few months Mississippi would pass its constitution, rejoin the Congress, and return to civil law. Therefore, Yerger's lawyer and the attorney general agreed to pause the case, keep Yerger in military custody while war powers continued, but then release him to the civil authorities once peace prevailed. When that happened, a local court granted Yerger bail, and he immediately fled to Baltimore; he was never prosecuted for his crime.[1]

As the Yerger case illustrated, war powers endured in beleaguered form between November 1868 and February 1871, when wartime finally ceased. The United States began a messy, confused exit from occupation. Military government remained, but its ability to intervene was weakened by Southern resistance and a growing legal opposition to war powers. Although six states had unambiguously returned to peacetime status in the summer of 1868, in Mississippi, Texas, and Virginia the nation continued to grasp the power to override civil law, make arrests, displace officeholders, and run military commissions. But those tools of occupation were fraying. They were weaker, more geographically constrained, less reliable, and less enduring than they had been only a year earlier. Peculiarly, some war powers survived in Georgia, which had seemingly been restored to peacetime in the summer of 1868 but in fact was placed under a mild form of military supervision on a technicality. During this final stage, congressmen engaged in the most intense debates about how long the government could hold defeated states in the grasp of war. Chastened by the problems in the South, some Republicans hoped to extend the war beyond 1871, perhaps even indefinitely.

As partisan insurgents launched increasingly violent campaigns, freedpeople, loyalists, officers, and congressmen asked how the government could protect rights in peacetime if it could not rely upon the military to override civil law. One answer lay in remaking the law itself through the Fifteenth Amendment, which promised to protect freedmen's voting rights from infringement based upon race or previous condition of servitude. This landmark expansion of rights grew from occupation. Like the Fourteenth Amendment, its ratification depended upon the coerced votes of military-supervised states. But the amendment was only the beginning. In debates over new civil rights or enforcement acts, some Republicans sought to grant the military the power to intervene to protect voting and civil rights; some contemplated a frequent use of martial law to put down the Ku Klux Klan. Other Republicans, however, believed these peacetime expansions of powers undermined the nation's system of government.

These fierce debates about the role of the military in peacetime turned upon the great question that the country faced at the end of the Civil War. Could it protect freedpeople in the exercise of the new rights the Constitution recognized? Educated by the extraordinary violence in the South, some

Republicans feared that civil rights and civil law were incompatible, that the United States would have to either utilize the military to enforce national law, or acknowledge that freedpeople's rights would be violated continuously. Others hoped to accomplish the same goal through federal courts and the newly created Department of Justice. Still other Republicans came to believe it was impossible to protect rights if large portions of a local population did not accept them. They faced these questions under the fiercest conditions imaginable, as white insurgents launched campaigns of assassination and terror. Their answers expanded the army's role in American life, but ultimately even these extraordinary measures would not be enough to beat back the combined work of Southern insurgents, Northern Democrats, and Supreme Court justices who sought to return the country to something closer to its antebellum status quo. As Congress ended formal war powers in 1870 and 1871, peacetime was on the horizon, but peace itself seemed far away.

The tensions between war powers and the return of civil authority surfaced from the moment Congress returned in December 1868. The first fight—and the one that took the longest to resolve—was over the baffling status of the war in Georgia. Because Georgia had been included in the bill of restoration that brought back the Carolinas, Arkansas, Alabama, Florida, and Louisiana in the summer of 1868, its congressmen had been seated in the House of Representatives. The army had restored civil law and withdrawn the state from the military district; wartime occupation seemed to have ended. But Georgia's senators did not arrive in time to be sworn in; this technically opened a window of opportunity for Congress. When Georgia's legislators expelled all twenty-nine sitting black members, outraged Republicans called for action. Among the legislators expelled were Sea Island leader Tunis Campbell, now a magistrate and power broker in coastal McIntosh County, and Henry McNeal Turner. The formidable Turner had been born free in South Carolina, served as chaplain to a U.S. Colored Troops regiment, wrote frequently for the *Christian Reporter,* worked for the Freedmen's Bureau, and had been elected to the legislature. Later, he would become an African Methodist Episcopal (AME) bishop and a prominent black nationalist. When the Georgia legislature voted to drive out all black members, Turner and other black Georgians petitioned Congress for help. In response to their complaints and the request of the Republican governor, the House now refused to seat any of the state's representatives. Georgia was "standing with one foot in the grave of rebellion and the other upon the rock of loyalty," a House Republican said. "We propose holding them in that position." With Georgia once again poised between war and peace, some congressmen introduced plans to reinstate military occupation there. But other Republicans feared that imposing military rule in Georgia would open the door to extending wartime in other restored states. In the end, Congress adjourned without resolving the situation; the state had no representation in Washington, but the army had not officially been empowered to reinstate occupation. Georgia was not yet returned to wartime but remained in a state of quasi-peace.[2]

In the unrestored states of Virginia, Mississippi, and Texas, war powers not only endured but expanded over 1869. Active military officers directly governed Virginia and Mississippi, while Texas's governor was a civilian appointed by the army. At his inauguration, President Grant signaled his commitment to occupation in his first appointments. In a symbolic warning to rebels, he ceremonially named Major General Philip Sheridan commander of the Department of Louisiana, before reassigning him to a much-higher-ranking position in the West. In the Department of the South, which oversaw Georgia, Grant replaced the cautious major general Meade with the interventionist brigadier general Alfred Terry. For Virginia, he displaced the equally cautious George Stoneman for Edward Canby, who had sustained military power in the Carolinas. In Mississippi he appointed the aggressive New Englander Adelbert Ames as commander. Congress in turn expanded the powers of occupation in those states by sweeping away all the civil officers who had supported secession. "I am for peace," an Illinois Republican said. But "now is the time to strike at every element of wrong and oppression in the land that is in reach of governmental action." This bill dismissed all but 885 of Virginia's 6,061 officials, leading to thousands of new military appointments, from judges down to street inspectors. But there were already fissures over the relationship between civil law and occupation; some peacetime Republicans wanted to rush a constitution through as way of avoiding making "the military government perpetual." Against this, Republican congressman Henry Dawes emphasized the necessity of force. "You may, if you have the power, make your framework of government here as perfect, as any ever Locke conceived in his chamber, but if you put it down in the State of Mississippi it will fall to pieces unless your Army goes down there to hold it up," he said.[3]

In Virginia, Mississippi, and Texas, the army remained the bulwark of civil rights and national power. In Virginia, the army voided racially discriminatory laws and stayed the collection of debts. Officers assumed control of many criminal matters as they expelled disloyal officeholders. Military commissioners heard cases, commanded sheriffs, and replaced magistrates. In Mississippi the military reduced the state's high poll taxes and finally extended jury service to freedpeople, at once expanding black rights and saving the army the trouble of running a full-fledged court system. The military was boldest in Texas, where it overturned the state's discriminatory apprenticeship and education laws, and also tried fifty-nine cases in front of military commissions between October 1868 and September 1869. When a state judge issued writs of habeas corpus for several Jefferson men who murdered a former U.S. officer and two freedmen, the state commander ignored the writs and kept the men in front of a military commission. "Let us have peace," he wrote, echoing Grant, "but let it be a peace based upon justice and the protection of the law-lovers against the law-breakers. Whatever that peace costs us we must conquer it." The most obvious sign of the war's endurance was the army's reach into the countryside. As Mississippi expanded from nine to fifteen posts and Virginia from thirteen to twenty, there were more posts in those two states by August 1869 than in the seven restored Confederate states combined. In Texas and Georgia, the army also maintained coverage, with thirty stations in Texas in 1869 and twenty in Georgia by late August 1869. Although the army did not tamp down all violence—particularly in Texas and Georgia—it created pockets of peace and stability.[4]

But in the restored states, the army's retreat allowed the Klan and other vigilante organizations to try to topple local governments. "Bloodshed + murder are things of common occurrence," an Alabama man wrote to the attorney general. Seeing portions of his state paralyzed by bold claims of authority, this man, like many others, looked once again to the national government and the army for deliverance. "Does this not amount to levying war against the U. States, + is it not treason? Then this County should be under the Marshal law. . . . Virtually we have no Government here." In eastern North Carolina, the Klan-like Constitutional Union Guard attacked jails, murdered prisoners, and assassinated a sheriff. As the partisan White Brotherhood invaded the state's central piedmont, forty men raided the town of Graham, firing wildly into houses, and Klansmen attacked sixty-two men in Rockingham County alone. By October 1869, Governor William Holden declared counties to be in a state of insurrection and pleaded for federal troops. In Jackson County, Florida, Klan-style organizations committed dozens of murders of politicians and civilians, sending a black state legislator fleeing for his life. But the army's assistance was limited to symbolic shows of force. By law, in peacetime the army had to wait for requests from sheriffs and judges, even when those officials were Klansmen. Slowly, the army began to expand its posts in the restored states in hopes that its mere presence would help. Without an official request, soldiers could only "quiet the public mind."[5]

In peacetime, states ideally created order through their militias, not the army. But this was easier said than done. Among the first to try was Arkansas. There, in the fall of 1868, a series of skirmishes along the Missouri line between rebel partisans and Missouri's loyal bands threatened to devolve into bloody conflict. In the final days before the November 1868 election, Klansmen murdered a congressman during a wave of 200 killings, and Governor Powell Clayton huddled with fellow Republicans for protection in the state capitol. Clayton was not cowering; he was holding his fire until the presidential election passed and he did not have to worry about inspiring a backlash among Northern voters. The day after the election, Clayton declared martial law in ten counties and organized a militia force of 2,000 men, including hundreds of African Americans in segregated units. Marching deep into the countryside where the Klan held sway, the militia held dozens of men for trial in front of state military commissions and executed three assassins. To break the Klan's support among taxpayers, Clayton ordered the militia to seize food and shelter from disloyal men. Although few of the cases went to trial, Clayton had shattered the Klan. As prominent Klansmen resigned, the legislature outlawed the organization. Across the river in Tennessee, Governor Brownlow, who had already declared martial law once in 1867, followed Arkansas's lead. In February 1869, Brownlow placed nine counties under martial law, regulated by a new 1,600-man militia, but days later he resigned the governorship to become a U.S. senator. His successor quickly restored civil law and restricted the state guard's powers; soon the Klan and its allies were back in command of large regions. The other state to try to quiet the violence was Texas, where Governor Edmund Davis declared martial law and sent black officers to arrest almost 6,000 civilians. But most Southern states could not obtain white volunteers and feared calling up black militiamen, so they were helpless against the insurgency. In the Senate, Democrats denounced these militias for relying upon "military power," not the law, for "preservation of the peace of society." In one of his last speeches before his death, William Fessenden mocked their qualms. "Talk of the moral effect of an election upon a people such as that! Why, sir, they care no more about it than for the whistling of an idle wind. It must be force, to be exercised by men who dare to exercise it." Fessenden lamented that Congress had been in a "very great hurry to reduce our military force" and had forgotten the necessity of placing "an armed force within the control of somebody for the preservation of order."[6]

But other Republicans still would not sustain the army. These Republicans came closest to matching novelist Albion Tourgée's description of their folly. He charged that they tried to build bricks without straw, to construct a national government without providing the necessary materials. The failure of Reconstruction, Tourgée argued, was due not to hypocrisy but blindness. They could not see the obligations their own policies put on them. In a series of tightly contested votes, Republican leader Benjamin Butler allied with Democrats to force deep cuts. Butler and his Democratic allies aimed to reduce the army immediately from 39,000 to 25,000 men. "This is a time of peace and not of war," one Democrat said. "It is the reconstruction policy of Congress which has necessitated the continuance of this vast Army at this enormous cost to the nation." But some Republicans still recognized the need to sustain the army they relied upon. Wartime Republicans led by Samuel Shellabarger derided the idea of cutting the army before there was "peace in the southern states." By holding the line and offering compromises, wartime Republicans beat back the Butler-Democratic alliance by a single vote, but they had paid a steep price. To forestall Butler's immediate cuts, they had agreed to stop recruitment until the army fell naturally to twenty-five regiments of infantry, five of cavalry, and five of artillery.[7]

To expand the peacetime meaning of rights, congressional Republicans once more changed the Constitution by adding a Fifteenth Amendment that prevented states from excluding voters based on race or previous condition of servitude. Instead of bayonets, they hoped it would be courts and constitutional language protecting voting rights. "We may sing and coo as dulcet as the dove, peace, peace; but the ugly fact will remain as stern, relentless, and terrible as ever that the rebel and master race at the South are not the lovers of this Union," Shellabarger said. To optimists who believed votes could protect rights, the amendment seemed the capstone to Reconstruction and the herald of the end of occupation. It was "the last as far as I can see of a series of great measures growing out of the rebellion, and necessary for the reorganization and pacification of the country," Republican congressman George Boutwell said. A Republican newspaper claimed that with this amendment, "the issues of the rebellion and the war pass away." Getting to the amendment had challenged Republican unity, as women's rights activists once again petitioned for inclusion. Some Republicans hoped to affirmatively guarantee the vote to all adult men. Others feared that extending rights that broadly would prevent Northeastern states from using educational or property qualifications against immigrants or Western states from excluding Chinese men. After months of squabbling, Republicans agreed on a narrow amendment that barred the exclusion of male voters on grounds of race or previous condition of servitude. This language opened the door to education and property qualifications that would be used against black men in the future.[8]

Ratifying the Fifteenth Amendment depended upon the war powers. As Democratic-controlled states rejected the amendment, Republicans required Virginia, Mississippi, Texas, and eventually Georgia to ratify the amendment in order to be restored to representation. The path to peace depended upon the military's power to force them to accept the terms of peace. With the support of those four states, plus the reconstructed states admitted in the summer of 1868, the amendment became law.[9]

As they signed off on the Fifteenth Amendment, Virginia, Mississippi, and Texas also passed new constitutions under military supervision. In his first weeks, Grant had urged Congress to clear a pathway for those states by letting commanders permit residents to vote separately on controversial clauses that would bar rebels from voting. This would get around the unpopularity of those clauses with whites, which had led Mississippi to reject its constitution in 1868 and Virginia's commander to prevent that state's constitution from coming to a vote. But the vote in Virginia revealed the thinness of peace, as residents struck down rebel disfranchisement by a huge margin and elected a coalition of Democrats and moderate Republicans. Although some legislators were technically ineligible because they could not take the proper oath,

Grant's attorney general pressed toward peace by preventing the army from expelling ineligible legislators. When Virginia Democrats then swept away their Republican partners, and Tennessee's Democrats did the same, Grant learned that peace had become something close to surrender. Therefore, in Mississippi and Texas, Grant backed Radical Republicans over moderate Democratic coalitions, even though the moderate group in Mississippi was led by his own brother-in-law. Under military guidance, Virginia, Mississippi, and Texas had remade their constitutions, passed the Fifteenth Amendment, and reconstructed their governments.[10]

But the path to peacetime stalled in Georgia. For 1869, the state had been held in legal purgatory, neither restored nor placed under direct military supervision. The state was not actually in peacetime, but because it had been included in the restoration act of 1868, the army ordered officers not to intervene against civil authorities. Events during the year made it clear that the military's work was not done. Led by Confederate major general John Gordon, the state Ku Klux Klan attacked a series of Republican officials in and around Warrenton, assassinating a neighboring sheriff, patrolling the streets of the town, driving the Warren County sheriff from office, and killing a freedman and his family. In response the army sent companies to restore the Warren County sheriff and arrest six Klan leaders, but it was stymied by its subservience to civil law. Because Georgia had not been placed back on a war footing, the officers had to obey a judge's writ of habeas corpus and release the killers. This, finally, was the impetus to restore war powers in Georgia. Exasperated, U.S. senator Henry Wilson asked Grant to use the army to stop the wave of "political murders." In reply to a request for information, Brigadier General Terry called for a return to "military control" since there was "practically no government," and he was powerless when local authorities sympathized with the Klan. But Terry's supervisor, Major General Henry Halleck, did not believe the army could reassert war powers on its own; only Congress could restart them. Meanwhile, in Greene County, twenty-five Klansmen attacked and crippled black legislator Abram Colby. The legislature in turn voted down the Fifteenth Amendment.[11]

When Congress returned in December 1869, Grant asked it to take control of the state. Peacetime Republican senator Lyman Trumbull and the Senate

Judiciary Committee proposed simply authorizing the army to help Georgia's governor reinstate the expelled black legislators. But Missouri Republican Charles Drake—increasingly a spokesman for the wartime position—wanted full military control over the state so that the rebels "may be made to feel that there is a power here that can hold them to their places under this Government." After House Republicans divided between those who favored bringing down "the hard hand of military power" and those who wanted minimal intervention, Republicans crafted an ambiguously worded bill that recognized the state's unusual legal position and empowered the army to help reorganize the legislature.[12]

President Grant interpreted that act broadly and ordered the army to resume war powers in Georgia. First, on Christmas Eve, he created a new District of Georgia under Brigadier General Terry. When Terry asked commanding general William T. Sherman to explicitly bestow "the powers given by the reconstruction acts," Grant then on January 4, 1870, countermanded the July 1868 order that had restored civil law in Georgia. The army now seemed to be operating on the same wartime footing it had used in Georgia and other Southern states from 1867 to the summer of 1868. Grant's order would "sustain you in the exercise of any authority that will maintain substantial good order until the State of Georgia is recognized," Sherman wrote. "Even then some lawful means will be found whereby we can defend our friends against the Kuklux or band of assassins. . . . You, on the spot, must be the judge of how far it is politic or wise to interfere." The state's governor believed that Grant had restored complete military government.[13]

Empowered by the president, but working under ambiguous congressional legislation, the army inaugurated a half-hearted occupation of Georgia. Fearing another Supreme Court intervention, Terry resisted calls to suspend habeas corpus completely, and he would not routinely authorize military commissions. But in other ways, he acted on his new status. Beyond the six permanent posts in Georgia, he moved troops into seventeen additional towns over 1870, as many posts as in Tennessee, Florida, Kentucky, South Carolina, and Alabama combined. In the Klan hotbed of Warren County, Terry created a special military subdistrict, reappointed the Klan-fighting sheriff, and dispatched additional troops. When that sheriff in turn was charged with taking bribes from Klan members, Terry tried him in front of a military court. As Klan partisans invaded the mountainous counties north of Atlanta and overwhelmed an army detachment guarding the Chattooga County jail, Terry

court-martialed the detachment commander, encouraged the governor to remove the local judge, and sent additional troops to restore order. Overall, he
replaced three sheriffs, arrested a handful of people for murder, and at times
refused individual state writs of habeas corpus. In the legislature, Terry's military aides barred about two dozen members from taking their seats and helped
establish a narrow Republican majority. But when Republicans complained
that judges undermined the state's color-blind laws by refusing to appoint black
jurors, Terry refused to intervene. The military was the ultimate authority,
but he did not want to "remedy every fault in the laws of this State."[14]

As Georgia returned to a form of military rule, representatives from Virginia
arrived in Washington and forced congressional Republicans to face the dilemmas of peace. If Congress seated them, then the war powers in that state
would end. That raised the question of which peace powers remained to protect the rights of the people there. Fearful of the white Southern insurgency
taking over the entire South, some Republicans tried to create new peacetime
powers that would endure after restoration. This split the Republican Party
among peacetime Republicans who wanted an end to war powers, wartime
Republicans who wanted to continue war powers temporarily but not remake
the government's normal peacetime authority, and a newly cohering band of
interventionists who focused on permanently expanding the federal government's peacetime powers. What was at stake was whether the antebellum constitutional order could survive the challenge of enforcing civil rights. Some
interventionists sought a broad reconfiguration of the government's role in
everyday life. These interventionists, led by the newly elected Oliver Morton in
the Senate, tried to put Virginia in a purgatorial status; it would be restored,
but could be stripped of its congressional representation (and therefore put
back under war powers) if it ever withdrew its support for the Fifteenth
Amendment. "If we have a right to reconstruct a State government that has
been destroyed by rebellion we have a right to protect it after it has been reconstructed," Morton said. But Senate Republicans, led by peacetime advocates
like Lyman Trumbull and Carl Schurz, successfully argued that those conditions would forever change the balance between federal and state powers. In
its final form, the bill required every member of the legislature to take a loyalty

oath, protected black men's right to hold office, and barred the state from elim-
inating public schools. The "question underlying all this controversy is a very
simple one," the Chicago *Tribune* wrote. "Is the war ended? Will it ever end?"[15]

When Mississippi's representatives arrived, Republicans clashed once more
over the government's power to intervene in restored states. Interventionist
leader Oliver Morton dismissed the idea that peacetime meant that the federal government could not protect rights. Instead of war powers, the government's authority would depend upon the Constitution's existing guarantee of
republican forms of government in the states. But peacetime Republicans beat
back the interventionists by five votes in the Senate and seventeen in the House
and imposed the same conditions in Mississippi that they had in Virginia.
With this, the Senate swore in Hiram Revels, the first African American
senator in U.S. history. Revels, born free in North Carolina, worked as an
AME minister in the North before the war, and then served as a chaplain for
a black regiment. Moving to Natchez, he was quickly elected alderman in the
1868 elections, then state senator. After delivering an impassioned prayer on
the legislature's opening day, Revels was almost immediately elected to the
U.S. Senate. When Texas's representatives arrived in March, Congress passed
a similar set of conditions, although Republicans also defeated an amendment
that stated that the federal government had no more power over the restored states than it did over any other state.[16] Narrowly and ambiguously,
some federal authority endured.

Still, Democrats and many Republicans feared that military power in the
South would transform the whole country. One issue surfaced in seating the
new senators from Mississippi. While Revels was sworn in with only mild
objections, the state's other elected senator, Adelbert Ames, raised more questions because he was serving as the military governor when he won office. The
Senate Judiciary Committee believed that Ames was ineligible since he had
never lived voluntarily in Mississippi but only served there at the army's orders.
Beyond that, Democrats charged that Ames used his military authority to
capture state politics. "May we not have this Chamber ultimately filled by
generals of the Army?" one Democrat asked. "Shall this be made one of the
legitimate fruits of reconstruction?"[17] Although Republicans overturned the
committee's recommendation and seated Ames, it was clear that worries about

the growth of military power were spreading not just among Democrats but also among Republicans.

These fears of militarization influenced Congress's debate over the size of the army. Worried congressmen pointed to President Grant, Senator Ames, and the prospect of military intervention in restored states to paint a dire picture of a democracy captured by the military. Republican congressman John Logan, a volunteer general during the war and a leader of the postwar veterans organization the Grand Army of the Republic, protested against "the iron bands of power" that the army used to influence policy, and feared that "this country shall be subverted into the hands of powerful military men who are to become aristocrats as they are in Europe." As he finished, there was "long continued applause upon the floor and in the galleries." The fight once again was over the pace of reduction. Newly seated Southern Republicans led the struggle to preserve the army's size. "If you want to give peace and safety to all the people of the South," a Republican senator from Alabama said, "I beg of you not to reduce the Army. . . . They are there as conservators of the peace." From Klan-torn North Carolina, Senator Joseph Abbott asked to expand the army to 50,000 men since "the nature of our Government is becoming more imperative, and we need more and more each year the element of force." But opposition to the army united both peacetime and interventionist Republicans, who disagreed about the federal government's role after restoration but disliked the reliance upon war powers and the army. With Radicals like Charles Sumner joining Democrats in voting for reduction, the effort to sustain the army died in the Senate by ten votes. Southern Republicans then tried to save the army by putting off any bill at all, and were joined by wartime supporters such as John Sherman and the increasingly influential Matthew Carpenter, but peacetime and interventionist Republicans united once again with Democrats to force the army's reduction to 30,000 men.[18] The Republicans who had united to save military authority—Thaddeus Stevens and William Fessenden— were now both dead. There were few people left to unambiguously defend the need for a large military. Without their leadership, the question of the army's role was fracturing the Republican Party in new ways.

To hold back the Klan, Congress tried to create new peacetime powers for the military. But this raised profound questions about the army's relationship to civil governments. Republicans recognized that abandoning freedpeople would make voting rights irrelevant. But deciding exactly how to provide protection in peacetime divided them. A new civil rights bill began as a simple, uncontroversial effort by House Republicans to make it a federal crime for private individuals to restrict black men's right to vote by "force, fraud, intimidation, or other unlawful means." Congressman John Bingham, typically a hardliner against changing the powers of peace, introduced this version as a basic extension of the powers created by the Fifteenth Amendment.[19]

But Senate Republicans wanted something much more extensive. Over nineteen hours of continuous debate, Republicans considered various ways to protect voting rights. North Carolina Republican John Pool proposed allowing the military to make arrests, hold defenders, and—most controversially—compel witnesses to testify. "It is the duty of the United States Government to go into the State, and by its strong arm to see that" a citizen "does have the full and free enjoyment of these rights." Southern Republicans celebrated the use of the army when the laws "are a dead letter" under the "dynasty of the knife and bullet." But Democrats and many Republicans opposed expanding the army's peacetime role. The Constitution did not enable the government "to use the arm of national authority for the purpose of realizing by force what conception each of us may entertain of the 'ideal republic,'" Carl Schurz said. Republican senator George Williams said that the war had compelled them to "subordinate the elections" to the "military power" in the past, but "it is our duty" as "soon as practicable to go back to the old system." Over the hours, interventionist Republicans, helped at times by wartime members like Matthew Carpenter, strengthened the bill by giving federal courts the power to overturn state elections, permitting the president to call out the army to prevent possible violations of the law, granting U.S. marshals the authority to arrest offenders, making it a crime to threaten to displace a tenant for voting against a landlord's interests, and outlawing conspiracies to go in disguise to injure or intimidate voters. They would not, however, permit the army to hold suspects for trial or compel witnesses to testify. Still, the bill was, Democratic senator Allen Thurman said, "so strange that nothing like it has ever been heard of before in the history of this Government."[20]

But House Republicans resisted the expansion of military powers. Many would not grant the president the preemptive power to call out the military to prevent potential future violations of the law. They wished to retain some peacetime barriers to the use of the army. Under pressure, the conference committee limited the president to using the military to assist "in the execution of judicial process," a simple extension of existing peacetime powers. Republican senators reluctantly accepted the compromise but promised more to come if the Klan did not stop attacks. In a sign of how sweeping peacetime military powers might be, they warned that this authority would not be confined to the rebel states but might be turned against the Irish Democratic political machines in New York. "We will make the effort to see if it is in the power of this Government to prevent its being turned into anarchy and confusion by a conspiracy in New York or Georgia or Louisiana," Republican senator William Stewart said. Although he embraced Grant's slogan, "Let us have peace," the crucial question was "Peace on what terms? The terms upon which we intend to have it, and the only terms upon which peace can be had, are that every citizen of the United States, without regard to color, shall have an equal opportunity to vote." It was a definition of wartime so broad that it could last everywhere and forever, and Democrats denounced it as "revolutionary." Later in the session, Republicans began to extend national power by inserting a provision into a Naturalization Act that would give marshals and federal attorneys the authority to intervene to preserve order on election days in New York City. In all, the national government and its army possessed a few new powers to intervene in domestic affairs, but they were still limited to responding to appeals from judges and local officials. Many Republicans had aimed to clothe the president, or even commanders, in effective authority to call out the military upon their own judgment, but that was not yet legal. Peacetime still placed the military, generally, at the call of local officials on the ground. Perilously, this reinforced white Southerners' commitment to take any measures necessary to overthrow Republican officeholders who might make such pleas for help.[21]

The most profound debates about rights and war powers came as Congress debated readmitting the state of Georgia. In concrete, if legalistic, ways, this was a debate about ending the Civil War. Georgia was the last place where war powers existed and where the army could exercise its unusual authority to overrule laws, displace officials, and arrest outlaws. The occupation that had once stretched from the Rio Grande to the Atlantic was now reduced to a single state. Under the Republican theory that wartime continued until Congress seated every state, the act of swearing in Georgia's representatives would end the war. Therefore, the debate about whether to restore Georgia was a debate about giving up on war powers altogether. Under this pressure, many wartime Republicans wanted to extend war powers as the only effective way to protect civil rights. Interventionist Republicans imagined new methods for permanently defending rights in peacetime. Some peacetime Republicans, in turn, looked forward to the end of the whole problem and the restoration of constitutional limits.

The debate about Georgia captured the relationship between force and enfranchisement. As Klans spread across the South, assassinating Republican leaders and intimidating black voters, Republicans knew what to expect if they left Georgia to its own devices. Without some intervention, white vigilantes would seize control of the state and try to unmake freedpeople's rights. The right to vote alone would be precious little protection. Already in Georgia, white Democrats had expelled black legislators, frightened black voters into staying home, killed leading Republicans, driven sheriffs from office, and crippled leading black politicians. Once the federal government loosened its hold on the state, worse would come until the white Democrats were fully in command.

Starting in February 1870, after Georgia's legislature reorganized itself, the question stayed in front of Congress for four and a half months of furious debate about the past, the present, and the future of the government's intervention in the rebel states. At once it was the entire fight over Reconstruction in microcosm and also a salvo in the upcoming struggle to define peace. Concretely, there seemed to be four options. Peacetime Republicans led by Bingham wanted simply to seat Georgia's representatives; because the state had been included in the 1868 restoration bill, it needed no additional legislation. Wartime Republicans by contrast hoped to continue military oversight long enough to beat back the Ku Klux Klan. Still other congressmen hoped to turn power from the military to state Republicans by deferring state elections until 1872. This would allow the incumbent government two more years in office to build up its strength and save black expelled legislators such as Henry McNeal Turner from running again in the fall. As the debate took on a life of its own, interventionists in turn tried to use Georgia as a model for expanding peacetime powers against the Klan. In the House, Benjamin Butler wanted to use Georgia to send a message that Congress would take control of any state where the Klan operated, but peacetime leader John Bingham allied with Democrats to block him. In the Senate, the Judiciary Committee likewise followed Bingham in voting simply to seat Georgia's representatives. Peace seemed around the corner.[22]

But on the Senate floor, the proximity of war's end prompted extraordinary and lengthy debates about the government's use of force to protect rights. Reconstruction had undermined many Republicans' faith in the law, a faith built up in New England and the Midwest but one that could not survive engagements with Southern partisans. Now, Vermont Republican George Edmunds said, they faced "one of the faults of republican or democratic government. . . . We have endeavored to protect law and property there by the force of provisional State law, by the force of provisional congressional law, and by the force of the armies of the United States." But "we have totally failed. . . . Then what are we to do?"[23]

One answer was to permanently remake the country by increasing the role of the military in everyday peacetime life. Missouri Republican senator Charles Drake, a strong radical from a state with a history of guerrilla warfare, wanted to reshape American government everywhere in order to save their new conceptions of rights. He would give the president the power to override civil law anywhere. Under his amendment to the Georgia bill, the president could authorize army commanders to suspend habeas corpus and "take all measures known to martial law," including military commissions, if a governor or legislature requested help. The army would no longer be a sheriff's posse in peacetime; it would be the commander of the realm. Taking a lesson from the Civil War battles against guerrillas, Drake's amendment allowed army commanders to directly levy fines on civilians who supported the Klan or other vigilantes. The amendment was extraordinary, he admitted, "but I claim the circumstances to which it is to apply are extraordinary." Senators should ask not whether it was constitutional but whether it would be effectual. "There is not now flagrant war in this country," he said, "but there are localities in the South . . . where there will be no peace until you make the disloyal, mutinous, and criminal population there feel the consequences of their acts." Although Drake attached his amendment to the Georgia bill, it applied everywhere.[24]

Although few Republicans could support such a drastic extension of military power, they saved Drake's amendment by modifying it. Senator Jacob Howard wanted to give the president sole power to suspend habeas corpus and to bar quartering, but he supported the bill. "What is this Government worth, what is your Constitution worth, what are your laws worth, if bands may wander about by day or night . . . to rob and plunder and murder?" Angrily, Republicans dismissed constitutional qualms as technicalities raised by "exceedingly legal gentlemen." The party should be guided by the "law of self-preservation." The "military was created for just such occasions and no other," another Republican said. "Let us meet the emergency of the hour like men." Baffled and outraged, peacetime Republicans like Carl Schurz, Lyman Trumbull, and George Williams denounced the bill as a revolutionary remaking of the military's power in a "time of peace." Although acceptable in wartime, this type of intervention "will not do as a general principle." By banding with Democrats, these peacetime Republicans defeated a modified version of Drake's bill by a single vote. Then, John Sherman saved it by tying the president's authority against the Klan to his preexisting constitutional power to use the military against insurrection or invasion. With these reduced but still potent powers to respond to a new category of requests for help, the bill carried by a 32–26 vote. The Senate by a single vote then protected the president's right to suspend habeas corpus against Klan-style violence. Klan-sympathizing local judges could no longer stymie investigations. "I do not want to violate the constitution," a North Carolina Republican said. "But we want something."[25]

Wary of further changes and fearful of the state of affairs in Georgia, some wartime Republicans tried to both save Georgia and normal peacetime powers by simply extending the state of war there. By this means, they hoped to preserve the national government's authority to use the military in Georgia without changing the broader legal limits on the use of the military in peacetime. Once again, occupation emerged as a way to accomplish otherwise impossible goals without undermining the republican system. The leader of this effort was the newly elected senator Matthew Carpenter of Wisconsin. Carpenter knew war powers as well as anyone, having penned an 1865 pamphlet on martial law for the army and argued for the extension of war powers in front of the Supreme Court in the 1868 *McCardle* case. Then, Carpenter had claimed, in a newspaper paraphrase, that the Supreme Court was "judicially bound to recognize war as still existing until Congress shall declare it to be terminated." A model of a wartime republican revolutionary, he was willing to go far beyond the Constitution in war but not to break its form in a time of peace. Better to act boldly through emergency war powers than to shelve the constitutional system of government or to surrender to Klansmen. The problem with the Georgia bill was that it ended war powers, something Congress should not do lightly. Once passed, the Georgia bill "consummates reconstruction, and closes the civil war. This act obliterates, as far as they can be obliterated, all traces of the civil war." Here, Carpenter distinguished between the legal meaning of wartime and the cultural memory of war. The "wounded hearts," "darkened homes," "desolated firesides," and graves could "never be obliterated nor forgotten," but the bill "so far as legislation is concerned" would "close the bloody drama." When "the war came," Carpenter said, "the Constitution went out." But once peace returned, so too would "the rights and blessings of peace, chief of which is constitutional protection. . . . The war is ended, and with this act of reconstruction is finished."[26]

Paradoxically, the safest way to protect Georgia and the constitutional order was to continue the war. To Carpenter, the talk of extending the state officers for two more years was absurd. If it was "not safe" to restore Georgia now, "what assurance have we that things will be better" in two years? The "one logical thing" would be to put aside the bill indefinitely and keep Georgia under military rule "until the elements lashed into fury by the war shall have subsided, order be restored, and peace established." Carpenter's speech was at once bold and conservative. He went farther than most Radicals in asserting the need for continued martial law and military commissions in Georgia, but did so by limiting the government's peacetime powers after restoration. Once restored, states regained their old right to self-rule. In response, Charles Sumner dismissed any limits on federal power. In an impassioned speech, he compared Carpenter's defense of state self-rule to secessionism. Sumner claimed that Carpenter wore "blood-spattered garments" of John C. Calhoun and championed ideas "buried under the apple tree of Appomattox." As in his earlier arguments with Fessenden, Sumner had mistaken Carpenter's constitutional caution for conservatism; in fact, Carpenter and Fessenden had offered more powerful, if less permanent, plans to defend rights in the South than Sumner ever did because they were not afraid of force. Their disagreement turned less upon Sumner's abstractions than upon their faith in the power of voting. To Carpenter, only force, not the franchise, could protect freedpeople.[27]

Now other wartime Republicans followed Carpenter in supporting the extension of war powers over Georgia. Once Carpenter finished, Kansas Republican Samuel Pomeroy introduced an amendment to send Georgia back into the Third Military District. Although peacetime Republicans complained bitterly, John Sherman supported the extension because, he said, "we are in no hurry" to end the war. A slim majority of Republicans backed the bill; to their surprise, eight Democrats joined them, in hopes of creating confusion and dividing the Republican caucus. Against them were many leading Radicals, who were wary of wartime powers and wanted to extend the legislature. With this act and the Klan amendment, a bill to restore Georgia and end the war had become a bill both to extend the war and to broaden the powers of peace. At two in the morning, the Senate finally took its vote on the complete bill. This time Democrats abstained, and the bill carried by two votes, with Lyman Trumbull and Charles Sumner voting together to try to block the extension of wartime.[28]

The question of war powers returned to the House of Representatives, as it had in struggles in 1866 and 1867. While Carpenter had replaced Fessenden as an unapologetic defender of war powers in the Senate, there was no Thaddeus Stevens to brace the House for the necessity of military power. Benjamin Butler, who had become the leader of the self-styled Radicals after Stevens's death, lacked Stevens's procedural savvy and, more importantly, his understanding of the utility of military power. An interventionist who believed both in the power of the vote and in the right of the federal government to take actions against new outrages in the future, Butler wanted no part of extending the war powers. In fact, he unsuccessfully introduced a general act of amnesty for Confederates. For two months, as the House sat on the Senate bill, Butler fought to restore Georgia to peace but to give its legislature the right to extend its term to 1872. Finally, the House and Senate compromised on ambiguous language; Congress neither forbade nor explicitly authorized the legislature to extend its term. The Senate's anti-Klan and wartime provisions had vanished. Instead of putting Georgia back into a state of war, Congress offered Georgia peace without any terms at all. The government's wartime power to interfere in the South seemed at an end.[29]

But the Georgia bill did not quite end the war. On July 15, as the House passed the legislation, a Republican submitted credentials for Georgia's two senators. If they had been seated, it would have concluded the conflict, but the Senate held them over until Congress met again in December. That afternoon, Congress adjourned for the summer and fall.[30] For another six months, wartime continued even though most of the powers of war had evaporated.

In those purgatorial months after Congress's July 1870 vote on Georgia, while war powers had all but slipped away, congressional Republicans witnessed the perils of peace. In the South, the governments that the army and the freed-people had made now tried to construct a sense of legitimacy. Everywhere but conservative-dominated Virginia, Reconstruction governments showed the fruits of occupation. For the first time ever in some states, these governments funded public schools, hospitals, jails, and orphan asylums. Many rewrote marriage laws to give women more property rights and more access to divorce. Buoyed by a black politics that emphasized state intervention and by a small but influential number of New England natives who assumed positions of power in the Southern Republican Party, governments from the state to the local level provided services that no Southerner, white or black, had ever received. Some states and towns offered free medical care. Legislators also rewrote labor law to restrict the meaning of vagrancy and to protect workers' rights to their crops. In an effort to promote economic development, they spent lavishly, and sometimes foolishly, on railroad development. All in all, it reflected the statist vision that emancipation taught Southern freedpeople. "They look to legislation," one Alabama newspaper wrote, "because in the very nature of things, they can look nowhere else." In North Carolina's legislature, Abraham Galloway—who had helped organize freedpeople at the massive presurrender settlements near New Bern and then helped established the Republican Party in Wilmington—had vaulted to the state legislature, where he served until he died at age thirty-three in September 1870.[31]

But peace would bring a carnival of violence. To forestall these Republican gains, a white Southern insurgency increased its partisan attacks. In North Carolina, where Republican governor William Holden presided over a remarkable biracial coalition that sought to modernize the state government, Klan-style partisans spread through the political battlegrounds of the state's interior. In desperation the army moved troops from Virginia into the Carolina countryside, but the Klan fought on. In the winter, the Klan set its sights on Wyatt Outlaw, the son of a white planter and a black woman. A mechanic and tavern keeper at the region's railroad shops, Outlaw set up a biracial Loyal Republican League that included both white Unionists and freedpeople. Outlaw, who had probably joined the U.S. Colored Troops during the war, was quickly elected town commissioner and state legislator. When white paramilitary organizations threatened him, he put the town of Graham under curfew and organized a patrol. Therefore, on February 26, 1870, Klansmen hanged him from a tree as a warning to other Republicans. In response Holden proclaimed a state of insurrection and asked Grant to suspend habeas corpus so that they could "have peace" by shooting a few Klansmen. But the Klan drove onward, choking and stabbing white Republican state senator John Stephens to death in the Caswell County courthouse. Desperately, Holden formed a militia of mostly white western Carolinians to put down the insurgency. Ignoring the state supreme court's writs of habeas corpus, Holden encouraged the militia to arrest about one hundred men, including two sheriffs, but he released them when a federal judge intervened. Soon the insurgent leaders walked free, helped by partisan juries. In despair, Holden disbanded the militia and lifted the state of insurrection. North Carolina had battled insurgents, and the insurgents had won.[32]

As the insurgents rose, the army retreated from the South. In the three newly restored states, the army rapidly centralized its troops, closing posts across Virginia, Mississippi, and eastern Texas. As the army shrank from 48,000 men in September 1868 to 34,870 in the fall of 1870 and to 30,000 by July 1871, it pulled back from large swaths of the South. From 12,000 soldiers in the non-Texas rebel states in October 1868, the number fell to 6,000 in 1869 and 4,300 by October 1870. From forty-four posts in October 1869, there were only thirty in the non-Texas rebel states by October 1870. For the first time since the start of the Civil War, the army actually shifted its emphasis overwhelmingly to the West. In 1868, about 30 percent of the nation's soldiers had been stationed in the Southern states east of the Mississippi; by 1870 the proportion was 14 percent. Counting the border states and Texas, the percentage of troops in the broader South had fallen from 346 companies—54 percent of the nation's force—to 143, or 30 percent of available troops (see Appendix 9). Under these pressures, the army launched a broad reorganization, closing posts in Kentucky and Tennessee, moving the states administratively into the Department of the South, and dispatching the 14th U.S. Infantry and other units to the Dakotas to fight Indians.[33]

The new peace powers that Congress constructed through its enforcement act could not replace the army, protect civil rights, or enforce federal law effectively. Part of the problem was the limitation of federal criminal law in the nineteenth century; cases of intimidation were too diffuse, the courts themselves too distant and too unreliable. As Senator Charles Drake had

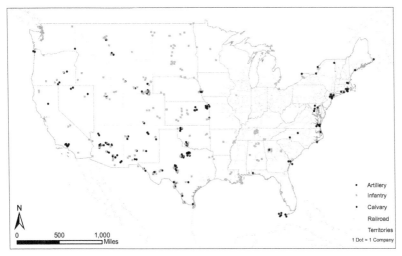

•	Artillery
░	Infantry
•	Calvary
	Railroad
	Territories
	1 Dot = 1 Company

N

0   500   1,000
Miles

U.S. Army presence, 1870. University of Richmond Digital Scholarship Laboratory.

predicted, U.S. marshals would be no better at preventing voter intimidation than they had been at enforcing the fugitive slave system in the 1850s. Unless it turned over more power to the army, the federal government lacked the capacity to defend rights in the countryside in peacetime. The threat of military intervention did have a mild impact in New York City, where the army mobilized troops to monitor the vote and prevent fraud by the Democratic city machine. Although the mayor negotiated a deal to keep the army off the streets, aggressive federal supervisors arrested twenty-six men for fraudulent voting, and turnout in the city dropped by more than 20,000 votes. Even there, it had taken a great many troops concentrated in a single spot to have an impact. Regulating the rural South would be much harder.[34]

The November 1870 elections exposed the control that white insurgents had over much of the South. Now that it was peacetime, the army's role was reduced to that of a bystander. Forced to defer to elected officials who were often Klansmen, the army was nearly helpless. As armed whites patrolled the streets of Laurensville, South Carolina, federal soldiers merely pleaded with local freedpeople not to provoke an attack. The day after the army left, thousands of mounted whites raided the town, killing twelve black men, including one legislator. In extreme cases, the army could still fight to defend itself; in Baton Rouge, two companies of the 19th Infantry drove back armed rioters who had threatened the U.S. marshal's home, tried to destroy ballot boxes, and attacked black politicians. At the end of the night, the army arrested thirty ringleaders, but partisan insurgents killed four Republicans and wounded the deputy U.S. marshal. "Had not the military acted with great promptness, every colored man in town would probably have been killed," a correspondent wrote.[35]

In Georgia, President Grant tried to utilize the last bits of war powers to save the fall election. Because war powers technically remained in place in Georgia, Grant ordered the army to protect election places. But the state commander, Brigadier General Terry, was tiring of occupation. He directed his soldiers to act "only when called upon" by a "proper civil official." In areas where troops were stationed, the Klan mostly kept quiet, but farther away, in places like the town of Sparta, whites crowded the polls and physically prevented black men from voting. The outcome was catastrophic for Republicans. Conservatives won roughly 80 percent of the legislative seats. Henry McNeal Turner, the fiery AME preacher, lost his spot in the state legislature along with many other black Republicans, though he held a job as postmaster thanks to national Republican patronage. Chastened by his experience, Turner lost faith in black people's prospects in the United States. Later he would become the most prominent spokesman for emigrating from the United States to Africa. As Turner exited the state legislature, five Democrats in Georgia, including the grand titan of the state Ku Klux Klan, gained seats in Congress.[36]

In other states, freedpeople's political power diminished, though it did not disappear. Republicans lost four congressional seats in North Carolina, one in Alabama, six in Tennessee, and two in Texas. In Alabama, after partisan attacks trimmed Republican margins by 2,000 votes in one county and 1,600 in another, Democrats captured one house of the legislature. In North Carolina militia patrols in Alamance and Caswell counties sustained Republican voting, but elsewhere paramilitary attacks frightened people into staying home. Democrats carried the legislature easily. Within weeks, the new legislature impeached Holden and by March expelled him from office in the first successful impeachment and removal of a governor in U.S. history. In Florida, partisans blockaded roads to Republican speeches. In bloody Jackson

County, where perhaps 150 black people were murdered between 1868 and 1871, terrorists drove down the Republican majority from 800 to 14. Although Republicans held a narrow edge in the Florida legislature, Democrats won two major state offices. In Tennessee, conservatives elected a Klan leader as governor and passed a constitution that eliminated rebel disfranchisement and threatened black civil rights. Republicans lost control of four Southern state legislatures and had little room for optimism anywhere except South Carolina, Mississippi, Louisiana, and Arkansas. Nationally, the Republicans ceded 25 seats in the House of Representatives, cutting their margin from 102 to 51. To add to the disaster, Missouri's Carl Schurz helped orchestrate an alliance with Democrats against radical Republicans led by Charles Drake. To the surprise of no one but Schurz, canny Democrats outmaneuvered him and elected arch–Reconstruction opponent Frank Blair to replace Drake.[37]

Weeks after the November elections, President Grant welcomed Congress back with a message about the end of the war and the powers of peace. He looked forward to the close of "the work of reconstruction" with the seating of Georgia's representatives. But he also warned Congress that "a free exercise of the elective franchise has by violence and intimidation been denied to citizens in exceptional cases in several of the States now in rebellion, and the verdict of the people thereby reversed."[38]

On the question of wartime, the issue had narrowed. Instead of asking whether Georgia would be represented, senators debated who would represent it. Although the House simply admitted the men who won the November election, the Senate faced a thornier problem. When the Georgia legislature met in the summer of 1868, it had chosen two senators; then the new legislature seated in 1870 by General Terry had elected two different men. The key fight was over Joshua Hill, a loyalist elected by the 1868 legislature before it expelled the black legislators; the other senator-elect from 1868 was technically ineligible because of his war service. What was at stake was not just his seat but Congress's judgment about the 1868 legislature. If it was legal, as implied in the federal government's recognition of its vote for the Fourteenth Amendment, then Hill should be seated. If not, then the Senate should recognize the later candidates.[39]

On February 1, 1871, nine years, nine months, and eighteen days after President Lincoln called for volunteers to enforce federal law in the rebellious states, wartime ended. After desultory debate, Democratic senator Willard Saulsbury said, "Let us have peace. Let us take a vote." By a 36–19 margin, the Senate seated Jonah Hill. When he took the oath, the war powers all but concluded in Georgia. With the closing of the Military District of Georgia three months later in May, the military recognized the end of war powers in the South. No rebel state remained under military control. Everywhere in the South, the army had to abide by its normal peacetime regulations; it could aid but not overthrow local governments; it could help enforce law but not make law; it could protect people in emergencies, but it generally depended upon local officials to ask for that help.[40]

Wartime had lasted almost ten years; the use of war powers after Appomattox had endured longer than the battlefield Civil War itself. Surveying the rebel states, there were fruits of occupation on the ground. Because of the use of military power, the Thirteenth, Fourteenth, and Fifteenth Amendments had been added to the Constitution. New, progressive governments existed in several Southern states, providing services unimaginable before the war. Through those amendments, as well as through the civil rights and enforcement acts and the Military Reconstruction acts, a new set of civil and voting rights existed both on paper and in practice. But the fragility of these rights and these gains was already evident. It was clear that white insurgents would likely take control of many, even most, Southern states, and would act to restrict black access to political power. If some Republicans had hoped that the vote alone would provide protection, the experiences of 1870 and 1871 had taught them that the wartime faction had been correct. It would take force, not just the franchise, to create defensible rights.[41]

As Northern Republicans and Southern freedpeople looked ahead, they saw that they would have to attack the problem of defensible rights without the tools of wartime. Instead of abandoning the project, they would instead search for new peacetime powers. The effort to build reliable rights without recourse to war powers would soon demonstrate how important those war powers had been. Without them, the government would find itself weaker and more constrained. There was reason indeed to wonder if peace might mean acquiescence or even surrender.

A GOVERNMENT WITHOUT FORCE

W ARTIME ENDS, but war's consequences do not. While the Civil War legally concluded in 1871, the fight over federal power, freedpeople's rights, and government force continued. But this struggle for power took place under new peacetime legal and political restraints. During the postsurrender wartime, the army had been able to intervene against civilian governments and laws. With the return of peace, those powers evaporated. No longer could officers override laws, depose officials, pull cases into military courts, or arrest murderers on their own judgment. Without that wartime authority, the military—and therefore the federal government—could be handcuffed by local and state officials. The return of peace meant the return of the primacy of governors, legislators, judges, sheriffs, and magistrates. Already, former rebels, under Democratic or Conservative party names and backed by a wave of terror and intimidation, controlled the legislatures of Virginia, North Carolina, Georgia, and Tennessee, and loyalists barely retained a hold over Florida, Texas, and, at times, Alabama. Only in Louisiana, South Carolina, Mississippi, and Arkansas did Republicans hang on to power, and even there they were already plagued by factional infighting.[1]

Although the turn to peacetime sapped a good deal of the federal government's power, some still abided. The struggle during the 1870s and 1880s would be over the army's authority to enforce federal laws and to protect federal rights during peacetime. Many Republicans hoped that the army would be able to utilize the broader peacetime powers established by Southern congressmen in the 1850 Fugitive Slave Act. Republicans in 1866 had turned those powers on their head in the Civil Rights Act. Just as the Fugitive Slave Act seemed to give federal marshals and commissioners the authority to call on the army as a posse to aid in capturing slaves, the Civil Rights Act gave them the power to call on the military to enforce civil rights. Additionally, an 1865 law authorized the military to protect election polling places. In the peacetime transitions in 1868, even President Johnson invoked those laws to defend the army's support for federal marshals and county sheriffs and its placement near voting precincts. Starting in 1870, Republicans built upon those peacetime powers in a series of Enforcement (or Civil Rights) Acts, a naturalization act, and an appropriations rider that allowed commissioners to use troops against criminals who prevented freedpeople from voting based on their race or color. A system of commissioners and marshals placed in the Southern countryside who could call upon military support might create sufficient peacetime powers to make the amendments meaningful.[2]

But these powers would not be enough against a rising Southern insurgency. In 1871 President Grant asked Congress to expand his authority, and Republicans in April passed the Ku Klux Klan Act, which reached back into wartime to authorize him to suspend habeas corpus and to deploy the military to protect the right to vote. "I reverence the Constitution," Senator Henry Wilson said, "but man is more than constitutions." Fearful of going too far, however, cautious Republicans limited Grant's right to suspend habeas corpus to two years. Beginning in late 1871, Grant struck at upcountry South Carolina, suspending habeas corpus and moving 1,000 soldiers into the stronghold of the Klan to help arrest more than 600 alleged conspirators. The Klan's actions "amount to war, and cannot be effectually crushed on any other theory," the attorney general wrote. But in fact it was not wartime; there would be no military commissions. In civilian courts, the legal system moved frustratingly slowly; at the end of 1872, more than 1,200 Klan or enforcement cases were still pending. Although the government launched a second wave of indictments in 1874 and utilized the army 350 times between 1871 and 1875, overwhelmed prosecutors moved to dismiss or settle thousands of cases. In response, white Southern insurgents shifted their strategies, discarding masks, minimizing extreme violence, and emphasizing fraud.[3]

Although the Klan acts worked, they also split the Republican Party in two. Peacetime Republicans like Carl Schurz and Lyman Trumbull, who had acceded to military authority during the war, now could no longer stomach it. In 1872, they (along with Charles Sumner) abandoned the party in protest of both President Grant's continued use of military power and allegations of corruption. Instead of joining Democrats, they fashioned a new Liberal Party that Democrats endorsed. Their candidate, Horace Greeley, lost nationally but cut significantly into Grant's margins in some Southern states, aided by intimidation and fraud. In three Georgia black majority counties, Grant did not receive a single vote. Although Grant still used the army to support besieged Republican governments in Arkansas, Alabama, Texas, and especially Louisiana, the military's presence dwindled in the countryside. In a coup against a Republican local government in Colfax, Louisiana, Democrats set fire to the courthouse and killed at least seventy black men. By the time the army arrived eight days later, it could do little more than watch. When rash speculation in railroad bonds and an international downtown sparked a massive 1873 depression, the Republicans took the political blame. In 1874, they suffered crushing defeats in the midterm elections and lost control of the House of Representatives.[4]

Before those new Democrats were sworn in, Republicans tried to extend the federal government's authority in a lame duck session in the winter of 1874–1875. Coups in Louisiana and Vicksburg, Mississippi, had showed them what was coming if they did not act. In Louisiana, insurgent White Leagues violently drove the governor and many local officials from their offices. In response, Lieutenant General Philip Sheridan, back on the scene once again, ordered 1,200 army troops to take control of the legislature, restored the deposed officeholders, and asked Congress for the power to try White League members by military commissions. This was at least one step too far in peacetime. But House Republicans did pass a bill that allowed the president to suspend habeas corpus for two years in four states. Fearful of losing support in the 1876 election, however, Senate Republicans let the force bill die. Instead they passed a civil rights act that banned segregation in public accommodations and other places. That fall, Democratic insurgents launched a new campaign of terror in Mississippi. Undermined by his own attorney general and fearful of electoral defeat, Grant did not send troops until it was too late. In black majority Yazoo County, where the Republican governor had won by 1,800 votes in 1873, Democrats prevailed 4,044 to 7. The federal government was losing its authority in the South.[5]

Although the infamous presidential election of 1876 is sometimes described as the end of Reconstruction, it was actually just one episode in a longer process of peeling back the federal government's authority. During the run-up

SHALL WE CALL HOME OUR TROOPS?
"We intend to beat the Negro in the battle of life, and defeat means one thing—EXTERMINATION."—*Birmingham (Alabama) News.*

During the 1875 crisis in Louisiana, *Harper's Weekly* portrays the U.S. Army as the only thing standing between freedmen and a war of extermination. *Harper's Weekly,* January 9, 1875. Library of Congress.

to the election, white rifle clubs massacred freedpeople at Hamburg and Ellenton, South Carolina. In response, the military stationed troops "practically every place on the map" in that state. When three Southern states produced two sets of election returns—one for Republican Rutherford B. Hayes and one for Democrat Samuel Tilden—there was talk of fraud and civil war. To protect threatened state governments, Grant stationed soldiers near the capitol buildings in South Carolina and Louisiana. After a commission awarded the disputed electoral votes—and thus the White House—to Hayes, the new president at his inaugural called for the "permanent pacification" of the country. By pacification, Hayes meant surrender, and in April the army withdrew from its positions. Democrats soon swept the Republican administrations in those states from power. "The time had come to put an end to bayonet rule," Hayes later wrote. "I saw things done in the South which could only be accounted for on the theory that the war was not yet ended." Still, it is easy to overstate the impact of the election. The army did not actually abandon the South; it moved in Louisiana from the Orleans Hotel to a camp outside the city, in South Carolina from the grounds of the statehouse to the barracks four blocks away. Even in 1877, a handful of soldiers remained, including 123 in Louisiana and 165 in South Carolina. The military would no longer sustain embattled state governments, but it still retained the power to respond to judges, sheriffs, and marshals. Recognizing this threat, Democrats in 1877 tried to "repeal all this military legislation" and "return where the Constitution intended." House Democrats insisted on cutting the military by almost one-third and limiting its authority. When Republican senators did not agree, no army appropriations bill passed, and the soldiers were not paid for months. In 1878, Democrats passed the Posse Comitatus Act, which seemed to strip away marshals' and commissioners' power to call out the military.[6]

For the next year, Democrats struggled to peel back more of the military's authority. In the early 1879 session, while Republicans still held on to the Senate, Democrats attached amendments to the government funding bill that would require the army to remove troops from the South, prevent the president from using the army or federal marshals to keep the peace at the polls, and repeal sections of the Ku Klux Klan Act. When Senate Republicans rejected those riders, Congress adjourned without allocating money to pay the government's expenses. On the verge of a shutdown, President Hayes called the new Congress into special session to fund the government. Having carried state legislative elections in the fall of 1878, Democrats now controlled the Senate for the first time since the Civil War. As the new Democratic-controlled Congress five times attached army-weakening riders to the appropriations bill, Hayes vetoed it five times. Although Democrats denounced the enforcement acts as "war measures," Hayes wrote in his diary that "it is for the victors to say what shall remain." Finally, Hayes accepted a vague rider that barred the use of soldiers as a police force. Still the fight was not finished. In 1880, Republican congressman James Garfield rode his defense of the army into the White House. But enforcement remained difficult. Although Garfield's successor empowered marshals to arrest more than 500 people for violating election laws in 1882 and 1883, the cases once again languished in civilian courts. Hemmed in on one side by Democratic congressmen, the military also was restricted by decisions of the U.S. Supreme Court. Between 1876 and 1883, the Court ruled that the enforcement acts and civil rights acts did not apply to private individuals and emptied out many of their protections.[7]

Although Congress had taken away some of the army's peacetime powers over the South, the military continued to play an important, if limited, role in the rest of the country. Called out by legislatures and governors, it intervened domestically about 125 times between 1877 and 1945. In the West, the army remained extraordinarily important. As soldiers retreated from the state-houses in South Carolina and Louisiana, Brigadier General O. O. Howard, former commissioner of the Freedmen's Bureau, led troops in a 1,700-mile chase after the Nez Percé Indians to force them from their northwestern homeland. So, too, would generals like Sheridan, Ord, and Pope become agents of federal power against natives, just as they had been agents of national force against rebels in the South. In the North, however, the situation was more complex. Although scholars sometimes contrast the army's retreat from the South with its intervention in the railroad worker-led Great Strike of 1877, President Hayes was reluctant to use the army in Northern cities and twice refused requests from local officials to deploy the military before acceding to calls for force. North or South, Hayes believed that in peacetime the president had to respond to the petition of a state government or federal judge, not act on his own volition. In the South, safely under control of Democrats, such requests to protect freedpeople were nonexistent. In the North, the military's role depended on the actions of the local government. In 1894 President Grover Cleveland did authorize the army to intervene against the Pullman strike without a request from state government, but Illinois's

THE "STRONG" GOVERNMENT 1869–1877.

This critique of bayonet rule shows the key images connected with the occupation of the South: the soldiers with pointed bayonets, the military tents, and the cannon that oversees the functioning of the law. *Puck*, May 12, 1880, 168–169. Library of Congress.

governor and many politicians sharply criticized this infringement on the state's authority.[8]

As white Southern Democrats launched a new wave of fraud and intimidation in the late 1880s, congressional Republicans tried one more time to expand the military's power in peacetime. In 1890, House Republicans passed a bill that increased the number of election supervisors, created a federal board of canvassers, and reaffirmed the president's right to use the army to uphold the law. "The Government which made the black man a citizen of the United States is bound to protect him in his rights as a citizen of the United States, and it is a cowardly Government if it does not do it," thundered Massachusetts Republican Henry Cabot Lodge. With only three Republicans voting against it, and no Democrats in favor, Lodge's force bill carried the House in July 1890. But a few Republican defections stymied the bill in the Senate, and did so again in the lame-duck session that followed.[9]

With this defeat, Republican efforts to intervene forcefully in the South essentially ended. From 1865 to 1870, Republicans had protected black rights by calling upon war powers. From 1871 to 1890, Republicans had struggled, with sporadic success, to wield the force of the federal government, including the military, to protect rights during a peacetime Reconstruction. They had pursued this course despite political defeat, negative Supreme Court rulings, the tainted presidential election of 1876, and Democrats' violent assertions of power in the South. But their acts had always rested on a thin foundation. Unlike war powers, peacetime authority was subject to constitutional and political limitations. As the war itself faded into the background, Northern voters no longer seemed willing to support the use of force. Despite these setbacks, at local levels, black political power endured and in some areas even grew in the 1870s and 1880s.

Those gains were precisely what white Southern Democrats meant to undo. As the Senate debated the Lodge force bill, Mississippi passed sweeping efforts at disfranchisement, including purportedly race-neutral poll taxes and literacy tests. When other states followed suit and the Supreme Court accepted their constitutionality in 1898 in *Williams v. Mississippi*, Southern black voting rights crumbled. By the early twentieth century, most Southern states prevented African Americans from voting. After the Supreme Court accepted the doctrine of separate but equal in *Plessy v. Ferguson* in 1896, most Southern states mandated segregation. By the early twentieth century, Democrats had stricken about 94 percent of the federal electoral-regulatory code from the books. With the death of the Lodge force bill, and the withdrawal of the threat of military intervention, the peacetime Reconstruction of 1871–1890 had come to a close. Without the fear of federal power, a new and bleak era of Jim Crow was dawning.[10]

More than a half century later, the army's role in enforcing federal rights expanded once again. Although grassroots social organizations and legal appeals drove the civil rights movement, the military provided the protection they demanded at some crucial moments. Buoyed by the army's increased firepower, its unprecedented popularity after World War II, shifting white Northern public opinion about legal segregation, and clear rulings from federal judges, the federal government used coercion effectively to restrain the white violence that had so long undermined African Americans' personal rights. When Arkansas officials resisted a 1957 federal court order to enroll nine black students in formerly all-white Central High School in Little Rock, President Dwight D. Eisenhower invoked a number of Reconstruction-era civil rights and enforcement acts, as well as older legal justifications, as he deployed a battle group of the 101st Airborne and nationalized units of the Arkansas National Guard. Five years later, President John F. Kennedy called out more than 9,300 U.S. soldiers to carry out a federal court ruling to integrate the University of Mississippi. Once again, however, relying on the military was controversial and expensive; the actions in Little Rock and Oxford cost $5 million each.[11]

The civil rights movement created both new conditions on the ground and new ways of understanding the past. Nowhere was this clearer than in portrayals of Reconstruction. Although some historians and intellectuals— especially W. E. B. Du Bois—had always defended Reconstruction, William Dunning and his students at Columbia University had successfully portrayed Reconstruction as a foolish failure from the earliest days of the twentieth century. They critiqued Reconstruction on many grounds, including its reliance upon military force. In early twentieth-century novels like *The Clansman* and films like *Birth of a Nation,* Reconstruction meant bayonet rule, and the South's liberation was cause for celebration. But the growth of black political power in the North, the World War II battle against fascism, and the grassroots attack on segregation in the South helped create space for a new, positive interpretation of Reconstruction. These revisionists celebrated the beneficial aspects of Reconstruction and also tore down the myths that surrounded it. Among the myths that revisionists dismissed was that of bayonet rule. Post–World War II scholars pointed out that the army often worked through local officials and rarely relied upon direct force. In time, this revised view edged into a claim that there had been no occupation at all. By the 1960s and 1970s, scholars who sympathized with Reconstruction asked why its outcomes had been so disappointing, its gains so evanescent. The argument that there had not been a serious occupation of the South helped explain why Reconstruction did not last. Working within the shadow of post-World War II Germany, Japan, and Little Rock, historians asked whether Reconstruction political leaders had simply not tried as hard to remake the 1860s South. They emphasized the role of ideological contradiction, personal motivations, racism, and will in limiting the gains of Reconstruction. Although Eric Foner's *Reconstruction: America's Unfinished Revolution* reasserted Reconstruction's surprisingly bold gains, recent scholarship has often returned to the premise that Reconstruction was not so radical, its leaders not so open-minded, and its limitations mostly internal. Historical amnesia about the occupation of the South helped confirm the notion that Reconstruction died of neglect.[12]

This book has told the story of the government's boldly extraconstitutional occupation. Reconstruction ended in disappointment, it is true, but not because its architects did not make a serious attempt. It is alluring to think that its limitations must be closely tied to their intentions, but reading backwards from policy outcomes to judge their political commitments confuses the issue. To see what Reconstruction did and did not do, we must abandon the presumption of perfect government efficacy—the idea that the state can accomplish what it wants if only its leaders want it badly enough. Instead we must treat government as an actor among other actors, one contested and sometimes defeated by powerful social forces. Reconstruction might have ended in disappointment even if it were manned by avenging angels. The tragedy of Reconstruction was not its leaders' imperfections, but the enormity of the obstacles they faced.[13]

We must begin by understanding what Reconstruction did and did not do. From the dawn of peace in 1871, or from our own vantage point, it is easy to be skeptical of the impact of the occupation. The occupation had been unable to create order in the rebel states. It was true that there was no concerted effort to overthrow the United States government, but there was also little basic safety for black and white loyalists and scant obedience to federal law. One congressman later estimated that more than 50,000 African Americans were murdered between emancipation and 1887. But the magnitude of the violence makes it perilously easy to overstate the failure of occupation. Relative to contemporary U.S. society, the South of 1871 was unusually dangerous for freedpeople, especially politically active ones. But looking backward at the whole of Southern history, the conditions appeared somewhat different. In 1860, slaves had been subject to nearly unmitigated violence at the hands of planters and patrollers. Rape of black women was both common and legal. During the 1860s, freedpeople successfully defended themselves in ways that made it more difficult for whites to police or oppress them. Although black people were far more likely to be murdered in 1871 than in 1860, in every other way they were safer from personal violence. A society in which whites had a nearly unlimited right to inflict violence was slowly, painfully becoming one where whites' access to force was declining. The end of slavery had opened up freedpeople's access to public spaces where they could create formal political communities. The carnival of violence against freedpeople after the close of battlefield fighting was a desperate effort to restore a sliver of the power planters held under slavery. It took whites much more work to achieve a far smaller level of control. [14]

The fruit of occupation was freedom, no matter how limited its terms. At the surrender of the Confederate armies, most African Americans remained enslaved. Without military rule and with the recognition of rebel state governments in the South—Sherman's plan—enslavement for some might still have continued; others would have suffered under a legally codified caste system. What was required was not just individual emancipation but the abolition of the institution. That demanded the tools of occupation. Although President Andrew Johnson eventually became a powerful obstacle to remaking the South, his protection of military rule, his support for army-led emancipation, and his requirement that new states end slavery and pass the Thirteenth Amendment were crucial for the legal abolition of slavery.

Had the occupation halted—as Andrew Johnson hoped—with the restoration of Southern white governments in the winter of 1865–1866, it is possible, although not certain, that order might have prevailed in the South. But

it would have been the order of the lash, the planters' recourse to physical bru-
tality to force freedpeople into bleak labor conditions and smaller portions of
freedom. In 1866, responding to the organized appeals of freedpeople and to
the violence in the South, Congress began to construct safeguards for freedom
that would alter the terms of the end of the war. By excluding rebel states,
Congress maintained the government's extraconstitutional hold over them.
Republicans used the absence of rebel representatives to remake civil law at
the federal level, defining the terms of freedom in the Civil Rights Act of
1866, embedding them in the Fourteenth Amendment, and extending wartime protection for freedpeople in the Freedmen's Bureau. Had white Southerners peacefully accepted those changes, as loyalists did in Tennessee, they
would probably have emerged from occupation quickly. But most white Southerners were not willing to accept them, and many Republicans were not willing
to let go of war powers.

Although President Johnson tried to force peace, Congress reasserted its
control over war powers in 1867. Between 1867 and 1870, occupation endured
and expanded, as Congress empowered the military and created new biracial
governments. The next fruit of occupation was the Fourteenth Amendment,
which Congress required rebel states to ratify. As they faced the Southern
counterattack in 1869, Republicans also compelled the final states under military rule to accept the Fifteenth Amendment, and this too would be a fruit
of occupation. By insisting that peace had not yet dawned, Congress and
black and white loyalists had changed the Constitution.

On the ground, occupation produced a new world for freedpeople and a
new South. Black Southerners vigorously protected their newfound authority
over their families, their working conditions, their churches, their property,
and their governments. Despite the failure of land redistribution, black Southerners built effective political and community organizations, putting together
some of the most cohesive political alliances in U.S. history in order to create
new activist governments in the South. The fruits of occupation—and of the
black mobilization that reshaped politics—could be seen in Robert Smalls,
who served five terms in Congress, representing the South Carolina district
where he was once a slave. But more important than any individual office-
holder was the remaking of social relations of power. By 1872, blacks won 15
percent of Southern political positions. Over Reconstruction, more than 1,500
black men served in office. Black political organizations elected magistrates
and judges who would listen to their complaints. With the potential to de-

fend their rights to make contracts, to move, and to marry, freedpeople built schools that taught hundreds of thousands to read and accumulated property at a pace fast enough that 20 percent of black farmers owned land by 1880. As they went about this work, black Southerners did not look to the army for guidance; they looked to it for the protection all free people need to make their rights meaningful.[15]

This extraconstitutional governmental action made the Civil War era in general, and the postsurrender era in particular, a revolution. As in other revolutions, political leaders went beyond the parameters of normal law and constitution to remake the political order. As elsewhere, the revolution drew upon social activism and also upon shifting parameters of the possible at the top of the political world. Like other revolutions, this one produced both startling changes and deep disappointments. And like many other revolutions, it depended upon force to do what law alone could not. Although Republicans sought to steer their revolution to a safe, peaceful end, they could not fully achieve that goal. Facing a powerful insurgency, they accomplished only part of what they desired. But it would be a mistake to read the lack of success as a lack of will or imagination. Even moderate Republicans were bolder—in their use of the Constitution and of force—than almost any American politicians from any other era in history. In their fight for liberal rights, they did not shy away from illiberal methods.

Proof of their boldness was that they relied upon the army, perhaps the least understood government institution of the 19th century. Republicans empowered the army to intervene throughout the region for most of the period between 1865 and 1868 (and to 1870 in four states), so the military could fundamentally disrupt social power relations in a rural, hierarchical region. The army had to remake life on the ground. This was the crucial promise of occupation, but also its gravest weakness. In trying to reshape daily life across a 750,000-square-mile region inhabited by 9 million people, the army faced a task that, as William T. Sherman had said, was nearly unprecedented and certain to inspire a ferocious counterattack by white Southerners. To some degree, the military succeeded. The army, with freedpeople, forced white Southerners to accept a new world. Into the 1870s, the army's continuing presence in a few towns helped sustain voting by black and white Republicans there.[16]

Even under the best of conditions, and with enormous resources, the army might well have failed at that task; history records fairly few examples of such sweeping efforts at societal transformation by military authority over a large, organized, and vehemently opposed population. Most occupations end in some form of accommodation to entrenched local elites who will pay nominal obeisance to the ruling power. Or they end in a spiral of flagrant wars.

But the army did not operate under the best of conditions. Beset by overconfidence, financial panics, and public wariness about military power, Congress steadily reduced the army. In Washington, the army had few truly reliable allies, either among President Johnson's circle or among Radical Republicans, and it had staggering responsibilities. Undoubtedly some of its officers—especially generals Hancock and Rousseau—behaved abominably under the influence of a bitter racism, but it is striking how many did not, whether from radicalism or from disgust at white Southern barbarity. As white Southern Republicans allied with Democrats, carpetbaggers headed home, missionaries shifted their attention westward, and Northern Radicals wavered, the army remained one of the very few allies of freedpeople. It was a bond forged not so much in sympathy as in shared dislike of common opponents. The credit for the staggering reformulation of black Southern society, and with it of the South and the nation itself, must go first to the freedpeople themselves, but then also to the army that provided basic protection, a counterweight to oppressive local law, and access to policy makers in Washington.

This is a peculiar moment to contemplate the period after Appomattox. Chastened by Iraq and Afghanistan, we are far more wary of the power of armies to remake societies. While historians have long agonized over the limits of Reconstruction, the relatively dismal record of contemporary occupations makes the difficulties of Reconstruction seem less mysterious. Rather than particular betrayals of the promise of Reconstruction, the failure to displace resistant local elites, to impose new laws and ideologies upon a conquered people, and to maintain domestic political support for paying the financial and human costs may be commonplaces of occupations. Skeptical of what occupations can accomplish, historians may now be well placed to rediscover the surprising things that Reconstruction did accomplish.

Thinking about Reconstruction in the current moment also poses another, graver challenge. Of course Reconstruction has meaning in and of itself, and the past cannot provide prescriptions for the present. Nevertheless, it would be cowardly not to acknowledge the contemporary conditions. Now, perhaps more than at any other time in a century, we have reason to doubt the legitimacy of war powers and the wisdom of extending wartime beyond the end of battles. Like ghosts from our attics, the tools of Reconstruction, including military commissions and restrictions on habeas corpus, rose again over the past decade, this time clothed less in tragedy than in horror. For those people who either endorse or oppose both contemporary and Reconstruction utilization of war powers, the juxtaposition between 2015 and 1865 poses no dilemma. And for people who, like me, are skeptical of the suspension of habeas corpus and the utilization of military commissions in the War on Terror but who wish Reconstruction had gone farther, it would be tempting to recast Reconstruction as a civil exercise, even a civics lesson. But it would not be true to history. The juxtaposition between these two moments is disturbing; it threatens to undercut both our wish that Reconstruction had accomplished more and our critique of the contemporary reliance upon war powers.

But this juxtaposition might inspire a sense of extreme irony that illuminates both past and present. The fears of constitutional overreach that Democrats and some Republicans expressed then may make more sense to us than we would like. Although many people who opposed Reconstruction were motivated by racism or partisan self-interest or class fears, there were also legitimate reasons to worry about its impact upon the nation. Conversely, the fact that Reconstruction's gains depended on a willingness to extend the war may undermine our own confidence that war powers and military commissions are always inappropriate. While it is safer to draw a bright line between virtue and vice, between civilian and military law, the example of Reconstruction may force a deeper reckoning with the troubling question of whether the dubious means of war powers are justified in pursuit of noble ends. Had Reconstruction stayed within constitutional lines, the conditions for black people would have been far worse. Contemplating that fact during a moment of grave, justified doubts about war powers forces us to reckon with the idea that some causes—though perhaps not many and probably not the ones in service of which we have deployed war powers during the last decade—are worth grave risks. Clean hands may simply preserve an unjust world. Proclaiming the desire for a world made new but disdaining the methods that might make it so is unsatisfying, perhaps untenable. From our experience of irony, we might become somewhat more willing to acknowledge that any serious effort to alter the world starts with the reckoning of costs, whether personal, political, financial, or otherwise. In dreams, as Yeats wrote, begins responsibility.[17]

The story of Reconstruction's occupation reminds us that the dangerous, coercive tools of government may also—terribly—be the only liberating instruments within our reach. Reconstruction serves as a warning that a government without force means a people without rights. While it is tempting to domesticate rights into congressional or constitutional debates, in fact rights are not so easily contained. They spring up from unlikely sources. And if they are to be meaningful, they also require force. Some of our most cherished rights are products of what scholars call law-creating violence, forceful moments that establish new parameters of the possible that in turn are integrated into the normal law of courts and congresses. Even those rights that were gained through political debate and courtroom decisions depend, as Little Rock revealed, upon the federal government's willingness and capacity to coerce opponents into submitting. This coercion—in hyperbolic terms—is what rebels and later Southern-sympathizing scholars denounced as bayonet rule, and what some Republicans and freedpeople celebrated as a revolutionary break. But relying upon coercion puts enormous demands on government to prevail over powerful social resistance.

Republicans risked a great deal when they relied upon the army and went beyond the Constitution, but they accomplished a great deal, and opened the possibilities for more. Republicans relied upon occupation and war powers out of a desperate attempt to discover the tools of effective government over a fractious and violent nation. While they had hopes that new laws would enforce themselves, they had good reason for skepticism, and little else to turn to but the army and the threat of force. They locked themselves in an unpleasant, morally ambiguous, but necessary embrace of the state not because they ignored the government's potential for abuse but because they understood the alternatives. By facing the force that undergirds our most precious rights, Republicans confronted truths we might rather ignore. After decades of critiques of power from both right and left, it is now second nature, even for many liberals and radicals, to diagnose government's coercions and its failures rather than its benefits. While this preserves a certain critical stance, it makes it impossible to understand how to construct meaningful rights. Liberated from force and treated as legal concepts or political rallying cries, rights become the invisible lubricants of society, independent of the structures of government that make them real. A liberation story becomes a libertarian one.

Republicans accepted the dangers of coercion because they understood the graver dangers of an impotent federal government. To end the war and create practical freedom, they had to—as Lee predicted at Appomattox Court House 150 years ago—march across the South two or three more times after surrender. To their credit, they did not shy from this. Perhaps we might wish they had marched a few more times before they sheathed their swords. Looking back after his presidency, Grant saw what had gone wrong and struggled to imagine a better solution. Instead of more democracy, he believed the country should have relied upon more force. Rather than enfranchising freedpeople, the government should have prevented everyone in the South from voting until federal power was secure. "The wisest thing would have been to continue for some time the military rule," he said privately. The problem was that "our people did not like it. It was not in accordance with our institutions." From a distance of 150 years since Appomattox, it is still hard to know whether Grant was celebrating or deploring the American wariness of force, whether he was trumpeting or lamenting Americans' faith in republican institutions. Even now Grant's judgment should loom over us as we look backward. At once, it is a brake against the cynical, if sometimes accurate, view that change is impossible, and also a guard against the optimistic view that change could be painless. It reminds us that government, despite its many sins, remains the only instrument that can make our freedom real.[18]

APPENDIXES

ABBREVIATIONS

NOTES

ACKNOWLEDGMENTS

INDEX

APPENDIX 1

Total U.S. Army posts by season, 1865

Quarterly posts	Mar./ Apr. '65	May '65	Summer '65 (June–Aug.)	Fall '65 (Sept.–Nov.)
North Carolina	13	25	26	17
South Carolina	8	8	42	47
Mississippi	12	18	50	36
Georgia	7	9	69	90
Alabama	17	26	30	25
Tennessee	35	40	40	13
Arkansas	12	17	18	19
Virginia	31	33	59	55
Louisiana	23	30	30	34
Florida	7	11	21	40
Confederacy without Texas	165	217	385	376
Texas	2	1	24	27
All Confederacy with Texas	167	218	409	403
Kentucky	25	22	28	12
Confederacy plus Kentucky	192	240	437	415

APPENDIX 2

Total U.S. soldiers by month, September 1865–January 1866

Total troops	Sept. '65	Oct. '65	Nov. '65	Dec. '65	Jan. '66
North Carolina	8,788	6,189	6,039	2,945	2,209
South Carolina	9,642	8,674	7,998	7,738	7,408
Mississippi	13,796	10,895	9,619	9,099	9,119
Georgia	15,779	12,328	10,086	9,403	2,764
Alabama	18,051	10,963	11,299	9,678	7,832
Tennessee	16,077	13,788	12,406	12,816	7,345
Arkansas	11,139	8,182	7,897	9,813	9,280
Virginia	20,760	18,733	12,512	7,280	3,293
Louisiana	23,747	19,434	15,667	16,644	9,772
Florida	8,703	7,550	5,343	2,830	2,813
Confederacy without Texas	146,482	116,736	98,866	88,246	61,835
Texas	43,424	31,851	26,341	23,042	25,085

APPENDIX 3

Total U.S. Army posts by month, August 1865–January 1866

Total posts	Aug. '65	Sept. '65	Oct. '65	Nov. '65	Dec. '65	Jan. '66
North Carolina	17	16	13	13	11	13
South Carolina	35	37	32	38	39	41
Mississippi	39	33	16	17	11	10
Georgia	68	75	74	60	45	14
Alabama	25	24	18	17	13	12
Tennessee	24	13	8	8	9	7
Arkansas	13	19	15	14	14	14
Virginia	48	50	41	30	22	39
Louisiana	29	33	33	24	17	14
Florida	14	24	37	25	27	27
Confederacy without Texas	312	324	287	246	208	191

APPENDIX 4

Size of U.S. Army in former Confederate states plotted against number of outposts, May–September 1865

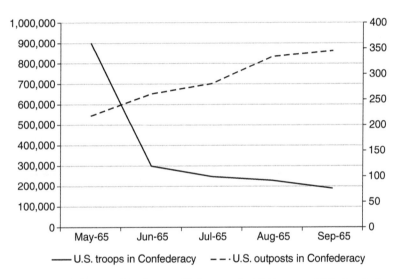

Data sources: Compiled from monthly and semimonthly departmental and division reports, RG 94, Records of the Adjutant General's Office, 1780s–1917, Entry 65, Returns and Station Books, 1690–1916, Returns of Civil War Army Corps, Divisions, and Departments, 1861–1865, NA.

APPENDIX 5

Size of U.S. Army in former Confederate states plotted against number of outposts, September 1865–January 1866

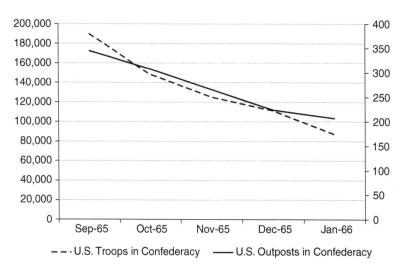

Data sources: Compiled from monthly and semimonthly departmental and division reports, RG 94, Records of the Adjutant General's Office, 1780s–1917, Entry 65, Returns and Station Books, 1690–1916, Returns of Civil War Army Corps, Divisions, and Departments, 1861–1865, NA.

APPENDIX 6

Total U.S. Army soldiers by month, January–December 1866

Total troops	Jan. '66	Mar. '66	May '66	Sept. '66	Dec. '66
North Carolina	2,209	2,212	1,870	1,454	1,132
South Carolina	7,408	5,613	3,173	1,991	1,624
Mississippi	9,119	4,292	439	593	747
Georgia	2,764	1,960	498	841	1,136
Alabama	7,832	5,525	1,088	810	831
Tennessee	7,345	4,687	1,349	1,663	1,698
Arkansas	9,280	5,789	4,051	2,075	1,442
Virginia	3,293	2,939	2,883	3,026	3,275
Louisiana	9,772	5,911	4,629	3,500	4,341
Florida	2,813	2,024	1,755	1,286	1,365
Confederacy without Texas	61,835	40,952	21,735	17,239	17,591
Texas	25,085	11,576	8,470	7,996	7,363
Confederacy	86,920	52,528	30,205	25,235	24,954

APPENDIX 7

Total U.S. Army posts by month, January–December 1866

Total posts	Jan. '66	May '66	Sept. '66	Dec. '66
North Carolina	13	16	10	10
South Carolina	41	29	14	15
Mississippi	10	5	5	6
Georgia	14	5	5	8
Alabama	12	9	7	7
Tennessee	7	3	3	6
Arkansas	14	8	8	9
Virginia	39	14	14	13
Louisiana	14	8	8	8
Florida	27	14	11	15
Confederacy without Texas	191	111	85	97
Texas	16	36	16	25
Total Confederacy	207	147	101	122

APPENDIX 8

Spread of troops across the country, by region, winter 1867–1868

Regions	Posts	Companies	Percentage of all companies
Northeast (CT, MA, DE, ME, NY, PA, NH, RI)	22	34	5.30
Border (DC, WV, KY, IN, MD, MO)	22	78.5	12.25
Confederacy without Texas	90	193	30.11
Texas	37	75	11.70
Midwest (MI, MN)	7	11	1.72
Pacific (CA, OR, WA)	27	34.5	5.38
Southwest (NM, NV, AZ, UT)	33	63	9.83
Plains (Dakota, CO, MT, NB, ID, KS)	39	144	22.46
Cherokee Territory	2	8	1.25
Broader regions			
The North—Northeast + Midwest	29	45	7.02
The South—Confederacy + Texas + border states	149	346.5	54.06
The West—Plains + Cherokee + Southwest + Pacific	101	249.5	38.92

Data sources: Army & Navy Journal, February 8, 1868, 399; February 15, 1868, 415; February 22, 1868, 431; February 29, 1868, 446.

APPENDIX 9

Spread of troops across the country, by region, fall 1870

	Posts	Companies	Percentage of all companies
Regions			
Northeast (CT, MA, DE, ME, NY, PA, NH, RI)	12	39	8.93
Border (DC, WV, KY, IN, MD, MO)	4	6	1.37
Confederacy without Texas	28	61.5	14.09
Texas	16	76	17.41
Midwest (MI, MN)	6	9	2.06
Pacific (CA, OR, WA)	15	30	6.87
Southwest (NM, NV, AZ, UT)	16	25	14.89
Plains (Dakota, CO, MT, NB, ID, KS)	47	130	29.78
Cherokee Territory	4	20	4.58
Broader Regions			
The North—Northeast + Midwest	18	48	11.39
The South—Confederacy + Texas + border states	48	143.5	30.38
The West—Plains + Cherokee + Southwest + Pacific	92	245	58.23

Data sources: Army & Navy Journal, November 19, 1870, 216; November 26, 1870, 232–233; December 3, 1870, 247.

ABBREVIATIONS

BRFAL	Bureau of Refugees, Freedmen, and Abandoned Lands
HSP	Historical Society of Pennsylvania, Philadelphia
LoC	Library of Congress, Washington, D.C.
NA	National Archives, Washington, D.C.
NAII	National Archives II, College Park, Maryland
NYHS	New-York Historical Society
NYPL	New York Public Library
OR	*The War of the Rebellion: A Compilation of the Official Records of the Union and Confederate Armies*, 128 vols. (Washington, D.C.: Government Printing Office, 1880–1901)
PAJ	*The Papers of Andrew Johnson*, ed. LeRoy P. Graf and Ralph W. Haskins (vols. 1–6), LeRoy P. Graf (vol. 7), and Paul H. Bergeron (vols. 8–16) (Knoxville: University of Tennessee Press, 1967–2000)
PUG	*The Papers of Ulysses S. Grant*, ed. John Y. Simon (Carbondale: Southern Illinois University Press, 1967–2009)
RG 48	Records of the Office of the Secretary of the Interior, National Archives, Washington, D.C.
	Entry 164, Letters Sent by the Indian Division, 1849–1903
RG 60	Department of Justice, National Archives II, College Park, Maryland
	Entry A1 9, President's Letters
	Entry 9, Office of the Attorney General, Letters Received, 1809–1870
	Entry 10, Office of the Attorney General, General Records, Letters Received, 1818–1870

RG 94   Office of the Adjutant General, National Archives, Washington, D.C.

Entry 4, Reports to the Secretary of War

Entry 62, Returns of Territorial Divisions, Departments, and Districts (Non–Civil War), ca. 1815–1916

Entry 65, Returns of Army Commands: War of 1812, Mexican War, Civil War

M617, Returns from Military Posts, 1806–1916

M619, Letters Received by the Office of the Adjutant General, 1861–1870

RG 105   Records of the Bureau of Refugees, Freedmen, and Abandoned Lands, National Archives, Washington, D.C.

M752, Register and Letters Received by the Commissioner of the Bureau of Refugees, Freedmen, and Abandoned Lands, 1865–1872

M843, Records of the Assistant Commissioner of the State of North Carolina, Bureau of Refugees, Freedmen, and Abandoned Lands

RG 393, Part 1   U.S. Army Continental Commands, 1821–1920, National Archives, Washington, D.C.

Entry 102, Letters Received, Department of Alabama, 1865–1866

Entry 265, Letters Received, Fourth Military District, 1867–1870

Entry 272, Letters, Reports, and Other Records of the Subcommands of the 7th Army Corps, 1863–1867, Department of Arkansas and 7th Army Corps and Fourth Military District, 1862–1870

Entry 293, Ration Reports Received, Department of Arkansas and 7th Army Corps and Fourth Military District, 1862–1870

Entry 297, Miscellaneous Records, Fourth Military District, 1867–1869, and Department of Arkansas, 1862–1870

Entry 926, Letters Received, Department of the Cumberland, Division and Department of Tennessee, 1862–1870

Entry 1664, General and Special Orders and Circulars, Department of Florida and District of Western Florida, 1860–1870

Entry 1691, Letters Received, Department and District of Florida, 1865–1869

Entry 1711, Letters Received, Department of Georgia, June 1865–May 1866

Entry 1756, Letters Received, Department of the Gulf, 1866–1867

Entry 1757, Records Received, Department of Louisiana, 1865–1866

Entry 2433, Letters Received, Department of Mississippi, 1864–1865

Entry 4111, Letters Received, Second Military District, 1867–1868

Entry 4134, General Orders and Special Orders Received from Posts, Second Military District, 1867–1868

Entry 4135, General Orders and Special Orders Received from Posts, Second Military District, 1867–1868

Entry 4161, Reports of Arrests of Civilians at Military Posts in South Carolina, 1866

Entry 4256, Register of Court-Martial Cases Tried by Field Officers and Provost Cases, 1867–1868

Entry 4306, Reports of Arrests in the Military Posts, South Carolina and North Carolina, 1867–1868

Entry 4498, Letters Received, Fifth Military District, 1867–1870

Entry 4509, Printed General Orders, Fifth Military District, 1867–1868

Entry 4521, Miscellaneous Reports, Fifth Military District, 1867–1870

Entry 4542, Reports of Inspections of Posts, Fifth Military District

Entry 4543A, Miscellaneous Papers, Inspector General's Office, Department of the Gulf

Entry 5103, Monthly Returns, First Military District

Entry 5260, Letters Received, Military Commissioner, First Division of Virginia, First Military District

Entry 5268, Letters Received, Military Commissioner, Third Division of Virginia, First Military District

Entry 5269, Letters Sent, Headquarters of the Military Commander of Warwick and Elizabeth City County, First Military District

Entry 5271, Letters and Reports, Military Commissioner, Fourth Division of Virginia, First Military District

Entry 5288, Record of Cases, Office of Military Commissioner, 31st Division

Entry 5738, Letters Received, Third Military District, 1867–1868

Entry 5741, Telegrams on Civil Government, Third Military District

Entry 5744, Documents Relating to the Murder of G. W. Ashburn, Third Military District

Entry 5749, Reports of General Meade and Others, Third Military District, 1868–1868

Entry 5757, Correspondence on Government of Georgia, Third Military District

USAMHI   United States Army Military History Institute, U.S. Army Heritage and Education Center, Carlisle, Pennsylvania

NOTES

INTRODUCTION

1 Ulysses S. Grant, *Personal Memoirs of U.S. Grant,* Vol. 2 (New York: C. L. Webster, 1885), 483–485; Horace Porter, *Campaigning with Grant* (New York: Century, 1897), 463–464; Brooks D. Simpson, *Let Us Have Peace: Ulysses S. Grant and the Politics of War and Reconstruction, 1861–1868* (Chapel Hill: University of North Carolina Press, 1991), 82; Elizabeth R. Varon, *Appomattox: Victory, Defeat, and Freedom at the End of the Civil War* (New York: Oxford University Press, 2013), 38–39; Joan Waugh, "'I Only Knew What Was in My Mind': Ulysses S. Grant and the Meaning of Appomattox," *Journal of the Civil War Era* 2, no. 3 (September 2012): 307–336; Benjamin P. Thomas, ed., *Three Years with Grant: As Recalled by War Correspondent Sylvanus Cadwallader* (New York: Alfred A. Knopf, 1955), 318–320; Edwin M. Stanton to Ulysses S. Grant, March 3, 1865, Roy P. Basler, ed., *Collected Works of Abraham Lincoln,* Vol. 8 (New Brunswick, N.J.: Rutgers University Press, 1953), 330–331.

2 Woodbury Davis, "Political Problems and the Conditions of Peace," *Atlantic Monthly,* August 1863, 254; *Army & Navy Journal,* May 27, 1865, 630; James Oakes, *Freedom National: The Destruction of Slavery in the United States, 1861–1865* (New York: W. W. Norton, 2012); Varon, *Appomattox.*

3 Alfred Bushnell Hart, series editor's preface to *Reconstruction: Political and Economic, 1865–1877,* by William Archibald Dunning (New York: Harper and Brothers, 1907), xiii.

4 *Army & Navy Journal,* May 27, 1865, 630; August 26, 1865, 8, 12; Congressional Globe, 39th Congress, 1st sess., 320–322; 41st Cong., 2nd sess., 2428–2430; *Official Opinions of the Attorneys General of the United States: Advising the President and Heads of Departments, in Relation to Their Official Duties* (Washington, D.C.: Government Printing Office, 1873), 13:60–67; Hugo Grotius, *The Rights of War and Peace: Including the Law of Nature and of Nations,* trans. A. C. Campbell (New York: M. W. Dunne, 1901), 17–18, 403–404; Thomas Hobbes, *Leviathan; or, The Matter, Form and Power of a Commonwealth, Ecclesiastical and Civil* (New York: George Routledge and Sons, 1886), 64.

The clearest descriptions of the extension of wartime and Reconstruction are Michael Les Benedict, *A Compromise of Principle: Congressional Republicans and Reconstruction, 1863–1869* (New York: W. W. Norton, 1974) and John Fabian Witt, *Lincoln's Code: The Laws of War in American History* (New York: Free Press, 2012), 305–323. On examinations of wartime and states of exception in the twentieth century, see Mary L. Dudziak, *War Time: An Idea, Its History, Its Consequences* (New York: Oxford University Press, 2012); Carl Schmitt, *Political Theology: Four Chapters on the Concept of Sovereignty* (Cambridge, Mass.: MIT Press, 1985); Giorgio Agamben, *State of Exception,* trans. Kevin Attell (Chicago: University of Chicago Press, 2005).

5 The best elaboration of the fluid but moderating influence of the Constitution on Reconstruction policy remains Michael Les Benedict, *Preserving the Constitution: Essays on Politics and the Constitution in the Reconstruction Era* (New York: Fordham University Press, 2006). See also Mark Neely's idea that wartime decisions needed "constitutional plausibility." Mark E. Neely Jr., *Lincoln and the Triumph of the Nation: Constitutional Conflict in the American Civil War* (Chapel Hill: University of North Carolina Press, 2011), 5; Robert W. Coakley, *The Role of Federal Military Forces in Domestic Disorders, 1789–1878* (Washington, D.C.: Center of Military History, 1988), 11–14, 20–22, 83, 102, 109, 127–129, 136–139, 171, 187, 228, 267.

6 "Proclamation," April 15, 1861, *OR,* Series 3, Vol. 1, 67; "Executive Order, No. 1," February 14, 1862, *OR,* Series 2, Vol. 2, 222; Abraham Lincoln to Erastus Corning and Others, [June 12], 1863, Roy P. Basler, ed., *Collected Works of Abraham Lincoln,* Vol. 6 (New Brunswick, N.J.: Rutgers University Press, 1953), 261–267. On the law of war and the Civil War, see Witt, *Lincoln's Code*; John Fabian Witt, "Law and War in American History," *American Historical Review* 115, no. 3 (June 1, 2010): 768–778; Oakes, *Freedom National,* 104–164; James Oakes, *The Scorpion's Sting: Antislavery and the Coming of the Civil War* (New York: W. W. Norton & Co., 2014), 104–165; Paul Finkelman, "Francis Lieber and the Modern Law of War," *University of Chicago Law Review* 80, no. 4 (Fall 2013): 2071–2132; William A. Blair, *With Malice toward Some: Treason and Loyalty in the Civil War Era* (Chapel Hill: University of North Carolina Press, 2014); Neely, *Lincoln and the Triumph of the Nation.*

7 For a recent, popular, and very flawed update of the old charge of Lincoln's tyranny, see Andrew P. Napolitano, *Dred Scott's Revenge: A Legal History of Race and Freedom in America* (Nashville: Thomas Nelson, 2009), 89–121. For balanced, if differing, scholarly accounts of the use of war powers, see James G. Randall, *Constitutional Problems under Lincoln* (New York: D. Appleton, 1926); Witt, *Lincoln's Code*; Benedict, *Preserving the Constitution*; Neely, *Lincoln and the Triumph of the Nation*; Blair, *With Malice toward Some*; Brook Thomas, *Civic Myths: A Law and Literature Approach to Citizenship* (Chapel Hill: University of North Carolina Press, 2007), 55–101.

8 Geo. W. Parker et al. to Andrew Johnson, April 29, 1865, *PAJ,* 7:657–658; David Robertson, *Debates and Other Proceedings of the Convention of Virginia, Convened at Richmond, on Monday the Second Day of June, 1788, for the Purpose of Deliberating on the*

Constitution Recommended by the Grand Federal Convention (Richmond: Ritchie & Worsley and Augustine Davis, 1805): 294; "Federalist Papers: No. 48," February 1, 1788, available at http://avalon.law.yale.edu/18th_century/fed48.asp.

9 On the utility of reading forward from the beginning of Reconstruction, rather than backward from its end, see Douglas R. Egerton, *The Wars of Reconstruction: The Brief, Violent History of America's Most Progressive Era* (New York: Bloomsbury, 2014), 16–17.

10 David M. Edelstein, *Occupational Hazards: Success and Failure in Military Occupation* (Ithaca, N.Y.: Cornell University Press, 2011), 3; William E. Birkhimer, *Military Government and Martial Law*, 3rd ed., rev. (Kansas City, Mo.: F. Hudson, 1914), 21.

11 Steven M. Goode, "A Historical Basis for Force Requirements in Counterinsurgency," *Parameters*, 39, no. 4 (Winter 2009): 45–57; Edelstein, *Occupational Hazards*, 16, 167; James Dobbins, *America's Role in Nation-Building from Germany to Iraq* (Santa Monica, CA: RAND, 2003), xvi–xvii; *The U.S. Army/Marine Corps Counterinsurgency Field Manual: U.S. Army Field Manual No. 3–24; Marine Corps Warfighting Publication No. 3–33.5* (Chicago: University of Chicago Press, 2007), 1–13.

12 The great portrayal of Reconstruction's transformative, even revolutionary, moment remains Eric Foner, *Reconstruction: America's Unfinished Revolution, 1863–1877* (New York: Harper and Row, 1988). Despite Foner's unparalleled capacity to show the interaction of social, political, and economic history, the emphasis on ideology reduces the army to the margins once the book moves past Appomattox. Although the army occasionally appears in the postsurrender sections, it takes a decided backseat to the much smaller Freedmen's Bureau.

This is a sharp turn from early Reconstruction history when virulently critical historians like Dunning School scholar Walter Fleming and journalist Claude Bowers used the army's occupation as proof of the folly of Reconstruction in sections titled "The Military Occupation" or "Army of Occupation." Where Fleming saw postsurrender occupation as tyrannical, revisionist 1960s scholars such as John Hope Franklin and Kenneth Stampp called it nonexistent. Although Richard Bensel credited military rule for protecting the vote, the point was undermined by his search for reasons that "Reconstruction failed." Despite a revival of scholarship on presurrender occupation, and fine recent work on Reconstruction by Brooks Simpson, James Hogue, Richard Zuczek, Mark Bradley, and Paul Cimbala, the army remains marginal to the broader narrative of the postsurrender period. Claude G. Bowers, *The Tragic Era: The Revolution after Lincoln* (Cambridge, Mass.: Houghton Mifflin, 1929); Walter L. Fleming, *The Sequel of Appomattox: A Chronicle of the Reunion of the States* (New Haven: Yale University Press, 1919); Dunning, *Reconstruction*; John Hope Franklin, *Reconstruction: After the Civil War* (Chicago: University of Chicago Press, 1961); Kenneth M. Stampp, *The Era of Reconstruction, 1865–1877* (New York: Knopf, 1965); Paul A. Cimbala, *Under the Guardianship of the Nation: The Freedmen's Bureau and the Reconstruction of Georgia, 1865–1870* (Athens: University of Georgia Press, 1997); James E. Sefton, *The United States Army and Reconstruction, 1865–1877* (Baton Rouge: Louisiana State University

Press, 1967); Harold Melvin Hyman, *A More Perfect Union: The Impact of the Civil War and Reconstruction on the Constitution* (New York: Knopf, 1973); Brooks D. Simpson, *The Reconstruction Presidents* (Lawrence: University Press of Kansas, 2009); Joseph G. Dawson III, *Army Generals and Reconstruction: Louisiana, 1862–1877* (Baton Rouge: Louisiana State University Press, 1982); Mark L. Bradley, *Bluecoats and Tar Heels: Soldiers and Civilians in Reconstruction North Carolina* (Lexington: University Press of Kentucky, 2009); William Alan Blair, "The Use of Military Force to Protect the Gains of Reconstruction," *Civil War History* 51, no. 4 (2005): 388–402; Robert Francis Engs, "The Missing Catalyst: In Response to Essays on Reconstructions That Might Have Been," *Civil War History* 51, no. 4 (2005): 427–431; Richard Franklin Bensel, *Yankee Leviathan: The Origins of Central State Authority in America, 1859–1877* (New York: Cambridge University Press, 1990), 305, 379–388; Richard Zuczek, *State of Rebellion: Reconstruction in South Carolina* (Columbia: University of South Carolina Press, 1996); James K. Hogue, *Uncivil War: Five New Orleans Street Battles and the Rise and Fall of Radical Reconstruction* (Baton Rouge: Louisiana State University Press, 2011); Jeremi Suri, *Liberty's Surest Guardian: American Nation-Building from the Founders to Obama* (New York: Free Press, 2011), 47–81; William L. Richter, *The Army in Texas during Reconstruction, 1865–1870* (College Station: Texas A&M University Press, 1987); Andrew F. Lang, "The Garrison War: Culture, Race, and the Problem of Military Occupation during the American Civil War Era," PhD diss., Rice University, 2013.

13 Congressional Globe, 41st Cong., 3rd sess., 1184.

14 Grant, *Personal Memoirs*, 2:494; Simpson, *Let Us Have Peace*, 85; Porter, *Campaigning with Grant*, 286; Joshua Lawrence Chamberlain, *The Passing of the Armies: An Account of the Final Campaign of the Army of the Potomac* (New York: G. P. Putnam's Sons, 1915), 196; William Marvel, *A Place Called Appomattox* (Chapel Hill: University of North Carolina Press, 2000), 259–263.

15 While Adam Fairclough attributed white Southern resistance to the extension of the vote to black men in 1867, historians have demonstrated conclusively that white Southern resistance had its roots in the period before Appomattox and continued throughout the period. Adam Fairclough, "Was the Grant of Political Suffrage a Political Error? Reconsidering the Views of John W. Burgess, William A. Dunning, and Eric Foner on Congressional Reconstruction," *Journal of the Historical Society* 12, no. 2 (June 2012): 155–188; Michael A. Ross and Leslie S. Rowland, "Adam Fairclough, John Burgess, and the Nettlesome Legacy of the 'Dunning School,'" *Journal of the Historical Society* 12, no. 3 (September 2012): 249–270; Mark Grimsley, "Wars for the American South: The First and Second Reconstructions Considered as Insurgencies," *Civil War History* 58, no. 1 (2012): 6–36; Hogue, *Uncivil War*, 10–12; Zuczek, *State of Rebellion;* Carole Emberton, *Beyond Redemption: Race, Violence, and the American South after the Civil War* (Chicago: University of Chicago Press, 2013), 168–205; Jason Phillips, *Diehard Rebels: The Confederate Culture of Invincibility* (Athens: University of Georgia Press, 2010).

16 Herman Melville, *Battle-Pieces and Aspects of the War* (New York: Harper and Brothers, 1866), 146–149; Stanton Garner, *The Civil War World of Herman Melville* (Lawrence: University Press of Kansas, 1993), 391–393.

Nearly a half century ago, James Sefton accurately wrote that the army was "by far the most important instrument of federal authority in the South" and that "it was the only enforcer of national reconstruction policy." In an important revision of previously negative portrayals of the military in Louisiana, Joseph G. Dawson III argued more than thirty years ago that the military "did a remarkable job, despite its inexperience, in administering an essentially hostile state . . . .The army—that most ungainly 'political engine'—had helped to establish the ground work of rights in the First Reconstruction that would form the basis of the Second Reconstruction a century later." William Blair echoed that sentiment a decade ago when he noted that "the central role of the military has been underappreciated in the histories of Reconstruction," which "rarely give the Army its due as the central agent for social and political change." Sefton, *United States Army and Reconstruction*, ix; Dawson, *Army Generals and Reconstruction*, 262; Blair, "Use of Military Force," 390.

17 Grant, *Personal Memoirs*, 2:496–98; Porter, *Campaigning with Grant*, 487–490.

1. AFTER SURRENDER

1 Winfield S. Hancock to H. W. Halleck, April 11, 1865, and Halleck to Hancock, April 11, 1865, *OR*, Series 1, Vol. 46, Part 3, 714.

2 David M. Edelstein, *Occupational Hazards: Success and Failure in Military Occupation* (Ithaca, N.Y.: Cornell University Press, 2011), 53.

3 The lists and maps and numbers here and elsewhere in the manuscript are drawn from a database the author personally compiled from tens of thousands of departmental and divisional returns in RG 94, Entry 62, and RG 94, Entry 65, as well as returns scattered through the individual department entries in RG 393, Part 1, all at National Archives I, Washington, D.C. Because data on the hundreds of outposts are drawn from thousands of monthly and biweekly reports, they will not all be cited individually. Instead, the author is developing a website with digital maps and datasets that will be available in 2015 at mappingoccupation.org.

4 General Orders No. 100: The Lieber Code, available at http://avalon.law.yale.edu /19th_century/lieber.asp.

5 Mark L. Bradley, *This Astounding Close: The Road to Bennett Place* (Chapel Hill: University of North Carolina Press, 2000).

6 William T. Sherman to Salmon P. Chase, May 6, 1865, *OR*, Series 1, Vol. 47, Part 3, 411–412; William Tecumseh Sherman, *Memoirs of General William T. Sherman*, Vol. 2 (New York: Appleton, 1875), 344.

7   *Army & Navy Journal,* June 3, 1865, 645–647; Joseph E. Johnston, *Narrative of Military Operations, Directed, during the Late War between the States* (New York: D. Appleton, 1874), 397–400; Sherman, *Memoirs,* 2:345–349; Martha Hodes, *Mourning Lincoln* (New Haven: Yale University Press, 2015).

8   Sherman, *Memoirs,* 2:354–356.

9   *Army & Navy Journal,* January 21, 1865, 340; June 3, 1865, 645–647; Sherman to James M. Calhoun, E. E. Rawson, and S. C. Wells, September 12, 1864, *OR,* Series 1, Vol. 39, Part 2, 418–419; Sherman to Chase, May 6, 1865, in *The Salmon P. Chase Papers,* ed. John Niven, Vol. 5 (Kent, Ohio: Kent State University Press, 1993), 42; Charles Royster, *The Destructive War: William Tecumseh Sherman, Stonewall Jackson, and the Americans* (New York: Knopf, 1991); Bradley, *This Astounding Close,* 46–47; Mark Grimsley, *The Hard Hand of War: Union Military Policy toward Southern Civilians, 1861–1865* (New York: Cambridge University Press, 1995); Anne Sarah Rubin, *Through the Heart of Dixie: Sherman's March and American Memory* (Chapel Hill: University of North Carolina Press, 2014).

10   *Army & Navy Journal,* June 3, 1865, 645–647; Sherman to Ulysses S. Grant, April 28, 1865, *OR,* Series 1, Vol. 47, Part 3, 335; Sherman to Chase, May 6, 1865, *OR,* Series 1, Vol. 47, Part 3, 410–411; Scott Reynolds Nelson and Carol Sheriff, *A People at War: Civilians and Soldiers in America's Civil War, 1854–1877* (New York: Oxford University Press, 2007); Scott Reynolds Nelson, "An American War of Incarceration: Guerrilla Warfare, Occupation, and Imprisonment in the American South, 1863–65," in *Inventing Collateral Damage: Civilian Casualties, War, and Empire,* ed. Stephen J. Rockel and Rick Halpern (Toronto: Between the Lines, 2009), 115–128.

11   Bradley, *This Astounding Close,* 206–219; Ulysses S. Grant, *Personal Memoirs,* Vol. 2 (New York: C. L. Webster, 1885), 506, 536.

12   The rejection of Sherman's armistice raises doubts about whether an emphasis upon union as the primary war aim can explain the United States' actions during Reconstruction. While scholars, especially Gary W. Gallagher, have accurately captured the centrality of national unity in shaping the Northern response to secession and the war's first years, an emphasis upon reunion cannot explain why everyone from President Andrew Johnson to General Grant rejected Sherman's armistice and demanded terms of peace that went beyond unification. For works that emphasize the centrality of union over other war aims, see Gary W. Gallagher, *The Union War* (Cambridge, Mass.: Harvard University Press, 2012) and Caroline E. Janney, *Remembering the Civil War: Reunion and the Limits of Reconciliation* (Chapel Hill: University of North Carolina Press, 2013). Mark W. Summers, *The Ordeal of the Reunion: A New History of Reconstruction* (Chapel Hill: University of North Carolina, 2014) was published as this book entered copyediting, too late to be fully incorporated here, but strives to balance an emphasis upon reunion with the broader issues raised by the government's actions during Reconstruction.

13 *Army & Navy Journal,* April 8, 1865, 521; April 29, 1865, 568; George Bancroft to Andrew Johnson, April 26, 1865, *PAJ,* 7:643.

14 P. H. Sheridan to Gordon Granger, June 13, 1865, *OR,* Series 1, Vol. 48, Part 2, 866–867; Chase to Johnson, April 11, 1865, *OR,* Series 1, Vol. 47, Part 3, 427–430; Joseph E. Brown to Johnson, May 7, 1865, *PAJ,* 8:40–41; Michael Perman, *Reunion without Compromise: The South and Reconstruction, 1865–1868* (New York: Cambridge University Press, 1973), 57–58.

15 Edwin M. Stanton to E. R. S. Canby, May 28, 1865, *OR,* Series 1, Vol. 48, Part 2, 640; William Smith to Grant, April 11, 1865, *OR,* Series 1, Vol. 46, Part 3, 704; J. J. Reynolds to Adjutant-General, U.S. Army, *OR,* Series 1, Vol. 48, Part 2, 627–628; "Executive Orders, May 9, 1865," available at www.presidency.ucsb.edu/ws/index.php?pid =72146.

16 Entries, April 11, 13, 16, 18, 21, 22, 24, 29, May 1, 1865, Marsena R. Patrick Journal, LoC; General Orders No. 31, Department of North Carolina, Army of the Ohio, April 27, 1865, Box 7, John McAllister Schofield Papers, LoC; Wm. Stewart to R. Marion Auten, June 9, 1865, RG 60, Entry 10, Vol. 10, Book D, NAII; Stanley G. Trott to Andrew Johnson, April 18, 1865, RG 60, Entry 9, Box 1, NAII; "Executive Order April 29, 1865," available at www.presidency.ucsb.edu/ws/index.php?pid=72057; George Henry Gordon, *A War Diary of Events in the War of the Great Rebellion, 1863–1865* (Boston: J. R. Osgood, 1882), 417–418; Brooks D. Simpson, *Let Us Have Peace: Ulysses S. Grant and the Politics of War and Reconstruction, 1861–1868* (Chapel Hill: University of North Carolina Press, 1991), 102.

17 67 U.S. 635; Gerald Mortimer Capers, *Occupied City: New Orleans under the Federals, 1862–1865* (Lexington: University Press of Kentucky, 1965); Peter Maslowski, *Treason Must Be Made Odious: Military Occupation and Wartime Reconstruction in Nashville, Tennessee, 1862–65* (Millwood, N.Y.: KTO Press, 1978); Stephen V. Ash, *Middle Tennessee Society Transformed, 1860–1870: War and Peace in the Upper South* (Baton Rouge: Louisiana State University Press, 1988); Stephen V. Ash, *A Year in the South: Four Lives in 1865* (New York: Palgrave Macmillan, 2002); Stephen V. Ash, *When the Yankees Came: Conflict and Chaos in the Occupied South, 1861–1865* (Chapel Hill: University of North Carolina Press, 1995); Daniel E. Sutherland, *Seasons of War: The Ordeal of a Confederate Community, 1861–1865* (New York: Free Press, 1995); Grimsley, *The Hard Hand of War,* 88; Judkin Browning, *Shifting Loyalties: The Union Occupation of Eastern North Carolina* (Chapel Hill: University of North Carolina Press, 2011); LeeAnn Whites and Alecia P. Long, *Occupied Women: Gender, Military Occupation, and the American Civil War* (Baton Rouge: Louisiana State University Press, 2009); Joseph G. Dawson III, *Army Generals and Reconstruction: Louisiana, 1862–1877* (Baton Rouge: Louisiana State University Press, 1982), 1–23; Edelstein, *Occupational Hazards,* 49.

18 *Army & Navy Journal,* January 7, 1865, 316; "General Orders, No. 100," April 24, 1864, *OR,* Series 3, Vol. 3, 148–164; John Fabian Witt, *Lincoln's Code: The Laws of War*

in American History (New York: Free Press, 2012); Giorgio Agamben, *State of Exception*, trans. Kevin Attell (Chicago: University of Chicago Press, 2005); Mary L. Dudziak, *War Time: An Idea, Its History, Its Consequences* (New York: Oxford University Press, 2012); Nelson and Sheriff, *A People at War*.

19   E. R. S. Canby to Howard, June 10, 1865, Reel 15, M752, RG 105, BRFAL, NA.

20   Special Field Orders No. 102, Army of the Tennessee, April 27, 1865, *OR,* Series 1, Vol. 47, Part 3, 324–325; H. W. Halleck to George Meade, April 30, 1865, *OR,* Series 1, Vol. 46, Part 3, 1016–1017; quoted in Perman, *Reunion without Compromise,* 47.

21   Q. A. Gillmore to John P. Hatch, *OR,* Series 1, Vol. 47, Part 3, 627; Gillmore to Stanton, May 29, 1865, with enclosures, *OR,* Series 1, Vol. 47, Part 3, 594–596; Geo. L. Hartsuff to Edward Ord, May 14, 1865, *OR,* Series 1, Vol. 46, Part 3, 1151; Ord to E. V. Sumner, May 17, 1865, *OR,* Series 1, Vol. 46, Part 3, 1166.

22   Chas. J. Baldwin to G. W. Baird, June 7, 1865, *OR,* Series 1, Vol. 47, Part 3, 639; Gillmore to E. L. Molineux, June 5, 1865, *OR,* Series 1, Vol. 47, Part 3, 629–630; Gillmore to I. Vogdes, May 29, 1865, *OR,* Series 1, Vol. 47, Part 3, 597; Vogdes to W. L. M. Burger, June 4, 1865, *OR,* Series 1, Vol. 47, Part 3, 622; J. W. Davidson to Capt. J. W. Miller, M321 Dept. Miss. 1865, RG 393, Part 1, Entry 2433, Box 1, NA.

23   On the fraught, imaginative nature of imperial sovereignties, see Lauren Benton, *A Search for Sovereignty: Law and Geography in European Empires, 1400–1900* (New York: Cambridge University Press, 2009); Lauren Benton and Richard Ross, "Empires and Legal Pluralism: Jurisdiction, Sovereignty, and Political Imagination in the Early Modern World," in *Legal Pluralism and Empires, 1500–1850,* ed. Lauren Benton and Richard Ross (New York: NYU Press, 2013): 1–20. For the most imaginative reading of legal experience in the nineteenth-century United States, see Laura F. Edwards, *The People and Their Peace: Legal Culture and the Transformation of Inequality in the Post-Revolutionary South* (Chapel Hill: University of North Carolina Press, 2009).

24   Grant to Philip Sheridan, May 28, 1865, *OR,* Series 1, Vol. 48, Part 2, 639; General Orders No. 63, Division of West Mississippi, *OR,* Series 1, Vol. 48, Part 2, 650; J. Schuyler Crosby to T. W. Sherman, May 29, 1865, *OR,* Series 1, Vol. 48, Part 2, 651–656; Special Orders No. 172, Division of Louisiana, *OR,* Series 1, Vol. 48, Part 2, 653; General Orders No. 21, Northern Division of Louisiana, *OR,* Series 1, Vol. 48, Part 2, 769–770; John Edwards to John Levering, May 24, 1865, *OR,* Series 1, Vol. 48, Part 2, 583–584; Chas E. Howe to H. Mattson, May 26, 1865, *OR,* Series 1, Vol. 48, Part 2, 612; Howe to Mattson, June 2, 1865, *OR,* Series 1, Vol. 48, Part 2, 733; Dawson, *Army Generals and Reconstruction,* 24–31.

25   P. Jos. Osterhaus to C. T. Christensen, June 19, 1865, *OR,* Series 1, Vol. 48, Part 2, 925–926; Osterhaus to Christensen, June 14, 1865, *OR,* Series 1, Vol. 48, Part 2, 877–878; J. W. Davidson to Capt. J. W. Miller, M321 Dept. Miss. 1865, RG 393,

Part 1, Entry 2433, NA; G. K. Warren to Christensen, May 18, 1865, *OR*, Series 1, Vol. 48, Part 2, 491.

26 Grant to Johnson, July 15, 1865, *PAJ*, 8:410; Gregory P. Downs, "The Mexicanization of American Politics: The United States' Transnational Path from Civil War to Stabilization," *American Historical Review* 117, no. 2 (April 2012): 387–409; Patrick J. Kelly, "The North American Crisis of the 1860s," *Journal of the Civil War Era* 2, no. 3 (2012): 337–368; Nicholas Guyatt, "'An Impossible Idea?': The Curious Career of Internal Colonization," *Journal of the Civil War Era* 4, no. 2 (2014): 234–263; Steven Hahn, "Slave Emancipation, Indian Peoples, and the Projects of a New American Nation-State," *Journal of the Civil War Era* 3, no. 3 (2013): 307–330.

27 *Army & Navy Journal*, June 3, 1865, 649; July 15, 1865, 74; September 16, 1865, 56; September 30, 1865, 88.

28 Vogdes to E. M. McCook, May 19, 1865, *OR*, Series 1, Vol. 47, Part 3, 538; W. L. Burger to C. G. Dyer, June 3, 1865, *OR*, Series 1, Vol. 47, Part 3, 619; Report of Lt. Col. Franklin A. Stratton, May 14, 1865, *OR*, Series 1, Vol. 46, Part 1, 1324–1325; General Orders No. 63, Department of the South, *OR*, Series 1, Vol. 47, Part 3, 498–499; General Orders No. 46, Department of North Carolina, *OR*, Series 1, Vol. 47, Part 3, 503; General Orders No. 22, May 24, 1865, District of Florida, *OR*, Series 1, Vol. 47, Part 3, 623–624; Gillmore to Hatch, May 27, 1865, *OR*, Series 1, Vol. 47, Part 3, 579; Bradley, *This Astounding Close*, 197.

29 General Orders No. 7, Division of the James, *OR*, Series 1, Vol. 46, Part 3, 1171–1172; Geo. D. Ruggles to Commanding Officer Second Corps, *OR*, Series 1, Vol. 46, Part 3, 877–878; J. M. Schofield to J. D. Cox, May 16, 1865, *OR*, Series 1, Vol. 47, Part 3, 511; Henry A. Hale to W. W. Wheeler, May 28, 1865, *OR*, Series 1, Vol. 47, Part 3, 587; Edwards, *People and Their Peace*; Paul D. Escott, *Many Excellent People: Power and Privilege in North Carolina, 1850–1900* (Chapel Hill: University of North Carolina Press, 1985).

30 Gordon, *War Diary*, 416; Henry Kyd Douglas, *I Rode with Stonewall: Being Chiefly the War Experiences of the Youngest Member of Jackson's Staff from the John Brown Raid to the Hanging of Mrs. Surratt* (Chapel Hill: University of North Carolina Press, 1940), 335–337.

31 Byron Strong to Sister Nellie, April 9, 1865, Byron Strong Papers 12225, New York State Library, Albany; F. N. Boney, ed., *A Union Soldier in the Land of the Vanquished: The Diary of Sergeant Mathew Woodruff, June–December 1865* (Tuscaloosa: University of Alabama Press, 1969), 32, 35–36.

32 Edmund L. Drago, *Black Politicians and Reconstruction in Georgia: A Splendid Failure*, illus. ed. (Baton Rouge: Louisiana State University Press, 1982), 1–15; Russell Duncan, *Freedom's Shore: Tunis Campbell and the Georgia Freedmen* (Athens: University of Georgia Press, 1986); David S. Cecelski, *The Fire of Freedom: Abraham Galloway and*

the Slaves' Civil War (Chapel Hill: University of North Carolina Press, 2012), 175–176; David C. Williard, "Executions, Justice, and Reconciliation in North Carolina's Western Piedmont, 1865–67," *Journal of the Civil War Era* 2, no. 1 (March 2012): 31–57.

33   Memoir, Charles W. Squires Papers, Box 23, Civil War Times Illustrated Collection, USAMHI; Doug J. Cater to Dear Cousin Laurence, May 16, 1865, Douglas J. and Rufus W. Cater Papers, LoC.

34   John Hatch to O. O. Howard, July 4, 1865, with enclosures, Reel 15, M752 RG 105, BRFAL, NA; Thavolia Glymph, "Rose's War and the Gendered Politics of a Slave Insurgency in the Civil War," *Journal of the Civil War Era* 3, no. 4 (December 2013): 501–532.

35   Alex H. H. Stuart, *A Narrative of the Leading Incidents of the Organization of the First Popular Movement in Virginia in 1865 to Re-Establish Peaceful Relations between the Northern and Southern States, and of the Subsequent Efforts of the 'Committee of Nine,' in 1869, to Secure the Restoration of Virginia to the Union* (Richmond: William Ellis Jones, 1888), 1–15; Gillmore to Stanton, May 29, 1865, *OR*, Series 1, Vol. 47, Part 3, 594–596; journal entry, May 4, 1865, Container 35, William C. Gorgas Papers, LoC; quoted in Dan T. Carter, *When the War Was Over: The Failure of Self-Reconstruction in the South, 1865–1867* (Baton Rouge: Louisiana State University Press, 1985), 10–11.

36   Stuart, "Narrative of the Leading Incidents of the Organization," 6–10; diary entries, March 17, April 21, May 11, June 5, June 9, 1865, John Brown Papers, Harrisburg Civil War Round Table Collection, Box 6, USAMHI; Col. Van E. Young to General Dana, May 16, 1865, Y D 25 Dept. Miss. 1865, Letters Received, Department of Mississippi, RG 393, Part 1, Entry 2433, Box 2, NA.

37   Lorenzo Sherwood to Johnson, May 29, 1865, *PAJ*, 8:138; James M. Rutland to Johnson, July 6, 1865, *PAJ*, 8:364; Chase to Stanton, in Niven, *Salmon P. Chase Papers*, 5:40; Brooks D. Simpson, LeRoy P. Graf, and John Muldowny, eds., *Advice after Appomattox: Letters to Andrew Johnson, 1865–1866* (Knoxville: University of Tennessee Press, 1987), 8; Perman, *Reunion without Compromise*, 18–25, 28.

38   Douglas Egerton, in his otherwise fine recent book, claims without convincing evidence that "a majority of whites either were grudgingly willing to recognize that the victorious North could make whatever demands it wished, or actually felt betrayed by the planter class and welcomed some Republican reforms." Douglas R. Egerton, *The Wars of Reconstruction: The Brief, Violent History of America's Most Progressive Era* (New York: Bloomsbury, 2014), 26–27, 388.

39   For views that emphasize the early resistance of white Southerners and that undercut portrayals of a window of opportunity, see George C. Rable, *But There Was No Peace: The Role of Violence in the Politics of Reconstruction* (Athens: University of Georgia Press, 1984), 188–191; Jason Phillips, *Diehard Rebels: The Confederate Culture of Invincibility* (Athens: University of Georgia Press, 2007); Lou Falkner Williams, *The*

Great South Carolina Ku Klux Klan Trials, 1871–1872 (Athens: University of Georgia Press, 2004), 1, 146; Perman, *Reunion without Compromise*, 18–28.

40 Richard Maury to My Dear Cousin, May 18, 1865, Container 21; R to Dear Cousin, June 18, 1865, Container 22; R to Miss M. Fontaine, July 26, 1865, Container 22; R to Dear Cousin, August 6, 1865, Container 22; S. Wellford Corgin to M. F. Maury, August 10, 1865, Container 22; Matthew F. Maury Papers, LoC.

41 Thurston to H. Wilson, January 10, 1866, Reel 9, M843, RG 105, BRFAL, NA; Maury to no name, May 20, 1865, Container 22, Maury Papers, LoC.

42 *Army & Navy Journal,* May 27, 1865, 632; Royster, *Destructive War,* 406–408.

43 Proclamation 135, May 29, 1865, available at www.presidency.ucsb.edu/ws/index.php ?pid=72403; Proclamation 134, May 29, 1865, available at www.presidency.ucsb.edu/ws /index.php?pid=72392.

2. EMANCIPATION AT GUNPOINT

1 M. F. Maury to no name, May 20, 1865, Container 22, Matthew F. Maury Papers, LoC; R. to Dear Sir, August 17, 1865, Container 22, Matthew F. Maury Papers, LoC.

2 T. W. Conway to Howard, May 26, 1865, Reel 14, M752, RG 105, BRFAL, NA; Edward Hatch to W. D. Whipple, June 22, 1865, H28 MDT 1865, RG 393, Entry 926, Box 1; Leon F. Litwack, *Been in the Storm So Long: The Aftermath of Slavery* (New York: Knopf, 1979), 113–118.

3 For works that aim to decenter freedom in the story of Reconstruction for other concepts such as equality, access, or survival, see Kate Masur, *An Example for All the Land: Emancipation and the Struggle over Equality in Washington, D.C.* (Chapel Hill: University of North Carolina Press, 2010); Gregory P. Downs, *Declarations of Dependence: The Long Reconstruction of Popular Politics in the South, 1861–1908* (Chapel Hill: University of North Carolina Press, 2011); Jim Downs, *Sick from Freedom: African-American Illness and Suffering during the Civil War and Reconstruction* (New York: Oxford University Press, 2012); Stephen Kantrowitz, *More than Freedom: Fighting for Black Citizenship in a White Republic, 1829–1889* (New York: Penguin, 2013). The great work of the freedom paradigm remains Eric Foner, *Reconstruction: America's Unfinished Revolution, 1863–1877* (New York: Harper and Row, 1988).

4 Stephen Skowronek, *Building a New American State: The Expansion of National Administrative Capacities, 1877–1920* (Cambridge: Cambridge University Press, 1982); Brian Balogh, *A Government out of Sight: The Mystery of National Authority in Nineteenth-Century America* (New York: Cambridge University Press, 2009); William J. Novak, *The People's Welfare: Law and Regulation in Nineteenth-Century America* (Chapel Hill: University of North Carolina Press, 1996); Theda Skocpol, *Protecting Soldiers and Mothers: The Political Origins of Social Policy in the United States* (Cambridge, Mass.: Harvard University

Press, 1992); Mark R. Wilson, *The Business of Civil War: Military Mobilization and the State, 1861–1865* (Baltimore: Johns Hopkins University Press, 2006); Gary Gerstle, "The Resilient Power of the States across the Long Nineteenth Century: An Inquiry into a Pattern of American Governance," in *The Unsustainable American State*, ed. Lawrence Jacobs and Desmond King (New York: Oxford University Press, 2009), 61–87.

5   Mark Grimsley, "Wars for the American South: The First and Second Reconstructions Considered as Insurgencies," *Civil War History* 58, no. 1 (2012): 6–36.

6   Ira Berlin et al., eds., *The Wartime Genesis of Free Labor: The Lower South* (New York: Cambridge University Press, 1990), 74–80; James Oakes, *Freedom National: The Destruction of Slavery in the United States, 1861–1865* (New York: W. W. Norton, 2012), 393–488; Edward E. Baptist, *The Half Has Never Been Told: Slavery and the Making of American Capitalism* (New York: Basic Books, 2014); Walter Johnson, *River of Dark Dreams: Slavery and Empire in the Cotton Kingdom* (Cambridge, Mass.: Harvard University Press, 2013); Joshua D. Rothman, *Flush Times and Fever Dreams: A Story of Capitalism and Slavery in the Age of Jackson* (Athens: University of Georgia Press, 2012); Scott Reynolds Nelson, *A Nation of Deadbeats: An Uncommon History of America's Financial Disasters* (New York: Alfred A. Knopf, 2012), 3–158.

7   Charles Bentzoni to Dear Sir, July 7, 1865, Reel 13, M752, RG 105, BRFAL, NA; Bentzoni to John Levering, July 3, 1865, enclosed in J. J. Reynolds to O. O. Howard, July 13, 1865, Reel 16, M752, RG 105, BRFAL, NA; Hatch to Whipple, June 22, 1865, H28 MDT 1865, RG 393, Part 1, Entry 926, Box 1, NA; J. W. Sprague to Howard, September 25, 1865, Reel 17, M752, RG 105, BRFAL, NA; J. M. Bowmler to Chas. E. Howe, November 23, 1865, Reel 2, M752, RG 105, BRFAL, NA.

8   Q. A. Gillmore to O. O. Howard, July 2, 1865, Reel 15, M752, RG 105, BRFAL, NA; Andrew J. Hamilton to Andrew Johnson, July 24, 1865, *PAJ*, 8:462; Hamilton to Johnson, August 30, 1865, *PAJ*, 8:674–679; Hamilton to Johnson, October 21, 1865, *PAJ*, 9:263–264; Carl Schurz to Johnson, July 28, 1865, in *Advice after Appomattox: Letters to Andrew Johnson, 1865–1866*, ed. Brooks D. Simpson, LeRoy P. Graf, and John Muldowny (Knoxville: University of Tennessee Press, 1987), 78–81.

9   Peter Randolph, *From Slave Cabin to the Pulpit: The Autobiography of Rev. Peter Randolph; The Southern Question Illustrated and Sketches of Slave Life* (Boston: J. H. Earle, 1893), 62; Luke E. Harlow, *Religion, Race, and the Making of Confederate Kentucky, 1830–1880* (New York: Cambridge University Press, 2014); Eugene D. Genovese, *A Consuming Fire: The Fall of the Confederacy in the Mind of the White Christian South* (Athens: University of Georgia Press, 1999).

10 D. W. Whittle to Howard, June 8, 1865, Reel 18, M752, RG 105, BRFAL, NA; Hatch to Genl. Woods, August 18, 1865, F 15 Dept. Ala. 1865, RG 393, Part 1, Entry 102, Box 1, NA; C. C. Andrew to Johnson, May 11, 1865, *PAJ*, 8:59; Joseph Bradley to Johnson, September 8, 1865, *PAJ*, 9:45; Abel Alderson to Johnson, December 3, 1865, *PAJ*, 9:458–459.

NOTES TO PAGES 44-49

11 Bentzoni to Dear Sir, July 7, 1865, Reel 13, M752, RG 105, BRFAL, NA; Samuel
S. Gardiner to Howard, July 28, 1865, Reel 15, M752, RG 105, BRFAL, NA; Hatch to
Whipple, June 22, 1865, H28 MDT 1865, RG 393, Part 1, Entry 926, Box 1, NA; Carl
Schurz to Johnson, July 28, 1865; Simpson, Graf, and Muldowny, *Advice after Appo-
mattox*, 78–81.

12 Congressional Globe, 38th Cong., 2nd sess., 120–22; *Atlantic Monthly*, July 1866,
120–122.

13 James McKaye, *The Mastership and Its Fruits: The Emancipated Slave Face to Face
with His Old Master: A Supplemental Report to Hon. Edwin M. Stanton, Secretary of War*
(New York: Wm. C. Bryant, 1864), 21–38.

14 *U.S. Statutes at Large*, Vol. 13, 507–509; Congressional Globe, 38th Cong., 2nd
sess., 487–488, 961, 985, 988–989; Michael Vorenberg, *Final Freedom: The Civil War,
the Abolition of Slavery, and the Thirteenth Amendment* (New York: Cambridge University Press, 2001); Oakes, *Freedom National*, 430–488.

15 Congressional Globe, 38th Cong., 2nd sess., 38–41, 84–86, 124–125.

16 Steven Hahn et al., eds., *Freedom: A Documentary History of Emancipation,
1861–1867: Land and Labor, 1865*, ser. 3 (Chapel Hill: University of North Carolina
Press, 2008), 1:19–20, 175–176.

17 M. F. Force to J. Warren Miller, September 25, 1865, F 139 Dept. Miss. 1865, RG
393, Part 1, Entry 2433, Box 1, NA.

18 Anthony E. Kaye, *Joining Places: Slave Neighborhoods in the Old South* (Chapel Hill:
University of North Carolina Press, 2009); G. Downs, *Declarations of Dependence*.

19 C. H. Van Wyck to Major Burger, September 1, 1865, enclosed in George Meade
to Secretary of War, September 20, 1865, A 1370, M619, RG 94, NA; John W. Ford to
Johnson, *PAJ*, 9:312–313; Samuel Thomas to Howard, October 12, 1865, Reel 22,
M752, RG 105, BRFAL, NA; *Equal Suffrage Address from the Colored Citizens of
Norfolk, Va., to the People of the United States: Also an Account of the Agitation among the
Colored People of Virginia for Equal Rights; With an Appendix concerning the Rights of
Colored Witnesses before the State Courts* (New Bedford, Mass.: E. Anthony and Sons,
1865), 4–5.

20 H. H. Moore to L. L. McHenry, June 12, 1865, Reel 16, M752, RG 105, BRFAL,
NA; C. W. Buckley to Thomas W. Conway, June 1, 1865, Reel 13, M752, RG 105,
BRFAL, NA; Journal entry, June 15, 1865, Container 35, William C. Gorgas Papers,
LoC; William A. Dobak, *Freedom by the Sword: The U.S. Colored Troops, 1862–1867*
(Washington, D.C.: U.S. Army Center of Military History, 2011), 461–462.

21 *Born in Slavery: Slave Narratives from the Federal Writers' Project, 1936–1938*,
Florida, Vol. 3, 103, available at http://memory.loc.gov/ammem/snhtml/mesnbibVolumes1
.html.

22 Louis Hughes, *Thirty Years a Slave: From Bondage to Freedom; The Institution of Slavery as Seen on the Plantation and in the Home of the Planter* (Milwaukee: South Side Printing, 1897), 172–187. Hughes explicitly states that all these events took place in 1865, but there is some reason for doubt, as he confused days of the week.

23 *Born in Slavery*, Texas, Vol. 16, Part 2, 133; Booker T. Washington, *Up from Slavery: An Autobiography* (Garden City, N.Y.: Doubleday, 1901), 19–23.

24 Washington, *Up from Slavery*, 19–23.

25 *Born in Slavery*, North Carolina, Vol. 11, Part 1, 23–24; *Born in Slavery*, South Carolina, Vol. 14, Part 1, 142–143, Part 3, 234–235.

26 Christopher G. Memminger to Johnson, September 4, 1865, *PAJ*, 9:22–25.

27 C. W. Buckley to Thomas W. Conway, June 1, 1865, Reel 13, M752, RG 105, BRFAL, NA; *Born in Slavery*, Arkansas, Vol. 2, Part 6, 97–98; *Born in Slavery*, Georgia, Vol. 4, Part 2, 55.

28 *Born in Slavery*, Texas, Vol. 16, Part 2, 133; Washington, *Up from Slavery*, 19–23; Randolph, *From Slave Cabin to the Pulpit*, 69; Elizabeth Keckley, *Behind the Scenes; or, Thirty Years a Slave and Four Years in the White House* (New York: G. W. Carleton, 1868), 139; Julie Saville, *The Work of Reconstruction: From Slave to Wage Laborer in South Carolina, 1860–1870* (New York: Cambridge University Press, 1994); Edward Magdol, *A Right to the Land: Essays on the Freedmen's Community* (Westport, Conn.: Greenwood Press, 1977); Steven Hahn, *A Nation under Our Feet: Black Political Struggles in the Rural South, from Slavery to the Great Migration* (Cambridge, Mass.: Belknap Press of Harvard University Press, 2003).

29 Robert S. Hudson to Johnson, November 2, 1865, *PAJ*, 9:332–333; Thos. C. Bennett to [J. F. Usher?], August 25, 1865, in *Freedom: A Documentary History of Emancipation; The Black Military Experience, 1861–1867*, ed. Ira Berlin, Joseph P. Reidy, and Leslie S. Rowland, Vol. 2 (New York: Cambridge University Press, 1983), 743.

30 *Army & Navy Journal*, September 2, 1865, 25; H. W. Halleck to E. M. Stanton, June 26, 1865, *OR*, Series 1, Vol. 46, Part 3, 1295–1297; Fields Cook, Richard Wells, Wm. Williamson, Wm. T. Snead, and T. Morris Chester to Johnson, June 10, 1865, *PAJ*, 8:211–214; H. M. Watterson to Johnson, June 7, 1865; Simpson, Graf, and Muldowny, *Advice after Appomattox*, 43–47.

31 General Orders No. 77, Department of Virginia, June 23, 1865, *OR*, Series 1, Vol. 47, Part 3, 1293; Simpson, Graf, and Muldowny, *Advice after Appomattox*, 42.

32 Q. A. Gillmore to C. Grover, May 10, 1865, *OR*, Series 1, Vol. 47, Part 3, 466–467.

33 General Orders No. 22, District of Florida, May 24, 1865, *OR*, Series 1, Vol. 47, Part 3, 623–624; Charles C. Soule to Howard, June 12, 1865, Reel 17, M752, RG 105, BRFAL, NA; Thomas W. Conway to Howard, May 26, 1865, Reel 14, M752, RG 105,

BRFAL, NA; Conway to Howard, July 21, 1865, Reel 14, M752, RG 105, BRFAL, NA; *Army & Navy Journal*, November 25, 1865, 208.

34 Bentzoni to Dear Sir, July 7, 1865, Reel 13, M752, RG 105, BRFAL, NA.

35 R. Saxton to O. O. Howard, June 4, 1865, Reel 17, M752, RG 105, BRFAL, NA; Reports of Outrages, 1865–1866, RG 393, Part 1, Entry 4158, NA; *Report of the Joint Committee on Reconstruction, at the First Session, Thirty-Ninth Congress*, Vol. 4 (Washington, D.C.: Government Printing Office, 1866), 63–68.

36 T. S. Free to Samuel Thomas, November 1, 1865, Reel 22, M752, RG 105, BRFAL, NA; J. H. Mathews to Stuart Eldridge, January 12, 1866, Reel 22, M752, RG 105, NA; Peter Osterhaus to Capt. M., August 2, 1865, 443 Dept. Miss. 1865, RG 393, Part 1, Entry 2433, Box 1, NA; Soule to Howard, September 8, 1865, Reel 17, M752, RG 105, BRFAL, NA; Schurz to Johnson, August 13, 1865, and Schurz to Johnson, September 4, 1865, in Simpson, Graf, and Muldowny, *Advice after Appomattox*, 90–97, 120–122.

37 *Army & Navy Journal*, December 30, 1865, 294; Randolph, *From Slave Cabin to the Pulpit*, 62–63; F. N. Boney, ed., *A Union Soldier in the Land of the Vanquished: The Diary of Sergeant Mathew Woodruff, June–December 1865* (Tuscaloosa: University of Alabama Press, 1969), 35–36, 48–50.

On the shifts in U.S. soldiers' views of Southerners, see Chandra Manning, *What This Cruel War Was Over: Soldiers, Slavery, and the Civil War* (New York: Knopf, 2007).

38 Orville Jennings to O. O. Howard, October 9, 1865, Reel 21, M752, RG 105, BRFAL, NA; E. M. Gregory to Howard, January 31, 1866, Reel 24, M752, RG 105, BRFAL, NA; Schurz to Johnson, August 13, 1865, in Simpson, Graf, and Muldowny, *Advice after Appomattox*, 96–97; James Rumley, *The Southern Mind under Union Rule: The Diary of James Rumley, Beaufort, North Carolina, 1862–1865*, ed. Judkin Browning (Gainesville, Fla.: University Press of Florida, 2009), 97–98; Josiah Turner Jr. to Jonathan Worth, January 12, 1866, in *The Correspondence of Jonathan Worth*, ed. Joseph Grégoire de Roulhac Hamilton, Vol. 1 (Raleigh: Edwards and Broughton Printing, 1909), 466; Joseph Grégoire de Roulhac Hamilton, ed., *The Papers of Randolph Abbott Shotwell*, Vol. 2 (Raleigh: North Carolina Historical Commission, 1931), 201–202, 213, 249.

39 Hugh P. Beach to Stanton, July 29, 1865, Reel 13, M752, RG 105, BRFAL, NA; Wager Swayne to Howard, August 21, September 11, 1865, Reel 17, M752, RG 105, BRFAL, NA; Soule to O. O. Howard, September 8, 1865, Reel 17, M752, RG 105, BRFAL, NA; Schurz to Johnson, August 29, 1865, in Simpson, Graf, and Muldowny, *Advice after Appomattox*, 108–109.

40 Jeremiah D. Tucker to Johnson, May 30, 1865, *PAJ*, 8:148; J. M. Simms to Dear Sir, May 25, 1865, enclosed in A. P. Ketchum to Stuart M. Taylor, July 1, 1865, Reel 17, M752, RG 105, BRFAL, NA; RJWC to O. O. Howard, January 2, 1866, Reel 23, M752, RG 105, BRFAL, NA; Steptoe B. Taylor to Howard, November 25, 1865, Reel

24, M752, RG 105, BRFAL, NA; James H. Ingraham and W. W. Lewis to S. A. Hurlbut, March 21, 1865, Reel 15, M752, RG 105, NA.

41   *Army & Navy Journal*, July 1, 1865, 706; August 5, 1865, 785; *OR*, Series 1, Vol. 47, Part 3, 560–561; James Redpath to Howard, July 21, 1865, Reel 16, M752, RG 105, BRFAL, NA; W. T. Bennett to L. A. Perry, July 15, 1865, and Bennett to Redpath, July 12, 1865, enclosed in O. Brown to Howard, July 8, 1865, Reel 13, M752, RG 105, BRFAL, NA.

42   *Army & Navy Journal*, October 21, 1865, 130–131.

43   Chas. A. Roxborough et al. to Johnson, June 9, 1865, *PAJ*, 8:204–205; John M. Palmer to Johnson, July 29 [27], 1865, *PAJ*, 8:487–490; Christopher C. Graham to Johnson, July 24, 1865, *PAJ*, 8:458; Annie E. Hutchcroft to Johnson, July 25, 1865, *PAJ*, 8:470–471; Charles Meng to Johnson, October 20, 1865, *PAJ*, 9:261; *Army & Navy Journal*, October 21, 1865, 130; October 28, 1865, 146; November 4, 1865, 162–163; John M. Palmer to Geo. W. Johnston, June 3, 1865, and General Orders No. 32, Department of Kentucky, May 11, 1865, and Chas. A. Roxborough et al. to Johnson, [June 1865], in *Freedom: A Documentary History of Emancipation: The Destruction of Slavery, 1861–1867*, ed. Ira Berlin et al., Vol. 1 (New York: Cambridge University Press, 1986), 619–620, 622, 624–625; Thomas James, *Life of Rev. Thomas James* (Rochester, N.Y.: Post-Express Printing, 1886), 17–19; Victor B. Howard, *Black Liberation in Kentucky: Emancipation and Freedom, 1861–1884* (Lexington: University Press of Kentucky, 1983), 80–83; Aaron Astor, *Rebels on the Border: Civil War, Emancipation, and the Reconstruction of Kentucky and Missouri* (Baton Rouge: Louisiana State University Press, 2012); Anne E. Marshall, *Creating a Confederate Kentucky: The Lost Cause and Civil War Memory in a Border State* (Chapel Hill: University of North Carolina Press, 2013); Harlow, *Religion, Race, and the Making of Confederate Kentucky*.

3. THE CHALLENGE OF CIVIL GOVERNMENT

1   Samuel Thomas to O. O. Howard, October 31, 1865, Reel 22, M752, RG 105, BRFAL, NA; William A. Dobak, *Freedom by the Sword: The U.S. Colored Troops, 1862–1867* (Washington, D.C.: U.S. Army Center of Military History, 2011), 476–479.

2   Thomas to Howard, October 31, 1865, Reel 22, M752, RG 105, BRFAL, NA; Dobak, *Freedom by the Sword*, 476–479.

3   Benjamin G. Humphreys to Andrew Johnson, November 1, 1865, *PAJ*, 9:319–320; T. S. Free to Howard, November 1, 1865, Reel 22, M752, RG 105, BRFAL, NA.

4   Johnson to Humphreys, November 17, 1865, *PAJ*, 9:397; Dobak, *Freedom by the Sword*, 479.

5   James Oakes, "Natural Rights, Citizenship Rights, State Rights, and Black Rights: Another Look at Lincoln and Race," in *Our Lincoln: New Perspectives on*

Lincoln and His World, ed. Eric Foner (New York: W. W. Norton, 2009), 109–134; Steven Hahn et al., eds., *Freedom: A Documentary History of Emancipation, 1861–1867: Land and Labor, 1865,* ser. 3 (Chapel Hill: University of North Carolina Press, 2008), 1:179–180.

6   See, especially, Robert W. Winston, *Andrew Johnson: Plebeian and Patriot* (New York: Henry Holt, 1928); Howard K. Beale, *The Critical Year: A Study of Andrew Johnson and Reconstruction* (New York: Harcourt, Brace, 1930); Paul H. Bergeron, *Andrew Johnson's Civil War and Reconstruction* (Knoxville: University of Tennessee Press, 2011).

7   See, especially, Eric McKitrick, *Andrew Johnson and Reconstruction* (New York: Oxford University Press, 1988); La Wanda Cox and John H. Cox, *Politics, Principle, and Prejudice, 1865–1866: Dilemma of Reconstruction America* (New York: Free Press, 1963); Michael Les Benedict, *A Compromise of Principle: Congressional Republicans and Reconstruction, 1863–1869* (New York: W. W. Norton, 1974); Hans L. Trefousse, *Andrew Johnson: A Biography* (New York: W. W. Norton, 1989); Annette Gordon-Reed, *Andrew Johnson* (New York: Henry Holt, 2011).

8   Tellingly, Eric Foner, the most careful political and social historian of this era, explained secessionists, Radicals, freedpeople, and Northern Democrats by analyzing their understanding of their self-interest but fell into psychoanalysis when it came to Johnson. Eric Foner, *Reconstruction: America's Unfinished Revolution, 1863–1877* (New York: Harper and Row, 1988), 176–185.

9   "Last Public Address," April 11, 1865, in *Collected Works of Abraham Lincoln,* ed. Roy P. Basler, Vol. 8 (New Brunswick, N.J.: Rutgers University Press, 1953), 403; William C. Harris, *With Charity for All: Lincoln and the Restoration of the Union* (Lexington: University Press of Kentucky, 1997), 236–237, 243–245; Benedict, *Compromise of Principle,* 89–97.

10   Charles Sumner to Parke Godwin, March 23, [1862], Box 11, Bryant-Godwin Papers, NYPL; "Message to Congress in Special Session," July 4, 1861, in Basler, *Collected Works of Abraham Lincoln,* Vol. 4 (New Brunswick, N.J.: Rutgers University Press, 1953), 434; "Last Public Address," April 11, 1865, in Basler, *Collected Works of Abraham Lincoln,* 8:403; *Report of the Joint Committee on Reconstruction, at the First Session, Thirty-Ninth Congress* (Washington, D.C.: Government Printing Office, 1866), xi; Herman Belz, *Reconstructing the Union: Theory and Policy during the Civil War* (Ithaca, N.Y.: Cornell University Press, 1969), 10–13.

These divergent theories are especially well covered in Harold Melvin Hyman, *A More Perfect Union: The Impact of the Civil War and Reconstruction on the Constitution* (New York: Knopf, 1973); Benedict, *Compromise of Principle;* McKitrick, *Andrew Johnson and Reconstruction;* Patrick W. Riddleberger, *1866, the Critical Year Revisited* (Carbondale: Southern Illinois University Press, 1979).

11   "Remarks at Vice-Presidential Swearing In," March 4, 1865, *PAJ,* 7:502–507; *Army & Navy Journal,* May 27, 1865, 633; Henry L. Dawes to My Own Dear Wife, April 16,

1865, Container 13, Henry L. Dawes Papers, LoC; Charles Sumner to John Bright, May 1, 1865, in *Memoir and Letters of Charles Sumner,* ed. Edward L. Pierce, Vol. 4 (Boston: Roberts Brothers, 1893), 242.

12 "The Grasp of War Speech, June 21, 1865, Basis for Reconstruction," in Richard Henry Dana Jr., *Speeches in Stirring Times, and Letters to a Son,* ed. Richard Henry Dana III (Boston: Houghton Mifflin, 1910), 246; Charles Francis Adams, *Richard Henry Dana: A Biography,* Vol. 2 (Boston: Houghton, Mifflin, 1891), 330–331.

13 J. G. Dodge to Johnson, June 20, 1865, *PAJ,* 8:263–264; South Carolina Black Citizens to Johnson, [June 29, 1865], *PAJ,* 8:317–318; Salmon P. Chase to John Schofield, May 7, 1865, in *The Salmon P. Chase Papers,* ed. John Niven, Vol. 5 (Kent, Ohio: Kent State University Press, 1993), 46, quoted in Benedict, *Compromise of Principle,* 102–103, 112–113, 124–125; Brooks D. Simpson, LeRoy P. Graf, and John Muldowny, eds., *Advice after Appomattox: Letters to Andrew Johnson, 1865–1866* (Knoxville: University of Tennessee Press, 1987), 4–5.

14 William H. Doherty to Johnson, May 9, 1865, *PAJ,* 8:50–51; John Binny to Johnson, December 16, 1865, *PAJ,* 9:511–513; Benjamin J. Lossing to Henry Wilson, June 19, 1865, Henry Wilson Papers, LoC; *Army & Navy Journal,* June 10, 1865, 661–662; Stanley Matthews to Chase, April 19, 1865, in Niven, *Salmon P. Chase Papers,* 5:28.

15 Richard Ownsby to Johnson, August 12, 1865, Box 1, Entry A1 9, RG 60, NAII; *Official Opinions of the Attorneys General of the United States: Advising the President and Heads of Departments, in Relation to Their Official Duties,* Vol. 11 (Washington, D.C.: Government Printing Office, 1873), 297–298, 301, 315; Brooks D. Simpson, *Ulysses S. Grant: Triumph over Adversity, 1822–1865* (Boston: Houghton Mifflin, 2000), 453; William A. Blair, *With Malice toward Some: Treason and Loyalty in the Civil War Era* (Chapel Hill: University of North Carolina Press, 2014), 234–267.

16 "Testimony," July 18, 1867, *PUG,* 17:224; entry, July 14, 1868; Col. William Moore, "Small Diary," Subseries 9-A, Reel 50, Andrew Johnson Papers, LoC; Gideon Welles to Johnson, July 27, 1869, *PAJ,* 16:74–83; Gideon Welles to Joseph S. Fowler, September 4, 1865, Box 1, Gideon Welles Papers, NYPL; Executive Order, May 9, 1865, available at www.presidency.ucsb.edu/ws/index.php?pid=72146; Brooks D. Simpson, *Let Us Have Peace: Ulysses S. Grant and the Politics of War and Reconstruction, 1861–1868* (Chapel Hill: University of North Carolina Press, 1991), 101; Gideon Welles, *Diary of Gideon Welles: Secretary of the Navy under Lincoln and Johnson,* ed. Howard K. Beale, Vol. 2 (New York: W. W. Norton, 1960), 281, 301–305; Benedict, *Compromise of Principle,* 98–99.

17 Proclamation 134, May 29, 1865, available at www.presidency.ucsb.edu/ws/index .php?pid=72392; Proclamation 135, May 29, 1865, available at www.presidency.ucsb .edu/ws/index.php?pid=72403; John H. Wheeler, *Reminiscences and Memoirs of North Carolina and Eminent North Carolinians* (Columbus, OH: Columbus Printing Works, 1884), 60–61.

18 "Recollections of President Andrew Johnson and His Cabinet," Box 7, Gideon Welles Papers, NYPL.

19 G. W. Ashburn to Thaddeus Stevens, May 29, 1866, Box 3, Thaddeus Stevens Papers, LoC; Judkin Browning, ed., *The Southern Mind under Union Rule: The Diary of James Rumley, Beaufort, North Carolina, 1862–1865* (Gainesville: University Press of Florida, 2009), 177–178, 181.

20 Quoted in Michael Perman, *Reunion without Compromise: The South and Reconstruction, 1865–1868* (New York: Cambridge University Press, 1973), 64–65, 110–111.

21 John Codman Hurd to Francis Church, November 14 [1867] and n.d. [Tuesday], Box 3, William Conant Church Correspondence, NYPL; *Army & Navy Journal*, July 15, 1865, 738–739; July 22, 1865, 754–756, 761; September 9, 1865, 37, 40–41; James E. Sefton, *Andrew Johnson and the Uses of Constitutional Power* (Boston: Little, Brown, 1980), 111.

22 James E. Sefton, *The United States Army and Reconstruction, 1865–1877* (Baton Rouge: Louisiana State University Press, 1967), 255–256.

23 D. P. Jenkins to Andrew Johnson, July 12, 1865, Box 1, Entry A1 9, RG 60, NAII; "General Orders, No. 100," April 24, 1864, *OR*, Series 3, Vol. 3, 148–164; *Official Opinions of the Attorneys General of the United States*, Vol. 8 (Washington, D.C.: W. H. & O. H. Morrison, 1872),365–370; John Fabian Witt, *Lincoln's Code: The Laws of War in American History* (New York: Free Press, 2012).

24 "Testimony," [May 12, 1865], *PUG*, 15:35; quoted in Hyman, *A More Perfect Union*, 152.

25 *Official Opinions of the Attorneys General of the United States*, 11:324–326.

26 James Johnson to Andrew Johnson, September 1, 1865, *PAJ*, 9:7–8; Perman, *Reunion without Compromise*, 114–117.

27 William W. Holden to Johnson, June 26, 1865, and Holden to Johnson, July 24, 1865, *PAJ*, 8:293–294, 463.

28 Perman, *Reunion without Compromise*, 118–119.

29 J. Madison Wells to Johnson, May 5, 1865; Wells to Johnson, July 3, 1865; Wells to Johnson, July 20, 1865; Wells to Johnson, August 25, 1865, *PAJ*, 8:33–34, 342, 504–505, 655–656; Hugh Kennedy to Johnson, August 1, 1865, *PAJ*, 8:661; Kennedy to Johnson, September 1, 1865, *PAJ*, 9:8; *Army & Navy Journal*, August 5, 1865, 785; October 14, 1865, 114; November 18, 1865, 192; Anthony M. Keiley to Johnson, June 25, 1865, *PAJ*, 8:291–292; Johnson to Francis H. Pierpoint, August 1, 1865, *PAJ*, 8:527; John W. Turner to Cyrus Comstock, August 26, 1865, Reel 1, Cyrus B. Comstock Papers, LoC; Report, Moses Stevens, August 12, 1865, Roll 14, M752, RG 105, BRFAL, NA; George Meade to Edwin Stanton, September 20, 1865, A1370, M619, RG 94, Letters Received

by the Office of the Adjutant General, NA; Carl Schurz to Johnson, September 15, 1865, in Simpson, Graf, and Muldowny, *Advice after Appomattox*, 142; James K. Hogue, *Uncivil War: Five New Orleans Street Battles and the Rise and Fall of Radical Reconstruction* (Baton Rouge: Louisiana State University Press, 2011), 21–22; Benedict, *Compromise of Principle*, 118–121; Joseph G. Dawson III, *Army Generals and Reconstruction: Louisiana, 1862–1877* (Baton Rouge: Louisiana State University Press, 1982), 5–30

30 *Army & Navy Journal*, September 16, 1865, 49; September 23, 1865, 65; October 5, 1865, 107; March 3, 1866, 445.

31 Simpson, Graf, and Muldowny, *Advice after Appomattox*, 16; Hyman, *A More Perfect Union*, 193, 198–201.

32 Cherokee County, Alabama, Citizens to Johnson, [ca. September 1865], *PAJ*, 9:3–4; Alexander Mcintosh, John Cannon, and Jno. T. Wallace to Johnson, August 2, 1865, *PAJ*, 8:534–535; *Army & Navy Journal*, September 2, 1865, 17; January 6, 1866, 311; Perman, *Reunion without Compromise*, 132–133.

33 Wager Swayne to Magistrates and Judges of Alabama, August 18, 1865, Roll 16, M752, RG 105, BRFAL, NA; Davis Tillson to O. O. Howard, November 1, 1866, Roll 32, Records of the Assistant Commissioner for the State of Georgia, BRFAL, NA; Clinton Fisk to Howard, September 13, 1865, Roll 14, M752, RG 105, BRFAL, NA; Samuel Thomas to Howard, August 4, 1865, Roll 18, M752, RG 105, BRFAL, NA; Samuel Thomas to Howard, September 21, 1865, Roll 22, M752, RG 105, BRFAL, NA; George Meade to Edwin Stanton, September 20, 1865, A1370, M619, RG 94, Letters Received by the Office of the Adjutant General, NA; T. W. Osborn to Howard, November 1, 1865, Roll 20, M752, RG 105, BRFAL, NA; Thomas Ruger to George Meade, September 19, 1865, enclosed in Meade to Stanton, September 20, 1865, A1370, M619, RG 94, NA; Report, Moses Stevens, August 12, 1865, Roll 14, M752, RG 105, BRFAL, NA; H. B. Quimby to John S. Bishop, October 6, 1865, Q 6 Dept. Miss. 1865, Box 1, Entry 2433, RG 393, Part 1, NA; *Army & Navy Journal*, August 19, 1865, 818; November 4, 1865, 162; Schurz to Johnson, August 29, 1865, and Harvey M. Watterson to Johnson, October 14 and October 20, 1865, in Simpson, Graf, and Muldowny, *Advice after Appomattox*, 106–107, 164–167; Perman, *Reunion without Compromise*, 141; William C. Harris, *Presidential Reconstruction in Mississippi* (Baton Rouge: Louisiana State University Press, 1967), 86–87.

34 W. L. Sharkey to H. W. Slocum, July 22, 1865, Box 2, Entry 2433, RG 393, Part 1, NA; *Army & Navy Journal*, December 2, 1865, 225; December 23, 1865, 278; James M. Tomeny to Johnson, November 21, 1865, *PAJ*, 9:416; Chase to Johnson, October 12, 1865, in Niven, *Salmon P. Chase Papers*, 5:70–72; John Niven, ed., *The Salmon P. Chase Papers*, Vol. 1 (Kent, Ohio: Kent State University Press, 1993), 606; Harris, *Presidential Reconstruction in Mississippi*, 86–87; Perman, *Reunion without Compromise*, 133.

35 *Army & Navy Journal,* October 14, 1865, 113; Isaac Murphy to Johnson, July 5, 1865, Folder 11, Box 73, Entry 9, RG 60, NAII; "Interview with Richmond Merchants," [July 8, 1865], *PAJ,* 8:371; Holden to Johnson, July 24, 1865, *PAJ,* 8:463; Hahn et al., *Freedom: Land and Labor, 1865,* 393–406.

36 Johnson to George H. Thomas, August 14, 1865, *PAJ,* 8:585; Johnson to O. O. Howard, August 24, 1865, *PAJ,* 8:648; Clinton B. Fisk to Johnson, September 1, 1865, *PAJ,* 9:6–7; Benedict, *Compromise of Principle,* 246–251; Hahn et al., *Freedom: Land and Labor, 1865,* 393–406; Russell Duncan, *Freedom's Shore: Tunis Campbell and the Georgia Freedmen* (Athens: University of Georgia Press, 1986).

37 Q. A. Gillmore to Howard, August 17, 1865, Roll 15, M752, RG 105, Register and Letters Received by the Commissioner, BRFAL; Benjamin F. Perry to Johnson, August 20, 1865, *PAJ,* 8:625–626; Johnson to George G. Meade, August 31, 1865, *PAJ,* 8:688; Meade to Edwin Stanton, September 20, 1865, A1370, M619, RG 94, Letters Received by the Office of the Adjutant General, NA; *Army & Navy Journal,* September 16, 1865, 49.

38 William L. Sharkey to Johnson, August 20, 1865; Johnson to Sharkey, August 21, 1865; Sharkey to Johnson, August 28, [1865], *PAJ,* 8:627–628, 635, 666–667; Johnson to Schurz, August 30, 1865, *PAJ,* 8:683; Johnson to Lewis E. Parsons, September 1, 1865, *PAJ,* 9:12; Schurz to Johnson, September 1, 1865, in Simpson, Graf, and Muldowny, *Advice after Appomattox,* 118; Perman, *Reunion without Compromise,* 100, 109; Harris, *Presidential Reconstruction in Mississippi,* 68–74.

39 *Army & Navy Journal,* September 2, 1865, 24–25; October 7, 1865, 104.

40 James B. Campbell to Johnson, September 18, 1865; James L. Orr to Johnson, October 2, 1865; Johnson to Holden, October 18, 1865; Holden to Johnson, October 20, 1865; Andrew Johnson to James Johnson, October 28, 1865; *PAJ,* 9:95, 166, 255, 260, 299; Andrew J. Hamilton to Johnson, March 17 [7], 1866, *PAJ,* 10:225–226; *Army & Navy Journal,* September 30, 1865, 82; November 11, 1865, 177; Benjamin C. Truman to Johnson, March 24, [1866], in Simpson, Graf, and Muldowny, *Advice after Appomattox,* 197; Perman, *Reunion without Compromise,* 74–77; Harris, *Presidential Reconstruction in Mississippi,* 52–54.

41 *Army & Navy Journal,* September 30, 1865, 82; Johnson to Sharkey, August 15, 1865, *PAJ,* 8:599–600; Harris, *Presidential Reconstruction in Mississippi,* 52–54.

42 Johnson to Perry, October, 31, 1865; Perry to Johnson, November 1, 1865; "Response to North Carolina Delegation," [November 10, 1865], *PAJ,* 9:314, 324–325, 369; *New York Times,* November 6, 1865, available at www.nytimes.com/1865/11/06/news /president-johnson-s-policy-and-the-democratic-party.html; Welles, *Diary of Gideon Welles,* 2:378–379; Benedict, *Compromise of Principle,* 128–129; Michael Vorenberg, *Final Freedom: The Civil War, the Abolition of Slavery, and the Thirteenth Amendment* (New York: Cambridge University Press, 2001); Oakes, *Freedom National,* 430–488.

43 C. R. Stickney to Thomas W. Conway, July 13, 1865, D 676, Dept. of Louisiana and Texas 1865, Box 1, Entry 1757, RG 393, Part 1, NA; Jas. L. Brisbin to Thaddeus Stevens, December 29, 1865, Box 3, Thaddeus Stevens Papers, LoC; W. G. Brownlow to George H. Thomas, July 24, 1865, T 384 MDT 1865, Box 2, Entry 926, RG 393, Part 1, NA; Joseph C. Bradley to Johnson, November 15, 1865, *PAJ*, 9:383–385; Central Committee of the Union Party of Tennessee to Johnson, ca. January 9, 1866, *PAJ*, 9:582–583; Parsons to Johnson, October 2, 1865, *PAJ*, 9:169–173; Hogue, *Uncivil War*, 26–27; Benedict, *Compromise of Principle*, 122.

44 Henderson Crawford to Johnson, November 5, 1865, *PAJ*, 9:344; Jonathan Worth to Johnson, March 4, 1866, *PAJ*, 10:213; Harris, *Presidential Reconstruction in Mississippi*, 131–135.

45 *Army & Navy Journal*, November 11, 1865, 177; Harris, *Presidential Reconstruction in Mississippi*, 58, 147–148; Perman, *Reunion without Compromise*, 79; Theodore Brantner Wilson, *The Black Codes of the South* (Tuscaloosa: University of Alabama Press, 1965), 61–80, 96–115; Hyman, *A More Perfect Union*, 419–420.

46 Johnson to Sharkey, November 17, 1865; Andrew Johnson to James Johnson, November 26, 1865; Perry to Johnson, December 2, 1865; James L. Orr to Johnson, December 21, 1865; *PAJ*, 9:400–441, 455–456, 527; McKitrick, *Andrew Johnson and Reconstruction*, 203; Perman, *Reunion without Compromise*, 74–77.

47 Thos J. Wood to W. D. Whipple, December 5, 1865, M686 MDT 1865, Box 2, Entry 926, RG 393, Part 1, NA; Wood to Whipple, December 14, 1865, M699 MDT 1865, Box 2, Entry 926, RG 393, Part 1, NA; *Army & Navy Journal*, December 30, 1865, 294; January 13, 1866, 326; Charles J. Jenkins to Johnson, January 1, 1866; Jenkins to Johnson, January 25, 1866; *PAJ*, 9:556–558, 638–640; Harris, *Presidential Reconstruction in Mississippi*, 77; David C. Williard, "Executions, Justice, and Reconciliation in North Carolina's Western Piedmont, 1865–67," *Journal of the Civil War Era* 2, no. 1 (March 2012): 48–50.

48 Daniel Sickles to Benjamin Perry, December 15, 1865, enclosed in Sickles to O. O. Howard, January 10, 1866, Reel 19, M752, RG 105, BRFAL, NA; H. R. Clitz to W. L. Burger, January 3, 1866, enclosed in Sickles to O. O. Howard, January 10, 1866, Reel 19, M752, RG 105, BRFAL, NA; *Army & Navy Journal*, January 6, 1866, 311; Perman, *Reunion without Compromise*, 79.

49 David Dudley Field to William C. Bryant, September 16, 1866, Box 6, Bryant-Godwin Papers, NYPL; "Reconstruction of the Rebel States," n.d., Container 5, Edward McPherson Papers, LoC.

4. AUTHORITY WITHOUT ARMS

1   John Hope Franklin, *Reconstruction: After the Civil War* (Chicago: University of Chicago Press, 1961), 35–37; Eric Foner, *Reconstruction: America's Unfinished Revolu-*

tion, 1863–1877 (New York: Harper and Row, 1988), 148, 153–155; Steven Hahn et al., eds., *Freedom: A Documentary History of Emancipation, 1861–1867: Land and Labor, 1865,* ser. 3 (Chapel Hill: University of North Carolina Press, 2008), 1:16–17, 173–176; René Hayden et al., eds., *Freedom: A Documentary History of Emancipation, 1861–1867: Land and Labor, 1866–1867,* ser. 3 (Chapel Hill: University of North Carolina Press, 2013), 2:2, 62–69.

2   Richard W. Stewart, *American Military History,* Vol. 1 (Washington, D.C.: Center of Military History, 2009), 373–375; Max Boot, *The Savage Wars of Peace: Small Wars and the Rise of American Power* (New York: Basic Books, 2002), 159–181; Hans Schmidt, *The United States Occupation of Haiti, 1915–1934* (New Brunswick, N.J.: Rutgers University Press, 1995); David G. Chandler and I. F. W. Beckett, eds., *The Oxford History of the British Army* (New York: Oxford University Press, 1996), 138, 161, 183–185; William Wilson Hunter, *The Indian Empire: Its Peoples, History, and Products* (New York: AMS Press, 1966), 361–362; Edward M. Spiers, *The Late Victorian Army, 1868–1902* (New York: St. Martin's Press, 1992), 216–217; T. A Heathcote, *The Military in British India: The Development of British Land Forces in South Asia, 1600–1947* (New York: St. Martin's Press, 1995), 120–121; Benjamin Claude Brower, *A Desert Named Peace: The Violence of France's Empire in the Algerian Sahara, 1844–1902* (New York: Columbia University Press, 2009), 43; John Ruedy, *Modern Algeria: The Origins and Development of a Nation* (Bloomington: Indiana University Press, 1992), 64–65; Gunther E. Rothenberg, *The Army of Francis Joseph* (West Lafayette, Ind.: Purdue University Press, 1976), 41–48; David M. Edelstein, *Occupational Hazards: Success and Failure in Military Occupation* (Ithaca, N.Y.: Cornell University Press, 2011); C. A. Bayly, *The Birth of the Modern World, 1780–1914: Global Connections and Comparisons* (Malden, Mass.: Blackwell, 2004); William Alan Blair, "The Use of Military Force to Protect the Gains of Reconstruction," *Civil War History* 51, no. 4 (2005): 388–402; Robert Francis Engs, "The Missing Catalyst: In Response to Essays on Reconstructions That Might Have Been," *Civil War History* 51, no. 4 (2005): 427–431; Charles S. Maier, "Consigning the Twentieth Century to History: Alternative Narratives for the Modern Era," *American Historical Review* 105, no. 3 (June 1, 2000): 807–831.

3   *Merchant's Magazine and Commercial Review,* January 1865, 22.

4   Ellis Paxson Oberholtzer, *Jay Cooke, Financier of the Civil War,* Vol. 1 (Philadelphia: G. W. Jacobs, 1907), 386, 478–486; Heather Cox Richardson, *The Greatest Nation of the Earth: Republican Economic Policies during the Civil War* (Cambridge, Mass.: Harvard University Press, 1997), 31–65.

5   John Sherman to Greeley, Feb 5, 1865, Container 3, Horace Greeley Papers, LoC; Richard Franklin Bensel, *Yankee Leviathan: The Origins of Central State Authority in America, 1859–1877* (New York: Cambridge University Press, 1990), 14, 237; Stephen Skowronek, *Building a New American State: The Expansion of National Administrative Capacities, 1877–1920* (New York: Cambridge University Press, 1982), 50–51; Robert P. Sharkey, *Money, Class, and Party: An Economic Study of Civil War and Reconstruction*

(Baltimore: Johns Hopkins University Press, 1959); Robert D. Hormats, *The Price of Liberty: Paying for America's Wars* (New York: Times Books, 2007), 79–86; Davis Rich Dewey, *Financial History of the United States* (New York: A. M. Kelley, 1968), 299, 329; James E. Sefton, *The United States Army and Reconstruction, 1865–1877* (Baton Rouge: Louisiana State University Press, 1967), 65, 207–208; Eric McKitrick, *Andrew Johnson and Reconstruction* (New York: Oxford University Press, 1988), 369–370; Mark Wilson, *The Business of Civil War Military Mobilization and the State, 1861–1865* (Baltimore: Johns Hopkins University Press, 2006), 202–203; Herbert Ronald Ferleger, *David A. Wells and the American Revenue System, 1865–1870* (Philadelphia: Porcupine Press, 1977), 6.

6   John A. Stewart to Hugh McCulloch, March 21, 1865, Vol. 1, Hugh McCulloch Papers, LoC; *Merchant's Magazine and Commercial Review*, April 1865, 287–290; Oberholtzer, *Jay Cooke, Financier*, 1:504–507.

7   H. D. Cooke to Jay Cooke and Fahnestock, March 20, 1865, Box 13, Folder 5, Jay Cooke Papers 148, HSP; McCulloch to Jay Cooke, March 21, 1865, Box 13, Folder 5, Cooke Papers, HSP; Henry Clews to My Dear Sir, March 21, 1865, Box 13, Folder 5, Cooke Papers, HSP; D. Crawford Jr. to Cooke, March 27, 1865, Box 13, Folder 6, Cooke Papers, HSP; Stewart to McCulloch, April 5 and 17, 1865, Vol. 1, McCulloch Papers, LoC; H. D. Cooke to Jay Cooke, July 11, 1865, Box 16, Folder 6, Cooke Papers, HSP; *Merchant's Magazine and Commercial Review*, May 1865, 383–385; *Merchant's Magazine and Commercial Review*, June 1865, 447; Oberholtzer, *Jay Cooke, Financier*, 1:529, 535; Hugh McCulloch, *Men and Measures of Half a Century: Sketches and Comments* (New York: C. Scribner's Sons, 1888), 244–245, 256.

8   H. D. Cooke to Jay Cooke and Fahnestock, March 28 and 29, 1865, Box 13, Folder 7; H. D. Cooke to Jay Cooke, April 8, 1865, Box 14, Folder 3, Cooke Papers, HSP; Samuel Wilkeson to Jay Cooke, April 11, 1865, Box 14, Folder 3, Cooke Papers, HSP.

9   *Army & Navy Journal*, October 28, 1865, 152; B. W. Brice to John A. Rawlins, May 20, 1865, *OR*, Series 1, Vol. 46, Part 3, 1180; H. D. Cooke to Jay Cooke, August 23, 1865, Box 17, Folder 6, Cooke Papers, HSP.

10   Steven M. Goode, "A Historical Basis for Force Requirements in Counterinsurgency," *Parameters*, Winter 2009, 45–57; *The U.S. Army/Marine Corps Counterinsurgency Field Manual* (Chicago: University of Chicago Press, 2007), xxvi; Edelstein, *Occupational Hazards*, 52.

11   George Carruthers to L. Thomas, April 30, 1865, George North Carruthers Papers, LoC; *Army & Navy Journal*, May 13, 1865, 600; William A. Blair, *With Malice toward Some: Treason and Loyalty in the Civil War Era* (Chapel Hill: University of North Carolina Press, 2014), 234–267.

12   "An Address Delivered by Major-General N. P. Banks at the Custom-House, New Orleans, on the Fourth of July, 1965," 7–8, Container 82, N. P. Banks Papers, LoC,

7–8; *Army & Navy Journal*, May 6, 1865, 584; *Army & Navy Journal*, July 22, 1865, 753, 760; Joseph Sumner to William Graham Sumner, August 20, 1865, Box 27, Folder 724, William Graham Sumner Papers, Yale University, New Haven, Connecticut; Herman Melville, *Battle-Pieces and Aspects of the War* (New York: Harper and Brothers, 1866), 146–149; Stanton Garner, *The Civil War World of Herman Melville* (Lawrence: University Press of Kansas, 1993), 391–393.

13 Report to Edwin Stanton, October 20, 1866, Official Reports of the Secretary of War, Entry 4, Vol. 7, 218–235, RG 94, Adjutant General's Office, NA; *Army & Navy Journal*, June 10, 1865, 661; T. W. Vincent to John Pope, June 2, 1865, L R 41 1865, Entry 272, RG 393, Part 1, NA; Vincent to George Thomas, telegram, July 12, 1865, A 11 DG 1865, Entry 1711, RG 393, Part 1, NA; Vincent to Thomas, August 23, 1865, telegram A 278 MDT 1865, Box 1, Entry 926, RG 393, Part 1, NA; Edwin Stanton to Andrew Johnson, November 22, 1865, *OR*, Series 3, Vol. 5, 495–520; *Annual Report of the Secretary of War* (Washington, D.C.: Government Printing Office, 1866), 27–28; William B. Holberton, *Homeward Bound: The Demobilization of the Union and Confederate Armies, 1865–1866* (Mechanicsburg, Penn.: Stackpole Books, 2000), 8, 153–154; Noah Andre Trudeau, *Out of the Storm: The End of the Civil War, April–June 1865* (Boston: Little, Brown, 1994), 377–378; E. D. Townsend, *Anecdotes of the Civil War in the United States* (New York: D. Appleton, 1884), 248.

14 *Army & Navy Journal*, July 15, 1865, 737; July 29, 1865, 770; December 9, 1865, 250–251; Gilbert H. McKibbin to J. M. Howard, May 16, 1865, *OR*, Series 1, Vol. 46, Part 3, 1159–1160; Q. A. Gillmore to Stanton, May 29, 1865, with enclosures, *OR*, Series 1, Vol. 47, Part 3, 594–596; Captain John A. Miller to Lieutenant J. W. Haight, October 6, 1865, M113 Dept. Ala. 1865, Box 1, Entry 102, RG 393, Part 1, NA; *Annual Report of the Secretary of War* (Washington, D.C.: Government Printing Office, 1865), 20, 41.

15 Theodore Edgar St. John to Dearest Janie, April 12, 1865, Theodore Edgar St. John Papers, LoC; Daniel Sterling to Dear Wife, May 25, 1865, Box 23, Civil War Times Illustrated Collection, USAMHI.

16 Bela St. John to Dear Parents, June 17, 1865, Bela T. St. John Collection, LoC; Francis Aber et al. to Admiral Lee, June 16, 1865, Container 45, Samuel P. Lee Papers, LoC; *Army & Navy Journal*, August 12, 1865, 811.

17 Major E. Grosskopff to Lt. Col. A. Schrader, November 1, 1865, Mem 343 Dept. Ala. 1865, Box 1, Entry 102, RG 393, Part 1, NA; *Army & Navy Journal*, December 2, 1865, 225; Robert D. Sawrey, *Dubious Victory: The Reconstruction Debate in Ohio* (Lexington: University Press of Kentucky, 1992), 104–106; Trudeau, *Out of the Storm*, 378–379.

18 See, especially, Gary W. Gallagher, *The Union War* (Cambridge, Mass.: Harvard University Press, 2011); Caroline E. Janney, *Remembering the Civil War: Reunion and the Limits of Reconciliation* (Chapel Hill: University of North Carolina Press, 2013).

19 Henry W. Gay to Dear Father and Mother, August 11, 1865, Henry W. Gay Papers, Box 45, Civil War Document Collection, USAMHI; entry, July 4, 1865, W. D. Latimer Diary, Newberry Library, Chicago.

20 J. R. Rey to Lizzie De Voe, June 3, 1865, Folder 1, MISC MSS Rudolph(e) Rey, NYHS; George H. Putnam to Mary Hillard Loines, May 29, 1865, Container 10, Low-Mills Family Papers, LoC; diary entries, May 17, 18, 20, August 9, 19, October 23, 1865, Edward H. Reynolds Papers, Box 21, Civil War Times Illustrated Collection, USAMHI.

21 *Army & Navy Journal,* August 26, 1865, 8, 12.

22 *Army & Navy Journal,* July 8, 1865, 721; July 15, 1865, 737; July 22, 1865, 753; July 29, 1865, 769; August 5, 1865, 785; August 19, 1865, 817.

23 *Army & Navy Journal,* August 26, 1865, 8–9; Andrew J. Hamilton to Johnson, August 30, 1865, *PAJ,* 8:674–679; Hamilton to Johnson, November 27, 1865, *PAJ,* 9:436–439; Barry A. Crouch, *The Freedmen's Bureau and Black Texans* (Austin: University of Texas Press, 1992); Barry A. Crouch, *The Dance of Freedom: Texas African Americans during Reconstruction* (Austin: University of Texas Press, 2007); James Smallwood, Barry A. Crouch, and Larry Peacock, *Murder and Mayhem: The War of Reconstruction in Texas* (College Station: Texas A&M University Press, 2003); Gregg Cantrell, "Racial Violence and Reconstruction Politics in Texas, 1867–1868," *Southwestern Historical Quarterly* 93, no. 3 (1990): 333–355.

24 P. H. Sheridan to John H. Foster, August 16, 1865, G 15 DF, Box 1, Entry 1691, RG 393, Part 1, NA; James Veatch to Crosby, July 21, 1865, V 26 DL 1865, Box 4, Entry 1757, RG 393, Part 1, NA; *Army & Navy Journal,* July 29, 1865, 774–775.

25 O. Brown to O. O. Howard, July 20, 1865, Reel 13, M752, RG 105, BRFAL, NA; Brown to Howard, August 16, 1865, Reel 13, M752, RG 105, BRFAL, NA; Augustus Watson to Howard, August 29, 1865, Reel 18, M752, RG 105, BRFAL, NA; E. Whittlesey to Howard, August 21, 1865, Reel 18, M752, RG 105, BRFAL, NA; Q. A. Gillmore to Rufus Saxton, August 10, 1865, Reel 17, M752, RG 105, BRFAL, NA; Samuel S. Gardner to Thomas W. Conway, July 3, 1865, Reel 15, M752, RG 105, BRFAL, NA; J. L. Fullerton to Howard, September 21, 1865, Reel 14, M752, RG 105, BRFAL, NA.

26 Elliott West, *The Last Indian War: The Nez Perce Story* (New York: Oxford University Press, 2009), xix–xx.

27 Edwin R. Capron to Dear Sister, April 18, 1865, Folder 5, Capron Papers, Newberry Library; *Army & Navy Journal,* July 22, 1865, 760; August 19, 1865, 821; October 7, 1865, 99; Jeffrey Ostler, *The Plains Sioux and U.S. Colonialism from Lewis and Clark to Wounded Knee* (New York: Cambridge University Press, 2004), 63–67; Heather Cox Richardson, *West from Appomattox: The Reconstruction of America after the Civil War* (New Haven, Conn.: Yale University Press, 2007), 33–37; Ari Kelman, *A Misplaced Massacre: Struggling*

over the Memory of Sand Creek (Cambridge, Mass.: Harvard University Press, 2013); Stacey L. Smith, *Freedom's Frontier: California and the Struggle over Unfree Labor, Emancipation, and Reconstruction* (Chapel Hill: University of North Carolina Press, 2013).

28 Thomas F. Meagher to Johnson, July 25, 1865, *PAJ*, 8:473; Meagher to Johnson, January 20, 1866, *PAJ*, 9:619–625; John C. Ferran to Theodore S. Bowers, July 24, 1865, *PUG*, 15:571; John Pope to William Sherman, February 25, 1865, Box 6, Folder 333, Orville E. Babcock Papers, Newberry Library; West, *Last Indian War.*

29 James Harlan to William Dole, June 22, 1865, Roll 5, M606, Entry 164, RG 48, NA; J. R. Doolittle, L. F. S. Foster, and L. W. Ross to Johnson, June 11, 1865, *PAJ*, 8:220; Johnson to James Harlan, June 22, 1865, *PAJ*, 8:270–271; *Army & Navy Journal*, September 9, 1865, 33; Fay A. Yarbrough, *Race and the Cherokee Nation: Sovereignty in the Nineteenth Century* (Philadelphia: University of Pennsylvania Press, 2008); C. Joseph Genetin-Pilawa, *Crooked Paths to Allotment: The Fight over Federal Indian Policy after the Civil War* (Chapel Hill: University of North Carolina Press, 2012); Charles Joseph Kappler, ed., *Indian Affairs: Treaties*, Vol. 2 (Washington, D.C.: Government Printing Office, 1904), 876–878, 883, 1051.

30 *Army & Navy Journal*, July 29, 1865, 770; September 2, 1865, 18; October 7, 1865, 99; October 14, 1865, 120; October 28, 147; *Annual Report of the Secretary of War*, 1866, 18–19; Holberton, *Homeward Bound*, 9.

31 Gillmore to George Meade, September 8, 1865; Thomas Ruger to Meade, September 19, 1865; Alfred Terry to George Ruggles, September 15, 1865; all enclosed in Meade to the Secretary of War, September 20, 1865, A1370, M619, RG 94, Letters Received by the Office of the Adjutant General, NA; Francis M. Bache to A. S. Webb, September 7, 1865, enclosed in Meade to the Secretary of War, September 20, 1865, A1370, M619, RG 94, Letters Received by the Office of the Adjutant General, NA; Peter Osterhaus to J. Warren Miller, August 29, 1865, M357 Dept. Miss. 1865, Box 1, Entry 2433, RG 393, Part 1, NA; Edward Hatch to Thomas Woods, August 18, 1865, F 15 Dept. Ala. 1865, Box 1, Entry 102, RG 393, Part 1, NA; Wager Swayne to Howard, August 28, 1865, Reel 17, M752, RG 105, BRFAL, NA; Brooks D. Simpson, LeRoy P. Graf, and John Muldowny, eds., *Advice after Appomattox: Letters to Andrew Johnson, 1865–1866* (Knoxville: University of Tennessee Press, 1987), 108–109, 121.

32 Alex S. Webb to Thomas Dodamead, April 25, 1865, *OR*, Series 1, Vol. 46, Part 3, 944; M. P. Ferrill to James Steedman, telegram, October 9, 1865, F 43 DG 1895, Entry 1711, RG 393, Part 1, NA; J. M. Brannon to S. B. Moe, August 1, 1865, S 21 DG 1865, Entry 1711, RG 393, Part 1, NA; *Army & Navy Journal*, September 16, 1865, 50; Schurz to Johnson, August 29, 1865, and Schurz to Johnson, September 4, 1865, in Simpson, Graf, and Muldowny, *Advice after Appomattox*, 108–109, 121.

33 Marvin A. Kreidberg and Merton G. Henry, *History of Military Mobilization in the United States Army, 1775–1945* (Washington, D.C.: Department of the Army, 1955), 109; *Annual Report of the Secretary of War*, 1865, 13.

34 James W. Morgan to W. Adams, August 20, 1865, Entry 293, RG 393, Part 1, NA; *Army & Navy Journal,* August 5, 1865, 792; September 9, 1865, 40–41; Salmon Chase to Charles Sumner, August 20, 1865, in *The Salmon P. Chase Papers,* ed. John Niven, Vol. 5 (Kent, Ohio: Kent State University Press, 1993), 65; David M. Jordan, *Winfield Scott Hancock: A Soldier's Life* (Bloomington: Indiana University Press, 1988); John F. Marszalek, *Sherman: A Soldier's Passion for Order* (New York: Free Press, 1993); Benson Bobrick, *Master of War: The Life of General George H. Thomas* (New York: Simon and Schuster, 2009); Freeman Cleaves, *Rock of Chickamauga: The Life of General George H. Thomas* (Norman: University of Oklahoma Press, 1948).

35 Ulysses S. Grant to Stanton, October 20, 1865, *PUG,* 15:357–359; *Army & Navy Journal,* October 21, 1865, 129; Entries, November 29, 30, December 1, 12, 1865, Reel 1, Cyrus Comstock Diary, LoC; Benjamin C. Truman to Johnson, October 13, 1865, in Simpson, Graf, and Muldowny, *Advice after Appomattox,* 155–156, 184–185, 212–213; Brooks D. Simpson, *Let Us Have Peace: Ulysses S. Grant and the Politics of War and Reconstruction, 1861–1868* (Chapel Hill: University of North Carolina Press, 1991), 123; *Annual Report of the Secretary of War,* 1866, 29.

36 Grant to George H. Thomas, November 4, 1865, *PUG,* 15:390–392; Grant to Meade, November 6, 1865, G 181 1865, enclosed in George Ruggles to Meade, November 16, 1865, R 934 1865, Roll 406, M619, , NA; Grant to Meade, November 6, 1865, *PUG,* 15:398–401.

37 *Army & Navy Journal,* January 20, 1866, 343; Simpson, *Let Us Have Peace,* 126–128; Simpson, Graf, and Muldowny, *Advice after Appomattox,* 220–221.

38 Report to Stanton, October 20, 1866, Official Reports of the Secretary of War, Entry 4, Vol. 7, 1865–1866, 218–235, RG 94, NA.

39 E. Whittlesey to Howard, October 15, 1865, Reel 23, M752, RG 105, BRFAL, NA; F. M. Crandal to Major W. Hoffman, November 6, 1865, C 420 FL 1865, Box 1, RG 393, Part 1, NA; Edward Canby to James Wells, January 31, 1866, N 13 DL 1866, Box 6, Entry 1757, RG 393, Part 1, NA; John Wible et al. to Canby, November 29, 1865, F 262 DL 1865, Box 2, Entry 1757, RG 393, Part 1, NA; Report, M. D. McAlister, November 7, 1865, E 52 DL 1865, Box 2, Entry 1757, RG 393, Part 1, NA; T. S. Free to W. A. Gordon, October 18, 1865, F 138 Dept. Miss. 1865, Box 1, Entry 2433, RG 393, Part 1, NA; Free to Samuel Thomas, November 1, 1865, Reel 22, M752, RG 105, BRFAL, NA; F. Grabenhorst to Henry E. Davies, November 25, 1865, G 93 Dept. Ala. 1865, Box 1, Entry 102, RG 393, Part 1, NA; Orville Jennings to Howard, October 9, 1865, Reel 21, M752, RG 105, BRFAL, NA; Henderson Crawford to Johnson, November 15, 1865, Reel 23, M752, RG 105, BRFAL, NA; Tillson to Howard, December 21, 1865, Reel 20, M752, RG 105, BRFAL, NA; Rufus Saxton to Howard, December 19, 1865, Reel 24, M752, RG 105, BRFAL, NA; *Report of the Joint Committee on Reconstruction, at the First Session, Thirty-Ninth Congress,* Vol. 4 (Washington, D.C.: Government Printing Office, 1866), 39–45.

40 W. L. Sharkey to Howard, October 10, 1865, Reel 22, M752, RG 105, BRFAL, NA; C. C. Soule to Howard, September 8, 1865, Reel 27, M752, RG 105, BRFAL, NA; *Army & Navy Journal*, July 22, 1865, 758; James Osgod, Jno. M. Davies, and T. B. James to Johnson, July 27, 1865, *PAJ*, 9:486–487; James M. Howry to Johnson, November 8, 1865, *PAJ*, 9:357–358; *Annual Report of the Secretary of War*, 1866, 53; Elijah P. Marrs, *Life and History of the Rev. Elijah P. Marrs First Pastor of Beargrass Baptist Church, and Author* (Louisville, Ky.: Bradley and Gilbert, 1885), 73–74.

41 George Meade to the Secretary of War, September 20, 1865, A1370, M619, RG 94, NA; Johnson to Thomas, September 4, 1865; Thomas to Johnson, September 7, 1865; Johnson to Thomas, September 8, 1865; *PAJ*, 9:26–27, 41, 48.

42 W. P. Richardson to W. L. Burger, December 26, 1865, enclosed in Daniel Sickles to Howard, January 10, 1866, Reel 19, M752, RG 105, BRFAL, NA.

43 *Army & Navy Journal*, November 18, 1865, 193; Whittlesey to Howard, December 8, 1865, Reel 23, M752, RG 105, BRFAL, NA; Charles Devens to W. L. Burger, December 28, 1865, and James Orr to Sickles, December 13, 1865, both enclosed in Sickles to Howard, January 10, 1866, Reel 19, M752, RG 105, BRFAL, NA; B. F. Perry to Sickles, December 7, 1865; Sickles to Perry, December 15, 1865, R. A. Bray to J. A. Clark, December 21, 1865; Orr to Clitz, n.d., all copies enclosed in Sickles to Howard, January 10, 1866, Reel 19, M752, RG 105, BRFAL, NA; Steven Hahn, "'Extravagant Expectations' of Freedom: Rumour, Political Struggle, and the Christmas Insurrection Scare of 1865 in the American South," *Past and Present*, no. 157 (1997): 122–158; Dan T. Carter, "The Anatomy of Fear: The Christmas Day Insurrection Scare of 1865," *Journal of Southern History* 42, no. 3 (1976): 345–364; Douglas R. Egerton, *The Wars of Reconstruction: The Brief, Violent History of America's Most Progressive Era* (New York: Bloomsbury, 2014), 122–123.

5. THE WAR IN WASHINGTON

1 Harold Hyman's otherwise fine work misses the implications of delay for occupation in deriding the Radical position as a "nay-saying stance." W. P. Fessenden to James S. Pike, April 6, 1866, James Shepherd Pike Papers, LoC; *Army & Navy Journal*, March 10, 1866, 460; Harold Melvin Hyman, *A More Perfect Union: The Impact of the Civil War and Reconstruction on the Constitution* (New York: Knopf, 1973), 306; Mark E. Neely Jr., *Lincoln and the Triumph of the Nation: Constitutional Conflict in the American Civil War* (Chapel Hill: University of North Carolina Press, 2011), 5. On the centrality of war powers to Reconstruction, see, especially, William Archibald Dunning, *Essays on the Civil War and Reconstruction and Related Topics* (New York: Macmillan, 1897); William Archibald Dunning, *Reconstruction, Political and Economic, 1865–1877* (New York: Harper and Brothers, 1907); John William Burgess, *Reconstruction and the Constitution, 1866–1876* (New York: C. Scribner's Sons, 1902); Eric McKitrick, *Andrew Johnson and Reconstruction* (New York: Oxford University Press, 1988); Michael Les

Benedict, *Preserving the Constitution: Essays on Politics and the Constitution in the Reconstruction Era* (New York: Fordham University Press, 2006); Herman Belz, *Reconstructing the Union: Theory and Policy during the Civil War* (Ithaca, N.Y.: Cornell University Press, 1969).

2   Congressional Globe, 39th Cong., 1st sess., 320–322, 363–364, 394–395, 619, 626, 631.

3   *Army & Navy Journal*, December 2, 1865, 224; Michael Les Benedict, *A Compromise of Principle: Congressional Republicans and Reconstruction, 1863–1869* (New York: W. W. Norton, 1974), 130–134; Georges Eugène Benjamin Clemenceau, *American Reconstruction, 1865–1870*, ed. Philippe Jules Fernand Baldensperger and Otto H. Olsen, trans. Margaret MacVeagh (New York: Da Capo Press, 1969), 52–53.

4   While David Donald perhaps goes too far in calling Johnson a "virtuoso of politics" during this period, his interpretation of the president's motivations is a useful counterweight to portrayals of Johnson that overemphasize his psychology or racism to a degree that makes it impossible to understand his actions as military governor of Tennessee or his prior success in politics. "Message to Congress," *PAJ*, 9:466–485; *Army & Navy Journal*, December 9, 1865, 242–243; H. D. Cooke to Jay Cooke, December 6, 1865, Box 19, Folder 1, Cooke Papers, HSP; La Wanda Cox and John H. Cox, *Politics, Principle, and Prejudice, 1865–1866: Dilemma of Reconstruction America* (New York: Free Press, 1963), 134–136; David Herbert Donald, *The Politics of Reconstruction, 1863–1867* (Baton Rouge: Louisiana State University Press, 1965), 23.

5   E. Hustains to N. P. Banks, November 19, 1865, Container 37, N. P. Banks Papers, LoC.

6   Congressional Globe, 39th Cong., 1st sess., 3–4, 296; Amasa Walker to Andrew Johnson, July 18, 1865, *PAJ*, 8:433; "Exchange with South Carolina Convention Delegates," October 13, 1865, *PAJ*, 9:238; Benedict, *Compromise of Principle*, 130–134; Cox and Cox, *Politics, Principle, and Prejudice*, 140–143.

7   Congressional Globe, 39th Cong., 1st sess., 5; quoted in Benjamin B. Kendrick, *The Journal of the Joint Committee of Fifteen on Reconstruction: 39th Congress, 1865–1867* (New York: Columbia University, 1914), 138–149; *Report of the Joint Committee on Reconstruction, at the First Session, Thirty-Ninth Congress*, Vol. 1 (Washington, D.C.: Government Printing Office, 1866), ii–vi; Gideon Welles, *Diary of Gideon Welles: Secretary of the Navy under Lincoln and Johnson*, ed. Howard K. Beale, Vol. 2 (New York: W. W. Norton, 1960), 387, 412.

8   W. P. Fessenden to James S. Pike, April 6, 1866, James Shepherd Pike Papers, LoC; Congressional Globe, 39th Cong., 1st sess., 25–27, 186, 726; appendix, 64–67; Robert Cook, *Civil War Senator William Pitt Fessenden and the Fight to Save the American Republic* (Baton Rouge: Louisiana State University Press, 2011); Charles Albert Jellison, *Fessenden of Maine, Civil War Senator* (Syracuse, N.Y.: Syracuse University Press, 1962); Benedict, *Compromise of Principle*, 38–39; James Gillespie

Blaine, *Twenty Years of Congress: From Lincoln to Garfield* (Norwich, Conn.: Henry Bill Publishing, 1886), 200.

9 Congressional Globe, 39th Cong., 1st sess., 137; *Army & Navy Journal*, January 13, 1866, 326–327; February 3, 1866, 380.

10 Congressional Globe, 39th Cong., 1st sess., 266–273; General Orders No. 3, January 12, 1866, *PUG*, 16:7–8; Ulysses Grant to Johnson, March 14, 1866; Grant to Johnson, February 14, 1866, *PUG*, 16:114, 458–459; Brooks D. Simpson, *Let Us Have Peace: Ulysses S. Grant and the Politics of War and Reconstruction, 1861–1868* (Chapel Hill: University of North Carolina Press, 1991), 128–129; Harold M. Hyman, "Johnson, Stanton, and Grant: A Reconsideration of the Army's Role in the Events Leading to Impeachment," *American Historical Review* 66, no. 1 (October 1960): 85.

11 "Interview with Delegation of Blacks," [February 7, 1866], *PAJ*, 10:41–48; *Report of the Joint Committee on Reconstruction,* 1866, 1:91–95, 120–121; Kendrick, *Journal of the Joint Committee of Fifteen,* 229–234; Welles, *Diary of Gideon Welles,* 2:432; Patrick W. Riddleberger, *1866, the Critical Year Revisited* (Carbondale: Southern Illinois University Press, 1979), 126–128; Brooks D. Simpson, *The Reconstruction Presidents* (Lawrence: University Press of Kansas, 2009), 92–97; Frederick Douglass, *The Life and Times of Frederick Douglass: From 1817–1882* (London: Christian Age Office, 1882), 390–394.

12 Congressional Globe, 39th Cong., 1st sess., 116, 320–322, 365–367, 619–626; Riddleberger, *1866, the Critical Year Revisited,* 68–73; Hyman, *A More Perfect Union,* 436–437.

13 Congressional Globe, 39th Cong., 1st sess., 393, 585–589, 656.

14 Joseph S. Fullerton to Johnson, February 9, 1866, *PAJ*, 10:64–69; "Freedmen's Bureau Veto Message," *PAJ*, 10:120–127.

15 *Army & Navy Journal,* February 24, 1866, 428–429; Congressional Globe, 39th Cong., 1st sess., 936–940; "Washington's Birthday Address," February 22, [1866], *PAJ*, 10:145–147; William H. Seward to Johnson, February 23, 1866; Thurlow Weed to Johnson, February 23, 1866; Jean Sylvanus Cobb Sr. to Johnson, March 7, 1866, *PAJ*, 10:164, 223–224; quoted in Michael Les Benedict, *The Fruits of Victory: Alternatives in Restoring the Union, 1865–1877* (Philadelphia: Lippincott, 1975), 164–165; Welles, *Diary of Gideon Welles,* 2:438–439; Benedict, *Compromise of Principle,* 145–147; Riddleberger, *1866, the Critical Year Revisited,* 85.

16 Congressional Globe, 39th Cong., 1st sess., 986–988; Kendrick, *Journal of the Joint Committee of Fifteen,* 251–256.

17 Congressional Globe, 39th Cong., 1st sess., 474–476, 1757–1760; George A. Rutherglen, *Civil Rights in the Shadow of Slavery: The Constitution, Common Law, and the Civil Rights Act of 1866* (New York: Oxford University Press, 2012), 51–59.

18 Congressional Globe, 39th Cong., 1st sess., 211–212, 478–480, 598–599, 603, 1118–1119, 1151–1153, 1782–1783.

19 "1866," 15–16, Col. William Moore, "Small Diary," Subseries 9-A, Reel 50, Andrew Johnson Papers, LoC; "Veto of Civil Rights Bill," *PAJ*, 10:312–320; Benedict, *Compromise of Principle*, 90–91; William C. Harris, *With Charity for All: Lincoln and the Restoration of the Union* (Lexington: University Press of Kentucky, 1997).

20 Proclamation 153—Declaring the Insurrection in Certain Southern States to Be at an End, April 2, 1866, available at www.presidency.ucsb.edu/ws/index.php?pid=71987; Welles, *Diary of Gideon Welles*, 2:473–474.

21 C. W. Woods to Joseph Holt, April 4, 1866, with enclosures, *OR*, Series 3, Vol. 5, 933; Congressional Globe, 39th Cong., 1st sess., 1753–1755; "Speech to Soldiers and Sailors," *PAJ*, 10:422–428; Salmon Chase to Flamen Ball, May 12, 1866; Chase to Jacob W. Schuckers, May 15, 1866; Chase to Gerrit Smith, May 31, 1866, in *The Salmon P. Chase Papers*, ed. John Niven, Vol. 5 (Kent, Ohio: Kent State University Press, 1993), 94–99; Welles, *Diary of Gideon Welles*, 2:473–474; Charles Fairman, *Reconstruction and Reunion, 1864–88* (New York: Macmillan, 1974), 143–146; Fred Charles Iklé, *Every War Must End* (New York: Columbia University Press, 2005); Gideon Rose, *How Wars End: Why We Always Fight the Last Battle; A History of American Intervention from World War I to Afghanistan* (New York: Simon and Schuster, 2010); Mary L. Dudziak, *War Time: An Idea, Its History, Its Consequences* (New York: Oxford University Press, 2012).

22 This shift in the window of radicalism suggests the difficulty of defining the Congress or its members as radical or moderate. Bills that would have seemed highly radical in 1865 became default Republican policy by 1866. While Michael Les Benedict, in particular, sees unanimity as proof of moderation, it is at least equally possible that the unanimity of the Republican Party reflected its radicalization. Fessenden to Pike, April 6, 1866, Pike Papers, LoC; Congressional Globe, 39th Cong., 1st sess., 3999; Riddleberger, *1866, the Critical Year Revisited*, 103; Hans L. Trefousse, *Andrew Johnson: A Biography* (New York: W. W. Norton, 1989), 247; Benedict, *Compromise of Principle;* Cox and Cox, *Politics, Principle, and Prejudice*, 208; W. R Brock, *An American Crisis* (New York: St. Martin's Press, 1963), 7.

23 Congressional Globe, 39th Cong., 1st sess., 1221, 1526.

24 On the Fourteenth Amendment, see especially William Edward Nelson, *The Fourteenth Amendment: From Political Principle to Judicial Doctrine* (Cambridge, Mass.: Harvard University Press, 1988); Garrett Epps, *Democracy Reborn: The Fourteenth Amendment and the Fight for Equal Rights in Post–Civil War America* (New York: H. Holt, 2006); Michael Kent Curtis, *No State Shall Abridge: The Fourteenth Amendment and the Bill of Rights* (Durham, N.C.: Duke University Press, 1986); Jacobus TenBroek, *The Antislavery Origins of the Fourteenth Amendment* (Berkeley: University of California Press, 1951).

25 Congressional Globe, 39th Cong., 1st sess., 2544; interview with *Lewiston Journal,* May 12, 1866, quoted in *PUG,* 16:257–259; Hannah Rosen, *Terror in the Heart of Freedom: Citizenship, Sexual Violence, and the Meaning of Race in the Postemancipation South* (Chapel Hill: University of North Carolina Press, 2009), 23–86; Altina L. Waller, "Community, Class and Race in the Memphis Riot of 1866," *Journal of Social History* 18, no. 2 (December 1, 1984): 233–246; James Gilbert Ryan, "The Memphis Riots of 1866: Terror in a Black Community during Reconstruction," *Journal of Negro History* 62, no. 3 (July 1, 1977): 243–257; Simpson, *Let Us Have Peace,* 136–137.

26 *Report of the Joint Committee on Reconstruction, at the First Session, Thirty-Ninth Congress,* Vol. 2 (Washington, D.C.: Government Printing Office, 1866), 16–17, 95–97; *Report of the Joint Committee on Reconstruction, at the First Session, Thirty-Ninth Congress,* Vol. 3 (Washington, D.C.: Government Printing Office, 1866), 5–10, 139; *Report of the Joint Committee on Reconstruction, at the First Session, Thirty-Ninth Congress,* Vol. 4 (Washington, D.C.: Government Printing Office, 1866), 8–11, 63–68, 72–76, 152–153. On the impact of testimony on the relationship between freedwomen and the national government, and the ways historians can use such testimony, see Rosen, *Terror in the Heart of Freedom.*

27 Congressional Globe, 39th Cong., 1st sess., 1078, 1753–1755, 2459–2460; Brock, *American Crisis,* 143; Kendrick, *Journal of the Joint Committee of Fifteen,* 199–200, 214–216; Riddleberger, *1866, the Critical Year Revisited,* 114–117; Faye E. Dudden, *Fighting Chance: The Struggle over Woman Suffrage and Black Suffrage in Reconstruction America* (New York: Oxford University Press, 2011); Ellen Carol DuBois, *Feminism and Suffrage: The Emergence of an Independent Women's Movement in America, 1848–1869* (Ithaca, N.Y.: Cornell University Press, 1978).

Although a legend sprang up that Fessenden's illness—the "varioloid"—had changed the history of the amendment, historians are right to be wary of Owen's claims, particularly since Stevens never agreed to Owen's terms of restoration. Robert Dale Owen, "Political Results from the Varioloid: A Leaf of History," *Atlantic Monthly,* June 1875, 660–670; Riddleberger, *1866, the Critical Year Revisited,* 133–135.

28 Congressional Globe, 39th Cong., 1st sess., 2461–2462, 2502–2503, 2532–2534, 2545, 2800–2804, 2869, 2899.

29 William Fessenden to Samuel Fessenden, May 4, 1866, Reel 1, Fessenden Collection, Bowdoin College; Congressional Globe, 39th Cong., 1st sess., 2286–2887, 3148.

30 O. H. Browning to Thomas Ewing, June 26, 1866, Container 18, Thomas Ewing Family Papers, LoC; "Speech at National Union Fair," [June 6, 1866], *PAJ,* 10:566; Welles, *Diary of Gideon Welles,* 2:535.

31 Congressional Globe, 39th Cong., 1st sess., 2776–2780, 3412–3413; *Army & Navy Journal,* June 30, 1866, 710; Simpson, *Let Us Have Peace,* 141.

32 Congressional Globe, 39th Cong., 1st sess., 3842, 3850.

33 Roy P. Basler, ed., *Collected Works of Abraham Lincoln*, Vol. 8 (New Brunswick, N.J.: Rutgers University Press, 1953), 408–409.

34 Grant to Edwin Stanton, October 20, 1865, *PUG*, 15:357–359; Grant to Henry Wilson, January 12, 1866, *PUG*, 16:11–13; Grant to Wilson, February 1, 1866, quoted in *PUG*, 16:42–43; Grant to Stanton, August 2, 1866, *PUG*, 16:274; Wilson to Grant, July 28, 1866, Series 10, Box 5, Ulysses S. Grant Papers, LoC; Congressional Globe, 39th Cong., 1st sess., 1975–1976, 2043, 2352, 3668–3669, 3684; Edward M. Coffman, *The Old Army: A Portrait of the American Army in Peacetime, 1784–1898* (New York: Oxford University Press, 1986), 216–220; Clayton R. Newell and Charles R. Shrader, *Of Duty Well and Faithfully Done: A History of the Regular Army in the Civil War* (Lincoln: University of Nebraska Press, 2011), 4, 62.

35 Those deep-laid financial anxieties sprang up also in the debates over the seemingly nonpartisan loan bill, another act that took an extraordinarily long time to wend its way through Congress. Philip Sheridan to Henry Wilson, June 29, 1866, Henry Wilson Papers, LoC; *Army & Navy Journal*, June 16, 1866, 684; Congressional Globe, 39th Cong., 1st sess., 971–973, 3554–3555, 3804.

36 Congressional Globe, 39th Cong., 1st sess., 3241, 3246–3248.

37 Congressional Globe, 39th Cong., 1st sess., 3241, 3246–3248, 3975–3981, 3994, 4008, 4056, 4113. For contrasting views, see Benedict, *Compromise of Principle*, 186–188; Howard K. Beale, *The Critical Year: A Study of Andrew Johnson and Reconstruction* (New York: Harcourt, Brace, 1930).

38 Congressional Globe, 39th Cong., 1st sess., 4304–4305; Kendrick, *Journal of the Joint Committee of Fifteen*, 353; Trefousse, *Andrew Johnson*, 251–256; Riddleberger, *1866, the Critical Year Revisited*, 146, 152–156.

39 Joseph Medill to Elihu B. Washburne, July 17, 1866, Box 1, Folder 2, ser. III-14, Joseph Medill Papers, Tribune Company Archives, Colonel Robert R. McCormick Research Center at Cantigny, Wheaton, Ill.; W. P. Fessenden to James S. Pike, April 6, 1866, James Shepherd Pike Papers, LoC.

6. A FALSE PEACE

1 "Incidents and Deductions from Army Life in the South West," 1864, George N. Carruthers Papers, LoC; Report, January 31, 1866, Carruthers Papers.

2 Report, February 28, 1866, Carruthers Papers.

3 Ulysses S. Grant to Edwin Stanton, January 29, 1867, *PUG*, 17:38–39; Michael Les Benedict, *A Compromise of Principle: Congressional Republicans and Reconstruction, 1863–1869* (New York: W. W. Norton, 1974), 22; James E. Sefton, *The United States*

Army and Reconstruction, 1865–1877 (Baton Rouge: Louisiana State University Press, 1967); William S. McFeely, *Yankee Stepfather: General O. O. Howard and the Freedmen* (New Haven, Conn.: Yale University Press, 1968), 291–296.

4   Grant to Stanton, January 29, 1867, *PUG*, 17:38–39; "Interview," [February 16, 1867], *PUG*, 17:51–52.

5   Clinton Fisk to O. O. Howard, February 14, 1866, Reel 21, RG 105, M752, RG 105, BRFAL, NA; Michael Perman, *Reunion without Compromise: The South and Reconstruction, 1865–1868* (New York: Cambridge University Press, 1973), 79.

6   Petition, Clem Murray et al., February 23, 1866, A 83 DF 1866, Box 1, Letters Received, 1865–1866, Department and District of Florida, RG 393, Part 1, NA; *Army & Navy Journal*, January 20, 1866, 351; February 17, 1866, 406; March 24, 1866, 487; "Petition of Many Colored Citizens," January 31, 1866, *PUG*, 16:445–447;William C. Harris, *Presidential Reconstruction in Mississippi* (Baton Rouge: Louisiana State University Press, 1967), 77; Harold Melvin Hyman, *A More Perfect Union: The Impact of the Civil War and Reconstruction on the Constitution* (New York: Knopf, 1973), 452–457.

7   Charles J. Jenkins to Andrew Johnson, January 25, 1866, *PAJ*, 9:638–640; Sterling R. Crockrill to Johnson, March 26, 1866, *PAJ*, 10:308–310; *Army & Navy Journal*, February 24, 1866, 422–423; Suzanne Stone Johnson and Robert Johnson, eds., *Bitter Freedom: William Stone's Record of Service in the Freedmen's Bureau* (Columbia: University of South Carolina Press, 2008), 15–16; Brooks D. Simpson, *Let Us Have Peace: Ulysses S. Grant and the Politics of War and Reconstruction, 1861–1868* (Chapel Hill: University of North Carolina Press, 1991), 128–129; Michael Les Benedict, *The Fruits of Victory: Alternatives in Restoring the Union, 1865–1877* (Philadelphia: Lippincott, 1975), 88–89.

8   Memoir, Samuel A. Craig Papers, Box 6, Civil War Times Illustrated Collection, USAMHI; *Army & Navy Journal*, March 3, 1866, 445; Johnson to Grant, February 17, 1866, *PAJ*, 10:110; "Endorsement," February 17, 1866, *PUG*, 16:70–73; Simpson, *Let Us Have Peace*, 130–131.

9   Entries, January 28, 30, February 2, 6, 10, 1866, Diary January–February 1866, Reel 1, Cyrus B. Comstock Papers, LoC; Grant to George Thomas, March 28, 1866, A 104 MDT 1866, Box 3, Entry 926, RG 393, Part 1, NA; Grant to Johnson, February 9, 1866, *PAJ*, 10:69; James M. Chambers to Johnson, February 15, 1866, *PAJ*, 10:95–97; Grant to Johnson, February 14, 1866, *PUG*, 16:458–459; Simpson, *Let Us Have Peace*, 130–131.

10   Return of the District of East Florida, June 1866, Box 72, Entry 65, RG 94, NA; Thomas R. Barry to Johnson, February 8, 1866, *PAJ*, 10:56.

11 J. B. Betz to F. H. Wilson, March 9, 1866, B 102 Dept. Ala. 1866, Box 1, Entry 102, RG 393, Part 1, NA; John T. Sprague to Charles Mundee, August 21, 1866, S 125 DF 1866, Box 3, Entry 1691, RG 393, Part 1, NA; Wager Swayne to O. O. Howard, January 31, 1866, Reel 19, RG 105, M752, RG 105, BRFAL, NA; Swayne to Charles Woods, December 28, 1865, S 130 Dept. Ala. 1866, Box 1, Entry 102, RG 393, Part 1, NA.

12 Grant to Thomas, March 28, 1866, A 104 MDT 1866, Box 3, Entry 926, RG 393, Part 1, NA; *Army & Navy Journal,* February 17, 1866, 406.

13 A. J. Edgerton to Nathaniel Burbank, May 31, 1866, E 41 DL 1866, Box 5, Entry 1757, RG 393, Part 1, NA; C. M. Hamilton to S. L. McHenry, April 30, 1866, enclosed in T. W. Osborn to Howard, May 8, 1866, Reel 27, RG 105, M752, RG 105, BRFAL, NA; E. M. Gregory to Howard, January 31, 1866, Reel 24, RG 105, M752, RG 105, BRFAL, NA; *Army & Navy Journal,* July 14, 1866, 743; Johnson and Johnson, *Bitter Freedom,* 9–11, 15–17, 30, 99–100.

14 Grant to Edward O. C. Ord, December 6, 1865, *PUG,* 16:400–406; Andrew J. Hamilton to Johnson, March 1, 1866, *PAJ,* 10:202–203; Settlers in Cherokee Neutral Lands to Johnson, December 2, 1865, *PAJ,* 9:457–458; Robert B. Mitchell to Johnson, [ca. August 1866], *PAJ,* 11:4–5; *Army & Navy Journal,* August 18, 1866, 12; August 25, 1866, 12.

15 William P. Mallett to Thaddeus Stevens, May 28, 1866, Box 3, Stevens Papers, LoC; John A. Bogert to S. B. Moe, February 22, 1866, C 36 DG 1866, Entry 1711, RG 393, Part 1, NA; B. H. Grierson to William Whipple, January 10, 1866, H 147 Dept. Ala. 1866, Box 1, Entry 102, RG 393, Part 1, NA; O. Brown to Howard, January 25, 1866, Reel 25, M752, RG 105, BRFAL, NA; Thomas Harley et al. to Joseph E. Oates, March 6, 1866, Reel 27, M752, RG 105, BRFAL, NA; J. H. Mathews to Stuart Eldridge, January 12, 1866, Reel 22, RG 105, M752, RG 105, BRFAL, NA; B. W. Hunter to Grant, August 7, 1866, *PUG,* 16:536–537.

16 Memoir, Samuel A. Craig Papers, Box 6, Civil War Times Illustrated Collection, USAMHI; William Logan to J. M. Sanna, May 18, 1866, L 17 DF 1866, Box 2, Entry 1691, RG 393, Part 1, NA; C. M. Hamilton to Major S. L. McHenry, April 30, 1866, enclosed in Osborn to Howard, May 8, 1866, Reel 27, M752, RG 105, BRFAL, NA; John Orcutt to Johnson, April 25, 1866, *PAJ,* 10:449–450.

17 Proclamation, April 2, 1866, *PAJ,* 10:349–352; G. W. Williams to Johnson, April 12, 1866, *PAJ,* 10:409–410; C. R. Woods to Joseph Holt, April 4, 1866, *OR,* Series 3, Vol. 5, 933; *Army & Navy Journal,* April 7, 1866, 524; Tillson to Howard, April 7, 1866, Reel 27, M752, RG 105, BRFAL, NA.

18 E. D. Townsend to Edward Canby, April 9, 1866, A 125 DL 1866, Box 4, Entry 1757, RG 393, Part 1, NA; Bland Ballard to Johnson, April 28, 1866, *PAJ,* 10:459–460; Humphrey Marshall to Johnson, May 2, 1866, *PAJ,* 10:470–471; Grant to Alfred H.

Terry, April 3, 1866, *PUG*, 16:149–150; Salmon Chase to Gerrit Smith, May 31, 1866, in *The Salmon P. Chase Papers*, ed. John Niven, Vol. 5 (Kent, Ohio: Kent State University Press, 1993), 98–99.

19 Edwin Stanton to Edward Canby, May 5, 1866, W 107 DL 1866, Box 6, Entry 1757, RG 393, Part 1, NA; General Orders No. 29, May 2, 1866, Box 2, Entry 1664, RG 393, Part 1, NA; General Orders No. 30, Dept. Fla., May 9, 1866, Box 2, Entry 1664, RG 393, Part 1, NA; General Orders No. 31, Dept. Fla., May 11, 1866, Box 2, Entry 1664, RG 393, Part 1, NA; General Orders No. 34, Dept. Fla., June 9, 1866, Box 2, Entry 1664, RG 393, Part 1, NA; L. L. Zulavsky to J. Brickle, June 15, 1866, enclosed in Zulavsky to Charles Mundee, June 20, 1866, Z 9 DF 1866, Box 3, Entry 1691, RG 393, Part 1, NA; James Janney to David S. Walker, June 25, 1866, J 38 DF 1866, Box 2, Entry 1691, RG 393, Part 1, NA; W. P. McKellar to Johnson, July 23, 1866, Box 5, Folder 5, President's Letters, 1866, Entry 9, RG 60, NAII; Case of Jefferson Lacey, June 27, 1866, Box 5, Folder 4, President's Letters, 1866, Entry 9, RG 60, NAII; *Army & Navy Journal*, April 28, 1866, 566; July 14, 1866, 742, 752; July 28, 1866, 774; August 18, 1866, 822; James Hughes to Johnson, January 19, 1866, *PAJ*, 9:609–610; Jonathan Worth to Johnson, July 11, 1866, *PAJ*, 10:673; W. P. McKellar to Johnson, July 23, 1866, *PAJ*, 10:717; Hyman, *A More Perfect Union*, 487–489; Simpson, *Let Us Have Peace*, 138.

20 James Speed to Johnson, July 13, 1866, *PAJ*, 10:688–689; Detlev Vagts, "Military Commissions: The Forgotten Reconstruction Chapter," *American University International Law Review* 23, no. 2 (January 1, 2007): 231–274.

21 Circular, August 10, 1866, Dept. Fla., Box 2, Entry 1664, RG 393, Part 1, NA; General Orders No. 44, [July 6, 1866], *PUG*, 16:228–230.

22 *Army & Navy Journal*, September 1, 1866, 30; Jacob Barker to Johnson, August 9, 1866, *PAJ*, 11:45; James K. Hogue, *Uncivil War: Five New Orleans Street Battles and the Rise and Fall of Radical Reconstruction* (Baton Rouge: Louisiana State University Press, 2011), 31–52; Joseph G. Dawson III, *Army Generals and Reconstruction: Louisiana, 1862–1877* (Baton Rouge: Louisiana State University Press, 1982), 36–43.

23 B. Dally to N. P. Banks, July 31, 1866, Container 38, N. P. Banks Papers, LoC; Guido Norman Lieber to Francis Lieber, August 13, 1866, Box 55, LI 5173, Francis Lieber Papers, Huntington Library, San Marino, California; *Army & Navy Journal*, August 11, 1866, 812.

24 Proclamation, August 20, 1866, *PAJ*, 11:100–104; "Speech in New York," [August 29, 1866], *PAJ*, 153–166; "Speech in Cleveland," [September 3, 1866], *PAJ*, 11:154–181; Simpson, *Let Us Have Peace*, 144.

25 Henry Stanbery to Johnson, October 12, 1866, *PAJ*, 11:345–356; *United States v. Anderson*, 9 *Wall.* 56; *McElrath v. United States*, 102 U.S. 426; *McKee v. Rains*, 10 *Wall.* 22; *The Protector*, 12 *Wall* 700; *Burke v. Mittenberger*, 19 *Wall* 519. Because of jurisdictional questions arising from Congress's revision of circuit court lines, however, Chase still

did not hold session in Virginia until 1867. Chase to Jacob W. Schuckers, September 24, 1866, in Niven, *Salmon P. Chase Papers*, 5:126–127.

26 George K. Leet to Philip Sheridan, October 17, 1866, A 103 DG 1866, Box 14, Entry 1756, RG 393, Part 1, NA; Leet to Sheridan, November 1, 1866, A 131 DG 1866, Box 14, Entry 1756, RG 393, Part 1, NA; Charles Griffin to George Hartsuff, January 31, 1867, E T 17 DG 1867, Box 17, Entry 1756, RG 393, Part 1, NA; J. G. Foster to Hartsuff, September 20, 1866, F 22 DG 1866, Box 14, Entry 1756, RG 393, Part 1, NA; Duff Green to Johnson, August 6, 1866, Box 105, Folder 2, Entry 9, RG 60, Department of Justice, NAII; *Army & Navy Journal*, October 13, 1866, 118; October 20, 1866, 144; Grant to Stanton, November 22, 1866, *PUG*, 16:389–392; Grant to Ord, December 6, 1866, *PUG*, 16:398–404; Robert J. Kaczorowski, *The Politics of Judicial Interpretation: The Federal Courts, Department of Justice and Civil Rights, 1866–1876* (Dobbs Ferry, N.Y.: Oceana, 1985), 34–36; Simpson, *Let Us Have Peace*, 144–146.

27 Special Orders No. 48, September 21, 1866; No. 63, December 31, 1866; No. 5, January 14, 1867, Post of Darlington, S.C., Entry 4135, RG 393, Part 1, NA; Reports of Arrests of Civilians at Military Posts in South Carolina, Entry 4161, RG 393, Part 1, NA; Special Orders No. 1, January 5, 1867, Post of Georgetown, S.C., Entry 4135, RG 393, Part 1, NA; Martin Flood to A. F. Hayden, September 10, 1866, F 50 BRFAL 1866, Box 15, Entry 1756, RG 393, Part 1, NA; Dover, Arkansas, Return, November 1866, M617, RG 94, Records of the Adjutant General, NA; Tillson to Howard, November 1, 1866, Reel 32, Records of the Assistant Commissioner for the State of Georgia, BRFAL; *Army & Navy Journal*, September 1, 1866, 22; September 15, 1866, 46; Grant to George H. Thomas, November 24, 1866, *PUG*, 16:392–393.

28 James Throckmorton to Stanbery, October 12, 1866, enclosed in Throckmorton to Stanbery, October 15, 1866, Box 135, Folder 8, Letters Received (Texas), 1848–1870, Entry 9, RG 60, NAII; E. C. Mason, Report of Board of Inquiry, October 2, 1866, M 140 DG 1866, Box 15, Entry 1756, RG 393, Part 1, NA; O. M. Roberts and D. G. Burnet to Johnson, December 6, 1866, *PAJ*, 11:529–533; Grant to Sheridan, September 21, 1866, *PUG*, 16:312–314.

29 John Martin to Major Woodruff, January 5, 1867, M 19 DG 1867, Box 16, Entry 1756, RG 393, Part 1, NA; Townsend to Stanton, October 20, 1866, *OR*, Series 3, Vol. 5, 1012–1013; Townsend to Grant, October 20, 1867, OR, Series 3, Vol. 5, 1047–1048.

30 S. M. Quincy to J. Schuyler Crosby, October 22, 1866, M 90 DG 1866, Box 15, Entry 1756, RG 393, Part 1, NA; W. H. Webster to C. R. Stickney, September 10, 1866, W 31 DG 1866, Box 16, Entry 1756, RG 393, Part 1, NA; D. Sturgis to A. A. Genl. District of Texas, December 18, 1866, S 26 DT 1866, Box 17, Entry 1756, Dept. of the Gulf, RG 393, Part 1, NA; Allen W. Trelease, *White Terror: The Ku Klux Klan Conspiracy and Southern Reconstruction* (New York: Harper and Row, 1971); Scott Reynolds Nelson, *Iron Confederacies: Southern Railways, Klan Violence, and Reconstruction* (Chapel Hill: University of North Carolina Press, 1999); Elaine Frantz Parsons,

"Midnight Rangers: Costume and Performance in the Reconstruction-Era Ku Klux Klan," *Journal of American History* 92, no. 3 (December 1, 2005): 811; George C. Rable, *But There Was No Peace: The Role of Violence in the Politics of Reconstruction* (Athens: University of Georgia Press, 1984); Carole Emberton, *Beyond Redemption: Race, Violence, and the American South after the Civil War* (Chicago: University of Chicago Press, 2013).

31 James Janney to General J. G. Foster, August 30, 1866, J 49 DF 1866, Box 2, Entry 1691, RG 393, Part 1, NA; Sprague to Hartsuff, February 28, 1867, F 1 FMD 1867, Box 1, RG 393, Part 1, NA; John Price to Foster, November 15, 1866, P 36 DG 1866, Box 15, Entry 1756, RG 393, Part 1, NA; John Martin to Major Woodruff, January 5, 1867, M 19 DG 1867, Box 16, Entry 1756, Department of the Gulf, RG 393, Part 1, NA; J. C. Emerson to D. Richards, January 11, 1867, Vol. 6, Reel 4, William Pitt Fessenden Papers, LoC; D. J. Baldwin to Henry Stanbery, February 2, 1867, Box 135, Folder 1, Letters Received (Texas), 1848–1870, Entry 9, RG 60, NAII; Grant to Stanton, January 29, 1867, *PUG*, 17:38–39.

32 Diary entries, September 22, October 12, 1866, Reel 1, Cyrus B. Comstock Papers, LoC; Harrison J. Campbell to William G. Brownlow, December 8, 1866, 354 C MDT 1866, Box 3, Entry 926, RG 393, Part 1, NA; Samuel B. Franks to Johnson, September 10, 1866, *PAJ*, 11:202–203; Trelease, *White Terror.*

33 W. T. C. Brannen to General Davis Tillson, October 15, 1866, Box 86, Folder 8, Letters Received (Georgia), 1811–1870, Entry 9, RG 60, NAII; John Erskine to Henry Fitch, December 12, 1866, Box 86, Folder 2, Letters Received (Georgia), 1811–1870, Entry 9, RG 60, NAII; Henry Fitch to Henry Stanbery, January 22, 1867, Box 86, Folder 2, Letters Received (Georgia), 1811–1870, Entry 9, RG 60, NAII; Worth to Johnson, November 30, 1866, *PAJ*, 11:498–499; Jonas H. Ramsey to Johnson, January 27, 1867, *PAJ*, 11:630–631.

34 Johnson and Johnson, *Bitter Freedom*, 31–33.

35 71 U.S. 2 (1866); Hyman, *A More Perfect Union*, 493–496; Brook Thomas, *Civic Myths: A Law and Literature Approach to Citizenship* (Chapel Hill: University of North Carolina Press, 2007), 102–124.

36 Aaron A. Bradley to Johnson, April 27, 1866, *PAJ*, 10:456–457; Stanton to Johnson, February 15, 1867, *PAJ*, 12:35; Kaczorowski, *Politics of Judicial Interpretation*, 31; Simpson, *Let Us Have Peace*, 167; Paul A. Cimbala, *Under the Guardianship of the Nation: The Freedmen's Bureau and the Reconstruction of Georgia, 1865–1870* (Athens: University of Georgia Press, 1997), 185–188; Russell Duncan, *Freedom's Shore: Tunis Campbell and the Georgia Freedmen* (Athens: University of Georgia Press, 1986).

37 *Army & Navy Journal*, September 1, 1866, 23, 28; Gordon Granger to Johnson, August 24, 1866, *PAJ*, 11:127–128.

38 *Army & Navy Journal*, October 6, 1866, 109; John William De Forest, *A Union Officer in the Reconstruction*, ed. David Morris Potter (Baton Rouge: Louisiana State University Press, 1997), 29–39.

39 Grant to Ord, March 1, 1867, *PUG,* 17:66–72.

40 "Interview," [February 16, 1867], *PUG,* 17:51–52.

7. ENFRANCHISEMENT BY MARTIAL LAW

1 Congressional Globe, 39th Cong., 2nd sess., 1366–1367, 1440–1441; appendix, 90–91.

2 Michael Perman, *Reunion without Compromise: The South and Reconstruction, 1865–1868* (New York: Cambridge University Press, 1973), 270–272; Michael Les Benedict, *A Compromise of Principle: Congressional Republicans and Reconstruction, 1863–1869* (New York: W. W. Norton, 1974), 240–241; Eric Foner, *Reconstruction: America's Unfinished Revolution, 1863–1877* (New York: Harper and Row, 1988); W. R Brock, *An American Crisis* (New York: St. Martin's Press, 1963); Benjamin B. Kendrick, *The Journal of the Joint Committee of Fifteen on Reconstruction: 39th Congress, 1865–1867* (New York: Columbia University, 1914); William Archibald Dunning, *Reconstruction, Political and Economic, 1865–1877* (New York: Harper and Brothers, 1907).

3 *Army & Navy Journal,* November 10, 1866, 189; Gideon Welles, *Diary of Gideon Welles: Secretary of the Navy under Lincoln and Johnson,* ed. Howard K. Beale, Vol. 2 (New York: W. W. Norton, 1960), 617.

4 J. J. Fisher to Benjamin Butler, February 25, 1867, Container 42, Benjamin F. Butler Papers, LoC; John C. O'Neill to Butler, March 11, 13, 1867, Container 42, Butler Papers, LoC; William Alexander to Butler, November 23, 1866, Container 41, Butler Papers, LoC; E. P. Upton to William P. Fessenden, December 24, 1866, Vol. 6, Reel 4, William P. Fessenden Papers, LoC; Congressional Globe, 39th Cong., 2nd sess., 1177–1180.

5 Congressional Globe, 39th Cong., 2nd sess., 250–253; David Herbert Donald, *The Politics of Reconstruction, 1863–1867* (Baton Rouge: Louisiana State University Press, 1965), 65–70.

6 Benjamin F. Perry to Andrew Johnson, November 10, 1866, *PAJ,* 11:449; Johnson to Lewis E. Parsons, January 17, 1867, *PAJ,* 11:611; Wager Swayne to Salmon P. Chase, December 10, 1866, in *The Salmon P. Chase Papers,* ed. John Niven, Vol. 5 (Kent, Ohio: Kent State University Press, 1993), 142–143; Brock, *American Crisis,* 183.

7 Congressional Globe, 39th Cong., 2nd sess., 3, 1290–1292; appendix, 2–3; Ulysses S. Grant to Edwin M. Stanton, October 27, 1866, *PUG,* 16:357–358.

8 Congressional Globe, 39th Cong., 2nd sess., 39–41, 63–64, 84, 105–109, 138, 313, 344.

9 Congressional Globe, 39th Cong., 2nd sess., 250–253, 349–352, 566–567, 594, 621–624, 814–815; Kendrick, *Journal of the Joint Committee of Fifteen,* 355–361.

10 Congressional Globe, 39th Cong., 2nd sess., 53, 116–117, 215–218, 596, 817; appendix, 78–79; Donald, *Politics of Reconstruction*, 65–81; Benedict, *Compromise of Principle*, 215–218; Gerard N. Magliocca, *American Founding Son: John Bingham and the Invention of the Fourteenth Amendment* (New York: New York University Press, 2013), 131–141.

11 Congressional Globe, 39th Cong., 2nd sess., 1130–1133, 1175, 1183–1184.

12 Kendrick believes that Fessenden's suggestion that the military bill might need amendment proves that he hoped to add a plan for restoration, but this reading does not fit Fessenden's opposition to those restoration plans over the rest of the session and seems to be based on a vestigial belief in Fessenden's conservatism. William P. Fessenden to Samuel Fessenden, January 19, 1867, Reel 1, Fessenden Collection, Bowdoin College; Congressional Globe, 39th Cong., 2nd sess., 1076, 1223–1224, 1302–1304; Benedict, *Compromise of Principle*, 223–225, 235–239; Kendrick, *Journal of the Joint Committee of Fifteen*, 125–129, 377–382, 406–410; Robert Cook, *Civil War Senator William Pitt Fessenden and the Fight to Save the American Republic* (Baton Rouge: Louisiana State University Press, 2011), 211–223; Donald, *Politics of Reconstruction*, 65–81.

13 *Army & Navy Journal*, February 9, 1867, 396–397; Congressional Globe, 39th Cong., 2nd sess., 1099, 1103–1104, 1181–1182.

14 Congressional Globe, 39th Cong., 2nd sess., 1098.

15 Congressional Globe, 39th Cong., 2nd sess., 1077–1078; appendix, 102–104.

16 Congressional Globe, 39th Cong., 2nd sess., 1082–1083, 1182–1183, 1210; appendix, 121–123; Kendrick, *Journal of the Joint Committee of Fifteen*, 394–396.

17 Congressional Globe, 39th Cong., 2nd sess., 53, 116–117, 215–218, 349–352, 596, 817; appendix, 78–79; *Nation*, November 29, 1866, 430; Benedict, *Compromise of Principle*, 222.

18 Congressional Globe, 39th Cong., 2nd sess., 1206–1210, 1213–1215; Kendrick, *Journal of the Joint Committee of Fifteen*, 403–405.

19 Congressional Globe, 39th Cong., 2nd sess., 1213–1215; Kendrick, *Journal of the Joint Committee of Fifteen*, 403–405.

20 Congressional Globe, 39th Cong., 2nd sess., 1223–1224, 1302–1304; Benedict, *Compromise of Principle*, 235–239; Kendrick, *Journal of the Joint Committee of Fifteen*, 406–410.

21 Congressional Globe, 39th Cong., 2nd sess., 1361, 1364, 1366–1369, 1384; Kendrick, *Journal of the Joint Committee of Fifteen*, 406–410.

22 Congressional Globe, 39th Cong., 2nd sess., 1398, 1459, 1467–1469; Kendrick, *Journal of the Joint Committee of Fifteen*, 406–410; Brock, *American Crisis*, 196–199.

23 While Michael Les Benedict—on the whole the most careful and convincing historian of the congressional struggle—attributes Fessenden's actions to his conservative desire to stick to the Fourteenth Amendment as terms, it is more useful to understand his actions, and the broader fight within Congress, as divisions over occupation and time, not simply fractures between Radicals and conservatives. With one exception, Fessenden and Sumner voted together for much of the rest of the session and on the key Reconstruction questions of the March 1867 session. Congressional Globe, 39th Cong., 2nd sess., 1316–1322, 1329; Cook, *Civil War Senator William Pitt Fessenden*, 217–218; Benedict, *Compromise of Principle*, 235–239; Kendrick, *Journal of the Joint Committee of Fifteen*, 411–414.

24 Early in the session, Navy Secretary Gideon Welles noted that Fessenden, despite his reputation for conservatism, supported Sumner's "measures when pressed to a decision." It was Fessenden's behavior at this session that led William R. Brock to say that Fessenden leaned, in "his cautious way, more definitely towards Radicalism." Notes [1868], Vol. 7, Reel 4, William P. Fessenden Papers, LoC; Congressional Globe, 39th Cong., 2nd sess., 1556–1563; Welles, *Diary of Gideon Welles*, 2:634–636; Brock, *American Crisis*, 175–176.

25 Congressional Globe, 39th Cong., 2nd sess., 1334–1336, 1357–1358, 1399, 1400, 1626–1627.

26 Congressional Globe, 39th Cong., 2nd sess., 1729–1733, 1972–1976; Brock, *American Crisis*, 196–199; Benedict, *Compromise of Principle*, 240–242.

27 Congressional Globe, 39th Cong., 2nd sess., 19–23, 944, 970, 1518, 1532–1535, 1849–1855; Hans L. Trefousse, *Andrew Johnson: A Biography* (New York: W. W. Norton, 1989), 277–281.

28 Congressional Globe, 39th Cong., 2nd sess., 1716–1720; Congressional Globe, 40th Cong., 1st sess., 630.

29 Gideon Welles, *Diary of Gideon Welles: Secretary of the Navy under Lincoln and Johnson,* ed. Howard K. Beale, Vol. 3 (New York: W. W. Norton, 1960), 18; Hans L. Trefousse, *Benjamin Franklin Wade, Radical Republican from Ohio* (New York: Twayne, 1963).

30 Congressional Globe, 40th Cong., 1st sess., 17, 49–52, 64.

31 Congressional Globe, 40th Cong., 1st sess., 62–67, 96–97, 110–111, 113, 118, 159–161, 163, 167–171, 200, 215.

32 Congressional Globe, 40th Cong., 1st sess., 304–305, 354–360, 441, 454.

33 Congressional Globe, 40th Cong., 1st sess., 203–206.

8. BETWEEN BULLETS AND BALLOTS

1   *New York Times,* May 15, 16, 28, 1867; *Army & Navy Journal,* June 1, 1867, 647, 653; Joseph H. Geiger to Andrew Johnson, May 15, 1867, *PAJ,* 12:270–271; Michael W. Fitzgerald, *Urban Emancipation: Popular Politics in Reconstruction Mobile, 1860–1890* (Baton Rouge: Louisiana State University Press, 2002), 96–98; Lonnie A. Burnett, *The Pen Makes a Good Sword: John Forsyth of the "Mobile Register"* (Tuscaloosa: University of Alabama Press, 2006), 157–159; Michael Perman, *Reunion without Compromise: The South and Reconstruction, 1865–1868* (New York: Cambridge University Press, 1973), 288; Ira V. Brown, "William D. Kelley and Radical Reconstruction," *Pennsylvania Magazine of History and Biography* 85, no. 3 (July 1, 1961): 325–327.

2   *Army & Navy Journal,* June 22, 1867, 400; Ulysses S. Grant to John Schofield, March 25, 1867, *PUG,* 17:419.

3   *Army & Navy Journal,* March 23, 1867, 493.

4   James Cronin to L. O. Parker, July 23, 1867, C 166 BRFAL La 1867, Box 1, Entry 4521, RG 393, Part 1, NA; Grant to Philip H. Sheridan, March 29, 1867, *PUG,* 17:91–93; William H. C. King to Johnson, May 2, 1867, *PAJ,* 12:250; Ulysses S. Grant, *Personal Memoirs of U.S. Grant,* Vol. 2 (New York: C. L. Webster, 1885), 582; Adam Badeau, *Grant in Peace: From Appomattox to Mount McGregor* (Hartford: S. S. Scranton, 1887), 95; Joseph G. Dawson III, *Army Generals and Reconstruction: Louisiana, 1862–1877* (Baton Rouge: Louisiana State University Press, 1982), 46–93.

5   Henry Stanbery to Johnson, February 13, 1867, *PAJ,* 12:25–26; Stanbery to Johnson, June 12, 1867, *PAJ,* 12:320–332; *Opinion of Attorney General Stanbery, under the Reconstruction Laws* (Washington, D.C.: Government Printing Office, 1867); Brooks D. Simpson, *Let Us Have Peace: Ulysses S. Grant and the Politics of War and Reconstruction, 1861–1868* (Chapel Hill: University of North Carolina Press, 1991), 181; James E. Sefton, *Andrew Johnson and the Uses of Constitutional Power* (Boston: Little, Brown, 1980), 156; Gideon Welles, *Diary of Gideon Welles: Secretary of the Navy under Lincoln and Johnson,* ed. Howard K. Beale, Vol. 3 (New York: W. W. Norton, 1960), 105; Martin E. Mantell, *Johnson, Grant, and the Politics of Reconstruction* (New York: Columbia University Press, 1973), 30–33.

6   *Army & Navy Journal,* June 29, 1867, 716; Grant to Pope, April 21, 1867, *PUG,* 17:117–121; Benjamin Platt Thomas and Harold Melvin Hyman, *Stanton: The Life and Times of Lincoln's Secretary of War* (New York: Knopf, 1962), 533–537.

7   James Hogue captures but overstates the breadth of the military power when he says the July 1867 act made the "generals into virtual dictators of conquered territories." Congressional Globe, 40th Cong., 1st sess., 517–518, 586, 614, 638, 642–644, 732–734, 747–748, 752; Robert Cook, *Civil War Senator William Pitt Fessenden and the Fight to Save the American Republic* (Baton Rouge: Louisiana State University Press, 2011), 223; James K. Hogue, *Uncivil War: Five New Orleans Street Battles and the Rise*

and Fall of Radical Reconstruction (Baton Rouge: Louisiana State University Press, 2011), 53–55.

8   Grant to Sheridan, June 7, 1867, *PAJ,* 17:185–188; Grant to Edward O. C. Ord, June 23, 1867, *PAJ,* 17:192; Army & *Navy Journal,* June 8, 1867, 661; Simpson, *Let Us Have Peace,* 181–182; Hogue, *Uncivil War,* 56–59; Sefton, *Andrew Johnson and the Uses of Constitutional Power,* 156.

9   Daniel R. Goodloe to J. M. Binckley, n.d., Box 125, Folder 1, Entry 9, RG 60, NAII; Grant to Daniel E. Sickles, August 24, 1867, *PUG,* 17:294; Salmon P. Chase to Sickles, September 19, 1867, in *The Salmon P. Chase Papers,* ed. John Niven, Vol. 5 (Kent, Ohio: Kent State University Press, 1993), 173–174.

10   Army & *Navy Journal,* September 14, 1867, 63; Grant to Ord, September 22, 1867, *PUG,* 17:354; "Proclamation *re* Supremacy of Civil Law," September 3, 1867, *PAJ,* 13:112–113; Mart H. Royston to Johnson, September 19, 1867, *PAJ,* 13:87–89; Michael Les Benedict, *A Compromise of Principle: Congressional Republicans and Reconstruction, 1863–1869* (New York: W. W. Norton, 1974), 253–256.

11   Army & *Navy Journal,* September 7, 1867, 37; Grant to Johnson, August 26, 1867, *PAJ,* 12:512; Grant to Sheridan, September 8, 1867, *PUG,* 17:316–317.

12   General Orders No. 40, Fifth Military District, November 29, 1867, Vol. 1, Entry 4509, RG 393, Part 1, NA; General Orders No. 1, Fifth Military District, January 1, 1868, Vol. 2, Entry 4509, RG 393, Part 1, NA; General Orders No. 3, Fifth Military District, January 11, 1868, Vol. 2, Entry 4509, RG 393, Part 1, NA; Elisha Pease to Joseph Reynolds, January 9, 1868, LR Vol. 1, S 1 D of T 1868, Book 116, Entry 4498, RG 393, Part 1, NA; Army & *Navy Journal,* December 14, 1867, 266; January 11, 1868, 326; Grant to Robert C. Buchanan, May 14, 1868, *PUG,* 18:254–255.

13   W. W. Nevin to Thaddeus Stevens, February 4, 1867, Box 4, Stevens Papers, LoC; Louis E. Granger to M. R. Jones, April 7, 1868, with enclosures, Box 125, Folder 1, Entry 9, RG 60, NAII; John Schofield to Adjutant General, October 5, 1867, Container 86, Schofield Papers, LoC; James L. Orr to Johnson, September 30, 1867, *PAJ,* 13:120–124; Jonathan Worth to Johnson, December 31, 1867, *PAJ,* 13:402–428; Thomas and Hyman, *Stanton,* 558; Perman, *Reunion without Compromise,* 321–323.

14   R. M. Patton to John Pope, June 11, 1867, LR 93 A 3 MD 1867, Box 1, Entry 5738, RG 393, Part 1, NA; circular, July 29, 1867, Container 57, Joseph Holt Papers, LoC; Army & *Navy Journal,* May 4, 1867, 581; June 15, 1867, 677–678; Augustus H. Garland to Johnson, July 9, 1867, *PAJ,* 12:389; Grant to John Pope, April 21, 1867, *PUG,* 17:118–121.

15   General Orders No. 3, First Military District, March 15, 1867, Entry 5271, RG 393, Part 1, NA; General Orders, November 2, 1867, Department of Florida, Box 1, Entry 1664, RG 393, Part 1, NA; Jos. J. Kennedy to Daniel Sickles, May 11, 1867, K 13 SMD 1867, Box 3, Entry 4111, NA; Army & *Navy Journal,* March 23, 1867, 486; May 4,

1867, 581; June 1, 1867, 646; June 22, 1867, 694; August 24, 1867, 5–6; September 21, 1867, 70; October 5, 1867, 102; October 12, 1867, 118; November 16, 1867, 204; December 14, 1867, 266; December 21, 1867, 278; December 28, 1867, 294; March 21, 1868, 486; April 11, 1868, 534; George S. Houston to Johnson, September 20, 1867, *PAJ*, 13:89–90; Suzanne Stone Johnson and Robert Johnson, eds., *Bitter Freedom: William Stone's Record of Service in the Freedmen's Bureau* (Columbia: University of South Carolina Press, 2008), 47–51; Hogue, *Uncivil War*, 56–59; Harold Melvin Hyman, *A More Perfect Union: The Impact of the Civil War and Reconstruction on the Constitution* (New York: Knopf, 1973), 501–502; William C. Harris, *Presidential Reconstruction in Mississippi* (Baton Rouge: Louisiana State University Press, 1967), 180.

16 Wager Swayne to H. Wood, October 4, 1867, A 184 3MD 1867, Box 1, Entry 5738, RG 393, Part 1, NA; Reports of Arrests in the Military Posts, South Carolina and North Carolina, 1867–1868, Box 1, Entry 4306, RG 393, Part 1, NA; John J. Turner to Johnson, May 30, 1867, *PAJ*, 12:293–295.

17 General Orders No. 31, First Military District, May 28, 1867, Entry 5271, RG 393, Part 1, NA; John Schofield to Adjutant General, October 5, 1867, Container 86, Schofield Papers, LoC; General Orders No. 102, December 23, 1867, Entry 5271, RG 393, Part 1, NA; J. Hamilton to H. W. Smith, March 20, 1867, H 2 2MD 1867, Box 2, Entry 4111, RG 393, Part 1, NA; John Pope to Joseph Holt, August 10, 1867, Container 57, Joseph Holt Papers, LoC; Howard E. Stansbury to Thos. H. Neill, September 14, 1868, S 21 DL 1868, Box 1, Entry 4521, RG 393, Part 1, NA; Special Orders No. 35, Post of Sumter, S.C., October 9, 1867, S 46 SMD 1867, Vol. 2, Box 9, Entry 4111, RG 393, Part 1, NA; E. W. Dennis to J. W. Clous, July 23, 1867, J 34 SMD 1867, Box 3, Entry 4111, RG 393, Part 1, NA; Register of Court-Martial Cases Tried by Field Officers and Provost Cases, 1867–1868, Entry 4256, RG 393, Part 1, NA; *Army & Navy Journal*, September 21, 1867, 70; December 7, 1867, 246–248; Worth to Johnson, December 31, 1867, *PAJ*, 13:402–428; Mark E. Neely Jr., *The Fate of Liberty: Abraham Lincoln and Civil Liberties* (New York: Oxford University Press, 1991), 175–179; Detlev Vagts, "Military Commissions: The Forgotten Reconstruction Chapter," *American University International Law Review* 23, no. 2 (January 1, 2007): 231–274.

18 Thomas Norton to J. F. Cunningham, August 27, 1867, N 17 4MD 1867, Box 10, Entry 265, RG 393, Part 1, NA; W. H. Smyth to R. C. Drum, February 28, 1868, 100 D TMD 1868, Box 5, Entry 5738, RG 393, Part 1, NA; Charles Griffin to George Hartsuff, July 27, 1867, LRB T 122 FMD 1867, Box 1, Book 15, Entry 4498, RG 393, Part 1, NA; Proceedings of Military Courts, Received at the Headquarters, Third Military District, Entry 5767, RG 393, Part 1, NA; Report of Civilians Tried by Military Commission in the Fourth Military District, enclosed in F. M. Cauley to William Atwood, November 10, 1869, N 6 4th MD 1869, Box 1, Entry 297, RG 393, Part 1, NA.

19 "Interview with *Cincinnati Commercial* Correspondent," December 31, 1867, *PAJ*, 13:397–398; Grant to Ord, March 1, 1867, *PUG*, 17:66–75.

20 Special Orders No. 50, June 15, 1867, Box 2, Entry 1664, RG 393, Part 1, NA; Grant to Ord, March 1, 1867, *PUG,* 17:71–75.

21 Johnson and Johnson, *Bitter Freedom,* 49; Thomas T. Smith et al., eds., *The Reminiscences of Major General Zenas R. Bliss, 1854–1876: From the Texas Frontier to the Civil War and Back Again* (Denton, Tex.: Texas State Historical Association, 2007), 389–390; Edward M. Coffman, *The Old Army: A Portrait of the American Army in Peacetime, 1784–1898* (New York: Oxford University Press, 1986), 244–245; Laura F. Edwards, *Gendered Strife and Confusion: The Political Culture of Reconstruction* (Champaign: University of Illinois Press, 1997).

22 Louis D. Watkins to George Hartsuff, April 22, 1867, Book 15, Box 1, Entry 4498, RG 393, Part 1, NA.

23 George Baldey to J. W. Forsyth, May 31, 1867; John B. Johnson to General Graham, March 11, 1868, Box 4, Entry 4543A, RG 393, Part 1, NA; Report of Inspections of Alexandria et al.; Report of an Inspection Made by John B. Johnson, Vol. 273, Entry 4542, RG 393, Part 1, NA; Reports from Commanders of B Company 20th Infantry at Marksville, Natchitoches, and Manning, Louisiana from May to September 1867, Box 2, Entry 4521, RG 393, Part 1, NA; *Army & Navy Journal,* October 5, 1867, 102; Charlotte C. Shepard to Johnson, September 14, 1867, *PAJ,* 13:66–69; Anson W. Hobson to Johnson, September 22, 1867, *PAJ,* 13:93–95.

24 Special Orders No. 23, September 26, 1867, Post of Columbus, Georgia, Entry 4134, RG 393, Part 1, NA; General and Special Orders, 1867–1868, Post of Columbus, Georgia, Entry 4134, RG 393, Part 1, NA; A. M. Martin to R. K. Scott, November 13, 1867, M 34, Vol. 3, SMD 1867, Box 11, Entry 4111, RG 393, Part 1, NA; Henry C. Brandt to the Commanding Officers, October 19, 1867, B 5, Vol. 3, SMD 1867, Box 11, Entry 4111, RG 393, Part 1, NA; T. F. Monroe to L. O. Parker, July 10, 1867, M 708 BFAL La 1867, Box 1, Entry 4521, RG 393, Part 1, NA; H. H. Foster to C. E. Compton, June 6, 1867, F 34 SMD 1867, Box 7, Entry 4111, RG 393, Part 1, NA; Joseph Reynolds to George W. Smith, November 15, 1867, LR (C) T 200 FMD, Box 3, Book 17, Entry 4498, RG 393, Part 1, NA; Joseph Reynolds to Thomas H. Neill, June 16, 1868, T 610 (d) FMD 1868, Box 8, Book 18, Entry 4498, RG 393, Part 1, NA.

25 Oscar Eastman to Jacob F. Chur, E 218 SMD 1867, Box 2, Entry 4111, RG 393, Part 1, NA; Thomas Satchford to J. C. DeGress, October 17, 1867, H 334 BRFAL 1867, Box 1, Entry 4521, RG 393, Part 1, NA; John Sprague to H. Clay Wood, December 5, 1867, 87 F TMD 1867, Box 1, Entry 5738, RG 393, Part 1, NA; Special Orders No. 8, October 29, 1868, Post of Tuscumbia, Entry 4134, RG 393, Part 1, NA; Special Orders No. 15, Post of Columbus, August 22, 1867, Entry 4134, RG 393, Part 1, NA; Special Orders No. 2, Post of Darlington, Entry 4135, RG 393, Part 1, NA; General Orders No. 16, Entry 4135, RG 393, Part 1, NA; circular, March 24, 1868, Box 7, Charles Alexander Nelson Papers, MSS Col 2114, NYPL; *Army & Navy Journal,* November 2, 1867, 172; Grant to Ord, May 11, 1867, *PUG,* 17:142–145; Edward McPherson, *Political*

Manual for 1868, Including a Classified Summary of the Important Executive, Legislative, Politico-Military, and General Facts of the Period, from April 1, 1867 to July 15, 1868 (Washington, D.C.: Philp and Solomons, 1868), 374; Douglas R. Egerton, *The Wars of Reconstruction: The Brief, Violent History of America's Most Progressive Era* (New York: Bloomsbury, 2014), 261–262.

26 Eric Foner, *Reconstruction: America's Unfinished Revolution, 1863–1877* (New York: Harper and Row, 1988), 316–326; Steven Hahn, *A Nation under Our Feet: Black Political Struggles in the Rural South, from Slavery to the Great Migration* (Cambridge, Mass.: Belknap Press of Harvard University Press, 2003), 206–215; Thomas C. Holt, *Black over White: Negro Political Leadership in South Carolina during Reconstruction* (Urbana: University of Illinois Press, 1977).

27 A. C. Wildrick to Louis Caziarc, September 25, 1867, H 31 SMD, Vol. 2, 1867, Box 7, Entry 4111, RG 393, Part 1, NA; Allen W. Trelease, *White Terror: The Ku Klux Klan Conspiracy and Southern Reconstruction* (New York: Harper and Row, 1971), 44–46, 68–69, 86–88, 103–104, 131–136; Hahn, *Nation under Our Feet*, 265–316.

28 Thomas Satchford to J. C. DeGress, October 17, 1867, H 334 BRFAL 1867, Box 1, Entry 4521, RG 393, Part 1, NA; B. J. Ogden et al. to Col. Cutts, August 19, 1867, C 33 FMD, Box 3, Book 17, Entry 4498, RG 393, Part 1, NA; George P. Screven et al. to Colonel Maloney, November 11, 1867, 136 S 3MD 1867, Box 2, Entry 5738, RG 393, Part 1, NA; B. J. Ogden et al. to Colonel Cutts, August 19, 1867, C 33 FMD, Box 3, Book 17, Entry 4498, RG 393, Part 1, NA; Citizens of Parish of St. Helena to Commanding General, January 3, 1868, S 1(c) FMD, Box 5, Book 17, Entry 4498, RG 393, Part 1, NA; W. A. Cameron to Louis Caziarc, November 17, 1867, S 91 SMD, Vol. 2, 1867, Box 9, Entry 4111, RG 393, Part 1, NA; B. Stokes et al. to E. Canby, n.d. [1868], S 24, Vol. 2, SMD 1868, Box 20, Book 11, Letters Received, Second Military District, 1867–1868, RG 393, Part 1, NA; Grant to Pope, August 3, 1867, *PUG*, 17:256–265; James Norcom to Johnson, October 9, 1867, *PAJ*, 13:148–149; John William De Forest, *A Union Officer in the Reconstruction*, ed. David Morris Potter (Baton Rouge: Louisiana State University Press, 1997), 127–128.

29 William Mills to George Meade, March 31, 1868, Entry 5744, RG 393, Part 1, NA; Mills to Meade, April 21, 1868, Entry 5744, RG 393, Part 1, NA; Meade to Henry Sibley, July 24, 1868, Entry 5744, RG 393, Part 1, NA; Meade to Grant, April 4, 1868, Entry 5744, RG 393, Part 1, NA; C. S. Trupell et al. to Meade, April 10, 1868, 53 T TMD 1868, Box 9, Entry 5738, RG 393, Part 1, NA; T. M. Hogan to George Meade, May 2, 1868, 183 H TMD 1868, Box 4, Entry 5738, RG 393, Part 1, NA; John T. Sprague to R. C. Drum, May 31, 1868, 193 F TMD 1868, Box 6, Entry 5738, RG 393, Part 1, NA; *Army & Navy Journal*, April 11, 1868, 533; Hogue, *Uncivil War*, 10; Trelease, *White Terror*, 86–88, 103–104; Hannah Rosen, *Terror in the Heart of Freedom: Citizenship, Sexual Violence, and the Meaning of Race in the Postemancipation South* (Chapel Hill: University of North Carolina Press, 2009); George C. Rable, *But There Was No Peace: The Role of Violence in the Politics of Reconstruction* (Athens: University of

Georgia Press, 1984); Mark Grimsley, "Wars for the American South: The First and Second Reconstructions Considered as Insurgencies," *Civil War History* 58, no. 1 (2012): 6–36; Carole Emberton, *Beyond Redemption: Race, Violence, and the American South after the Civil War* (Chicago: University of Chicago Press, 2013), 136–205.

30 Johnson to Amos Layman, October 9, 1867, *PAJ*, 13:146; Benedict, *Compromise of Principle*, 272–276; Hans L. Trefousse, *Impeachment of a President: Andrew Johnson, the Blacks, and Reconstruction* (Knoxville: University of Tennessee Press, 1975), 90–91.

31 Thomas Ruger to Richard Drum, July 4, 1868, 175 R TMD 1868, Box 8, Entry 5738, RG 393, Part 1, NA; *Army & Navy Journal*, March 28, 1868, 508; "Third Annual Message," December 3, 1867, *PAJ*, 13:280–306; John Forsyth to Johnson, December 12, 1867, *PAJ*, 13:327–328; John Forsyth and Lewis E. Parsons to Johnson, May 5, 1868, *PAJ*, 13:60–62; Grant to Sheridan, April 5, 1867, Grant to George G. Meade, January 6, 1868, *PUG*, 18:94–97; Gideon Welles, *Diary of Gideon Welles: Secretary of the Navy under Lincoln and Johnson*, ed. Howard K. Beale, Vol. 2 (New York: W. W. Norton, 1960), 242–243.

32 J. L. Pennington to Thaddeus Stevens, March 22, 1868, Box 4, Stevens Papers, LoC; Congressional Globe, 40th Cong., 2nd sess., 1314, 2213–2214, 3213; appendix, 84.

33 Congressional Globe, 40th Cong., 2nd sess., 1847, 2119–2122; John B. Haskin to Johnson, January 16, 1868, *PAJ*, 13:471; Hyman, *A More Perfect Union*, 503–505; Vagts, "Military Commissions"; Thomas and Hyman, *Stanton*, 533–537; Gerard N. Magliocca, *American Founding Son: John Bingham and the Invention of the Fourteenth Amendment* (New York: New York University Press, 2013), 140.

34 David O. Stewart, *Impeached: The Trial of President Andrew Johnson and the Fight for Lincoln's Legacy* (New York: Simon and Schuster, 2009), 145.

35 Stewart, *Impeached*, 92–93, 101–105, 140–142, 148–154; Badeau, *Grant in Peace*, 71; Michael Les Benedict, *The Impeachment and Trial of Andrew Johnson* (New York: W. W. Norton, 1973), 73–75, 102–105; Benedict, *Compromise of Principle*, 296–299; Trefousse, *Impeachment of a President*, 123–129, 135.

36 Benjamin Perley Poore, *Trial of Andrew Johnson, President of the United States, before the Senate of the United States, on Impeachment by the House of Representatives for High Crimes and Misdemeanors*, Vol. 1 (Washington, D.C.: Government Printing Office, 1868), 328, 377; Benjamin Perley Poore, *Trial of Andrew Johnson, President of the United States, before the Senate of the United States, on Impeachment by the House of Representatives for High Crimes and Misdemeanors*, Vol. 3 (Washington, D.C.: Government Printing Office, 1868), 30–31, 328; Hiram Ketchum Sr. to Johnson, April 7, 1868, *PAJ*, 14:21–22; Benedict, *Compromise of Principle*, 134; Benedict, *Impeachment and Trial of Andrew Johnson*, 178–179.

37 Poore, *Trial of Andrew Johnson President*, 3:14–16, 142–144, 346–347; Stewart, *Impeached*, 160–165; Trefousse, *Impeachment of a President*, 138–139.

38 The hypothetical case that a quick conviction would have been possible rests upon Lyman Trumbull, who cheered impeachment in February but voted against it in May, but other senators who abstained from the February Senate resolution in turn voted for conviction, making it impossible to judge with certainty. Benedict, *Impeachment and Trial of Andrew Johnson*, 178–179.

39 Congressional Globe, 40th Cong., 2nd sess., 1861; Benedict, *Compromise of Principle*, 284, 310–312; Brooks D. Simpson, *The Reconstruction Presidents* (Lawrence: University Press of Kansas, 2009), 123–127; Trefousse, *Impeachment of a President*, 158–159.

40 Trefousse, *Impeachment of a President*, 168–171; Gene Smith, *High Crimes and Misdemeanors: The Impeachment and Trial of Andrew Johnson* (New York: Morrow, 1977), 293–295; Stewart, *Impeached*, 254–265; Mark Wahlgren Summers, *The Era of Good Stealings* (New York: Oxford University Press, 1993), 36–43; Benedict, *Impeachment and Trial of Andrew Johnson*, 170–173.

41 Although Michael Les Benedict believes Johnson's actions forced Republicans to accept a quick restoration of the states, the chance for long-term occupation had probably expired a year earlier with the defeat of the military bill in 1867. Congressional Globe, 40th Cong., 2nd sess., 2412–2413, 2628–2629, 2836, 2904, 2938, 3331, 3363, 3484–3485; Benedict, *Compromise of Principle*, 321.

42 The precise date of the Fourteenth Amendment's ratification depends upon how one deals with the two state legislatures that rescinded their earlier ratifications. If they are counted, the amendment was ratified on July 9; if not, the ratifications in Alabama and Georgia pushed the amendment over the threshold on July 21, and on July 28 the secretary of state certified the amendment. Congressional Globe, 40th Cong., 2nd sess., 3389, 3607.

43 Congressional Globe, 40th Cong., 2nd sess., 2133, 3732, 3814, 4245, 4493; Albion W. Tourgée, *A Fool's Errand, by One of the Fools* (New York: Fords, Howard, & Hulbert, 1879), 152.

44 Congressional Globe, 40th Cong., 2nd sess., 3871–3872, 3975.

45 George Thomas to John Schofield, September 23, 1868, 658 Cumberland 1868, enclosed in Meade to Grant, A 375 1868, Reel 609, M619, RG 94, NA; *Army & Navy Journal*, November 18, 1868, 235; A. O. P. Nicholson to Johnson, July 24, 1868, *PAJ*, 14:419–421; Robert P. Cypert to Johnson, August 18, 1868, *PAJ*, 14:512–513; Grant to Johnson, March 13, 1868, *PUG*, 18:196–197; Robert W. Coakley, *The Role of Federal Military Forces in Domestic Disorders, 1789–1878* (Washington, D.C.: Center of Military History, 1988), 300–306; Trelease, *White Terror*, 44–46.

46 Meade to General Schriver, July 21, 1868, Entry 5741, RG 393, Part 1, NA; Henry S. Gansevoort to Dear Brewster, June 11, 1868, Box 163, Gansevoort-Lansing Collection, NYPL; W. H. Smith et al. to John Schofield, August 1, 1868; John Rawlins to

Grant, August 5, 1868; Meade to Townsend, August 24, 1868; Meade to Schofield, August 5, 1868; all enclosed in Meade to Grant, A 375 1868, Reel 609, M619, RG 94, NA; Meade to Grant, October 9, 1868, 875 South Dept. 1868 with attachments filed in A 375 1868, Reel 609, M619, RG 94, NA; Meade to John Rawlins, October 31, 1868, Entry 5749, RG 393, Part 1, NA; *Army & Navy Journal*, May 9, 1868, 598; July 19, 1868, 758; August 1, 1868, 790; August 8, 1868, 806; August 29, 1868, 18; Grant to Edward R. S. Canby, June 26, 1868, *PUG*, 18:296–297; Harrison Reed to Johnson, July 13, 1868, *PUG*, 14:351–352.

47 Meade to Sprague, August 8, 1868, Entry 5741, RG 393, Part 1, NA; *Army & Navy Journal*, December 5, 1868, 250; Reed to Johnson, July 13, 1868, *PAJ*, 14:351–352; Grant to Robert C. Buchanan, June 27, 1868, *PUG*, 18:299–303.

48 William Evarts to John Schofield, August 21, 1868, 401 A 1868, and William Evarts to Alex Magruder, August 20, 1868, 195 M Florida 1868, enclosed in Grant to Meade, June 27, 1868, 375 A 1868, M619, Roll 609, Letters Received by the Office of the Adjutant General, 1861–1870, RG 94, NA; *Army & Navy Journal*, August 19, 1868, 25; September 12, 1868, 50; December 12, 1868, 266; Coakley, *Role of Federal Military Forces*, 132–133, 300–301.

49 Meade to Grant, July 20, 1868, enclosed in Grant to Meade, June 27, 1868, 375 A 1868, M619, Roll 609, Letters Received by the Office of the Adjutant General, 1861–1870, RG 94, NA; William Mills to R. C. Drum, September 29, 1868, Entry 5757, RG 393, Part 1, NA; Meade to Rufus Bullock, October 3, 1868, RG 393, Part 1, Entry 5757, NA; *Army & Navy Journal*, October 17, 1868, 132; Henry C. Warmoth to Johnson, August 1, 1868, *PAJ*, 14:472–474; Foner, *Reconstruction*, 342–343.

50 General Orders No. 27, Department of the South, October 8, 1868, Entry 5741, RG 393, Part 1, NA; George Meade to John Rawlins, October 31, 1868, Entry 5749, RG 393, Part 1, NA; Returns of the Department of the Cumberland, March 1867–February 1869, Box 16, Entry 62, RG 94, NA; *Army & Navy Journal*, October 17, 1868, 130.

51 Schofield to Lovell Rousseau, October 29, 1868, Container 49, John M. Schofield Papers, LoC; *Army & Navy Journal*, December 5, 1868, 241, 243; Trelease, *White Terror*, 117–119, 131–136; Foner, *Reconstruction*, 343; Benedict, *Compromise of Principle*, 328–330.

52 U. Ozanne to Stevens, July 9, 1868, Box 5, Stevens Papers, LoC; Record of Cases, Office of Military Commissioner, 31st Division, Entry 5288, RG 393, Part 1, NA; General Orders No. 98, August 20, 1868, Entry 5271, RG 393, Part 1, NA; N. P. Young to Q. M. Fleming, May 8, 1868, Entry 5268, RG 393, Part 1, NA; Benjamin G. Humphreys to Johnson, June 22, 1868, *PAJ*, 14:246–247; Grant to Irvin McDowell, June 5, 1868, *PUG*, 18:279–282; Perman, *Reunion without Compromise*, 337–341.

9. THE PERILS OF PEACE

1   *Army & Navy Journal,* July 18, 1869, 760, October 30, 1869, 164; *New York Times,* June 15, 1869, July 15, 1869, August 4, 1869; W. S. M. Wilkinson, *Trial of E. M. Yerger: Before a Military Commission for the Killing of Bv't-Col. Joseph G. Crane, at Jackson, Miss., June 8th, 1869* (Jackson, Miss.: Clarion Book and Job Printing, 1869), 19–21; *Official Opinions of the Attorneys General of the United States: Advising the President and Heads of Departments, in Relation to Their Official Duties* (Washington, D.C.: Government Printing Office, 1873), 13:60–67.

2   Congressional Globe, 40th Cong., 3rd sess., 7, 568, 675–677; Michael Les Benedict, *A Compromise of Principle: Congressional Republicans and Reconstruction, 1863–1869* (New York: W. W. Norton, 1974), 328–330.

3   *Army & Navy Journal,* March 13, 1869, 465; C. A. Hartwell to J. T. Randlett, June 24, 1869, Entry 5260, RG 393, Part 1, NA; H. R. Putnam to Wm. B. Jones, January 20, 1869, Entry 5269, RG 393, Part 1, NA; Congressional Globe, 40th Cong., 3rd sess., 406–408, 428, 434, 544, 652, 680; *Annual Report of the Secretary of War* (Washington, D.C.: Government Printing Office, 1869), 14–17; Edward McPherson, *The Political History of the United States of America during the Period of Reconstruction (from April 15, 1865 to July 15, 1870)* (Washington, D.C.: Solomons and Chapman, 1875), 425–427; James E. Sefton, *The United States Army and Reconstruction, 1865–1877* (Baton Rouge: Louisiana State University Press, 1967), 189–198.

4   C. A. Hartwell to J. T. Randlett, June 24, 1869, Entry 5260, RG 393, Part 1, NA; H. R. Putnam to Wm. B. Jones, January 20, 1869, Entry 5269, RG 393, Part 1, NA; T. E. Rose to Wm. Atwood, April 19, 1869, R 62 4MD 1869, Box 2, Entry 297, RG 393, Part 1, NA; *Army & Navy Journal,* November 14, 1868, 203; November 21, 1868, 210; December 12, 1868, 266–267; January 2, 1869, 314–315; June 5, 1869, 664; July 10, 1869, 745; August 14, 1869, 822; Roster of Troops Serving in the Department of Louisiana, September 10, 1869, Box 2, Entry 4521, RG 393, Part 1, NA; George Baldey to J. C. Bates, January 9, 1869, Box 2, Entry 4521, RG 393, Part 1, NA; Roster of Troops Serving in the Department of the South, October 1869, Box 2, Entry 297, RG 393, Part 1, NA; Distribution of Troops Serving in the Fourth Military District, Department of Mississippi, December 1, 1869, Box 2, Entry 297, RG 393, Part 1, NA; Rosters of Troops Serving in the First Military District, August 31, 1869, Box 2, Entry 297, RG 393, Part 1, NA; *Annual Report of the Secretary of War,* 1869, 14–18; Edward McPherson, *Political History,* 425–430; Allen W. Trelease, *White Terror: The Ku Klux Klan Conspiracy and Southern Reconstruction* (New York: Harper and Row, 1971), 140–147.

5   D. Woodruff to E. Hoar, August 30, 1869, Box 71, Folder 9, Entry 9, RG 60, NAII; *Annual Report of the Secretary of War,* 1869, 80–89, 97–98; Trelease, *White Terror,* 189–207, 240–246; Daniel R. Weinfeld, *The Jackson County War: Reconstruction and Resistance in Post–Civil War Florida* (Tuscaloosa: University of Alabama Press, 2012); Sefton, *United States Army and Reconstruction,* 217.

6   Congressional Globe, 40th Cong., 3rd sess., 82–83, 86, 1819; *Army & Navy Journal,* January 16, 1869, 338; Robert W. Coakley, *The Role of Federal Military Forces in Domestic Disorders, 1789–1878* (Washington, D.C: Government Printing Office, 1988), 300–306; Derek W. Frisby, "A Victory Spoiled: West Tennessee Unionists during Reconstruction," in *The Great Task Remaining before Us: Reconstruction as America's Continuing Civil War,* ed. Paul Alan Cimbala and Randall M. Miller (New York: Fordham University Press, 2010), 20–21; Eric Foner, *Reconstruction: America's Unfinished Revolution, 1863–1877* (New York: Harper and Row, 1988), 440–441; Trelease, *White Terror,* 151–153, 170–173, 178–183; George C. Rable, *But There Was No Peace: The Role of Violence in the Politics of Reconstruction* (Athens: University of Georgia Press, 1984), 104–106.

7   Congressional Globe, 40th Cong., 3rd sess., 1328, 1587, 1857; appendix, 189–190; Edward M. Coffman, *The Old Army: A Portrait of the American Army in Peacetime, 1784–1898* (New York: Oxford University Press, 1986), 216–220; Albion W. Tourgée, *Bricks without Straw: A Novel,* ed. Carolyn L. Karcher (Durham: Duke University Press, 2009).

8   Congressional Globe, 40th Cong., 3rd sess., 555, 742–745, 1044; appendix, 96–99; quoted in Rable, *But There Was No Peace,* 144; Ellen Carol DuBois, *Feminism and Suffrage: The Emergence of an Independent Women's Movement in America, 1848–1869* (Ithaca, N.Y.: Cornell University Press, 1978); Faye E. Dudden, *Fighting Chance: The Struggle over Woman Suffrage and Black Suffrage in Reconstruction America* (New York: Oxford University Press, 2011); Xi Wang, *The Trial of Democracy: Black Suffrage and Northern Republicans, 1860–1910* (Athens: University of Georgia Press, 2012), 30–48; Richard H. Abbott, *The Republican Party and the South, 1855–1877: The First Southern Strategy* (Chapel Hill: University of North Carolina Press, 1986), 205–208.

9   Congressional Globe, 41st Cong., 1st sess., 660, 700.

10   Special Orders No. 251, Department of the South, November 10, 1869, S 11 4MD 1869, Box 9, Entry 265, RG 393, Part 1, NA; Special Orders No. 1, 2nd Infantry, November 21, 1869, S 117 4MD 1869, Box 9, Entry 265, RG 393, Part 1, NA; S. R. Whitall to Wm. Atwood, November 28, 1869, W 216 4MD 1869, Box 9, Entry 265, RG 393, Part 1, NA; Monthly Returns of the First Military District, State of Virginia, March–December 1869, Entry 5103, RG 393, Part 1, NA; Congressional Globe, 41st Cong., 1st sess., 605; *Army & Navy Journal,* November 20, 1869, 206; November 27, 1869, 224; Rable, *But There Was No Peace,* 140–142; Foner, *Reconstruction,* 413–415; William Gillette, *Retreat from Reconstruction, 1869–1879* (Baton Rouge: Louisiana State University Press, 1982), 83–84.

11   Congressional Globe, 41st Cong., 2nd sess., 257; *Annual Report of the Secretary of War,* 1869, 89–94; Trelease, *White Terror,* 226–242; Alan Conway, *The Reconstruction of Georgia* (Minneapolis: University of Minnesota Press, 1966), 185–186.

12   Congressional Globe, 41st Cong., 2nd sess., 3–4, 165–166, 287, 292, 325.

13 Congressional Globe, 41st Cong., 2nd sess., 328; Rufus Bullock to William Lawrence (copy), January 20, 1870, Box 51, Benjamin Butler Papers, LoC; Sefton, *United States Army and Reconstruction*, 199–207.

14 Congressional Globe, 41st Cong., 2nd sess., 4790; *Annual Report of the Secretary of War* (Washington, D.C.: U.S. Government Printing Office, 1870), 37–39; Edwin Campbell Woolley, *The Reconstruction of Georgia* (New York: Columbia University Press, 1901), 73–80; Coakley, *Role of Federal Military Forces*, 307–310; Conway, *Reconstruction of Georgia*, 187–188; Sefton, *United States Army and Reconstruction*, 199–207; Trelease, *White Terror*, 226–242.

15 Congressional Globe, 41st Cong., 2nd sess., 353, 443–444, 448, 473–474, 598, 644; quoted in Michael Les Benedict, *The Fruits of Victory: Alternatives in Restoring the Union, 1865–1877* (Philadelphia: Lippincott, 1975), 49–55.

16 Congressional Globe, 41st Cong., 2nd sess., 1257, 1324–1325, 1330, 1366, 1970, 2272.

17 Congressional Globe, 41st Cong., 2nd sess., 2307–2308.

18 Congressional Globe, 41st Cong., 2nd sess., 2274–2280, 3409, 5343, 5401–5405.

19 Congressional Globe, 41st Cong., 2nd sess., 3503–3504.

20 Congressional Globe, 41st Cong., 2nd sess., 3568, 3607–3609, 3613, 3657, 3668–3669, 3678–3679, 3683–3684, 3688.

21 In the midst of this debate, Senator Charles Sumner tried to amend the bill to strike the word "white" from naturalization laws. When Western Republicans protested that this would enfranchise Chinese workers, Republicans amended it to extend naturalization only to aliens of African descent. Congressional Globe, 41st Cong., 2nd sess., 3755, 3805–3806, 3808; Wang, *Trial of Democracy*, 55–77; Charles W. Calhoun, *Conceiving a New Republic: The Republican Party and the Southern Question, 1869–1900* (Lawrence: University Press of Kansas, 2006), 18–27; George A. Rutherglen, *Civil Rights in the Shadow of Slavery: The Constitution, Common Law, and the Civil Rights Act of 1866* (New York: Oxford University Press, 2012), 81–83.

22 Congressional Globe, 41st Cong., 2nd sess., 1701–1705, 1770–1771, 1927–1929, 2677; appendix, 291; Woolley, *Reconstruction of Georgia*, 83–85.

23 Congressional Globe, 41st Cong., 2nd sess., 1957–1960.

24 Congressional Globe, 41st Cong., 2nd sess., 2065–2067, 2742–2746.

25 Congressional Globe, 41st Cong., 2nd sess., 2068, 2089–2092, 2645–2648, 2722–2724, 2826–2829; appendix, 291–293.

26 Congressional Globe, 41st Cong., 2nd sess., 2428–2430; *New York Times*, March 5, 1868; Frank Abial Flower, *Life of Matthew Hale Carpenter: A View of the Honors and*

Achievements That, in the American Republic, Are the Fruits of Well-Directed Ambition and Persistent Industry (Madison, Wisc.: D. Atwood, 1884), 111–114, 132–133.

27 Congressional Globe, 41st Cong., 2nd sess., 2428–2430, 2748–2749.

28 Congressional Globe, 41st Cong., 2nd sess., 2606, 2710, 2820–2822, 2827–2829.

29 Congressional Globe, 41st Cong., 2nd sess., 4752, 4793, 4797.

30 Congressional Globe, 41st Cong., 2nd sess., 5583, 5621, 5634.

31 Quoted in Foner, *Reconstruction*, 364–370; David S. Cecelski, *The Fire of Freedom: Abraham Galloway and the Slaves' Civil War* (Chapel Hill: University of North Carolina Press, 2012).

32 *Army & Navy Journal*, July 9, 1870, 734; Ulysses S. Grant to William W. Holden, July 22, 1870, *PUG*, 20:210–213; Rable, *But There Was No Peace*, 104–106; Trelease, *White Terror*, 189–225.

33 *Army & Navy Journal*, February 12, 1870, 399; March 26, 1870, 494; April 9, 1870, 526; June 4, 1870, 654; November 19, 1870, 216; November 26, 1870, 232–233; December 3, 1870, 247–248; United States War Department, *Report of the Secretary of War: Being Part of the Message and Documents Communicated to the Two Houses of Congress at the Beginning of the Second Session of the Forty-Second Congress* (Washington, D.C.: Government Printing Office, 1871), iii–iv, 16–17, 41; Trelease, *White Terror*, 275–278.

34 *Army & Navy Journal*, November 12, 1870, 198, 205; Wang, *Trial of Democracy*, 79; Trelease, *White Terror*, 380–388; Benedict, *Fruits of Victory*, 49–55.

35 *Army & Navy Journal*, March 11, 1871, 472; November 19, 1870, 214; Trelease, *White Terror*, 270–273, 339–366.

36 *Army & Navy Journal*, December 31, 1870, 310; Woolley, *Reconstruction of Georgia*, 97–98; Sefton, *United States Army and Reconstruction*, 199–207; Foner, *Reconstruction*, 421–424; Gillette, *Retreat from Reconstruction*, 88–91; Trelease, *White Terror*, 226–242.

37 Weinfeld, *Jackson County War*; Paul Ortiz, *Emancipation Betrayed: The Hidden History of Black Organizing and White Violence in Florida from Reconstruction to the Bloody Election of 1920* (Berkeley: University of California Press, 2006), 24; Rable, *But There Was No Peace*, 150; Foner, *Reconstruction*, 413–415; Gillette, *Retreat from Reconstruction*, 166; Trelease, *White Terror*, 210–225, 240–246, 270–273.

38 Congressional Globe, 41st Cong., 3rd sess., 5–6.

39 Congressional Globe, 41st Cong., 3rd sess., 822–823.

40 Congressional Globe, 41st Cong., 3rd sess., 873, 1184.

41 For a discussion of the role of personal force, including access to guns, in defending rights, see Carole Emberton, *Beyond Redemption: Race, Violence, and the*

American South after the Civil War (Chicago: University of Chicago Press, 2013), esp. 150; W. E. B. Du Bois, *Black Reconstruction in America, 1860–1880* (New York: Free Press, 1999).

CONCLUSION

1   Douglas R. Egerton, *The Wars of Reconstruction: The Brief, Violent History of America's Most Progressive Era* (New York: Bloomsbury, 2014), 296, 304.

2   Guido Norman Lieber, *The Use of the Army in Aid of the Civil Power* (Washington, D.C.: Government Printing Office, 1898), 16; James E. Sefton, *The United States Army and Reconstruction, 1865–1877* (Baton Rouge: Louisiana State University Press, 1967), 32–33, 218–219; Robert W. Coakley, *The Role of Federal Military Forces in Domestic Disorders, 1789–1878* (Washington, D.C.: Center of Military History, 1988), 272, 300–301.

3   Congressional Globe, 41st Cong., 3rd sess., 571, 575; appendix, 125; *Army & Navy Journal,* September 2, 1871, 35; Coakley, *Role of Federal Military Forces,* 308–313; William Gillette, *Retreat from Reconstruction, 1869–1879* (Baton Rouge: Louisiana State University Press, 1982), 25–26, 29–37, 41–43, 53; Charles W. Calhoun, *Conceiving a New Republic: The Republican Party and the Southern Question, 1869–1900* (Lawrence: University Press of Kansas, 2006), 20–22, 26–33; Sefton, *United States Army and Reconstruction,* 221–228; Brooks D. Simpson, *The Reconstruction Presidents* (Lawrence: University Press of Kansas, 2009), 155–157; Allen W. Trelease, *White Terror: The Ku Klux Klan Conspiracy and Southern Reconstruction* (New York: Harper and Row, 1971), 374–380, 399–418; Richard M. Valelly, *The Two Reconstructions: The Struggle for Black Enfranchisement* (Chicago: University of Chicago Press, 2004), 106–107; Eric Foner, *Reconstruction: America's Unfinished Revolution, 1863–1877* (New York: Harper and Row, 1988), 454–457; Lou Falkner Williams, *The Great South Carolina Ku Klux Klan Trials, 1871–1872* (Athens: University of Georgia Press, 2004), 44–47, 85–88; Xi Wang, *The Trial of Democracy: Black Suffrage and Northern Republicans, 1860–1910* (Athens: University of Georgia Press, 1996), 49–133; *Annual Report of the Secretary of War* (Washington, D.C.: Government Printing Office, 1871), 2–4, 16–17; Robert Goldman, *A Free Ballot and a Fair Count: The Department of Justice and the Enforcement of Voting Rights in the South, 1877–1893* (New York: Fordham University Press, 2001); Robert J. Kaczorowski, *The Politics of Judicial Interpretation: The Federal Courts, Department of Justice and Civil Rights, 1866–1876* (Dobbs Ferry, N.Y.: Oceana Publications, 1985), 87–89; Stephen Budiansky, *The Bloody Shirt: Terror after Appomattox* (New York: Viking, 2008).

4   Coakley, *Role of Federal Military Forces,* 323–324; LeeAnna Keith, *The Colfax Massacre: The Untold Story of Black Power, White Terror, and the Death of Reconstruction* (New York: Oxford University Press, 2008); Charles Lane, *The Day Freedom Died: The Colfax Massacre, the Supreme Court, and the Betrayal of Reconstruction* (New York: Henry Holt, 2008); Andrew L. Slap, *The Doom of Reconstruction: The Liberal Republicans in the Civil War Era* (New York: Fordham University Press, 2006).

5   Coakley, *Role of Federal Military Forces*, 328–330; Gillette, *Retreat from Reconstruction*, 96, 102, 107–127, 139–149, 158–163; Calhoun, *Conceiving a New Republic*, 40–77; Sefton, *United States Army and Reconstruction*, 222–246; Simpson, *Reconstruction Presidents*, 158, 174, 177; Keith, *Colfax Massacre*, 109, 113, 149; Egerton, *Wars of Reconstruction*, 305, 314, 322–323; James K. Hogue, *Uncivil War: Five New Orleans Street Battles and the Rise and Fall of Radical Reconstruction* (Baton Rouge: Louisiana State University Press, 2011); Nicholas Lemann, *Redemption: The Last Battle of the Civil War* (New York: Farrar, Straus and Giroux, 2006), 23–27, 95–100; George C. Rable, *But There Was No Peace: The Role of Violence in the Politics of Reconstruction* (Athens: University of Georgia Press, 1984), 148–152; Joe Gray Taylor, *Louisiana Reconstructed, 1863–1877* (Baton Rouge: Louisiana State University Press, 1974); Joseph G. Dawson III, *Army Generals and Reconstruction: Louisiana, 1862–1877* (Baton Rouge: Louisiana State University Press, 1982), 183–185; Michael Perman, "Counter Reconstruction: The Role of Violence in Southern Redemption," in *The Facts of Reconstruction: Essays in Honor of John Hope Franklin*, ed. Eric Anderson and Alfred A. Moss (Baton Rouge: Louisiana State University Press, 1991), 121–139; Ted Tunnell, *Crucible of Reconstruction: War, Radicalism, and Race in Louisiana, 1862–1877* (Baton Rouge: Louisiana State University Press, 1984).

6   Heather Cox Richardson, "Hemingway, South Carolina, and Reconstruction," http://histsociety.blogspot.com/2013/01/hemingway-south-carolina-and.html; Coakley, *Role of Federal Military Forces*, 333–339; Calhoun, *Conceiving a New Republic*, 141–145; Sefton, *United States Army and Reconstruction*, 247–251; Valelly, *Two Reconstructions*, 95; Everette Swinney, *Suppressing the Ku Klux Klan: The Enforcement of the Reconstruction Amendments, 1870–1877* (New York: Garland, 1987), 190; Simpson, *Reconstruction Presidents*, 191, 226; L. F. Williams, *Great South Carolina Ku Klux Klan Trials*, 129; Richard Zuczek, *State of Rebellion: Reconstruction in South Carolina* (Columbia: University of South Carolina Press, 1996); Egerton, *Wars of Reconstruction*, 324; T. Harry Williams, ed., *Hayes: The Diary of a President, 1875–1881, Covering the Disputed Election, the End of Reconstruction, and the Beginning of Civil Service* (New York: D. McKay, 1964), 269–270; Vincent P. DeSantis, "Rutherford B. Hayes and the Removal of Troops and the End of Reconstruction," in *Region, Race and Reconstruction: Essays in Honor of C. Vann Woodward*, ed. J. Morgan Kousser and James M. McPherson (New York: Oxford University Press, 1982); Dawson, *Army Generals and Reconstruction*, 216–260.

7   Richardson, "Lessons from the First National Shutdown," *New York Times*, Room for Debate, December 18, 2013, www.nytimes.com/roomfordebate/2013/12/18/the-history-and-lessons-of-congressional-crises/lessons-from-the-first-national-shutdown; Calhoun, *Conceiving a New Republic*, 160–165, 172–173, 191, 196–197, 229–230; Lieber, *Use of the Army*, 16–17; Richardson, *Wounded Knee: Party Politics and the Road to an American Massacre* (New York: Basic Books, 2010); Valelly, *Two Reconstructions*, 66–68; Simpson, *Reconstruction Presidents*, 222; T. H. Williams, *Diary of a President*, 219; Wang, *Trial of Democracy*, 134–215; Pamela Brandwein, *Rethinking the Judicial Settlement of Reconstruction* (New York: Cambridge University Press, 2011); Keith, *Colfax Massacre*, 144–146, 155–157; Lawrence Goldstone, *Inherently Unequal: The Betrayal of*

Equal Rights by the Supreme Court, 1865–1903 (New York: Bloomsbury, 2011); Donald G. Nieman, *Promises to Keep: African-Americans and the Constitutional Order, 1776 to the Present* (New York: Oxford University Press, 1991).

8 Clayton D. Laurie and Ronald H. Cole, *The Role of Federal Military Forces in Domestic Disorders, 1877–1945* (Washington, D.C.: Center of Military History, 1997), 33–46, 66; Gary Felicetti and John Luce, "The Posse Comitatus Act: Liberation from the Lawyers," *Parameters* 34, no. 3 (2004): 100; Candidus Dougherty, "'Necessity Hath No Law': Executive Power and the Posse Comitatus Act," *Campbell Law Review* 31, no. 1 (Fall 2008): 1–50; Lieber, *Use of the Army*, 10–13; Coakley, *Role of Federal Military Forces*, 342–348; Calhoun, *Conceiving a New Republic*, 56, 157–160; Charles Doyle, *The Posse Comitatus Act and Related Matters: The Use of the Military to Execute Civilian Law* (Washington, D.C.: Congressional Research Service, 2012), 19–20; Elliott West, *The Last Indian War: The Nez Perce Story* (New York: Oxford University Press, 2009); Foner, *Reconstruction*, 583; Charles Fairman, *Reconstruction and Reunion, 1864–88* (New York: Macmillan, 1974), 1371–1378; Gillette, *Retreat from Reconstruction*, 294–297; Valelly, *Two Reconstructions*, 66–67, 117–119.

9 Calhoun, *Conceiving a New Republic*, 235–239; Valelly, *Two Reconstructions*, 121–122; Wang, *Trial of Democracy*, 216–252.

10 Calhoun, *Conceiving a New Republic*, 284; Wang, *Trial of Democracy*, 294–299; Egerton, *Wars of Reconstruction*, 326; J. Morgan Kousser, *The Shaping of Southern Politics: Suffrage Restriction and the Establishment of the One-Party South, 1880–1910* (New Haven, Conn.: Yale University Press, 1974); Steven Hahn, *A Nation under Our Feet: Black Political Struggles in the Rural South, from Slavery to the Great Migration* (Cambridge, Mass.: Belknap Press of Harvard University Press, 2003).

11 Michael Vorenberg generously guided me toward the statutory connections between Little Rock and the 1870s Reconstruction legislation. Paul J. Scheips, *The Role of Federal Military Forces in Domestic Disorders, 1945–1992* (Washington, D.C: Center of Military History, 2005), 28, 31, 47, 51, 66, 120–121, 134; Valelly, *Two Reconstructions*, 11–12; Doyle, *Posse Comitatus Act*, 40.

12 John Hope Franklin, *Reconstruction: After the Civil War* (Chicago: University of Chicago Press, 1961); Kenneth M. Stampp, *The Era of Reconstruction, 1865–1877* (New York: Knopf, 1965); Bruce E. Baker, *What Reconstruction Meant: Historical Memory in the American South* (Charlottesville: University of Virginia Press, 2007); John David Smith and J. Vincent Lowery, eds., *The Dunning School: Historians, Race, and the Meaning of Reconstruction* (Lexington: University of Kentucky Press, 2013).

13 Other works that emphasize Reconstruction's revolutionary potential, to different ends, include Hahn, *Nation under Our Feet;* William Archibald Dunning, *Reconstruction, Political and Economic, 1865–1877* (New York: Harper and Brothers, 1907); W. E. B. Du Bois, *Black Reconstruction in America, 1860–1880* (New York: Free Press, 1999). Works that emphasize the limitations of Reconstruction and its continuities with what

came before and after include Leon F. Litwack, *Been in the Storm So Long: The Aftermath of Slavery* (New York: Knopf, 1979); Jim Downs, *Sick from Freedom: African-American Illness and Suffering during the Civil War and Reconstruction* (New York: Oxford University Press, 2012); Susan Eva O'Donovan, *Becoming Free in the Cotton South* (Cambridge, Mass.: Harvard University Press, 2010); Franklin, *Reconstruction;* Stampp, *Era of Reconstruction.*

14 Egerton, *Wars of Reconstruction*, 296, 304; Weinfeld, *Jackson County War;* Ortiz, *Emancipation Betrayed*, 24.

15 Michael W. Fitzgerald, *Splendid Failure: Postwar Reconstruction in the American South* (Chicago: Ivan R. Dee, 2007), 157–158; Egerton, *Wars of Reconstruction*, 20–21, 31–32, 142; Eric Foner, *Freedom's Lawmakers: A Directory of Black Officeholders during Reconstruction* (New York: Oxford University Press, 1993), xxv; Sharon Ann Holt, *Making Freedom Pay: North Carolina Freedpeople Working for Themselves, 1865–1900* (Athens: University of Georgia Press, 2000); Loren Schweninger, *Black Property Owners in the South, 1790–1915* (Urbana: University of Illinois Press, 1990); Adrienne Monteith Petty, *Standing Their Ground: Small Farmers in North Carolina since the Civil War* (New York: Oxford University Press, 2013).

16 Richard Franklin Bensel, *Yankee Leviathan: The Origins of Central State Authority in America, 1859–1877* (New York: Cambridge University Press, 1990), 287–290; Mark R. Wilson, *Business of Civil War: Military Mobilization and the State, 1861–1865* (Baltimore: Johns Hopkins University Press, 2006).

17 On law-creating violence, see Carl Schmitt, *Political Theology: Four Chapters on the Concept of Sovereignty*, trans. George Schwab (Chicago: University of Chicago Press, 2006); Georges Sorel, *Reflections on Violence*, ed. Jeremy Jennings, trans. Thomas Ernest Hulme (New York: Cambridge University Press, 1999); Antonio Negri, *Insurgencies: Constituent Power and the Modern State*, trans. Maurizia Boscagli (Minneapolis: University of Minnesota Press, 1999); Walter Benjamin, "Critique of Violence," in *Reflections: Essays, Aphorisms, Autobiographical Writings*, ed. Peter Demetz, trans. Edmund Jephcott (New York: Harcourt Brace Jovanovich, 1978); Giorgio Agamben, *Homo Sacer: Sovereign Power and Bare Life*, trans. Daniel Heller-Roazen (Palo Alto, Calif.: Stanford University Press, 1998).

18 John Russell Young, *Around the World with General Grant: A Narrative of the Visit of General U.S. Grant, Ex-President of the United States, to Various Countries in Europe, Asia, and Africa, in 1877, 1878, 1879; To Which Are Added Certain Conversations with General Grant on Questions Connected with American Politics and History*, Vol. 2 (New York: American News Company, 1879), 362–363; Joan Waugh, *U.S. Grant: American Hero, American Myth* (Chapel Hill: University of North Carolina Press, 2009).

ACKNOWLEDGMENTS

I have depended too much on too many people. Although the faults of the book are mine, the virtues are in large part theirs.

I have depended a great deal upon archivists. Their assistance led me to entirely rethink the premises of my book. I began with the idea of asking why there was not a robust occupation at the end of the Civil War. Seeking basic information on the placement and size of army outposts in the rebel states, I found myself flummoxed that this data did not actually exist. I received some extremely generous help from National Archives staff who listened patiently to my questions, guided me through the research lists, and, most importantly, walked the back rooms in search of boxes that might be relevant. After a great deal of trial and error, they gave me a list of one hundred boxes that I could utilize to construct the outpost size and locations in the years after Appomattox. As I slowly began to piece together that information, I realized that my initial question was misguided. There was a more geographically expansive, intrusive, and long-lasting occupation than I expected to find. The assistance they gave led me to entirely reverse the interpretations of the book. From a study of an occupation that did not launch, it turned into an exploration of the causes, consequences, and downfall of a surprisingly robust occupation. The dataset that formed the basis of this study, and which will be published in a collaborative website funded by the American Council of Learned Societies, was a product of the patience and generosity of the many researchers at National Archives I in Washington, D.C. Additionally, I depended a great deal upon archivists at National Archives II in College Park, the Library of Congress, the Huntington Library, the Historical Society of Pennsylvania, the United States Army Military History Institute at the U.S. Army Heritage and Education Center, the New-York Historical Society, the New York Public Library (especially Thomas Lannon), and the New York State Archives. For photographs, Jenny Watts, Bob Zeller, and Garry Adelman provided advice. At Louisiana State University, Germain Bienvenu and Judy Bolton went above and beyond in assisting me, as did Karla Lang at Palestine Public Library and Kristy Phillips at the University of North Texas Library's Portal to Texas History.

I realized the implications of the spread of the military only when I saw the data I had collected turned into the maps that grace these pages. Scott Nesbit from the beginning saw the potential for producing maps from these data and coordinated our application for an American Council of Learned Societies grant that will help us produce interactive, digital maps in 2015 with the assistance of the Willson Center Lab for Digital Humanities at the University of Georgia. At the University of Richmond Digital Scholarship Lab, Nate Ayers and Justin Madron handled all my requests with grace. Ed Ayers believed in the project and committed the university and the lab to helping me. I am grateful to all of them.

For financial support that made this project possible, I am grateful to the National Endowment for the Humanities for a Summer Stipend, the Gilder Lehrman Center for the Study of Slavery, Resistance, and Abolition for a Post-Doctoral Fellowship, the New York Public Library for an Archives Research Fellowship, the Huntington Library for an Andrew W. Mellon Foundational Fellowship, the National Endowment for the Humanities for an NEH Award for Faculty, the PSC-CUNY for grants to cover research, and the CCNY Dean of Arts and Humanities Office under Fred Reynolds, Geraldine Murphy, and Eric Weitz for support of conference travel.

I am also grateful for the hospitality and sharp questions at many scholarly gatherings where the nebulous ideas at the center of this project took shape, including talks at the University of Pennsylvania, Johns Hopkins University, Princeton University, University of Cambridge, Ohio State University, University of California at Irvine, University of Florida, University of Tennessee, Pennsylvania State University, the Huntington Library, the U.S. Capitol Historical Society, the New York Military Affairs Symposium, the White Plains Historical Society, the Gilder-Lehrman Center, the Graduate Center and City College of the City University of New York, the American Social History Project, the CUNY Chancellor's Salon, the Organization of American Historians, the Clements Center for Southwest Studies at Southern Methodist University, the Autry National Center's Institute for the Study of the American West, the Association for the Study of African American Life and History, the Against Recovery Conference at NYU, the Society of Civil War Historians, the Future of Civil War History Conference at Drew University, and the After-Slavery Conference at Charleston, South Carolina. Among the many people who made these trips pleasurable were John Brooke, Dodie McDow, Brook Thomas, William Link, Bill Blair, Tony Kaye, Barby A. Singer, David Blight, Kevin Waite, Roberto Saba, Emma Teitelman, Phil Morgan, Angus Burgin, Nathan Connolly, and Luke Harlow.

The highest tribute an intellectual peer can pay is to take one's ideas seriously enough to expose their limitations. For their (sometimes gleeful!) assistance, I am grateful to Luke Harlow, Daniel Amsterdam, Gayle Rogers, Sam Schaffer, Scott Nelson, and Elaine Parsons who read sections of the book. Colleagues at City College—Adrienne Petty, Emily Greble, Cliff Rosenberg, Andreas Killen, Beth Baron, Craig Daigle, Lale Can, Jennifer Roberts Onyedum, Richard Boles, Darren Staloff, Anne Kornhauser, and, especially, Judith Stein—read sections and offered wisdom, reading lists, and encouragement. My former student, Will Hickox, read the manuscript with great care near the end of the process and made helpful suggestions.

Especially helpful were discussions with Bill Link and Jim Broomall for an essay on the nature of freedom in a collection they will publish; with Adam Arenson and Andy Graybill for a piece on Texas after Appomattox they are publishing in *Civil War Wests: Testing the Limits of the United States;*, and with Bruce Baker and Brian Kelly for some suggestions on occupation and the geography of power they published in *After Slavery: New Scholarship on Race, Labor, and Politics after the Civil War.* I am also grateful to the many fine historians I have not met whose work in military and political history made this book conceivable, particularly Brooks Simpson, Michael Les Benedict, Mark Grimsley, James Sefton, Joseph G. Dawson III, and Paul Bergeron.

My pals Erik Gellman, Guy Ortolano, Gayle Rogers, David Smith, and Abram Van Engen kept my elbows sharp and my ego deflated on our annual "basketball" trips. Michael A. Washburn lived with my Kentucky triumphalism even in a victory over his hometown Louisville Cardinals, and kept my ears buzzing and my liver rebelling at shows all over the region, including his own. And Anthony Guinyard has been a true friend since we were united by the mysteries of the first-year housing office.

Steve Hahn remains my intellectual inspiration. As I took on a project that threatened at once to lead me into both the dusty army archives and old books on the occupation of Hungary, Steve encouraged me to follow my curiosity even if it led me toward arguments different from his own. At crucial points he helped me narrow the questions I was asking here, conceptualize future projects that would make use of the comparative work I had begun, and hold to the belief that the questions worth asking are the unsettling ones that are hard to answer.

Friends who read an entire manuscript are friends indeed. I want to thank Harvard University Press's two thorough and supportive reviewers. One of them, David Blight, not only revealed himself to me after writing a very useful report but went out of his way to talk to me about the book on several occasions; the other anonymous reader's report helped the book grapple with occupation studies and military history to its great benefit. Jeremy Kryt generously took time off from his journalistic work on contemporary Latin American civil wars (and his own novel writing) to ask the very broadest questions about the relationship between the Civil War and civil wars in general. Michael Vorenberg volunteered to read my entire draft the first time we met. His responses were gracious and generous. Stacey Smith was kind enough to take time from her own work to read my manuscript and to reflect upon the interconnections between Southern and Western history during this period. Andrew Zimmerman helped me connect the particular story of the post-Appomattox United States to broader questions about state power in the nineteenth century, and the relationship between law and violence.

In a tour de force eighteen-page single-spaced response to the manuscript, Laura Edwards guided me firmly through the thickets of legal history. She asks the broadest questions and seeks answers in the densest sources; no one I know can move so quickly from account books to the nature of the law, from a receipt to the structure of nineteenth-century society.

Bill Blair has been a cheerleader, a skeptical reader, and a mentor throughout the process. He generously shared ideas with me that he had developed in a pathbreaking article on occupation a decade ago, let me read sections of his important book on disloyalty while it was still in manuscript, pushed me to capture the role of court trials in shaping the decision to continue the war, and nudged me toward concision and clarity. Furthermore, he funded a conference on Reconstruction at Penn State University that sparked many ideas that carry through this book.

I co-organized that conference with Kate Masur, who talked about this book with me so many times and then read the manuscript so frequently that she would deserve a coauthorship if she agreed with all its conclusions. Kate has been a remarkable friend, a careful editor, a sharp critic, and the most interesting thinker about the post–Civil War period in the field.

Finally, Jim Oakes also read the book multiple times. He encouraged me to read more deeply in the congressional debates, advice that changed the book dramatically and turned it from an on-the-ground history into a study of the interaction between high policy and social conditions. His work on emancipation and abolition is a model for clear writing and sharp argumentation. And he has been, besides, a dedicated friend.

At Harvard University Press, Joyce Seltzer has championed, critiqued, and guided the book with admirable dedication and her famously sharp wit. In one of our first conversations, she helped me see the book in bolder, more ambitious terms than I had imagined. In our later conversations, she helped me keep my feet on the ground, my prose on the level, and my eye on the details upon which the book will rise or fall. Brian Distelberg, Kimberly Giambattisto, and many others helped steer the book to completion.

The other person who read the entirety of the manuscript, Diane Downs, is someone I am grateful for in ways I cannot properly express. She is a joy and an inspiration, a delight and a true companion. Over tacos and burritos and nachos and cheese fries and soup dumplings and chicken curry and dal makhani and too many delicious, unhealthy foods to name, she showed an unimaginable tolerance for discussions about the post–Civil War South. Here's to some time off before I burden you with the next one, Diane. Our daughters, Sophia Marie and Gabriella Francesca, are our greatest distraction and our most joyful burdens, whether they are waking us up in the middle of the night, or demanding more playground time after school, or pleading for just one more playdate, or skipping ahead of us down the sidewalk as we chase futilely behind. To their question "When will Daddy *ever* be finished?" they at last have an answer.

My father, Monty Downs, never doubted that my perambulations through writing and history would lead to a shelf of books bearing our last name. And he never doubted the importance and the beauty of a life of the mind. When a cautious father might have encouraged a profession that made more sense, he always urged me both in his words and in his deeds to do what I love, to do it well, and to keep doing it over and over. The stubborn, perhaps foolish, ambition behind this book is a legacy of my mother, Ann Patterson Howard, but the discipline to do and do and do until it is finally done is something I learned on the back roads of Kauai from my father a long time ago. Aloha and mahalo.

INDEX

Abbott, Joseph, 223
acquiescence, myth of white Southern, 9, 12–13, 34
Alabama, post-surrender occupation of, 39, 43, 49, 55, 57, 103; provisional government of, 71, 75–76, 80–81, 83; reduction of cavalry in, 96; reduction of troops in, 106–108, 142; black troops in, 109; conditions during 1866 in, 143, 145; and opposition to Fourteenth Amendment, 164; during Military Reconstruction, 179–180, 195–196, 198, 207; restoration of, 202–203, 205–206; after 1868, 215–217, 234, 239
Algeria, 91
American Freedmen's Inquiry Commission, 45
Ames, Adelbert, 209, 214, 222–223
amnesty, 69–70
anarchy, 17, 21–22, 28, 33, 154, 181
Anderson, Mary, 51
Anthony, Susan B., 129
Appomattox Court House, 1, 8, 94
Arkansas, loyalist government of, 21, 41, 65, 70; post-surrender occupation of, 27, 42, 54–55; reduction of troops in, 100, 106–108, 142, 189; black troops in, 109; conditions during 1866 in, 144, 158; during Military Reconstruction, 186–189, 195–196, 207; restoration of, 202–203, 205–206; after 1868, 216–217, 234–235, 239, 245

armed forces, use of in peacetime, 4, 12, 124–125, 183–185, 204–210, 212, 215–217, 224–230, 232–235, 237–246
Army & Navy Journal, 19, 71
Ashburn, George, 196
Ashley, James, 177

Baird, Absalom, 149
Bancroft, George, 116
Banks, Nathaniel, 75, 95
Barnard, R. W., 120
Bean, John, 58
Bentzoni, Charles, 42, 44, 54–55
Bingham, John, 124, 224; fights for peace terms, 162, 166–170, 176, 203, 226–227; shifts view on impeachment, 199–200
Birth of a Nation, 245
Black Codes, 84–87, 123–125, 139
Black Horse Cavalry, 154
Blaine, James, 166, 169–170, 172–174, 199–200
Blair, Francis Jr., 235
Bliss, Zenas, 191
Boutwell, George, 170, 172, 218
Boynton, Charles B., 165
Bozeman Trail, 101, 144
Bradley, Aaron, 196
Brooks, James, 46, 118
Brown, Drury, 61–62
Brown, Joseph, 20
Brownlow, William, 155, 204, 216
Bryant, William Cullen, 44
Bullock, Rufus, 206

Division of the Atlantic, 72
Division of the Gulf, 72
Division of the Mississippi, 72
Division of the Tennessee, 72
Dominican Republic, 91
Douglas, Henry Kyd, 30
Douglass, Ambrose, 49
Douglass, Frederick, 121
Drake, Charles, 220, 227, 232, 235
Du Bois, W. E. B., 245
Dunning, William, 245

Edmunds, George, 227
Eisenhower, Dwight D., 245
elections of 1866, 163–164
elections of 1867, 197
elections of 1868, 206–208
elections of 1870, 233–235
elections of 1872, 238–239
elections of 1874, 239
elections of 1876, 239–240
Eliot, Thomas, 131
emancipation, martial law and, 4, 9, 39–40,
    44–46, 50, 53, 58–60
Emancipation Proclamation, 43
Enforcement bill (1870). *See* Civil Rights
    Act (1870)
Enforcement bill (1871). *See* Civil Rights
    Act (1871)
enfranchisement, and fears of Northern
    backlash, 67–68, 162, 197; in 1867,
    165–166, 302n22; as end to wartime,
    169–170, 218–219; as product of
    military force, 176, 324n41
Ewing, Thomas, 23
Ex Parte McCardle, 198–199, 228
Ex Parte Milligan, 148, 156–157, 164, 187

federal elections (Lodge) bill, 244
Fessenden, William, 164, 217, 223, 311n12,
    312nn23–24; and enfranchisement, 67;
    determination to extend wartime of in
    1866, 114, 118–119, 121, 123, 126,
    167–168; alliance with Thaddeus
    Stevens, 120–121, 162, 167–168,
    172–173; fights to extend wartime in
    1867, 167–168, 172–173, 176–177;

opposes impeachment, 177, 184,
    200–201
Fifteenth Amendment, 113, 212, 217–218,
    248
financial fears, 90–93, 133, 304n35
Five-twenties, 92–94
Flanigan, Harris, 21
Florida, post-surrender occupation of,
    25, 49, 54; provisional government
    of, 71, 74–75, 86, 140; reduction of
    troops in, 100, 106–108, 142, 153,
    189; conditions during 1866 in,
    143, 145, 148, 154; during Military
    Reconstruction, 189, 195–196,
    207; restoration of, 202–203,
    205–206; after 1868, 216–217, 235,
    239–241
Foner, Eric, 246, 273n12
Force, Manning F., 47
Fourteenth Amendment, 113, 127–130,
    133–134, 161, 164–165, 202–203, 248,
    319n42
Freedmen and Southern Society Project, 41
Freedmen's Bureau. *See* Bureau of Refu-
    gees, Freedmen, and Abandoned
    Lands
freedom, as access to the state, 5, 40, 44–46,
    49–51, 247–253; as accessible rights,
    40, 49, 54, 103–104, 122, 247–251;
    definitions of, 51–53, 281n3; and notion
    of practical freedom, 54–55, 115, 121,
    123–125, 168; as land redistribution,
    78–79
freedpeople, mobilization of, 10, 52–53,
    67–68, 78–79, 110–111, 145–146,
    248–249; numbers at surrender, 41;
    political mobilization during Military
    Reconstruction, 179–180, 193, 195–196,
    207–208, 231–232
French Revolution, 20, 118
Fugitive Slave Law of 1850, 4, 124, 206,
    233, 237–238

Galloway, Abraham, 31, 231
Garfield, James, 119, 129, 168, 172, 203, 242
Gay, Henry, 97
General Orders Number 3 (1866), 120, 139

Milton Keynes UK
Ingram Content Group UK Ltd.
UKHW040707120324
439192UK00001B/42

9 780674 241626